READER'S DIGEST
PHOTOGRAPHIC FIELD GUIDE
BIRDS
OF AUSTRALIA

Text by Jim Flegg with Steve Madge
Photographs supplied by the National Photographic Index
of Australian Wildlife at the Au...

The publishers, author and consultant gratefully acknowledge the assistance of all those involved in the compilation of this book. Thanks are due not just to all the photographers but also to Sally Bird for her enormous help in collating the photographs. Tribute must be paid, too, to those who participated so effectively in compiling the Royal Australasian Ornithologists Union *Atlas of Australian Birds*, from which the majority of the maps were derived. Finally, special thanks must go to Caroline Flegg. This book is dedicated to Camilla and Thomas Bird in Armidale.

Revised edition
First published in Australia in 1995 by
Reader's Digest (Australia) Pty Limited
26–32 Waterloo Street, Surry Hills, NSW 2010

The National Library of Australia Cataloguing-in-Publication data

Flegg, Jim.
Reader's Digest photographic field guide to the birds of Australia.

Rev. ed.
Bibliography.
Includes index.
ISBN 0 86438 939 6.

1. Birds - Australia - Identification. 2. Birds - Australia - Pictorial works.
I. Madge, Steve. II. Reader's Digest (Australia). III. National Photographic Index of Australian Wildlife. IV. Title. V. Title: Photographic field guide to the birds of Australia. VI. Title: Birds of Australia.

598.2994

Conceived and produced by New Holland (Publishers) Ltd
Commissioning Editor: Charlotte Parry-Crooke
Project Manager: Ann Baggaley
Editor: Martyn Bramwell
Design: ML Design, London
Cartography: ML Design, London
Artwork: Janet Baker; Martin Woodcock
Index: Paul Barnett

Typeset by ML Design, London
Reproduction by HBM Print Pte Ltd, Singapore
Printed and bound in Singapore by Kyodo Printing Co (Singapore) Pte Ltd

CONTENTS

INTRODUCTION

Birds are the most colourful and easily observed of all wild creatures. Almost any situation - town or country - is full of interest for the enthusiastic birdwatcher. Even the most casual observer can experience the satisfaction to be gained from a growing familiarity with birds and a developing ability to recognize individual species.

Budgerigars in massed flight above a waterhole

There is much to be marvelled at: an albatross, watched offshore from a prominent headland, planing effortlessly, with hardly a wingbeat, low over the waves, is lost to sight with startling rapidity so fast is its ocean-spanning progress. There is much that is sheer spectacle: the stunning vista of an ephemeral inland lake, re-established by recent rains and almost immediately packed with countless thousands of pelicans, cormorants, ducks, geese and waders all reaping the rich but brief harvest of food and establishing huge breeding colonies. More mundane perhaps, and certainly more frequently encountered, but no less of a spectacle, are the sights and sounds over farmed land and open woodland as large flocks of galahs, corellas and cockatoos and the like gather at a dam to drink. Even in the city suburbs flocks of rosellas, king parrots and lorikeets demonstrate colourfully their ability to co-exist with man.

On the other hand, there is also much interest - inevitably coupled to enjoyment - to be gained by watching individuals or groups of birds going about their daily lives. Using the fairy wrens as just one example of many, it is not simply the beauty of the colours of a male in breeding plumage seen at close range that is the attraction, but more the privilege of sharing in, and trying to understand, the patterns of interplay between their ecology and behaviour that shape their day.

This *Photographic Guide* covers all the species that you are likely to encounter in Australia, even in a lifetime of birdwatching. Included are more than 760 individual species which breed in or

Included are more than 760 individual species which breed in or regularly visit or pass through some part of the country - even those which have occurred only once or twice, or which are, sadly, on the brink of extinction, one or two maybe beyond that tragic edge.

The main guide, pages 42-353, contains the photographs of the birds in characteristic habitats, together with detailed descriptions and maps showing where each species is most likely to occur. Many species are also illustrated with extra photographs depicting the plumage variations that may appear according to age, sex or time of year. How to use the guide and interpret the maps and symbols is described in the following section.

Other introductory sections provide essential background information. *Bird Biology* identifies and illustrates the physical features of birds and describes the functions of plumage. *Bird Habitats* summarizes the major types of terrain and explains in general terms which bird families are represented in particular habitats. *Bird Names and Classification* examines the internationally accepted system of classification under which the birds in this book are arranged. Finally, *Family Characteristics* describes the taxonomic groupings into which the Australian birds included here are divided and outlines the family likenesses that should be readily recognized in the field.

At the end of the guide there are useful sections on choosing and using equipment, such as binoculars, for the field, and an outline of the current status of conservation in Australia. Addresses of organizations of interest to birdwatchers, and a selective bibliography of recommended titles, conclude the guide.

How to Use the Guide

The species included in the guide are arranged according to the widely accepted order described on page 25 under *Bird Names and Classification*. The guide begins in the conventional way with the emus and cassowaries (family Casuariidae) and ends with the ravens and crows (family Corvidae).

Each species included in the guide is illustrated with one or more photographs and described in a detailed text. Each text is accompanied by a distribution map and a range of habitat symbols. All the elements relating to each species are displayed together for ease of use.

Detailed texts provide full descriptions of the birds, their life-styles, habits, voices and distribution

Photographs show the birds in typical stance and habitat, as well as plumage variations, in flight or at the nest

Maps show the birds' distribution

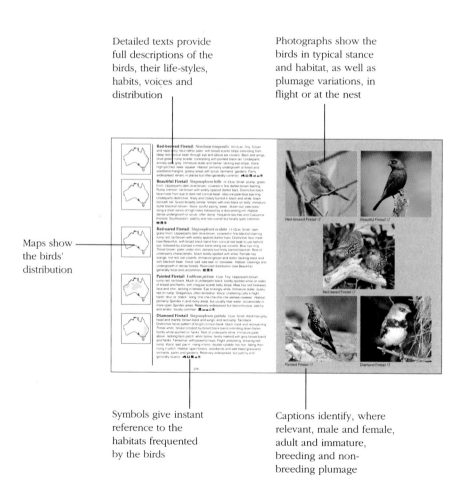

Symbols give instant reference to the habitats frequented by the birds

Captions identify, where relevant, male and female, adult and immature, breeding and non-breeding plumage

The Photographs and Captions

Each species is illustrated with at least one photograph. Where plumage substantially differs between males, females and immatures, and between breeding and non-breeding birds, the precise plumage stage is identified in the captions, and additional photographs are often provided. Species which are almost always seen in flight are depicted thus. In the case of species that are either very rare, perhaps extinct, or extremely difficult to photograph, artwork drawn to photographic standards and illustrating precise details has been included.

The Maps

Distribution maps are included in the left-hand columns of the text pages, the areas shaded in blue giving a broad indication of where each species in the guide is most likely to be found. It should be emphasized that a particular species may occur only in widely separated regions within the shaded area; its range may also vary within the area according to breeding habits or seasonal changes in local climate and conditions. These maps are derived from the Royal Australasian Ornithologists Union *Atlas of Australian Birds* and represent tens of thousands of hours of fieldwork by hundreds of ornithologists.

The distribution of seabirds is, for the most part, shown only by shaded areas along the coastlines which they frequent. However, the ranges of many species will extend far beyond Australia.

A number of species, often seabirds arriving at random intervals and unpredictable areas around the coast, are seen in Australia only from time to time. To indicate such vagrants (see, for example, the Fulmar Prion, page 62) the accompanying maps are marked with cross-hatching.

The Descriptions

Detailed information is provided for each species in the guide. The popular, or common, name is printed in **bold** type followed by the scientific name in *italics*. The measurement refers to the length of the bird from beak-tip to tail-tip. A general description covers physical appearance and there are notes on flight pattern and any distinctive behavioural characteristics. Songs and calls, important aids to identification, are described phonetically where possible. Habitat and abundance information, followed by habitat symbols, conclude the description.

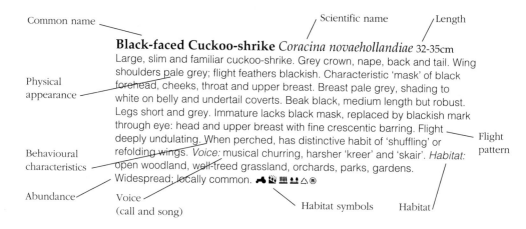

Common name

Scientific name

Length

Black-faced Cuckoo-shrike *Coracina novaehollandiae* 32-35cm

Physical appearance

Large, slim and familiar cuckoo-shrike. Grey crown, nape, back and tail. Wing shoulders pale grey; flight feathers blackish. Characteristic 'mask' of black forehead, cheeks, throat and upper breast. Breast pale grey, shading to white on belly and undertail coverts. Beak black, medium length but robust. Legs short and grey. Immature lacks black mask, replaced by blackish mark through eye: head and upper breast with fine crescentic barring. Flight deeply undulating. When perched, has distinctive habit of 'shuffling' or refolding wings. *Voice:* musical churring, harsher 'kreer' and 'skair'. *Habitat:* open woodland, well-treed grassland, orchards, parks, gardens. Widespread; locally common.

Flight pattern

Behavioural characteristics

Abundance

Voice (call and song)

Habitat symbols

Habitat

The common names given for the birds in this guide are in popular use and widely recognized. However, as many species have alternative names which may be equally well-used, it is advisable to note also the scientific names - which here follow the most up-to-date information available on the classification of Australian birds.

The starting point for identification of a bird is a comparison of its size and shape with that of another, familiar, species. Next comes recognition of the particular details that distinguish one species from another, male from female, or adult from immature. These details, or fieldmarks, include colour and pattern of plumage, length and shape of bill and legs, shape of wings and tail. In addition to physical characters, many clues can be gained from observing the general behaviour of a bird when perching or feeding, or in flight, when further plumage details may be revealed.

Not least, *where* a bird is sighted is an important guide to its identity. Each description includes notes on the types of habitat in which a bird is likely to be found, and indicates the chances of seeing that bird. There are, of course, always exceptions - birds are highly mobile and their movements are not always safely predictable from year to year. Spotting the unusual or unexpected is just one of the pleasures of birdwatching.

The Symbols

As explained above, symbols representing the major types of habitat are included at the end of each species description. To make cross-reference easier, these also appear alongside the appropriate information in the section on *Bird Habitats*. In addition, three further symbols are used to show at a glance whether a bird is migratory, nomadic or resident.

Cities, towns and gardens

Farmland

Wetlands

Coasts

Estuaries

Mangroves

Rainforest

Closed woodland

Open woodland

Scrubland

Heathland

Grassland

Desert

Migrant

Nomad

Resident

Bird Biology

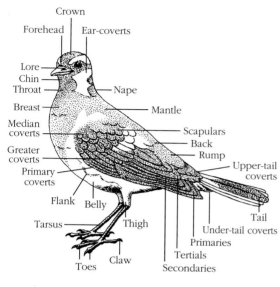

Crown
Forehead
Ear-coverts
Lore
Chin
Throat
Nape
Breast
Mantle
Median coverts
Scapulars
Back
Greater coverts
Rump
Primary coverts
Upper-tail coverts
Flank
Belly
Tarsus
Thigh
Tail
Under-tail coverts
Primaries
Tertials
Toes
Claw
Secondaries

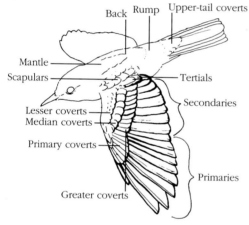

Back
Rump
Upper-tail coverts
Mantle
Scapulars
Tertials
Lesser coverts
Median coverts
Secondaries
Primary coverts
Greater coverts
Primaries

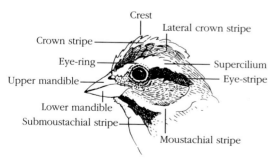

Crest
Lateral crown stripe
Crown stripe
Eye-ring
Supercilium
Upper mandible
Eye-stripe
Lower mandible
Submoustachial stripe
Moustachial stripe

Birds and mammals are highly evolved and very efficient animals, and although both branched off from a common ancestral reptilian stock at about the same time – around 130 million years ago – they have achieved their success by very different evolutionary routes. Both are warm-blooded and maintain their body warmth by means of an insulating coat, but while this is provided by fur or hair in the mammals, the birds are insulated by feathers. In some ways the birds have departed rather less from their reptilian ancestors than have the mammals, and indeed the newly hatched young of many birds closely resemble reptiles in appearance. The shelled egg is itself a reptilian feature, abandoned by all but the most primitive mammals, and in many ways the modern bird can be thought of as a highly specialized, well-tuned reptile.

The bird's skeleton consists primarily of a central box structure formed by the backbone, ribs and sternum, in which are grouped all the bird's vital organs. This provides protection and, perhaps more important, places the weight centrally between the wings – an ideal configuration for effective flight. Attached to this box structure are the wings – one of the most distinctive features of birds, yet one that is by no means unique in the animal kingdom.

The size and shape of the wing vary enormously, but the underlying skeletal structure is the same in all birds and can easily be related to the human (or any other mammalian) arm and hand. The 'shoulder' of a wing – the forward-protruding joint – is in fact the 'wrist' beyond which is a much-reduced and highly modified 'hand'. Differences in wing shape reflect function and flight style. Gamebirds, and some of the pigeons, have short rounded wings for quick take-off; oceanic gliders such as the albatrosses have extremely long, straight, narrow wings; while the soaring birds of prey

Wing Shapes

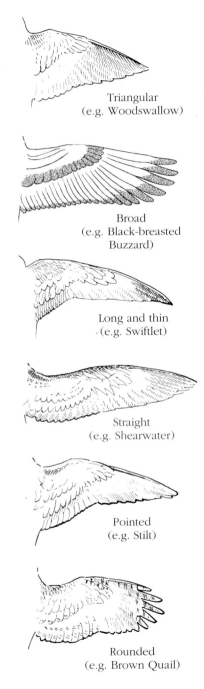

Triangular
(e.g. Woodswallow)

Broad
(e.g. Black-breasted
Buzzard)

Long and thin
. (e.g. Swiftlet)

Straight
(e.g. Shearwater)

Pointed
(e.g. Stilt)

Rounded
(e.g. Brown Quail)

have huge, long, broad, heavily 'fingered' wings that enable them to 'ride' for hours on rising air currents. Each wing outline is characteristic of a particular way of life, and individual variations of wing shape can be of great value in field identification.

Flight may not be unique to birds, but feathers certainly are. Made of the protein keratin, and possibly derived from the scales of their reptilian ancestors, they windproof and waterproof the bird, provide superb thermal insulation, and above all provide the 'variable geometry' that makes the birds so much more successful in flight than any other flying creature – or any flying device yet invented by man. Often beautifully coloured, they give birds plumages that allow them to recognize one another, that can provide astonishingly effective camouflage, and that can be used in display or for sending contact or warning signals through a flock. Although their flexibility is a great asset, it does also mean that feathers wear out over the year and must be changed regularly in the process of moult. Thus, although feathers create the plumages we use as key identification features, wear and tear and the annual moult, by altering these plumages (which may also vary with age and sex), can add a further layer of complexity to bird identification.

Attached to the end of the bird's body is the tail, of major importance in flight for steering but also used in display and communication. Its shape, colour, and the way it is held or moved, can be a useful identification aid. At the other end are the neck and head. Interestingly, compared with the mammals, which all have seven neck vertebrae (even in the giraffe), birds have anything up to 25 in the case of the Black Swan. Beak adaptations are also enormously varied, and most are valuable field guides, even if they only place the bird in a broad group or family. The range of adaptation is fascinating in its own right – but even more so when it is realized that in order to take to the air with such superlative skill the birds 'abandoned' the hands which would otherwise have been used in food-gathering and manipulation.

Finally, the legs and feet: once again enormously varied in their adaptations and again a useful – often essential – identification feature in the field. Length, colour, the shape and configuration of the toes, all play a part – from the long legs of the herons and waders through the talons of the eagles and owls to the webbed toes of the waterbirds, so different in the grebes and ducks. In the bird,

Tail Shapes

Square
(e.g. Varied Sittella)

Notched
(e.g. Spangled Drongo)

Rounded
(e.g. Bell Miner)

Wedge-shaped
(e.g. Wedge-tailed Eagle)

Forked
(e.g. Barn Swallow)

Pointed
(e.g. Australasian Gannet)

although the leg bones – like the wing – closely relate to the mammalian hind limb, their proportions differ markedly. The true thigh is short, and normally completely hidden beneath the body feathers, while what appears to be the thigh is actually the shin (tibio-fibula) and what looks like the 'knee' (only the wrong way round) is actually the ankle. The long, horny-covered bone below the ankle, called the tarsus, is derived from parts of the ankle and the upper ends of the toes.

Finally, a note about the birds' year and its influence on their plumages. In the south and away from the arid centre, most birds breed during the summer months – broadly speaking from September to March. At this time, adults can be seen in good plumage, song can be heard at its best, and display behaviour observed as pairs come together and perhaps defend their nesting area. As the eggs hatch and nestlings fledge, increasing numbers of birds can be seen in juvenile and immature plumages, usually much drabber than the adults' and sometimes quite strikingly different. Contrary to popular belief, unlike young marsupials (and humans) almost all young birds fledge (leave the nest) much the same size as their parents. These inconspicuous immature plumages will be shed in a moult which sometimes involves all the feathers but more often principally those on the head and body. During moult, plumage variations are to be expected. Adults, too, change their feathers in a moult, usually once a year in small and medium-sized species; over a longer period in larger birds. Some really large birds of prey (eagles) and seabirds (albatrosses) may take four or five years, or even longer, to achieve adult plumage.

In the north, breeding is less likely to be dependent on our months or seasons. In the arid central regions, rain is the most important factor: shortly after the rains come, the nomadic species start to breed with astonishing speed. A substantial number of species, particularly ducks and waders, visit Australia as migrants from their Northern Hemisphere breeding grounds. For much of the time, some will be in their comparatively drab non-breeding plumage, but as they arrive during the last three months of the year, some may still be moulting from their breeding plumage, and prior to their departure northwards again in the

Beak Shapes

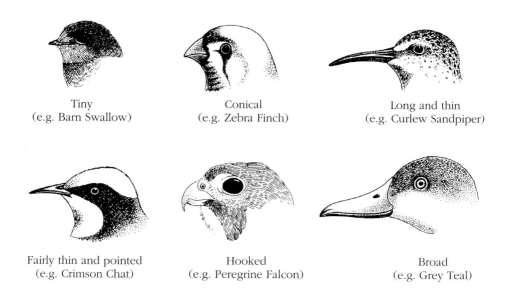

Tiny
(e.g. Barn Swallow)

Conical
(e.g. Zebra Finch)

Long and thin
(e.g. Curlew Sandpiper)

Fairly thin and pointed
(e.g. Crimson Chat)

Hooked
(e.g. Peregrine Falcon)

Broad
(e.g. Grey Teal)

first three months of the year, some may begin the process of moulting into the much brighter breeding plumage, all of which adds to the hazards of identification (especially of waders). Some Australian birds (e.g. the grebes) have distinct, dull, non-breeding plumages, and several ducks (actually drakes) have a short-lived 'eclipse' plumage when they moult into a drab female-like plumage for better concealment whilst their flight is impaired by the moulting of their wing feathers.

Bird Habitats

Australia is a unique continent, one of the world's driest overall, second only to Antarctica, with almost one-third of its land surface on average receiving less than 25cm of rainfall annually. Rivers are few and far between, unpredictable in their flow (which may cease for extended periods), and apart from the Murray-Darling system, remarkably short for the size of the land mass. Much to the fascination of the early explorers (who suspected a major 'inland sea') a number of these rivers flow towards the red heart of the country, feeding swamps and lakes, sometimes saline, often as unpredictable in their occurrence as they are in their duration. In the arid interior, droughts may persist for years, to be broken suddenly in a local torrential deluge or subject to floods resulting from rains a considerable distance away. The adaptability of wildlife of all forms in these conditions is amazing, and makes a fascinating study in itself. For ornithologists, perhaps the most striking feature is the unusually large proportion of nomadic birds, ever mobile and able to exploit the flush of plant and animal growth after the rains, wherever it may occur.

Australia is also a sizeable continent, covering an area approaching one-third the size of North America. Situated astride the Tropic of Capricorn (Alice Springs, often regarded as the centre of the continent geographically, lies just south of the Tropic) and spanning some 33 degrees of latitude, it naturally experiences a very varied climate, from tropical monsoons in the north to temperate, even cool temperate, in the far south. In the tropical north, the summers are hot and wet, the winters cooler and dry. In the south, the summers are hot, though generally somewhat cooler than the far north, but dry, while the winters are appreciably cooler and also wetter. Frosts do occur in the south in winter, and high-altitude areas of the southeast and Tasmania have regular snowfalls. The Great Dividing Range has its influence on the aridity of the Australian heartland, extracting such rainfall as may be brought with the cycle of depressions coming in off the Pacific Ocean, and year-round exerting an unpredictable local influence on the weather along the eastern coastal strip, home to much of Australia's human population.

Topographically, the Great Dividing Range is the only mountain feature to disrupt the generally flat continent. It runs, in quite a broad belt, from Cape York in the far north, southwards to Tasmania. At its southern extremes, some areas can be described as genuinely alpine, but for most of its length it constitutes little of an impediment to creatures as mobile as birds despite creating an appearance of impenetrability to mankind. There are other isolated upland areas – Kimberly in the northwest, the Darling and Stirling Ranges in the southwest, the Macdonnells in the centre and the Gawler and Flinders Ranges in the south. The most hostile areas, to any life-forms, are the massive desert or semi-desert areas across the interior, but even these have their specialist survivors, and all are subject to 'colonization' by nomads after any rainfall.

In any geographical area, the vegetation has developed under a number of constraints, some of them (like isolation) stretching back many millions of years. In most cases soil type, climate and the topography of the landscape are likely to be the dominant factors. Australia's long isolation has given it a flora as unusual as its marsupial population, with two evergreen tree/shrub genera, *Eucalyptus* and *Acacia*, predominating, but its varied and warm climate ensures that there is a continuous supply of flowers, seeds and fruit and their attendant insect populations. In the paragraphs that follow, the major habitat divisions are outlined and described, but only in the broadest terms, not least because the boundaries of any man-defined habitat are inevitably going to be indistinct as one habitat grades into another, or as other forces – for example soil type, or the presence of water – exert their effects. Most habitat types will contain a range, often a wide range, of plant species, but it must be remembered, from the 'birds' point of view', that the suitability of a habitat depends on rather more than the food plants or animals it contains: the availability of water, of suitable cover, of nest sites and roosting places will all play a part, together with innumerable specialized requirements for particular species, many of them unknown to us.

Although many birds are catholic in their choice of habitat, and although their powers of flight mean that a travelling bird may turn up just about anywhere (especially during the migration seasons or immediately after periods of stormy weather), a knowledge of bird habitats – how they are structured and what kinds of bird may be expected there – can be of tremendous assistance to the birdwatcher. Such information allows for a better planning of birdwatching excursions, as well as easing a surprising number of potential identification problems. A knowledge of the distribution of species subtly similar in plumage (for example the Frilled and Pied monarchs) or those often difficult to see well enough and for long enough to check all the relevant plumage details (for example the pittas), can be of considerable use in identification. This is where species distribution maps become of additional value over and above their intrinsic interest. Equally subtle habitat preferences often help shape the distribution patterns of birds related within the same genus or family.

Cities, Towns and Gardens

Interesting birdlife does not necessarily cease on the outskirts of a town or city. A number of bird species (some of them quite surprising) have managed to penetrate these predominantly human preserves, and despite the many hazards have adapted very successfully to their new habitat.

The unusual hazards of urban or suburban life include a shortage of natural foods and an abundance of alien predators such as cats, rats and dogs. Perhaps the car should also be

placed in this category. But there are benefits too: the plants that gardeners grow, for example, being cultivated rather than wild, often have larger fruits or seeds, and seem to be perfectly palatable and nutritious. In addition, many householders feed birds with kitchen scraps.

Best-known of the town birds is the Magpie Lark, perhaps the most adaptable of all Australian birds and certainly one of the most widespread. Others that have successfully overcome the problems, and often appear to flourish in their man-made surroundings, include several robins, woodswallows, currawongs and crows, some of the honeyeaters, Double-barred and Crimson finches, the King Parrot and several of the rosellas and lorikeets, and one or two of the doves. These span pretty well the range of avian diets, from nectar, seeds and fruit through to insects. Omnivores are well represented by the opportunist currawongs, butcherbirds, magpies and crows, and the Silver Gull would also fall in this category. Predators, too, are represented, the most striking examples being the Australian (or Nankeen) Kestrel and the Southern Boobook.

Farmland

On farmland, as in no other rural habitat, human hands have shaped the environment. Changes to the landscape – and thus to both the macro- and micro-habitats it contains – may be sudden and sweeping. Often they are of annual occurrence as crop succeeds crop. Even the grazing of stock on grasslands can have profound effects on the natural habitat, especially if attempts are made to 'improve' the nutritional quality of the grasses and other herbs of the natural flora. It is all too easy today to be critical of farmers for the destruction of the natural landscape: for creating 'prairie' regions, and for the over-use of pesticides, herbicides and fertilizers. There are undoubtedly instances where such criticism is valid, but many others where it is not, particularly when you consider that today's consumers demand high-yielding, cheap crops with little or nothing in the way of pest and disease blemishes. Much the same applies to the cost-effective production of quality meats and dairy products.

Even naturally, these open landscapes are not the richest of bird habitats, but a number of groups flourish, some expected, such as various quails and Richard's Pipit; others less so,

such as the Masked and Banded Lapwings – shorebirds or waders that have forsaken the habitat of most of their relatives for inland terrain with minimal water. Others, such as the Australian Bustard, seem far less tolerant of human presence and have been driven from all but the most sparsely settled areas.

Over much of these dry grassland areas, now predominantly used for grazing, the influence of the settlers has not been totally negative, particularly in the provision of boreholes and dams. Some of the latter are large enough and permanent enough to bring in genuine wetland birds. There is also a self-inflicted problem, in that extensive monocultures, particularly of cereals provided with artificial water sources at regular intervals, encourage seed-eating bird populations to expand, often to the point of exploding beyond naturally sustainable levels. At this point, the sight of flocks of hundreds, frequently thousands, of parrots or finches ceases to be a spectacle and translates the birds concerned into pests. Often the damage that is caused can be substantial, but it must always be remembered that it was the farming community that initiated the environmental changes. Amongst the seed-eaters, it is the Galahs, corellas and cockatoos that cause damage, while in fruit-growing or vineyard areas, fruit-eating parrots like the King Parrot and various rosellas can wreak havoc. On grazing land, a secondary problem has arisen. Introduced rabbits have provided an unexpected food source for native predators – particularly the Wedge-tailed Eagle, which flourishes to the extent that it is perceived by property owners as a major threat to lamb production. Though occasional attacks on lambs do occur, they cannot be regarded as a justification for the widespread and largely thoughtless persecution to which the Wedge-tailed Eagle has been subjected.

⚒ Wetlands

Of all bird habitats, 'wetlands' must form the broadest category. Covering streams from their sources, often high in the hills, until they discharge as rivers into the sea, it also includes lakes, ponds, marshes and swamps. Add to these the man-made water areas, the reservoirs, mineral extraction lakes, waterholes and dams. Even under these headings there are sub-divisions, for the upland stream clattering down a rocky hillside differs greatly in nature and in birdlife from the sluggish, turbid waters of the lowlands, just as the ephemeral waters

inland (sometimes fresh, sometimes brackish, occasionally saline) differ from each other and from permanent freshwater areas.

Australia's wetlands differ substantially in their structure and distribution from those anywhere else in the world, although the impact of this is seen more in the vagaries of bird occurrence (in numbers and in timing) than in the species involved, which underlines yet again the biological and behavioural adaptability (and capability) of many of our birds. From north to south, Australian wetlands fall into four major groupings, largely determined by region. In the tropical zone, which stretches across northern Australia and for practical purposes also down the east coast of Queensland almost to the New South Wales border, the climate is not of the winter/summer type but dictated by the monsoon into 'wet' and 'dry', the wet beginning with October and November rains followed by the typical monsoon deluges that occur between December and March. As the dry season begins, the swamp waters recede but leave a substantial food-rich, moist, fertile and lush margin of green vegetation which delights, among many other birds, spectacular species like the Magpie Goose, Brolga and Sarus Crane.

In the arid heart of Australia, rainfall is on average extremely low, but by no means evenly

18

distributed, so that years of drought may be ended by a substantial deluge that creates, initially, sometimes vast lakes and swamps, which normally last for no more than a few months, but which as they dry cause the spectacular growth, flowering and seeding of numerous ephemeral plant species. These become food for substantial gatherings of nomadic seed-eaters, primarily finches and the smaller parrots, and none more spectacular than the vast flocks of Budgerigars. The floodwaters also contain rapidly expanding fish and amphibian populations, adapted to survive extended drought and to flourish, fast and furious in their reproduction, within days of the rains beginning to fall. Onto these substantial but short-lived food stocks nomadic waterbirds descend, from pelicans and cormorants to ibises, egrets, spoonbills and ducks, as well as numerous smaller birds. Swiftly into their breeding routine, these birds usually accomplish a successful breeding season before parched conditions return, perhaps to endure for several years.

The Murray-Darling basin, with many important permanent waters fed by the melting snows of the Dividing Range, supports the hard core of Australian waterbirds on a regular basis. The species involved are frequently similar to those that exploit the rains of the interior, and include several duck species, cormorants, spoonbills, ibises, herons, egrets and the Black Swan. However, the variety is greater, and the permanence of water and dense marginal vegetation encourages other, less mobile, wetland birds such as crakes and rails.

Farther south still are the permanent fresh waters of the temperate southeast in New South Wales, Victoria, South Australia and Tasmania. Though permanent, many are ecologically less rich than the Murray-Darling swamplands, and are typified by Black Swans (often in considerable numbers), Australian Shelduck, Chestnut Teal and the strange Musk Duck.

Over the last two centuries, human intervention has wrought havoc in the wetlands of Australia by draining many and constraining and channelling others, all with the goal of improving agricultural performance. In consequence, the large natural or semi-natural wetlands that do remain are of immense interest to naturalists because of the numbers and variety of birds and other wildlife that they support. Some, indeed, would feature prominently on a list of the world's top areas for birdwatching, and most, if not all, should be ranked as a major component of the natural heritage.

On the credit side, though, has been man's creative role in the wetland story, which revolves around the creation of dams and boreholes. Even the unprepossessing sewage farm normally makes an extremely good birdwatching site to the birdwatcher, far from being a scar on the landscape. Over the country as a whole, huge numbers of birds of a tremendous range of species depend on natural and artificial wetlands. Particularly in the arid interior, man-made waters add substantially to the carrying capacity of the land so far as bird populations are concerned, alleviating some of the problems presented by rainfall that is as unpredictable in its quantity as it is in its timing.

⋘ Coasts

The coast of Australia is very varied, and in consequence provides varied habitats and equally varied (if sometimes difficult to access) birdwatching. By their nature, coasts of almost all types are exposed habitats, particularly those bearing the brunt of storms originating in the Pacific or Indian oceans. Like the wetlands, the Australian coastal habitat can be subdivided into several more or less distinct types, often as diverse in the birds they attract as they are to the eye.

Rocky islands provide safe breeding ledges for several larger birds, out of reach of predators, but on them small birds are generally scarce. The number of species involved is not large, but is broadly representative of seabird groups, ranging from the Shy Albatross, Australasian

Gannet, Fairy Prion, Red-tailed Tropicbird and Black-faced Cormorant to the Osprey and White-breasted Sea Eagle. In addition, cliff promontories and headlands jutting into the sea provide the best opportunity (other than from a boat) of seeing seabirds actually at sea, a far more typical environment than the cliffs. Sea-watching from such a site allows views of seabirds exercising their mastery over this environment. A wide horizon is needed to appreciate the energy-saving gliding prowess of the larger albatrosses. On the associated rocky shores can be found breeding colonies of some tern species (Black-capped, Bridled and Crested) and the Sooty Oystercatcher.

At the other extreme are sandy or muddy shores, often backed by dune systems. This is a harsh, very exposed habitat ecologically, with the sand substrate shifting continuously before the wind. Food can be difficult to find, and in some areas human pressures, in the various shapes of recreational developments, are already – or are set to become – the major threat to wildlife. Amongst the breeding birds in remoter areas are Little Penguins (themselves a major

tourist attraction, but with the human visitors to the sand dunes under strict control), several terns, the Hooded Dotterel and Beach Stone-curlew.

Along the tropical northern coast, the shores in many places are fringed with mangroves, often backed by saltmarshes. Mangroves offer a far more sheltered environment than other coasts, reflected in the numerous members of the heron family that roost, nest or feed among them; and in the four kingfishers and other small birds (several warblers, especially the Mangrove Gerygone, and honeyeaters) that flourish among them.

Estuaries

Estuaries are broad, shallow, sheltered areas, often of considerable size, where slow-moving rivers join the sea. They have a number of attributes that make them superb bird habitats. As it winds through the landscape, the river collects run-off water rich in various nutrients: in the estuary, sheltered and even in the south relatively warm, these terrestrial nutrients mingle with those brought in by the sea, and the combination produces salt or brackish water and mud or sand flats extremely rich in minute (often microscopic) plant and animal life. On these tiny life forms and on the detritus in the settling silt flourish countless millions of larger creatures – shellfish, shrimps and the like. It is these, and the specialist estuary plants and seaweeds, that support a considerable fish population and often a large number of birds.

Ecologically speaking, it is in summer (the Northern Hemisphere winter) that estuaries are of greatest value to birds – especially waders, as many of these breed in the far north of Eurasia and North America and overwinter south of the Equator. For the long-haul migrants, anxious to get back to their breeding grounds quickly and in good condition, but with several thousand kilometres to fly, estuaries serve as vital staging posts, where, in sheltered surroundings, the birds – waders in particular – may enjoy the rich feeding and prepare rapidly for the next northward stage of their journeys. Moving southwards is a more leisurely affair, but the staging posts and the food they offer are, of course, just as necessary as in spring. Many waders will pause on migration to moult, a process that the brief Arctic summer does not allow time for.

Clearly, the best results will come from visiting estuaries in summer, when the range of birds to be seen will be at its greatest. There can be no better way of getting to grips with the problems of identifying waders than by watching an array of species close together. To this can be added the sheer thrill of watching smoke-like mobs of waders twisting and turning with perfect timing across the open estuary sky.

By their very nature, estuaries are a scarce type of habitat, but nevertheless of extreme importance to many birds. Thus it is that government and conservation bodies must view with great alarm the increasing demands to industrialize or recreationalize these (in land developers' eyes) barren and useless features of our landscape.

Forests, Woodlands and Scrublands

On the basis of plant community structure, climate and other factors, botanists are able to define a range of tree-covered environments, from tropical rainforest down to scrubland with occasional trees, with a degree of precision far above that required by ornithologists and beyond the botanical capability of many of them. The evidence also seems to point to the conclusion that though there are some specialists, many of the birds frequenting tree-covered habitats are also less discerning than the botanists, basing their habitat requirements more on the quantity and continuity of supply of their food and water and the provision of appropriate nesting, and perhaps also roosting, sites. In consequence, the divisions chosen here are broad, and overlapping between categories is to be expected. With birds as mobile and as opportunist in their feeding as they often are, the boundaries cannot be expected to be either well-defined or rigidly adhered to by bird populations.

🐾 Rainforest

Though the usual concept of Australian rainforest is as a relict area on the eastern coast of Queensland, rainforests of various types are distributed irregularly along the eastern coast and the Great Dividing Range, stretching from Tasmania in the south up to Cape York in Queensland. For practical purposes, they can be divided into three main types.

Tropical Rainforest: one of the most complex, and species-rich, of all plant communities and restricted to Queensland. Many tree species are involved, usually tall and reaching up to 30m in height, normally with a closed canopy where the outermost branches of neighbouring trees touch. Trees of lesser stature but equal variety, including palms, form the understorey; creepers and climbers like lianas are common, and the ground flora is usually a rich mixture

of mosses and ferns. Typical birds would include the Southern Cassowary, Australian Brush-turkey, Palm Cockatoo, and various pittas, fruit pigeons and bowerbirds.

Subtropical Rainforest: this form occurs farther south, with fewer tree species, often in two layers. Frequently a single tree species may dominate the canopy over a large area (e.g. Coachwood, *Ceratopetalum*). Climbers are less evident, but there are often large numbers of epiphytic ferns growing on the trunks and branches of major trees. Typical birds would again include the Australian Brush-turkey, together with whipbirds, scrubwrens and the Golden Whistler.

Temperate Rainforest: this third type occurs in the southeast and south, and is generally species-poor, dominated often by a single tree species such as the Antarctic Beech, *Nothofagus*. Generally speaking, temperate rainforests hold substantially fewer birds than those farther north, but *Zoothera* thrushes, yellow robins and lyrebirds could be nominated as typical.

👥 Open Forests and Woodlands

This term also covers a substantial range of habitats, among which several major types can be identified.

Dry Sclerophyll Forests: these are usually dominated by eucalypt trees of medium height, forming an open-canopy forest on poor soils in moderate or low rainfall areas (75-100cm annually). Like the tough-leaved eucalypts, the understorey is also drought-tolerant and there is little in the way of leaf litter. Typical birds could include thornbills, Spotted Pardalote and Scarlet Robin.

Wet Sclerophyll Forests: occur in higher-rainfall areas (over 100cm annually). These forests are again eucalypt-dominated, but the species are more varied, usually taller (up to 30m), and normally form a closed canopy. The understorey is of tree ferns and shrubs, with a deep moist leaf litter on the forest floor. Typical birds could include King Parrot, yellow robins, Rufous Bristlebird and various flycatchers.

In general, sclerophyll forests tend to favour insect-eaters such as the flycatchers, and are poorer habitats for seed-eaters such as finches. There may be plants in flower all year, which provides good habitats for nectar- and pollen-feeders like honeyeaters and lorikeets.

Woodland: above all others, this term covers a multitude of habitats where trees are present, ranging from sparsely distributed to open-canopy, and sometimes to closed-canopy. The underlying soils vary equally greatly; rainfall ranges from semi-arid to wet; and the climatic conditions from tropical to temperate. Differences from the forest types above are sometimes clear, sometimes subtle. Woodlands often have eucalypts as their dominant tree species, sometimes with native pines or *Casuarina* interspersed. Rarely are the trees much more than 10m high except when growing as isolated specimens. A fairly substantial scrub understorey is typical, in some areas (often the more arid ones or on poorer soils) reduced to a sparse covering of perennial grasses and herbs.

The best of these woodlands are excellent bird habitats, some research studies showing them to carry three times the number of bird species as rainforest or sclerophyll forest. This is

an interesting anomaly, contradicting what might be expected as the forests are botanically substantially richer habitats. Woodlands seem to hold perhaps more than the normal population of specialist birds. In many cases, almost half the species present may be very largely dependent on the woodland habitat, and on the food it offers all year (from pollen and nectar to fruit and seed, and all the associated insects), or if they are migrants, during their stay. The birds involved range from kookaburras and rosellas to fantails and thornbills in temperate and tropical woodland, through semi-arid regions where Red-capped Robin, Red-rumped Parrot, Ringneck and Golden Whistler would be expected, to arid-zone woodlands where Red-backed Kingfisher, Mulga Parrot, the woodswallows, various babblers and the yellow robins occur.

The graduation from woodland to scrubland is rarely sharply defined: the distinction is slight between woodland with widely-spaced trees over a well-developed understorey and a dense scrub community of low trees, often with a closed canopy.

▥ Scrubland

There are two widely recognized major scrubland types, based on the dominant low tree species. Mallee is composed of a handful of species of multi-stemmed eucalypts, with a shrub and grass understorey, often augmented by ephemerals after the rains. The other, mulga, is composed of a similar multi-stemmed growth, but of various *Acacia* species rather than *Eucalyptus*. Typical birdlife is frequently common to both these major scrubland types, and other scrub, and includes various whistlers, babblers, fairy wrens and honeyeaters, Pink Cockatoo, Bourke's Parrot and of course the mound-building Malleefowl.

⛰ Heathland

Heathland plant communities are usually very diverse botanically, their diversity being due in large part to the poor nutrient levels in the soils on which heathland becomes established. In one sense, this has been their salvation as little attempt has been made to convert them to farmland. Even extensive fertilizer application may not produce worthwhile grazing. Some heathlands, however, are vulnerable to mineral and sand extraction, and others to pressures from tourism, particularly to damage from casually or accidentally started fires. Their plant diversity results in an abundant food supply, ranging from pollen and nectar to fruit and seeds, and in a plentiful and varied insect fauna. Fairy-wrens, emu-wrens, scrubwrens and honeyeaters are frequently present, often in some numbers.

🌾 Grasslands

Native grasslands range from the comparatively small areas of alpine or subalpine grass in the highlands of the southeast, not at all richly populated with birds, to the much more extensive *Spinifex* and Mitchell-grass plains and communities of arid and semi-arid regions. Of these, birds like the grasswrens, emu-wrens, Spinifexbird and the elusive Night Parrot could be described as typical. Other more generalized grasslands, often at least in part influenced by man and his grazing stock, are home to birds such as various quail and button-quail, finches, the Australian Bustard and the ubiquitous Masked and Banded Lapwings.

🏜 Deserts

Much of the enormous area of the arid interior of Australia can be subdivided into *Spinifex*, saltbush and bluebush. In rainfall terms, the last two, occurring in the inland southeast, are better classified as semi-arid, with average rainfalls in the range 20-50cm per year. The shrubs are widely spaced to allow extensive root-runs for water-gathering, and after the rains (which

are irregular) there is a flush of ephemeral grasses and flowering plants, and the Orange Chat could be a typical bird. Mitchell-grass plains occur in the north, nourished by monsoon rains in the summer. *Spinifex* is more a plant of dunes and rocky ground in the centre and northwest of Australia.

True desert, where the rainfall averages only 20-25cm per year, and where some years may pass between rains in many areas, is less common. Best-known of such habitats is the stony or gibber desert, where vegetation and birds are normally in scant supply, but where the astonishing Desert Chat (or Gibberbird), Australian Pratincole and Australian or Inland Dotterel (sometimes called Desert Plover) manage to survive. Fully drought- or desert-adapted birds are few in number, but nomads (an Australian speciality) are far more numerous, and after the rains, whenever and wherever they occur, nomadic species such as some of the finches, parrots, woodswallows and chats are swiftly on the spot to exploit the sudden food supply, and equally swiftly embark on a breeding cycle capitalizing on the short-lived flush of growth.

Bird Names and Classification

The placing of bird species within groups, and the gathering of these groups together at progressively higher levels, is a scientific exercise undertaken by specialist ornithologists called taxonomists. The established classification system operates as follows: closely related species are placed in the same genus (plural genera). Related genera are grouped together in Families, and families in turn combine to form Orders, the largest grouping of all. Australia's national bird emblem is the Emu, the solitary living member, species *novaehollandiae*, of the genus *Dromaius* and of the family Dromaiidae. This is grouped with the other huge flightless birds of the world – the ratites – including the Rheas, Kiwis and the Ostrich, in the order Struthioniiformes, which contains ten species from four families. At the other extreme, the order Passeriformes, world-wide, contains several thousand species in dozens of families. Thus the Black Tern *Chlidonias niger* (*niger* = black) joins the White-winged Tern *Chlidonias leucopterus* (*leuco* = white, *pterus* = wing) in the genus *Chlidonias*. The first part of the scientific name is always the genus, the second refers to the species. Related genera are grouped in families – so *Chlidonias* (marsh terns) joins *Sterna* (sea terns) and *Larus* (gulls) in the family Laridae, which contains about eighty different species world-wide. Laridae belong, together with fourteen other families, to the Order Charadriiformes.

Technically a species may be defined as a group of animals that breed with others similar, but not with different animal groups. Thus Masked Finches and Long-tailed Finches, though obviously related to each other as finches, with broadly similar plumage, beaks, feet and habits, never interbreed in the wild. We can recognize them as distinct from each other, so it comes as no surprise that so can they. Several factors prevent interbreeding, including courtship behaviour, plumage and song. A Masked Finch only recognizes the song and plumage colours and patterns of another Masked Finch when selecting a mate. The courtship display reinforces this. A displaying male Long-tailed Finch would mean nothing to a female Masked Finch, which reacts to a completely different display programme. There are slight but subtly powerful ecological barriers in their habitats, and in the biology of the two species. For example, their nest structures are different, the Masked Finch constructing a bulky, untidy nest lacking an entrance spout, on or close to the ground, while the Long-tailed builds an altogether neater nest, with a sophisticated entrance spout, high in scrub or trees. Thus there are two distinct groups of birds, Masked Finches and Long-tailed Finches, which for a variety of reasons do not interbreed: each of these groups is a species.

If a species occurs over a wide geographical range, variations in plumage (and song) can occur. Each of these variants may be called a subspecies, or a race. Usually there will be a barrier of some sort separating them from others of their kind: often a mountain range, a desert, or a substantial stretch of sea. In the Long-tailed Finch, for example, birds from Western Australia have yellow beaks, while those from western Queensland have red beaks. In the related Double-barred Finch, eastern birds have a prominent white rump patch, while those from west of the Gulf of Carpentaria have an equally conspicuous black rump. Sometimes the plumage differences between races or subspecies are really striking, as between the various regional forms of sittellas *Daphoenositta*. These populations vary in colour and pattern of the head, colour of the wing stripe, markings of the back and underparts, and patterns of sexual dimorphism. For many years each distinct form was considered a distinct species, or six in all. Studies have shown, however, that wherever different forms meet, they freely hybridise. This, combined with similarities in aspects of their biology, have led scientists to now treat all the forms as a single species, *Daphoenositta chrysoptera*.

The birds in this book are arranged in the internationally widely accepted order published by the R.A.O.U. in 1975. Each family is treated separately, beginning with the Emu, which is considered to be the oldest in terms of evolution, and ending with the families Cractidae and Corvidae of the Order Passeriformes, or perching birds, which contains more recent and generally more advanced birds.

Family Characteristics

The biological features of birds used by researchers as the basis of taxonomic groupings are sometimes quite obvious and useful to the birdwatcher in the field; but often they are minute details, of internal anatomy and today even of cellular biochemistry, and thus of little field use. However, there *are* family likenesses that, once memorized, can be of immense value in field identification. The webbed feet of the ducks and swans, for example, help you to place a bird in the right family quickly: then you can scan the finer details to establish a final identification. But beware – there are some pitfalls: closely similar though the swallows and swifts may appear in shape and behaviour, they are only very distantly related. Their similarities are the result of ages of evolution shaping each to much the same way of life, and are purely superficial.

The family likenesses outlined below are all ones which should be readily recognizable by birdwatchers in the field. Especially in the larger Orders of the non-passerines, and in the massive Order Passeriformes (containing about half of all the world's birds), the common features that group families within an Order are often obscure. A good example is the Order Charadriiformes, which holds the various wader or shorebird families, each distinctive enough in its own right, together with the gulls, terns and skuas, and, for example, with the Northern Hemisphere auk family thrown in for good measure. This is a logical grouping in taxonomists' eyes, based on sound anatomical, biochemical and physiological detail, but one which forms a confusingly diverse assemblage to the birdwatcher. Consequently, outlines here are given of family-level characteristics, as these have more practical value. Where it is of additional practical help (e.g. for waterfowl, or birds of prey) the major features of the various subfamilies are given.

Emus and Cassowaries: Family Casuariidae (*see* pages 42-3)
Huge flightless birds with a long neck and long powerful legs with three-toed feet. Each inner toe of the Cassowary is armed with a sharp talon-like claw used in defence. Both have shaggy plumage of coarse, loose feathers, giving a distinctive heavy-tailed appearance. The head and neck of the Cassowary have bare colourful skin; head with a tall horny casque or helmet. Omnivorous. Emus usually found in open or lightly wooded areas, Cassowaries in dense rainforests. Sexes similar in plumage, but females larger than males.

Ostriches: Family Struthionidae (*see* pages 42-3)
Huge, unmistakable flightless birds, with a long bare neck, long powerful legs, and feet with only two toes. Distinctive bare muscular 'thighs' (actually shins). Loose coarse plumage. Omnivorous. Usually found on open plains and pastoral land. Sexes dissimilar.

Grebes: Family Podicipedidae (*see* pages 44-5)
Medium-sized specialized diving waterbirds with longer slimmer necks than most other waterfowl. All have medium or short dagger-shaped beaks and small wings. Often swim with bodies almost submerged, using powerful feet with lobed toes, set back near the stumpy fluffy tail, rarely coming ashore. Dive frequently. Although many migrate, they fly infrequently once settled in a wetland area, requiring a long take-off run. Nests are characteristically floating rafts of waterweed moored to nearby emergent vegetation. Courtship displays are elaborate and noisy. Carnivorous, eating all forms of small water animals. Found on most types of fresh, brackish or coastal salt waters. Distinct non-breeding plumage. Sexes similar, but males brighter in breeding plumage.

Penguins: Family Spheniscidae (*see* pages 46-9)
Mostly medium-sized flightless seabirds, heavily built with an insulating blubber layer, but well streamlined for underwater swimming using stiff paddle-like wings for propulsion. Feet set back near the tail; stance upright on land with a distinctive waddling walk. Plumages tend to be dark-backed, pale-

bellied, with distinctive features mostly on the head during the breeding season. Penguins have much more uniform non-breeding plumages, and may then be difficult to identify. Come ashore usually only to breed, in dense, huge colonies, though the Little Penguin is often found ashore resting or sheltering. Carnivorous, eating fish, squid and free-swimming crustaceans. Sexes similar.

Albatrosses: Family Diomedeidae (*see* pages 50-3)
Very large, superficially gannet-like, oceanic birds with large heads and beaks, stout bodies, short tails, and characteristically extremely long, straight slender wings. Distinctive fast gliding flight low over the sea, with wings held at right-angles to the body with minimal flapping. Underwing patterns are often useful diagnostically, but immatures take several years to acquire full adult plumage, which can cause confusion. Come ashore only to breed. Carnivorous, eating all forms of free-swimming marine animals, and maritime carrion. Sexes similar.

Fulmars, Petrels, Prions, Shearwaters: Family Procellariidae (*see* pages 54-67)
Oceanic seabirds and in some ways a diverse grouping, varying in size from small to very large, but with characteristic beaks showing outward signs of segmentation and prominent paired tubular nostrils on the ridge of the beak. Come ashore only to breed on remote islands and headlands, or occasionally when storm-driven. Fulmars and shearwaters are master gliders, sweeping low over the sea on wings held stiffly at right-angles to the body. They dive shallowly, often from the surface, to reach food. The giant petrels superficially resemble albatrosses, but lack their elegant flight, frequently scavenging maritime offal. The *Pterodroma* petrels are called gadfly petrels because of their fast, swooping, erratic flight with bursts of rapid, shallow wingbeats. Prions are specialist plankton feeders, some with beaks highly specialized for filter-feeding. They feed by diving, by swimming on the surface with head submerged, or by characteristic bouncing flight, touching down to the surface intermittently to feed. Most are nocturnal on their breeding grounds, with weird cackling and cooing songs. Many have characteristic musty odours. Carnivorous, eating all forms of marine animal life from zooplankton upwards. Some feed on carrion. Sexes similar.

Storm-Petrels: Family Hydrobatidae (*see* pages 68-71)
Small, dark, oceanic petrels, some with white rumps or underparts, all with small, dark, hooked beaks with long tubular nostrils on the ridge. Flight varies from tern-like swooping to apparently feeble moth-like fluttering with long legs trailing and touching the surface. Feed from a buoyant swimming position picking from surface in flight or by shallow dives. Carnivorous, mostly eating zooplankton. Sexes similar.

Diving-Petrels: Family Pelecanoididae (*see* pages 70-1)
Dumpy small to medium petrels, in several ways similar to the Northern Hemisphere auk family (Alcidae) in structure and behaviour as a result of convergent evolution, but retaining a petrel-like beak. Feed by diving and chasing food underwater, propelled by the wings. Carnivorous, feeding on larger zooplankton, crustaceans and small fish. Sexes similar.

Pelicans: Family Pelecanidae (*see* pages 72-3)
Very large and unmistakable waterbirds, with a huge beak with a capacious pouch. Swim strongly, plunging their heads underwater to scoop up food (unlike some, Australian Pelicans do not dive for food). On land, waddle clumsily, with stocky legs set well back on the body and large feet with all four toes joined by webbing. Fly powerfully on long, broad, heavily fingered wings, often in V-formation, frequently soaring effortlessly in a wide spiral to great height. Nest in remote, usually large colonies. Carnivorous, feeding on fish and crustaceans. Sexes similar.

Gannets and Boobies: Family Sulidae (*see* pages 72-3)
Large, well-streamlined maritime birds with cigar-shaped bodies, long dagger-like beaks and relatively long pointed tails, and with long, comparatively slender, pointed wings. Gannets are white in adult plumage, with black wingtips and tail. The boobies are more tropical in distribution, more varied in plumage coloration, and frequently have the bare skin of the face and feet (all four toes joined by webbing) brightly and diagnostically coloured. Immatures may take some years to attain adult plumage.

Carnivorous, feeding predominantly on fish, often caught deep underwater following a spectacular dive from metres above the sea. Sexes broadly similar.

Darters: Family Anhingidae (*see* pages 74-5)
Large waterbirds, broadly similar to cormorants but slimmer, with a long slender snake-like neck, often with a kink, and a thinner dagger-like beak. Often swim with body submerged. Dive frequently, swimming fast underwater using large feet, all four toes joined by webbing. Emerge and perch to dry with broad, fingered wings spread wide. Seen on most types of open water inland, and on coastal lagoons, but rarely on the open sea. Carnivorous, largely on fish. Males darker than females.

Cormorants: Family Phalacrocoracidae (*see* pages 74-5)
Largely all-black or black-and-white waterbirds with species occupying all types of fresh, brackish and salt waters. Body elongated, with feet set well back near the tail. Neck long; head with long hooked beak. Swim low in the water, diving frequently to hunt, propelled by large feet with all four toes joined by webbing. Emerge to dry with broad fingered wings outstretched. Usually communal at roosting and breeding sites. Carnivorous, feeding on aquatic creatures of all types. Sexes similar.

Frigatebirds: Family Fregatidae (*see* pages 76-7)
Large, dark seabirds with very long narrow wings usually held in a broad 'W', and with long, deeply forked tails. Neck comparatively short but flexible; head with a long sharply hooked beak. Spend much time on the wing and despite their size are among the most agile of fliers, able to snatch flying fish in mid-air or pick up nesting material without touching down. Rarely land (except on the nest) and rarely alight on the sea. Carnivorous, obtaining much of their food by skua-like piratical attacks on other seabirds, but also catching their own, including snatching in flight the nestlings of other seabirds. Males have a bare skin crimson inflatable throat sac in the breeding season which the larger female lacks.

Tropicbirds: Family Phaethontidae (*see* pages 76-7)
Large white seabirds, the size of a large gull but as elegant in flight as a tern, with extremely long slender central tail feathers. Relationship to other Pelecaniformes, rather than to gulls and terns, is confirmed by all four toes being joined by webbing. Unlike gulls, the legs are set far back and tropicbirds can only shuffle about on land. Flight direct and fast, with steady stiff wingbeats, occasionally hovering, frequently plunging gannet-like for food caught in the strong serrated beak. Carnivorous, feeding on fish and crustaceans. Sexes similar.

Herons, Egrets and Bitterns: Family Ardeidae (*see* pages 78-83)
Medium to large wading birds with long legs, long necks, and straight dagger-shaped beaks. Some acquire long plumes in breeding plumage. Hunt by stalking their prey, pacing slowly and often wading, securing it by a sudden fast stab. Flight is deceptively leisurely on long, broad, heavily fingered wings, with legs outstretched behind the tail and head and neck characteristically folded back between the shoulders. Carnivorous and opportunist, mostly on water or marshland creatures of all types, the Cattle Egret often far from water. Sexes broadly similar.

Storks: Family Ciconiidae (*see* pages 84-5)
Huge and well-known long-legged, long-necked birds with heavy dagger-like beaks, more massive in all respects than the herons and cranes. Catholic in their habitat choice, depending on available food. Flight slow and powerful, on long, broad, heavily fingered wings, legs trailing but with neck, head and beak extended. Carnivorous and opportunist, feeding on any available animal life. Sexes similar.

Spoonbills and Ibises: Family Threskiornithidae (*see* pages 84-5)
Large, long-legged and long-necked wading birds, spoonbills with distinctive spatulate beaks, ibises with equally characteristic long down-curved beaks. Fly with necks and legs extended, frequently in flocks (large flocks in the case of ibises) and often in straggling V-formation. Ibises probe curlew-like for food, while spoonbills characteristically sweep their beaks from side to side in shallow water. Spoonbills have either crests or body plumes during the breeding season. Carnivorous, feeding on small aquatic or

wetland creatures of all types. Sexes similar.

Magpie Goose: Family Anseranatidae (*see* pages 86-7)
A family containing only one species, unique to Australia. The Magpie (or Pied) Goose is large, long-necked and comparatively long-legged. It has striking black-and-white plumage. Distinctive knobbed beak. Flight heavy on broad, fingered wings. Often in large noisy flocks. Largely vegetarian. Sexes similar.

Swans, Ducks and Geese: Family Anatidae (*see* pages 86-95)
Wetland birds with characteristic webbed feet involving the three front toes and with characteristic 'duck-like' beaks. As a very dry continent, it is not surprising that Australia holds comparatively few, about one-sixth, of the world's species, but more surprisingly, ten of the thirteen subfamilies are represented. Descriptions of these subfamilies follow.

Whistling-Ducks: Subfamily Dendrocygninae (*see* pages 86-7)
Medium-sized, long-legged, long-necked ducks with a rather upright stance. Often in flocks. Swift-flying, with long neck drooping distinctively and legs protruding beyond tail; usually with continuous whistling calls. Largely vegetarian. Sexes similar.

Swans: Subfamily Cygninae (*see* pages 86-7)
Huge waterfowl with distinctively long necks and short powerful legs with large webbed feet. Swim buoyantly with necks gracefully curved. Often up-end for food and frequently graze away from water. Flight powerful, on long, broad, fingered wings, neck outstretched. Largely vegetarian. Sexes broadly similar.

Freckled Duck: Subfamily Stictonettinae (*see* pages 86-7)
Monotypic subfamily, unique to Australia. Medium-sized dark duck, buoyant on the water, with a short neck, large distinctive angular head, and beak concave in profile. Often in flocks, sometimes large. Omnivorous, eating wetland vegetation and small aquatic animals. Sexes similar.

Cape Barren Goose: Subfamily Cereopsinae (*see* pages 88-9)
A subfamily unique to Australia, containing only one species. The Cape Barren Goose is large and long-necked, with a distinctively short stout wedge-shaped beak almost covered by the fleshy greenish cere. Characteristically rapid shallow wingbeats. Largely terrestrial, rarely venturing onto water. Vegetarian. Sexes similar.

Shelducks: Subfamily Tadorninae (*see* pages 88-9)
Long-necked, rather goose-like, medium-large brightly plumaged ducks. Strong flight with comparatively slow wingbeats for a duck. Omnivorous, feeding on wetland plants and small aquatic creatures, especially snails. Sexes similar in one species, dissimilar in the other.

Dabbling Ducks: Subfamily Anatinae (*see* pages 88-93)
The medium-sized 'typical' ducks that feed by dabbling in mud, up-ending in the shallows or occasionally grazing close to the water. Omnivorous, feeding on wetland plants and small aquatic creatures of all types. Sexes may be similar or dissimilar.

Diving Ducks or Pochards: Subfamily Aythyinae (*see* pages 92-3)
Medium-sized, dumpy-bodied ducks, swift in flight with rapidly beating comparatively small wings, favouring larger areas of deep freshwater, in which they dive frequently. Omnivorous, feeding on water plants and seeds, and small aquatic animals. Sexes broadly similar in Australia.

Perching Ducks: Subfamily Cairininae (*see* pages 92-5)
Small to medium-sized ducks, usually boldly patterned. Comparatively broad-winged in flight. May occur among trees, frequently nesting in tree holes. Omnivorous, feeding on water plants, grassland, and

insects and other small animal life. Sexes dissimilar.

Stifftails: Subfamily Oxyurinae (*see* pages 94-5)
Medium-sized, dumpy-bodied ducks with long stiff tails, usually carried flat on the water except in display, when raised vertically and spread. Dive frequently, fly swiftly low over the water but rarely in daylight. Omnivorous, feeding on aquatic plants and animals. Sexes dissimilar.

Birds of Prey: Orders Accipitriformes, Falconiformes (*see* pages 96-105)
The Australian day-flying birds of prey are grouped in eight families or subfamilies. All have typically sharply hooked beaks, and most have relatively long legs with strong feet and powerful talons. They range in size from small to huge; females are often larger than males, sometimes considerably so.

Order Accipitriformes

Osprey: Family Pandionidae (*see* pages 96-7)
The world-wide fish-hawk, large, with distinctively angled fingered wings and characteristic hunting technique of plunging for its fish prey. Fish are often carried torpedo-like in flight, head forwards, grasped by long powerful talons on particularly rough-soled feet. Carnivorous, feeding exclusively on fish. Sexes similar.

Hovering Kites: Subfamily Elaninae (*see* pages 96-7)
Medium-sized elegant falcon-like birds of prey, characterized by pale plumages and habit of hovering, rather heavily compared with a kestrel, legs dangling. Carnivorous, most prey taken on the ground. Sexes similar.

Bazas or Cuckoo Falcons: Subfamily Leptodontinae (*see* pages 96-7)
Medium-large birds of prey with comparatively short, broad, fingered wings and a distinctive crest. Soar frequently. Spectacular tumbling display flight. Often hunt in foliage canopy. Carnivorous, favouring insects and small reptiles. Sexes slightly dissimilar.

Soaring Kites: Subfamily Milvinae (*see* pages 96-9)
Medium-large birds of prey with long, often angled, fingered wings and long tails, characterized by effortless soaring and great manoeuvrability in low-level flight. May occur singly or in gatherings at a rich food source. Carnivorous, sometimes hunting, frequently taking carrion. Sexes usually similar.

Hawks: Subfamily Accipitrinae (*see* pages 98-101)
Medium to medium-large, long-tailed birds of prey, with short or medium-length rounded wings. Characterized by fast direct flight, bursts of wing flaps interrupted by glides. Often hunt from a semi-concealed perch with a good view, securing their prey on the ground or after a swift, agile pursuit. Soar during courtship display. Carnivorous, favouring birds but also taking mammals and reptiles. Sexes similar in plumage but females are markedly larger.

Eagles: Subfamily Buteoninae (*see* pages 100-1)
Large or very large birds of prey, with powerful flight on long, broad, heavily fingered wings. Beak comparatively massive – as long as the head. Legs feathered, feet powerful. Soar frequently. Immatures take some years to reach adult plumage: intermediate immature plumages can be confusing. Carnivorous, hunting prey of all types but also taking carrion.

Harriers: Subfamily Circinae (*see* pages 102-3)
Large, comparatively slim, long-winged, long-legged birds of prey with rather small, owl-like heads with a clear facial disc of feathers. Hunt low over open landscapes, gliding frequently on wings held stiffly in a shallow V. Carnivorous, most prey taken by surprise and secured in a quick pounce. Sexes broadly similar.

Order Falconiformes

Falcons: Family Falconidae (*see* pages 102-5)
Medium to medium-large, fast-flying birds of prey characterized by longish, pointed wings and comparatively short tails. Soar high before swooping at speed with wings part-closed on prey passing below, or use sheer speed to overtake prey, often killing in flight. Kestrels also hover expertly. Carnivorous, some taking largely birds, others including mammals, reptiles and larger insects in their diet. Sexes generally similar except in the Australian Kestrel.

Mound Builders: Family Megapodiidae (*see* pages 106-7)
Large or very large chicken-like birds with small heads and large, powerful legs and feet. Tend to run if threatened but can fly well, if noisily. Unique in building mounds of earth and vegetation in which the large clutch of eggs is incubated. Omnivorous. Sexes broadly similar, but males may be brighter in breeding season.

Quails and Pheasants: Family Phasianidae (*see* pages 106-9)
Quails are small, plump, terrestrial birds with small heads, short beaks and strikingly rounded wings. All are secretive and cryptically plumaged, but have usefully distinctive, often far-carrying calls. The introduced Common Pheasant is appreciably larger, longer-legged, and has a long pointed tail. Omnivorous. Sexes broadly similar in quail except for King Quail; markedly dissimilar in the Common Pheasant where males are boldly plumaged, females cryptically coloured.

Button-quails: Family Turnicidae (*see* pages 110-13)
Small, plump, terrestrial birds resembling the true quail in shape and behaviour but differing in anatomical detail. Similarities are considered to be the result of convergent evolution. Omnivorous. Sexes broadly similar, but larger females are usually more brightly coloured.

Plains-wanderer: Family Pedionomidae (*see* pages 112-13)
A uniquely Australian family of one genus with a single species, and of uncertain affinities with other birds. Medium-small, and best described as quail-like, but with an upright stance and the long legs of a wader! Booming voice similar to Button-quails. Apparently omnivorous, taking all types of seeds and small animals. Sexes dissimilar, the female being larger and brighter.

Crakes and Rails: Family Rallidae (*see* pages 114-19)
Medium or small birds with comparatively long necks and small heads, and with long legs ending in feet with long toes, lobed in the Coot. Frequent a wide variety of habitats, but wetland species have bodies markedly flattened from side to side to ease passage between reed stems. Short tail usually flicked while walking or swimming. Flight apparently feeble on short rounded wings, with legs trailing, but some are nevertheless long-haul migrants. Many are secretive, but most have usefully distinctive strident calls. Omnivorous. Sexes similar.

Cranes: Family Gruidae (*see* pages 120-1)
Huge, long-legged, long-necked birds, generally stork-like in appearance and in flight, with neck and legs extended, and broad, fingered wings beating steadily but shallowly. Characterized by extended secondary wing feathers drooping over the tail in a bulky 'bustle' and by their leaping, dancing displays. Frequently highly vocal, with loud trumpeting calls. Rarely wade into water or fish. Omnivorous. Sexes similar.

Bustards: Family Otididae (*see* pages 120-1)
Very large open-landscape birds, with long thick neck, comparatively small beak, and long stout legs with comparatively small feet. Walk sedately. Rely on camouflage or run when disturbed, but if they take flight, wingbeats are strong. Among the heaviest of flying birds, requiring a take-off run to get airborne. Omnivorous. Males much larger and appreciably bolder-plumaged than females.

Lotusbirds or Jacanas: Family Jacanidae (*see* pages 120-1)
Medium-small, rail-like, wetland birds, with small head and beak, long slim neck, and characteristically long slender legs with extremely long-toed feet, allowing safe passage across floating vegetation (hence 'lily-trotter'). May submerge if alarmed. Fly with legs dangling. Omnivorous, feeding on aquatic vegetation and small animals. Sexes similar, although females are usually larger than males.

Waders or Shorebirds: part of the Order Charadriiformes (*see* pages 122-49)
The Charadriiformes is a complex and diverse Order, containing besides the familiar 'wader' grouping the gulls, terns and skuas (and in the Northern Hemisphere, the auks). Within the Australian waders – sometimes called shorebirds though frequently inappropriately – lie eight families. Six are small, and their members are distinctive: these are the stone-curlews, painted snipe, oystercatchers, stilts and avocet, phalaropes, and pratincoles. The two larger groups are the plovers, a cohesive band of varying sizes but all with distinctive stubby beaks, and the *Scolopacidae*. This is a diverse family in all respects: some have long, curved beaks, others have them short and stubby, or even straight and needle-like; many have long necks or legs, others are much shorter in all respects. Wader identification, because of their open coastal, wetland or inland habitats and natural wariness, is often a longish-range task. Important features to note – besides size and plumage colour – are the patterns (if any) visible on the wings and tail in flight; the length and particularly the colour of the legs; the length and shape of the beak; and any calls given. Waders feed (usually on small animals such as worms, shrimps and shellfish in wetlands, or on terrestrial invertebrates in drier habitats) with a fascinating variety of techniques, using beaks ranging from short and stubby (plovers), to needle-fine and upturned (avocet) or extremely long and downcurved (curlew). This range of structural and behavioural adaptation allows them to share the food available without undue competition, and at the same time provides most useful identification features.

Stone-curlews or Thick-knees: Family Burhinidae (*see* pages 122-3)
Medium-sized but among the larger waders, with a plover-like short beak, and large yellow-irised eyes indicative of a nocturnal life. Long legs with conspicuously bulky ankle joints (hence 'thick-knee'). Walk sedately. Rely on cryptic plumage for concealment, but if flushed, flight is fast and direct on narrow, downcurved, pointed wings with bold wingbars. Vocal, usually at night, with wailing or shrieking calls. Carnivorous, feeding on all types of small animals in both wetland and open landscapes. Sexes similar.

Painted Snipe: Family Rostratulidae (*see* pages 122-3)
Small wading birds, superficially snipe-like but with some similarity in secretive behaviour and appearance to the rails. Beak and legs of medium length for a wader. Omnivorous, probably favouring small aquatic animals. Sexes dissimilar, with females slightly larger and appreciably brighter than males.

Oystercatchers: Family Haematopodidae (*see* pages 122-3)
Medium-sized but among the larger waders, either pied or black in plumage, with sturdy, medium-long, laterally flattened straight beaks, and medium-length stout legs. Vocal, with penetrating piping calls. Omnivorous, favouring molluscs and crustaceans, occasionally annelid worms. Sexes similar.

Plovers and Dotterels: Family Charadriidae (*see* pages 124-31)
Medium (plovers) or small (dotterel) waders, with dumpy bodies, short necks, rounded heads, typically short stubby beaks distinctively slightly swollen at the tip, and medium-length legs. The feet lack a hind claw. Typically feed on drier substrates, running a few paces before jabbing at prey on or near the surface. Flight often swift and direct. Frequently form flocks. Carnivorous, feeding on small, usually invertebrate animals. Sexes similar, but marked differences are apparent between bright breeding and drab non-breeding plumages.

Stilts and Avocets: Family Recurvirostridae (*see* pages 130-1)
Tall, slim, medium-sized waders, distinctively long-legged (especially in stilts) and long-necked, with finely pointed medium-long beaks (characteristically upturned in avocet). Vociferous, with distinctive plaintive yelping calls, particularly if suddenly disturbed or near the nest. Carnivorous, feeding on small, usually aquatic, creatures. Sexes similar.

Sandpipers, Stints, Snipe and Curlews: Family Scolopacidae (*see* pages 132-47)
The largest and most diverse of wader families, ranging from small to large in size and with varied beak lengths. Sandpipers are small to medium-sized waders, graceful in appearance, with medium-long legs and medium-long beaks, usually straight or only slightly curved (up or down) and usually slim. Stints are the smallest of waders, the size of a chat or many honeyeaters: comparatively their legs are of medium length, their beaks short, straight and fine. Godwits are large waders with long legs and very long straight or almost straight, quite robust beaks. Curlews also tend to be large, and have comparatively very long characteristically downcurved beaks and mottled brown plumages varying little with season. Snipe too vary little with season, and have excellently camouflaged buff and brown plumages. Dumpy and comparatively short-legged, they have the longest, straightest beaks for their size of any wader. Many Scolopacidae are long-haul migrants. Carnivorous, occasionally taking plant food. Sexes similar, but marked differences may occur between breeding and non-breeding plumages. Note that migrants may be moulting into or out of adult or juvenile plumage, which can add to identification problems.

Phalaropes: Family Phalaropodidae (*see* pages 148-9)
Small aberrant waders, spending much of their time swimming buoyantly on water, often well out to sea. Long-necked, with short, usually fine beaks, they swim neck erect like a tiny gull, often spinning to obtain food. Carnivorous, but occasionally taking plant matter. Females slightly larger and appreciably brighter than males in breeding season; usually indistinguishable in non-breeding plumage.

Pratincoles: Family Glareolidae (*see* pages 148-9)
Medium-sized aberrant waders, usually found on dry inland plains, saltpans etc. In many ways they resemble long-legged terns with short beaks, and with their long wings and forked tails they hawk on the wing for food, like giant swallows. Carnivorous, usually taking insects. Sexes similar.

Skuas: Family Stercorariidae (*see* pages 150-1)
Medium to large gull-like seabirds with brown or fawn-and-white plumage, with bold white flashes distinctive in the wings in flight. Adults of some species have elongated central tail feathers. Agile in flight, securing much of their food by piratical attacks on other seabirds. Carnivorous, taking fish; sometimes predatory, taking young birds, eggs. Sexes similar.

Gulls and Terns: Family Laridae (*see* pages 152-63)
Gulls are well-known medium to large seabirds, usually with white and grey or black adult plumage, and with webbed feet. Swim buoyantly. Terns and noddies have a similar range of plumages, are mostly appreciably smaller, slimmer-winged and all are noticeably shorter in the leg. Though their feet are webbed they swim rarely, hunting for prey in flight, dipping to the water surface or plunge-diving for prey. Some gulls visit inland grassland, while some terns prefer fresh water, others salt. Subtle plumage details are often important in identification. Predominantly carnivorous on aquatic animals of many types, sometimes taking carrion, sometimes predatory. Sexes similar.

Pigeons and Doves: Family Columbidae (*see* pages 164-73)
Medium-small to medium-large birds, with plump, heavy bodies and comparatively small heads on longish necks. 'Pigeon' is usually applied to the larger species. Forest species are usually brilliantly coloured; open-land species much drabber, usually with buff or grey plumages. Often gregarious. Calls may be a useful identification aid. Omnivorous, but usually concentrating on fruit (forest) or seeds (open land), with occasional insects etc. Sexes similar in some species, dissimilar in others.

Cockatoos: Family Cacatuidae (*see* pages 174-9)
Medium to large parrots, usually simply patterned, only occasionally brightly coloured. All have prominent erectile crests; typical parrot hooked beaks, sometimes large; and typical parrot feet with two toes pointing forwards, two back. Often gregarious, usually harshly noisy. Omnivorous. Sexes similar in some species, dissimilar in others.

Parrots: Family Psittacidae (*see* pages 178-9)
Medium-sized short-tailed woodland and forest parrots, with characteristic parrot beak and feet. Brightly coloured, noisy and gregarious. Vegetarian, primarily fruit-eating. Sexes dissimilar, in one case markedly so.

Lorikeets: Family Loriidae (*see* pages 180-3)
Characteristically fast-flying small to medium-small parrots, predominantly green and with long pointed tails. Small characteristic parrot beak, but with brush-tipped tongue for feeding on nectar in blossoms. Gregarious, often in large noisy flocks, inhabiting forests and woodlands of all types. Vegetarian, favouring fruit and flowers, occasionally eating insects. Sexes similar.

Fig-Parrots: Family Opopsittidae (*see* pages 182-3)
Tiny – the smallest Australian parrot. Robustly built with a comparatively large head and strong parrot-type beak. Tail short, triangular. Fast-flying, comparatively secretive and quiet. Races separated by head patterns. Vegetarian. Sexes dissimilar.

Longtailed Parrots: Family Polytelitidae (*see* pages 182-5)
Medium-large to large colourful parrots, with long broad or pointed tails. Often gregarious, occupying a range of habitats from sub-desert to rainforest. Distinctive calls are also a useful identification feature. Primarily vegetarian. Sexes dissimilar.

Broadtailed Parrots: Family Platyceridae (*see* pages 186-97)
A large grouping of small to large, usually colourful, parrots from a wide range of habitats, with comparatively small beaks and long pointed or broadly pointed tails. Swift undulating flight. Often gregarious, sometimes with loud distinctive calls. Predominantly vegetarian. Sexes similar in some species, dissimilar in others.

Cuckoos and Coucals: Family Cuculidae (*see* pages 198-203)
A diverse grouping of small to large birds with long tails, elongated bodies, which coupled with short legs give a distinctive 'horizontal' perching posture. Flight usually swift, and their short wings often give a characteristically hawk-like flight silhouette. Calls are often loud and distinctive, and are a valuable identification aid. All but the Coucal are nest parasites of other birds. Primarily insectivorous, but some also eat small animals and fruit. Sexes sometimes similar, in other cases dissimilar.

Owls: Family Strigidae (*see* pages 204-5)
Large-headed, plump-bodied birds, small to large in size, usually with an upright perching stance. Most are nocturnal hunters. Eyes large, forward-looking, often with a bright yellow or gold iris, set in a distinct facial disc. Legs feathered, ending in large feet with powerful talons. Often vocal. Calls can be monotonous but are a valuable indicator of their presence after dark and a useful aid to identification. Carnivorous. Sexes broadly similar.

Barn Owls: Family Tytonidae (*see* pages 206-7)
Large-headed, almost top-heavy birds, medium to medium-large in size, with distinctively long, slim, 'knock-kneed' legs and powerful talons. Stance upright. Facial disc prominent, heart-shaped; eyes large and all-dark, forward-looking. Rarely vocal except in breeding season. Carnivorous. Sexes similar.

Frogmouths: Family Podargidae (*see* pages 208-9)
Strange, extremely well camouflaged birds, broadly resembling nightjars but with more than a hint of owl in their character. Medium to large in size, short-legged, with an upright, usually motionless, perching stance. Huge but inconspicuous beak. Eyes large, often closed or part-closed in daylight, with red or yellow iris. Nocturnal or crepuscular. Often solitary. Predominantly insectivorous, but eats other small animals. Sexes similar.

Owlet-nightjars: Family Aegothelidae (*see* pages 208-9)
Small, well camouflaged birds, more closely resembling long-tailed owls than the nightjars, with large forward-facing eyes set in a large head, often twisted from side to side. Nocturnal or crepuscular. Call a valuable indicator of their presence and identity. Predominantly insectivorous. Sexes similar.

Nightjars: Family Caprimulgidae (*see* pages 210-11)
Small to medium-sized, well-camouflaged nocturnal or crepuscular birds with long tails and short legs giving a characteristically horizontal perching posture. Stiff-winged hawk-like flight, in agile pursuit of insects. White patches in wing and tail, if present, are a useful identification guide. Calls are characteristic and distinctive. Insectivorous. Sexes broadly similar.

Swifts: Family Apodidae (*see* pages 210-13)
The most aerial of birds, small to medium-small in size, generally swallow-like in appearance with a comparatively stout, blunt-headed but well-streamlined body and exceptionally long, slender, sickle-shaped wings. Often gregarious. Flight fast. Legs tiny, rarely perching except at the nest. Tail shapes and position of white plumage patches are good identification guides. Insectivorous. Sexes similar.

Kingfishers: Family Alcedinidae (*see* pages 214-19)
Small to medium-large birds, usually short-tailed and plump, with an upright perching stance. Apparently oversized head and beak, and comparatively tiny feet. One subfamily (*Alcedininae*) hunts over water, the other (*Daceloninae*) primarily in dry habitats, in both cases from a prominent perch. Often brightly coloured. Calls penetrating or harsh laughing, usefully distinctive. Often solitary. Carnivorous, with a wide selection of prey (including snakes) caught by plunge-diving or in a swoop to the ground. Sexes broadly similar.

Bee-eaters: Family Meropidae (*see* pages 218-19)
Represented by a single species in Australia. Medium-sized, characteristically harlequin-coloured, with a pointed downcurved beak, elongated central tail feathers, and a swooping swallow-like flight. Distinctive call, useful as an early warning of its presence. Often gregarious. Insectivorous, taking most prey in acrobatic flight. Sexes broadly similar.

Rollers: Family Coraciidae (*see* pages 218-19)
Another colourful family represented by a single Australian species, the Dollarbird. Medium-sized and heavily built, with a shortish powerful beak. Tail square-cut. Wings a mixture of brilliant blues with diagnostic white spot in flight feathers. Distinctive harsh call. Often solitary. Carnivorous, taking prey on the ground after swooping from regularly used prominent perch. Sexes similar.

Pittas: Family Pittidae (*see* pages 220-1)
Distinctively brilliantly-coloured ground-living forest or scrub birds, thrush-like but almost tail-less in appearance, with comparatively long strong legs. Secretive, but calls are a useful guide to both their presence and their identity. Omnivorous, taking various seeds and fruits, and small terrestrial animals. Hard seeds and snails may be smashed open on regularly-used 'anvil' stones. Sexes similar.

Lyrebirds: Family Menuridae (*see* pages 220-1)
Very large and distinctive, even famous, ground-living forest birds, confined to Australia, with chicken-like bodies, heads and feet, and a long tail, amazingly developed into the 'lyre' in one species. Complex courtship rituals on display grounds, including dancing and well-developed song with wide range of mimicry. Primarily carnivorous. Sexes similar, but females have shorter, simpler tails.

Scrub-birds: Family Atrichornithidae (*see* pages 222-3)
Distinctively Australian, smallish, brownish babbler-like birds of dense undergrowth. Noisy in behaviour, fossicking through leaf litter, and powerfully vocal, but extremely elusive in sightings. Range and voice determine identity. Probably largely carnivorous, feeding on terrestrial invertebrates. Females lack black chest/throat markings of males, otherwise similar.

Larks: Family Alaudidae (*see* pages 222-3)
Small, sandy-brownish, open-grassland birds, running actively. Beak comparatively stout; feet with long hind claw. Songs usually melodious, sometimes repetitive and with mimicry, produced in soaring song flight, but a useful distinguishing feature. Tail shows white edges in flight. Omnivorous. Sexes similar. Skylark is an introduced species.

Swallows and Martins: Family Hirundinidae (*see* pages 224-5)
Familiar small birds, most often seen in flight when their characteristically rather long and slender curved wings show to good effect as they swoop after insect prey. Most species (swallows) have deeply forked tails with long streamers. Martins have shorter shallowly forked tails. Distribution of white areas of plumage is a useful identification guide. Frequently gregarious. Insectivorous. Sexes broadly similar.

Pipits and Wagtails: Family Motacillidae (*see* pages 226-7)
Small, fast-running, terrestrial birds with distinctive habit of wagging their long or longish tails up and down. Pipits are drab browns and streaked; wagtails distinctively coloured and patterned. All have distinctive flight calls: valuable identification aids. Deeply undulating flight. Carnivorous, usually feeding on terrestrial invertebrates. Sexes similar in pipits, dissimilar (sometimes subtly so) in wagtails.

Cuckoo-shrikes and Trillers: Family Campephagidae (*see* pages 228-31)
Medium or medium-small birds, usually greyish or blackish plumaged, with comparatively long tails giving a cuckoo-like appearance in flight. Beak of medium length but strong and slightly hooked (like a shrike). Legs usually comparatively short. Plumage patterns and voice are good identification pointers. Omnivorous. Sexes generally similar, more distinctive in trillers.

Bulbuls: Family Pycnonotidae (*see* pages 230-1)
One medium-sized introduced species, long-tailed and perky, with a distinctive head pattern and crest. Calls simple but melodic and distinctive. Sometimes gregarious. Omnivorous. Sexes similar.

Flycatchers, Thrushes, Whistlers and allies: Family Muscicapidae
(*see* pages 232-57)
World-wide, the largest of all bird families and also diverse, best considered in readily recognizable groups.
Thrushes (*see* pages 232-4): generally plump, medium-small or medium, slim-beaked songbirds, often terrestrial in habits. The 'true thrushes' are melodious and, apart from the introduced Blackbird, brownish with boldly speckled breasts. Scrub-robins are Australian endemics, thrush-like in behaviour but longer in the tail, and more strikingly terrestrial. Omnivorous, taking fruit and small invertebrates of many kinds. Sexes similar.
Australian Robins (*see* pages 234-43): small, usually colourful, plump birds with comparatively long slender legs and appreciably slimmer beaks than the Monarch Flycatchers (see below). The robins have an upright posture and slightly drooped wings and characteristically flick their tails. The red-breasted robin males are easily identified; females and immatures present considerable challenges and demand attention to finer details of plumage and distribution. They watch for food on the ground from a prominent perch. Yellow robins are normally tame, frequently perching on vertical tree trunks watching for food on the ground below. The *Microeca* flycatchers have characteristic flycatcher behaviour and typically flattened beak, and comparatively soft plumage colours. Primarily insectivorous. Sexes dissimilar in the red-breasted robins, usually broadly similar in the remainder.
Shrike-tit (*see* page 243): small-medium, robust and colourful bird with a comparatively large, crested, boldly patterned head and stout, notched and slightly hooked beak. Omnivorous. Sexes broadly similar.
Whistlers and Shrike-thrushes (*see* pages 244-49): comparatively heavy-headed, short-legged, small-medium sized songbirds with rather stout slightly hooked beaks. Whistlers usually have males more boldly coloured than females, sometimes substantially so, and often hunt food among the leaves. Flight strong and undulating. Song distinctive in both melodic content and explosive volume. Shrike-thrushes are more sombrely plumaged, actively hunting prey on trunks, branches and the ground, with songs comparable to whistlers in musical quality but briefer. The sexes are broadly similar in plumage.

Carnivorous, with a wide range of prey.

Monarch Flycatchers (*see* pages 250-55): distinctive flycatchers with characteristic longish broad beaks fringed with bristles, very small to medium-small in size. Hunt from prominent perches, with tail quivered sometimes side to side, sometimes up and down, dashing out to catch prey in flight or on foliage. Voice simple, with harsh or whistling calls. Primarily insectivorous. Sexes sometimes similar, or broadly so; sometimes strikingly dissimilar.

Fantails (*see* pages 256-7): small, often familiar flycatchers with characteristically long tails, often held partly cocked and frequently opened and closed like a fan, showing distinguishing tail and rump patterns. Confiding birds with characteristically jerky movements as they hunt methodically through the foliage. Songs vigorous, some ascending, some descending, and a useful field guide. Primarily insectivorous. Sexes similar.

Chowchillas, Whipbirds, Wedgebills, Quail-thrushes: Family Orthonychidae
(*see* pages 258-61)
Small-medium or medium-sized terrestrial songbirds, rather secretive in behaviour and generally comparatively long-tailed. Males generally have bolder black-and-white head patterns than females. Voices usually high-pitched and thin, sometimes with mimicry but far-carrying. Beak comparatively robust. In whipbirds and wedgebills, sexes are similar with a distinctive crest. Carnivorous, with a wide range of invertebrate prey.

Australian Babblers: Family Pomatostomidae (*see* pages 262-3)
Vocal, medium-sized and plump terrestrial birds, with comparatively stout legs and long tails. Beak pointed, slightly downcurved. Often gregarious, living in characteristic cooperative groups up to about a dozen strong. Move in close-knit flocks, flying low and direct with whirring wingbeats followed by glides. On ground, move noisily in high bouncing hops. Subtle differences in head, breast and wing pattern, and in calls, aid identification. Omnivorous. Sexes similar.

Old-World Warblers: Family Sylviidae (*see* pages 264-7)
Small to small-medium, generally inconspicuous, grassland or reed-bed birds, slim-beaked, sombrely coloured, some plain, some streaked. Songs and calls are usefully distinctive, ranging from repetitive harsh to melodic warbles. Primarily insectivorous, occasionally eating fruit or seeds. Sexes similar.

Australian Warblers: Family Maluridae (*see* pages 268-75)
A grouping of small (some medium-small) insectivorous birds peculiar to the Australasian region. The fairy-wrens are familiar, with their tiny bodies and long cocked tails. Males are extremely brightly plumaged during the breeding season but duller, like the females, for the rest of the year. Gregarious and cooperative in breeding. Range and habitat can help sort similarly-plumaged females. Emu-wrens also have tiny bodies, but their long scanty tails have a distinctively fragile, bristly appearance. Males have characteristic blue throats. Secretive, rarely leaving dense scrub cover. Range helps with identification. Grasswrens are larger and darker, generally with comparatively shorter, stouter tails. Range and habitat are valuable aids to identification.

Scrubwrens, Fairy Warblers, Thornbills and allies: Family Acanthizidae
(*see* pages 276-91)
Another diverse grouping of Australian endemics, generally 'normal small bird' in appearance, mostly carnivorous (insects predominating), some taking nectar, tiny to small in size. The 'Sandstone Warblers' are brown above, cinnamon below. They are tame and terrestrial, almost mouse-like, and have distinctive songs. Habitat is a useful identification aid. Scrubwrens are birds of dense undergrowth, sombre in plumage apart from their distinctive head patterns and comparatively long beaks. Their tails are of normal length and not carried cocked. Some have distinctive and musical songs. The Weebill and the *Gerygone* warblers have short-pointed insectivorous beaks and often take their prey in flight around the outer leaves of the canopy. Tiny and slimly-built, most have usefully distinctive and attractive songs. Plumage and eye colours and head and tail patterns are primary identification guides. The thornbills are tiny brownish or yellowish birds, sometimes streaked. Identification rests on the presence or absence of

streaks, rump colour, eye colour, head pattern and overall body colour. Songs are often characteristic and a useful guide, and may contain mimicry. The whitefaces are similarly diminutive, but have distinctive, easily identifiable plumages. Their beaks are stouter than thornbills', reflecting a terrestrial life and a diet including seeds. Bristlebirds are larger, more sombrely plumaged and a little babbler-like in appearance. Their far-carrying calls are useful indicators of both presence and identity, and range is also a valuable aid.

Sittellas: Family Neosittidae (*see* pages 290-1)
Small, short-tailed, agile climbing bird with strong feet and dagger-like, slightly upturned beak. Wings comparatively large and rounded, both wings and tail with distinctive patterns best visible during display or in flight, which is deeply undulating. Gregarious and noisy, with several distinctive calls. Plumages vary considerably across the country. Carnivorous, predominantly eating insects and their larvae. Sexes similar.

Australian Treecreepers: Family Climacteridae (*see* pages 292-3)
An Australian family of small to small-medium, generally dark-plumaged birds with long strong claws for tree-creeping and slightly downcurved, comparatively long and finely pointed beaks for seeking food in bark crevices. Usually in ones or twos, climbing trunks in upward spirals, before gliding off to begin a new trunk near the base. Some species feed on the ground. Plumage colours and streaking and eye-stripe size and colour are useful identification aids, as is range. Predominantly insectivorous, with some seeds. Sexes dissimilar.

Honeyeaters: Family Meliphagidae (*see* pages 294-317)
One of the largest and most typically Australian bird families, ranging from tiny to large in size, and varied in habitat choice, behaviour and plumage. All have an elongated appearance, with slim bodies often held almost horizontally, comparatively long tails, and relatively long but strong downcurved beaks. Their legs are strong, babbler-like. All are active birds, always on the move, often in groups. Many species have bare areas of skin on the face, and some have fleshy wattles. Most are noisy, some have distinctive songs or calls. Usually plumage features, particularly around the head, are the best identification guide, and where differences are subtle, distribution maps can often help greatly. The brush-tipped tongue that facilitates nectar feeding, though characteristic of the family, is of little help in identification. Omnivorous, with insects, nectar and pollen, and fruits predominating. Sexes similar.

Australian Chats: Family Epthianuridae (*see* pages 318-21)
A small endemic family of tiny or small, often gregarious, brightly-coloured birds. Frequently seen on low scrub or on the ground where they run swiftly with a characteristic 'swagger'. Flight is strong, with bursts of wingbeats. Plumage features easily identify males: differences are sometimes subtle between females and immatures. Predominantly insectivorous. Sexes dissimilar.

Sunbird: Family Nectariniidae (*see* pages 320-1)
The sole Australian representative of a large Afro-Asian family, the Sunbird is typically brilliantly coloured, with a metallic sheen to its purple-black throat. Tiny, with a distinctively long, downcurved beak for sucking nectar, frequently from trumpet-shaped flowers. Darting flight. Distinctive high-pitched calls and song. Omnivorous, taking nectar and small invertebrates. Sexes dissimilar.

Flowerpecker: Family Dicaeidae (*see* pages 320-1)
Another tiny sole Australian representative of a large Afro-Asian family. This species, the Mistletoebird, is characteristically dumpy and short-tailed, distinctively plumaged, restlessly active. Often seen near mistletoe, a favourite food. Calls and song are useful identification features. Usually solitary or in pairs. Omnivorous, taking fruit, nectar and insects. Sexes dissimilar.

Pardalotes: Family Pardalotidae (*see* pages 322-3)
Tiny, short-tailed, dumpy birds with whirring flight and short, stout beaks. Though plumages are distinctively spotted, speckled or striped, pardalotes may be difficult to spot in the foliage. Often

gregarious. Calls are often a useful guide to their presence and identity. Predominantly insectivorous, with other small invertebrates. Sexes broadly similar.

White-eyes: Family Zosteropidae (*see* pages 324-5)
Small, highly active, vocal and often gregarious birds, warbler-like in shape, with short, fine, slightly downcurved beaks. Plumages are greenish above, whitish below, with a bold characteristic white eye-ring. Calls and songs are usefully distinctive. Omnivorous, taking insects, fruits and nectar. Sexes similar.

Finches: Family Fringillidae (*see* pages 326-7)
Small seed-eaters (but larger than native grass-finches) with robust conical beaks capable of cracking hard-shelled seeds. Two introduced species, one unmistakably brilliantly plumaged, the other more sombre. Calls, song and distribution are useful aids. Predominantly vegetarian, but feed young on insects. Sexes broadly similar.

Old-World Sparrows: Family Passeridae (*see* pages 326-7)
Small seed-eaters, with thick conical beaks, robustly and compactly built. Calls and songs harsh and simple, but distinctive. Two introduced species, comparatively sombrely plumaged in browns and fawns. Often gregarious. More or less omnivorous. Sexes similar in one case, dissimilar in the other.

Grass-finches and allies: Families Ploceidae and Estrildidae (*see* pages 326-35)
Tiny to small seed-eaters, with stout conical seed-crushing beaks. Apart from the introduced Bishop and Wydah (Ploceidae), these are active, colourful or boldly patterned birds, some with long pointed tails. All build complex domed nests of woven grasses. Often gregarious, in fast-flying active flocks. Plumage details are usually readily diagnostic. Omnivorous, eating seeds and small invertebrates. Females usually less brightly coloured or boldly patterned than males.

Starlings and Mynahs: Family Sturnidae (*see* pages 336-7)
Small-medium, dark (often glossy) plumaged, robustly built birds with medium-length dagger-shaped beaks. Of the three species two are introduced. Often gregarious, usually vocal, sometimes with much mimicry. Fast in flight. Omnivorous. Sexes broadly similar.

Orioles and Figbirds: Family Oriolidae (*see* pages 336-7)
Broadly similar in shape to starlings and thrushes but slightly larger in size, with longish, quite robust, slightly downcurved beaks, often pink in colour. Some have bare patches of facial skin. Usefully distinctive songs and calls. Omnivorous, chiefly eating fruits and insects. Sexes dissimilar.

Drongos: Family Dicruridae (*see* pages 338-9)
Distinctive, all-black, medium-sized birds with broad strong beaks, characteristically short legs, and longish, broadly forked tail. Calls harsh and metallic. Tend to sit motionless apart from occasional tail flicks on prominent perches, dashing off to catch prey. Aggressive. Omnivorous, food ranging from nectar to small animals, predominantly insects. Sexes similar.

Bowerbirds: Family Ptilonorhynchidae (*see* pages 338-41)
Medium-sized, largely terrestrial birds with shortish stout beaks and comparatively strong legs. Males tend to have bright or iridescent plumage or coloured short nape-crests, while females are much drabber. Distinguished by the fascinating building of 'bowers' – made by males for display and mating, using available vegetation, natural items (berries, stones) and artifacts (rings from beer cans even). Structure of bower (avenue or maypole) and predominant ornamentation colours give identification guidance, as does distribution. Omnivorous. Sexes dissimilar.

Birds of Paradise: Family Paradisaeidae (*see* pages 342-3)
Medium-large, famously spectacular birds, most species native to New Guinea. Australian members are generally dark-plumaged and iridescent, with amazing arboreal displays. Voice harsh, loud and distinctive. Omnivorous. Sexes dissimilar.

Woodswallows: Family Artamidae (*see* pages 344-5)
Medium-small birds, resembling a cross between a swallow and a starling, with all the grace of the former in flight yet with the markedly triangular wings of the latter. Robustly built, they have short pointed beaks, blue with black tips. Gregarious. Underside plumages are distinctive in flight and an excellent identification aid. Predominantly insectivorous. Sexes similar.

Mud-nesters: Family Corcoracidae (*see* pages 346-7)
Large or medium-large birds, endemic to Australia. Always gregarious, they are cooperative breeders. Apart from building large cup-shaped mud nests cemented to a branch, the two species are not closely similar in looks, but both are long-tailed and have the look of the Icterids of the Americas. One is black, the other grey; one has a longish, slender, downcurved beak, the other an altogether shorter and stouter one. Omnivorous, predominantly feeding on small animals of all types. Sexes similar.

Magpie-Larks: Family Grallinidae (*see* pages 346-7)
Medium-sized birds, neither magpie nor lark but of uncertain affinities. Characteristically boldly patterned, pied plumage, with black-tipped white tail distinctive in flight. Aggressive, yet often feeds in company with other gregarious birds. Distinctive call. Predominantly carnivorous on all sorts of small animals. Sexes broadly similar.

Butcherbirds and Currawongs: Family Cracticidae (*see* pages 346-51)
Medium to large birds, usually with strikingly patterned grey, black and white plumages. Relatively long tails and stout, straight, longish and slightly hooked beaks are characteristic. Voices are loud and usefully distinctive. Widespread and often gregarious. Omnivorous, often predatory on any smaller animal, also eating fruits. Sexes similar.

Ravens and Crows: Family Corvidae (*see* pages 350-3)
Familiar all-glossy-black large birds with heavy longish straight beaks, usually showing rather rounded fingered wings in flight. Calls loud, harsh and simple variants of 'caw'. Correct identification calls for attention to structure and behaviour as well as voice. Range may also help. Omnivorous, often predatory or scavenging. Sexes similar.

BIRDS

OF AUSTRALIA

Emu *Dromaius novaehollandiae* 160-190cm Enormous, familiar and unmistakable, and Australia's national bird emblem. Long-necked, with a comparatively small head. Bare skin of sides of head, neck and throat bluish-grey. Body grey-brown, bulky, with distinctively coarse shaggy feathering and bulbous drooping tail. Breeding females are darker, with bristly blackish feathers on head and neck. Flightless, with no discernible wings. Legs long, strong; runs powerfully with characteristically bouncing, rolling gait. Surprisingly, swims well. Chicks have striped plumage. *Voice:* male has deep grunts; female a thumping drumming. *Habitat:* catholic in habitat choice, avoiding desert areas, dense forests and human settlements. Sometimes solitary; sometimes in flocks, occasionally large. Widespread; locally quite common. 🏍 ♙♙ ⅏ 🛏 ♙♙ ⓡ △

Southern Cassowary *Casuarius casuarius* 120-150cm Enormous and distinctive. Neck long and comparatively thick; head with characteristic dark casque or helmet. Bare skin of face and throat blue, nape scarlet. Reddish fleshy wattles droop from front of neck. Body bulky, purplish black, with coarse drooping feathers. Female slightly larger, with brighter-coloured fleshy patches. Flightless, with no discernible wings. Legs dark grey, long and strong, with dagger-like inner toenail used in offence and defence. Runs swiftly and swims well. Chicks have strongly linear striped plumage. *Voice:* harsh coughs, piercing whistles, often at night. *Habitat:* tropical rainforest, often by stream-sides and in clearings. Shy, usually in family groups. Generally uncommon except in undisturbed habitat. 🐾 ⓡ

Ostrich *Struthio camelus* 220-250cm Enormous and familiar, the largest living bird, with a long almost bare pinkish or greyish neck topped by a smallish head with large eyes and a flattened beak. Body black in male, with conspicuous white plumes on wings and tail. Female grey, lacking plumes. Legs long and powerful, with distinctive 'muscular thighs' (actually shins); runs swiftly with characteristic prancing strides, with rudimentary wings held outstretched. Flightless. Chicks have blackish bodies with buff and black striped head and neck. *Voice:* male has booming roar. *Habitat:* plains, grazing land, open woodlands. Introduced; scarce; all known feral birds are now captive. 🏍 ♙♙

Emu (adult)

Emu (adult and immatures)

Southern Cassowary ♂

Ostrich ♂

Great Crested Grebe *Podiceps cristatus* 50cm Large, distinctive slender-necked, slim-bodied waterbird; largest of the grebes. Adults have black crest and broad chestnut and black 'ear tufts' drooping to form a ruff. Some non-breeding birds have greatly reduced ruff and crest. Beak pinkish yellow; long, slim and dagger-like. Body brown above, buff shading to white below, with distinctive 'tail-less' appearance. Eye chestnut. Immatures lack chestnut ruff, have only a vestige of the crest, and a yellowish beak. Legs bluish, set well back on body; feet with lobed toes. Dives frequently and neatly. Characteristic humpbacked appearance in flight, with head and neck drooping; prominent white leading and trailing edges to the inner half of the wing are distinctive. *Voice:* barking and rattling calls, vocal during breeding season with elaborate courtship displays. *Habitat:* most types of large inland and coastal waters. Often gregarious. Irregular in numbers and distribution, sometimes locally common. 🌊⚓🐟△®

Hoary-headed Grebe *Poliocephalus poliocephalus* 30cm Medium-large grebe, with typical slim-bodied fluffy-tailed appearance. Appreciably shorter-necked than Great Crested, with shorter, stouter, dagger-shaped beak. Breeding adult has black head with fine white streaks, black beak with whitish tip. Neck and belly white, flanks buff, back brown. Eye white. Non-breeding birds have dark brown crown and back of neck sharply demarcated from white face and throat; beak pinkish grey. Dives frequently and neatly. In flight appears plumper and shorter-necked than Great Crested, showing broad white wingbar running the full length of the wing. Characteristically flies to escape danger. *Voice:* rarely vocal. *Habitat:* larger fresh waters of most types and sheltered coastal seas. Widespread; fairly common, sometimes locally numerous. 🌊⚓🐟△®

Australasian Grebe *Tachybaptus novaehollandiae* 24cm Medium-sized, but the smallest and dumpiest of the grebes. Head and short neck blackish, with chestnut patches on side of neck visible in good conditions. Beak stubby, black with small whitish tip and with conspicuous yellow patch of bare skin at gape. Eye golden. Breeding adult dark in appearance, brown above, dark buff on the flanks, shading to white on the belly. Winter birds are greyer, with white face, throat and front of neck shading into grey-brown crown and nape. Beak pinkish grey. Dives frequently, and to escape danger (see Hoary-headed). *Voice:* characteristic shrill whinnying chatter. *Habitat:* usually on fresh waters. Sometimes gregarious with Hoary-headed. Widespread; in many places common. 🌊△®

Great Crested Grebe

Hoary-headed Grebe (breeding)

Hoary-headed Grebe (non-breeding)

Australasian Grebe (breeding)

Australasian Grebe (non-breeding)

King Penguin *Aptenodytes patagonica* 90cm Very large, and unmistakably a penguin, upright and robustly built. Large size; long, straight dagger-like beak, and black head with yellowish patches on sides of nape are all good distinguishing features. Upperparts steel-blue, underparts white in adult. Immatures are greyer overall, with rather shorter beaks, streaked pink on lower mandible. Crown greyish, nape patches dull cream. *Voice:* vocal only on sub-Antarctic breeding grounds. *Habitat:* oceanic, straying into coastal waters. Vagrant. ✎

Gentoo Penguin *Pygoscelis papua* 73cm Very large, but medium-sized for a penguin. Dumpy, upright, with distinctive comparatively short, slim, dagger-like yellowish-orange beak and yellowish-orange legs. Upperparts black, with black head; underparts white. Diagnostic white band running from eye to eye round back of crown. Immature paler and greyer, with less white on head, and with shorter, paler yellow beak and paler feet. *Voice:* vocal only on Antarctic and sub-Antarctic breeding grounds. *Habitat:* oceanic, straying into coastal waters. Vagrant. ✎

Chinstrap Penguin *Pygoscelis antarctica* 72cm Very large, but medium-sized for a penguin. Head pattern diagnostic, with white face, black crown and nape, and thin but conspicuous black stripe - the chin strap - running from the nape across the cheeks and throat. Beak short, slim and blackish. Upperparts dull black, underparts white, with pink feet. Immature greyer, with speckling of dark feathers on face and throat. *Voice:* only on Antarctic and sub-Antarctic breeding grounds. *Habitat:* oceanic, straying into coastal waters. Vagrant. ✎

Adelie Penguin *Pygoscelis adeliae* 74cm Very large, but medium-sized for a penguin. Head pattern diagnostic, lacking any crest, all-black including throat, with a striking white eye-ring. Forehead characteristically steeply sloped. Beak short and black, with orange at base. Upperparts black, underparts white, with pink feet. Immature greyer, with white throat; lacks eye-ring. *Voice:* vocal only on Antarctic breeding grounds. *Habitat:* oceanic, straying into coastal waters. Vagrant. ✎

Magellanic Penguin *Spheniscus magellanicus* 70cm Very large, but medium-sized for a penguin. Beak robust, black with a white vertical mark near the tip. Upperparts black; underparts white with a distinctive black horseshoe-shaped band round upper breast, which with black and white head, face and throat pattern, is diagnostic. Legs black. Immature greyer, lacking the distinctive head pattern. *Voice:* vocal only on breeding grounds. *Habitat:* oceanic, straying into coastal waters. Vagrant. ✎

Royal Penguin *Eudyptes schlegeli* 68cm Very large, but medium-sized for a penguin. Crown black, cheeks diagnostically smoky grey or grey-flecked, with often indistinct but sometimes bulky, loose, long and straggling golden crest as 'eyebrow' over red eye. Beak long stout and deep, pink; legs pink. Upperparts black; underparts white. Immature greyer, lacking crests, with smaller dull brown or reddish beak. Cheeks and throat often smoky grey. *Voice:* vocal only on Antarctic and sub-Antarctic breeding grounds. *Habitat:* oceanic, straying into coastal waters. Vagrant. ✎

King Penguin (breeding)

Gentoo Penguin (breeding)

Chinstrap Penguin (breeding)

Adelie Penguin (breeding)

Magellanic Penguin (breeding)

Royal Penguin (breeding)

Rockhopper Penguin *Eudyptes chrysocome* 54cm Very large, but smallish for a penguin. Long straggling bristling golden crest over each eye, characteristically starting as a slim line only just in front of the eye. Throat black. Beak stubby but deep; dark pink. Legs pale pink. Black above, white below. Immature greyer, with pale tip to pinkish-brown beak and with whitish throat heavily streaked with grey. Lacks eyestripe. *Voice:* vocal only on breeding grounds. *Habitat:* oceanic, but regular winter visitor as singles or in small groups to southern coastal seas. ≼

Fiordland Penguin *Eudyptes pachyrhynchus* 50-70cm Very large, but medium-sized for a penguin. Dense yellow crest, bristling at nape, running over each eye, characteristically starting as a broad line at the base of the pink beak. Throat and cheeks black, with diagnostic white scaly markings below eye. Black above, white below. Immature greyer, with whitish throat. Unlike immature Rockhopper has defined whitish stripe over eye. *Voice:* vocal only on breeding grounds in New Zealand and farther south. *Habitat:* oceanic, but possibly fairly regular if scarce visitor to southeastern coastal waters. ≼

Erect-crested Penguin *Eudyptes sclateri* 70cm Very large, but medium-sized for a penguin. Dense yellow crest characteristically bristles upwards, starting as a thick line close to the base of the beak and running back onto nape. Beak reddish brown, lined with pale whitish bare skin round gape. Black above, white below, with black throat. Feet pale pink with black soles. Immature has whitish throat and much less developed cream crest. *Voice:* vocal only on breeding grounds on southern islands. *Habitat:* oceanic, occasionally straying into coastal waters. Vagrant. ≼

Snares Penguin *Eudyptes robustus* 70cm Very large, but medium-sized for a penguin. Black above, white below, with a black throat. Similar to but more robustly built than Fiordland, with a drooping yellow crest starting close to the base of the reddish brown beak. Bare line of pinkish skin round gape, and lack of white cheek flecks of Snares, help separate this species from adult Fiordland. Immature Snares greyer, with defined eye-stripe. *Voice:* vocal only on breeding grounds on New Zealand islands. *Habitat:* oceanic, straying into coastal waters. Vagrant. ≼

Little Penguin *Eudyptula minor* 33cm Large, but the smallest of all penguins. Adult distinctly blue-grey above shading to white below; flippers blackish above with a white trailing edge, white below. Beak black, pointed; feet pinkish with black soles. Adult at end of breeding season distinctly browner. Immature has upperparts even bluer. Swims very low in water, sometimes with only head and neck and tail protruding. Often gregarious, especially near colonies. *Voice:* puppy-like yelping, deep growls and donkey-like braying - all useful indicators of its presence on land, as colony visits are nocturnal. *Habitat:* coastal seas offshore from Western Australia to central Queensland. Breeds in burrows on islands. Locally abundant. ≼ ®

Rockhopper Penguin (breeding)

Fiordland Penguin (immature)

Erect-crested Penguin (breeding)

Snares Penguin (breeding)

Little Penguin (breeding)

Wandering Albatross *Diomedea exulans* 100-130cm Enormous, with perhaps the greatest wingspan of any seabird, often reaching 3.5m. Distinctive albatross silhouette and flight pattern. Plumages variable, from almost all-dark immature with whitish face and underwing over as long as ten years, to all-white full adult plumage save for black wingtips. Sheer size, effortless flight and angular flying-cross silhouette are with experience the best distinguishing features. See similar Royal. *Voice:* seldom vocal at sea. *Habitat:* oceanic, breeding on sub-Antarctic islands. Follows ships and fishing boats. Regular but rarely numerous visitor off southern coasts, mostly in winter and spring. 🐟

Royal Albatross *Diomedea epomophora* 95-130cm Enormous. Closely resembles immature Wandering. All plumages have white head and body and dark upperwing contrasting with white saddle. Wandering is similar in some plumage stages but has black tail band (little or none in Royal), greyish crown patch and mottled saddle. Mature Royal has white area along upper forewing, this is attained progressively from leading edge inwards; whereas Wandering develops white patches in centre of dark upperwing, spreading later to leading edge. Combination of mostly dark upperwing and white tail diagnostic of Royal. At very close range look for diagnostic narrow black "smile line" along cutting edges of mandibles. *Voice:* seldom vocal at sea. *Habitat:* oceanic, breeding on islands off New Zealand. Follows fishing boats but rarely ships. Occasional off southern and southeastern coasts. 🐟

Black-browed Albatross *Diomedea melanophrys* 90cm Very large, but comparatively dumpy, thick-necked albatoss. Beak yellow, with pink tip visible at close range. Characteristic black marking through and over eye. Body white, with black tail and black uppersides to wings. Back black, as in other mollymawks, distinguishing them from white-backed Royal and Wandering. Underwing distinctively white centrally, with broad black margins. Immature greyer, with grey nape and sides of breast and grey underwing. Beak blackish. Flight distinctively precise, almost shearwater-like. *Voice:* seldom vocal at sea. *Habitat:* oceanic, breeding on many sub-Antarctic islands and off New Zealand, following ships and visiting inshore waters along the south coasts. Widespread, particularly during the winter: the most numerous Australian albatross. 🐟

Buller's Albatross *Diomedea bulleri* 85cm Very large, comparatively heavily built albatross. Dark eye-patch and pale forehead contribute to a distinctive 'capped' appearance. At close range, beak black with prominent yellow culmen and underside. Adult underparts and rump white, with black tail, grey head, throat and mantle. Upperwing dark grey, underwing characteristically white with narrow black margins. Immature brownish-grey with all-black beak, but shows distinctive underwing pattern of adult. *Voice:* seldom vocal at sea. *Habitat:* oceanic, very occasionally visiting coastal waters in the southeast. 🐟

Wandering Albatross (older immature)

Royal Albatross (immature)

Black-browed Albatross

Buller's Albatross

Grey-headed Albatross *Diomedea chrysostoma* 85cm Very large robustly-built albatross. Head, nape and throat dove grey, with black mark through eye. Beak black with narrow yellow culmen stripe. Adults with underwing pattern similar to Black-browed but black and white more clearly demarcated. Underparts and rump white, tail black. Immature browner, with all-dark beak; white underwing patch suffused with grey. *Voice:* seldom vocal at sea. *Habitat:* oceanic, breeding on many sub-Antarctic islands. Regular winter visitor to southern inshore waters; occasionally comparatively numerous off southwest of Tasmania. ◄

Yellow-nosed Albatross *Diomedea chlororhynchos* 75cm Very large, but smallest of the 'mollymawk' albatrosses. Head and body white, with black upperwings and tail. Dark smudge through eye. Underwing white, narrowly bordered black. Beak long and slender, black with yellow stripe along ridge. Immature greyer, with all-black beak. *Voice:* seldom vocal at sea. *Habitat:* oceanic, breeding on several southern ocean islands. Regular winter visitor to southern coasts, occasionally in flocks off the southwest. ◄

Shy (White-capped) Albatross *Diomedea cauta* 100cm Very large, with a wingspan often exceeding 2m. Variable amounts of pale grey wash to head, nape and throat. Dark smudge through eye. Body white, with blackish tail. Back and upperwing characteristically uniform dark grey, contrasting with predominantly white underwing with very narrow dark margins. Beak greyish-yellow. Immature greyer. Avidly follows ships and particularly fishing boats, taking offal. *Voice:* harsh gurgles (and beak-clattering) in breeding season. *Habitat:* breeds on remote southeastern islands, dispersing widely but remaining fairly common along the south and southeast coasts. ◄ ®

Sooty Albatross *Phoebetria fusca* 90cm A distinctly slim, graceful, all-dark albatross with a relatively long, almost pointed, tail. Plumage entirely chocolate brown, darkest around the head. At close range, pale shafts to primaries can be seen, as can white eye-ring. Beak blackish with a narrow yellow stripe on lower mandible. Immature has buffish scaly markings on mantle. *Voice:* seldom vocal at sea. *Habitat:* oceanic, with breeding colonies on islands in southern Atlantic and Indian Oceans; occasionally occurring along southern coasts. ◄

Light-mantled Sooty Albatross *Phoebetria palpebrata* 90cm Very similar to Sooty in size and graceful flight, with similar slender-winged, long-tailed appearance. Uniformly dark brown, with white eye-ring visible at close range, but with nape, mantle, back and rump all dove grey. Black beak has pale bluish line along lower mandible. Immature similar, but with buff scaly markings on back. *Voice:* seldom vocal at sea. *Habitat:* oceanic, breeding on southern islands and ranging farther south to pack-ice margins. Very rare along the south coast. ◄

Grey-headed Albatross

Yellow-nosed Albatross

Shy (White-capped) Albatross

Sooty Albatross

Light-mantled Sooty Albatross

Southern Giant-Petrel *Macronectes giganteus* 90cm Largest of the petrels, with a 2m wingspan. Immediately separable from albatrosses by comparatively clumsy, heavily flapping flight on kinked wings. Adult has two colour phases: all-white with black flecks, and dark - all sooty brown save for brown-flecked greyish head. In both cases beak yellow with green tip, bulbously heavy, clearly segmented, with nostril tube on ridge. Immature entirely sooty brown with yellow beak. Faint whitish speckling on leading edge of wing. *Voice:* guttural croaks and whining cries. *Habitat:* oceanic, breeding on sub-Antarctic islands. Disperses northwards in winter, when immatures can be frequent winter and spring visitors to coasts south of the Tropic of Capricorn. Adults are rare; the white morph very rare. ⚓ ⸖

Northern Giant-Petrel *Macronectes halli* 90cm Very large, and almost identical to the Southern Giant-Petrel. Recognized only recently as a distinct species. Dark-plumage adult has denser crown markings than Southern, giving a subtle 'capped' appearance, and the beak tip (visible only at close range) is reddish pink or horn, not greenish. There is no white form. Lacks whitish leading edge to wing. Immature usually inseparable. *Voice:* guttural croaks and whining cries. *Habitat:* oceanic; breeding range farther north than Southern, dispersing north in winter and spring, when immatures can be frequent visitors to coastal seas. May be more numerous than Southern. ⚓ ⸖

Southern Fulmar *Fulmarus glacialoides* 50cm Large, heavily built petrel, flying on relatively short straight wings, held at right-angles to the body and often slightly downcurved. Glides extensively, with few distinctively stiff and shallow wingbeats except close to cliffs. Adult and immature pale grey above shading to white below. Wings have dark grey tips, with a pale panel distinctive on primaries in flight. *Voice:* seldom vocal at sea. *Habitat:* oceanic; breeds on Antarctic and sub-Antarctic coasts. Rare visitor to southern coastal waters, usually in winter. ⚓

Antarctic Petrel *Thalassoica antarctica* 45cm Large petrel, similar to Cape Petrel but distinctively blackish, fading to brown with wear, above. White below. Characteristic broad white unbroken bar running full length of wing, with only a very slim dark trailing edge, making a strikingly diagnostic flight pattern with dark-tipped white tail. Flight fulmar-like, with stiff-winged shallow beats. *Voice:* seldom vocal at sea. *Habitat:* oceanic, breeding close to Antarctica. Vagrant to Victorian coastal waters. ⚓

Cape Petrel *Daption capense* 35-40cm Large speckled petrel. Head and neck black, with black head less robust than Antarctic Petrel. Flight fast, low over the water, with quick rigid wingbeats. Upperparts diagnostic: back and rump white, boldy spotted black; tail white with black terminal bar. Wings black, with bold white patches on inboard half (with black flecks) and at base of primaries. Floats high on water, showing distinctive speckled back and wings. *Voice:* seldom vocal at sea. *Habitat:* oceanic; breeds widely on islands in southern oceans and on Antarctic coasts. Quite common as winter and spring visitor to coastal waters south of the Tropic of Capricorn. ⚓

Snow Petrel *Pagodroma nivea* 35cm Large all-white petrel, with a slim, short, black beak and black smudge through the eye. Comparatively longer-winged than Cape Petrel; wings held slightly more angled, and with different flight, with fluttering erratic phases interspersed with glides. *Voice:* seldom vocal at sea. *Habitat:* oceanic, breeding on Antarctic coasts and islands. Vagrant. ⚓

Southern Giant-Petrel (juvenile)

Northern Giant-Petrel

Southern Fulmar

Antarctic Petrel (fresh plumage)

Cape Petrel

Snow Petrel

Great-winged Petrel *Pterodroma macroptera* 40cm Large dark brown petrel, slim-bodied with large head and longish, slightly pointed tail. Small pale face patch (larger in New Zealand race *gouldii*). Wings long and pointed, held angled forwards, almost tern-like in outline, dark brown above, paler below, with a glossy darker brown central bar. Flight is anything but tern-like, sweeping up to a considerable height before swooping down again, often in flocks. *Voice:* vocal and varied on breeding grounds from staccato chatter to whistles and braying. *Habitat:* oceanic, but rarely pelagic, not ranging far from colonies. Breeds in Western Australia, where present all year round in locally large numbers. Elsewhere along south coast is present regularly, usually in winter, sometimes in flocks.

White-headed Petrel *Pterodroma lessonii* 43cm Large and distinctively-plumaged petrel. Head white, shading to grey on nape; black patch through eye. Long, slim tern-like wings. Upper wing largely brown with grey back extending onto forewing; underwing brown with darker central bar. Tail pale grey, square-cut. Underparts white. Flight fast, swooping and wheeling. *Voice:* not vocal at sea. *Habitat:* oceanic, breeding on remote coasts and islands. Regular but uncommon winter visitor to coastal seas south of the Tropic.

Providence Petrel *Pterodroma solandri* 40cm Large, gracefully-flying petrel. Body grey-brown, with brownish tail and brown head, with white flecking giving a pale-faced appearance. Wings long and pointed, with characteristic white patch at base of primaries giving a skua-like pattern. *Voice:* not vocal at sea. *Habitat:* oceanic, breeding on Lord Howe Island, dispersing northwards. Frequent southeastern coastal waters.

Kermadec Petrel *Pterodroma neglecta* 40cm Large variable petrel with two distinct plumage phases. Dark form similar to Providence Petrel but brown (not grey-brown) bodied, with prominent white flashes visible at bases of primaries in upperwing, also with characteristic white leading edge to the underwing. Pale form has white underparts with pale grey head and nape. Wings, rump and tail brown. Feet pale whitish or grey, contrasting with dark undertail. Intermediate forms occur, but with the characteristic wing pattern. *Voice:* not vocal at sea. *Habitat:* oceanic, breeding on islands in South Pacific. Vagrant to eastern coastal waters.

Herald Petrel *Pterodroma arminjoniana* 36cm Large variable petrel with two distinct plumage phases. Dark form similar to Kermadec Petrel but dark grey-brown, with distinctive white double bar running the length of the underwing, which also has a whitish leading edge. Pale form is grey-brown above, with a paler whitish forehead and darker smudge through the eye, shading to white below, sometimes with a greyish incomplete chest band. Intermediate plumage forms occur, but all with the characteristic underwing pattern and typical gadfly petrel swooping, soaring flight. *Voice:* not vocal at sea. *Habitat:* oceanic, breeding on scattered islands in the southern oceans, including Raine Island (Great Barrier Reef). Vagrant elsewhere along north-eastern offshore waters.

Tahiti Petrel *Pterodroma rostrata* 36cm Large distinctive petrel, entirely dark glossy brown on upperparts, with glossy brown head, neck and breast and blackish tail contrasting sharply with white belly and undertail coverts. Faint whitish bar visible in underwing at close range. Flight typical of gadfly petrel. Beak robust and bulbous. *Voice:* not vocal at sea. *Habitat:* oceanic, breeding in New Caledonia area, apparently not ranging far afield. Vagrant to northern and eastern seas.

Great-winged Petrel

White-headed Petrel

Providence Petrel

Kermadec Petrel (dark form)

Herald Petrel (pale form)

Tahiti Petrel

Kerguelen Petrel *Pterodroma brevirostris* 34cm Large petrel with distinctive silhouette, with heavy head, diminutive dark beak, and longish almost pointed tail. Uniformly greyish-brown, with paler face and dark brown glossy bar running centrally the length of the underwing, contrasting with paler leading edge of inner part of wing. Flight often solitary and high, 'swiftlike'. *Voice:* not vocal at sea. *Habitat:* oceanic, breeding on sub-Antarctic islands. Regular winter visitor to southern coastal seas; commoner in southwest. ◣ ▮

Soft-plumaged Petrel *Pterodroma mollis* 34cm Large gadfly petrel, grey to grey-brown above with characteristic whitish forehead and a short white stripe over a darker smudge through the eye. Underparts white, with a distinctive grey breast band, sometimes incomplete. Underwing grey-brown, with darker central band and paler greyish leading edge to inner half of wing. Legs and feet whitish. Often gregarious, flying, low and fast. *Voice:* not vocal at sea. *Habitat:* oceanic, breeding on sub-Antarctic islands, regularly ranging north and sometimes quite common in southwestern and southern coastal seas. ◣ ▮

Mottled Petrel *Pterodroma inexpectata* 33cm Medium-large gadfly petrel. Dark grey above with white face, shading to white below, with grey on belly and flanks. Undertail whitish. Upper surface of wings grey, underside white, with narrow black trailing edge. On both surfaces a characteristic bold but narrow black M marking is a useful feature. Wingbeats flickering, with towering and frequent glides. *Voice:* not vocal at sea. *Habitat:* oceanic, breeding off New Zealand and on sub-Antarctic islands. Rare visitor, usually in summer to southeastern coastal waters. ◣

Gould's Petrel *Pterodroma leucoptera* 30cm Medium-large petrel with rather shearwater-like flight, banking and twisting with rapid wingbeats and frequent glides. Upperparts grey-brown, greyer on back, rump and tail. Face and underparts white, with brownish collar marks. Underwing white, with black margins and distinctive diagonal black mark running from 'wrist' towards legs. *Voice:* various repetitive insect-like buzzings and varied whistles on breeding grounds; silent at sea. *Habitat:* breeds on rocky islands off NSW and New Caledonia, occasionally seen in summer off southeast coasts. Rare. ◣

Black-winged Petrel *Pterodroma nigripennis* 30cm Medium-large petrel, broadly similar in appearance to Gould's, but paler grey above, with a longer, almost pointed tail. Grey collar marks, white face with dark eye patch, white underparts. *Voice:* repetitive 'peet' calls over breeding grounds, sometimes disyllabic 'pee-er'; silent at sea. *Habitat:* breeds on rocky islands off NSW, New Zealand and elsewhere, occasionally seen in summer off southeast coast. Rare. ◣

Cook's Petrel *Pterodroma cookii* 28cm Medium-large slightly wedge-tailed petrel, pale blue-grey above, with whitish forehead and black smudge through eye; pale grey collar marks. Upper surface of wings blue-grey, with blackish primaries and a distinctive dark grey M marking. Underwing white, narrowly outlined in black, with a short thin black mark extending part way from 'wrist' towards legs. *Voice:* not vocal at sea. *Habitat:* oceanic, breeding on offshore islands in New Zealand and elsewhere, ranging in summer as a vagrant to eastern coastal waters. ◣

Kerguelen Petrel

Soft-plumaged Petrel

Mottled Petrel

Gould's Petrel

Black-winged Petrel

Cook's Petrel

White-necked Petrel *Pterodroma externa* 40cm Large, slightly wedge-tailed petrel; a larger, capped version of Cook's. Upperparts blue-grey, but with white collar and blackish crown joined to blackish smudge through eye. Forehead white. Blue of shoulders extends onto sides of breast as half-collars. Upperwing darker blue-grey than Cook's, with broad blackish M marking. Underwing very similar to Cook's. *Voice:* not vocal at sea. *Habitat:* oceanic, vagrant to eastern coastal waters. ≼

Blue Petrel *Halobaena caerulea* 28cm Medium-large petrel, broadly similar to Cook's. Upperparts pale grey-blue, darker on nape and crown giving something of a capped appearance; forehead white. Upperwings blue-grey, with a blackish M marking. Tail blue, with a dark blue-grey band above distinctive white tail tips. Underwing all-white, with black markings on leading edge. Flight long-winged, strong and direct. Often gregarious, and often in company with prions. Follows ships. *Voice:* not vocal at sea. *Habitat:* oceanic, breeding on sub-Antarctic islands, visiting southern coasts as an uncommon (but occasionally numerous) winter and spring visitor. ≼

Broad-billed Prion *Pachyptila vittata* 28cm Medium-large, the largest of the prions. Heavy-headed and slightly wedge-tailed. Blue-grey above with dark crown separated by whitish eyestripe from dark cheek streak. Tail black-tipped. Upperwing blue-grey, with narrow black M marking. Underparts white. Amazingly broad beak, with short nostril tube, visible at close range. Typical prion in behaviour, diving frequently, or swimming forward, head submerged, in search of plankton, using wings for extra propulsion. Sometimes gregarious. *Voice:* not vocal at sea. *Habitat:* oceanic, breeding on islands off New Zealand and elsewhere, reaching southern coastal waters as rare winter visitor. ≼

Salvin's Prion *Pachyptila salvini* 26cm Medium-large prion, only slightly smaller than Broad-billed, from which separation is often very difficult other than in the hand. Beak slightly smaller and narrower, head paler. *Voice:* not vocal at sea. *Habitat:* breeds on islands in southern Indian Ocean, dispersing east and southeast. Reasonably common winter visitor to western and southern coasts. ≼

Antarctic (Dove) Prion *Pachyptila desolata* 27cm Medium-large prion, extremely difficult if not impossible to separate in the field from the two broad-billed species, but has more extensive grey collar. In the hand, separable on beak features. *Voice:* not vocal at sea. *Habitat:* oceanic, breeding on Antarctica and sub-Antarctic islands, ranging widely around Southern Hemisphere. Reasonably common winter visitor in offshore waters along the southwest, southern and southeastern seaboard. ≼

Slender-billed Prion *Pachyptila belcheri* 25cm Medium-large but one of the smaller prions; similar in plumage and behaviour to other members of the group, particularly the Antarctic Prion. At close range appreciably thinner beak (which lacks filtering lamellae) and longer, downcurved eye-stripe may help, as may its greyish rather than blue-grey back. *Voice:* not vocal at sea. *Habitat:* oceanic, breeding on islands in South Atlantic and southern Indian oceans; an uncommon winter and spring visitor to southern coastal seas, particularly southernmost Western Australia. ≼

White-necked Petrel

Blue Petrel

Broad-billed Prion

Salvin's Prion

Antarctic (Dove) Prion

Slender-billed Prion

Fulmar Prion *Pachyptila crassirostris* 25cm Medium-large. Closely similar to Fairy Prion, smallest of the prions, but with a deeper, broader beak. Other distinguishing beak features are of use only in the hand. *Voice:* not vocal at sea. *Habitat:* oceanic, breeds on sub-Antarctic islands. Vagrant, but records are held in doubt. ✒

Fairy Prion *Pachyptila turtur* 25cm Medium-large, but the smallest prion. Typical prion behaviour and plumage, but beak short and narrow, with the nostril tube occupying one third of its length. In flight, broad black terminal band (about half the tail length) is a useful distinguishing feature from other prions (except Fulmar Prion). Bouncing flight, dipping to the surface to take plankton, is also distinctive. In windy weather, snakes at speed with wings rigid, rocking shearwater-like from side to side showing first blue, then white, then blue and so on. *Voice:* soft 'cuck-cuck, coo-er' on breeding grounds; silent at sea. *Habitat:* breeds Bass Strait and other southeastern islands, and elsewhere. Common offshore Victoria and southern NSW; infrequent elsewhere on southern seaboard. ✒ ❙ ®

Grey Petrel *Procellaria cinerea* 49cm A large, robust, rather shearwater-like petrel, but with long slim pointed wings often held angled at the 'wrist'. Upperparts palish grey-brown, paling to off-white on belly, contrasting with grey-brown underwing. Tail wedge-shaped. Plumage otherwise distinctively featureless! Beak greenish with black nostril tube and ridge; feet pinkish with yellow webs. Often flies high, sometimes with feet protruding to give slightly fork-tailed look. Dives frequently, often plunging at shallow angles from several metres. Sometimes follows ships; often solitary. *Voice:* not vocal at sea. *Habitat:* oceanic, breeding on sub-Antarctic islands, ranging north as vagrant to southwestern and southeastern coastal seas. ✒

Black Petrel *Procellaria parkinsoni* 46cm Large, wedge-tailed petrel with feet protruding beyond tail tip. Apparently distinctively all-black apart from black-tipped yellowish beak. Legs and feet black. In practice difficult to distinguish from such seabirds as Flesh-footed Shearwater (slimmer beak, pale feet), Great-winged Petrel (shorter beak, pale face) and particularly the Westland Petrel (differs only in size). *Voice:* not vocal at sea. *Habitat:* oceanic, breeding on New Zealand and offshore islands. Vagrant to eastern coastal seas. ✒

Westland Petrel *Procellaria westlandica* 53cm Large, wedge-tailed petrel with feet protruding beyond tail tip in flight. All-black plumage, with black legs and feet and black-tipped pale yellowish beak. As Black Petrel, difficult to separate from Flesh-footed Shearwater and Great-winged Petrel, and almost impossible to separate from Black Petrel unless accurate size estimation is possible. *Voice:* not vocal at sea. *Habitat:* oceanic, breeding South Island, New Zealand. Vagrant to eastern seaboard. ✒

White-chinned Petrel *Procellaria aequinoctialis* 56cm Large, wedge-tailed petrel with feet protruding beyond tail tip in flight. Body plumage entirely sooty black except for pale throat and sometimes face patches. These vary in extent and in prominence, so confusion is possible with the species mentioned above. With experience, the distinctively large all-pale beak, and lazy, comparatively broad-winged flight, are useful guides. Follows ships; can be aggressive among other birds. *Voice:* not vocal at sea. *Habitat:* oceanic, breeding on sub-Antarctic islands. Vagrant to southeastern seaboard. ✒

Fulmar Prion

Fairy Prion

Grey Petrel

Black Petrel

Westland Petrel

White-chinned Petrel

Flesh-footed Shearwater *Puffinus carneipes* 48cm One of the largest shearwaters. Very dark brown or blackish above and below, with a dark-tipped pale beak and strikingly pale pink feet set against a slightly rounded black tail. Flight distinctive and sedate for a shearwater, with slow stiff-winged flaps alternating with glides. *Voice:* breathing 'coo-kee-aarh' around colonies. *Habitat:* oceanic, breeding widely in Southern Hemisphere including islands off the Australian south coast. Widespread along south coast summer and autumn; locally common. ≤®

Wedge-tailed Shearwater *Puffinus pacificus* 42-46cm Large and distinctively wedge-tailed, with grey beak and pale pink legs and feet. Two colour forms: dark - entirely chocolate brown (sometimes with white breast); wedge tail and contrasting pink feet are useful features; pale: grey-brown above, white below, with black-bordered white underwings with grey speckling in 'armpits'. Flight buoyant and supple on bent wings. *Voice:* crooning and wailing calls at breeding colonies; silent at sea. *Habitat:* oceanic, breeding on tropical and subtropical islands, including those off western and eastern Australian coasts. Common locally; rare on northern and southern seaboards. ≤®

Buller's Shearwater *Puffinus bulleri* 43-45cm Large, but among the smaller shearwaters. Upperparts blue-grey, with black cap; thick black M marking across upperwing, black primaries, and grey rump contrasting with relatively long wedge-shaped black tail. Flight distinctively leisurely. *Voice:* silent at sea. *Habitat:* oceanic, breeding off northern New Zealand. Scarce but regular and increasingly frequent summer visitor to southeast coasts. ≤

Sooty Shearwater *Puffinus griseus* 47-50cm Large shearwater. Heavily built but with relatively long narrow wings. Uniformly sooty brown above, paler grey-brown below. Underside of wing dark brown, with distinctive paler central stripe. Tail short and rounded, feet usually protrude beyond tip. *Voice:* three-syllabic 'coo-roo-aah' crooning on breeding grounds; not vocal at sea. *Habitat:* oceanic, widely distributed around the world's oceans. Small breeding colonies on offshore islands, NSW and Tasmania. Regular, occasionally locally quite common, off southern and eastern coasts except in winter. ≤®

Short-tailed Shearwater *Puffinus tenuirostris* 39-43cm Large, resembling an appreciably smaller version of Sooty. Sooty brown above and below, with pale patches in underwing less pronounced than in Sooty and sometimes almost invisible. Some forms have various paler patches on breast or throat. Beak distinctively short and slim. Often gregarious, some flocks huge. Flies with smooth wingbeats alternating with glides; in windy weather fast and weaving, with short bursts of rapid flapping. *Voice:* nocturnal on breeding grounds, 'coo-ka roo-ka raah' and varied crooning. Silent at sea. *Habitat:* oceanic, breeding on offshore islands. Widespread along southern coast, often common off southeastern corner and Tasmania, but largely absent May-September. ≤ ∤®

Streaked Shearwater *Calonectris leucomelas* 50cm The largest Australian shearwater: heavy-bodied, large-headed and short-tailed giving a rather albatross-like appearance accentuated by straight-winged gliding flight. Upperparts grey-brown with darker flight feathers and tail; paler on head, with white forehead. Underparts white. *Voice:* seldom vocal at sea. *Habitat:* oceanic; now recognized as a scarce but regular visitor to northern and eastern coastal waters. ≤

Flesh-footed Shearwater

Wedge-tailed Shearwater (dark form)

Buller's Shearwater

Sooty Shearwater

Short-tailed Shearwater

Streaked Shearwater

Manx Shearwater *Puffinus puffinus* 36-40cm Large, relatively narrower-winged than Hutton's. Striking black and white colouration suggested by smaller and stockier Little, but dusky sides of head envelopes eye and flight action less fluttering. Undertail coverts and underwing white, the latter cleanly dark bordered. Legs pale pink and grey; beak blackish, comparatively robust. *Voice:* seldom vocal at sea. *Habitat:* oceanic, breeding on North Atlantic islands. Single amazing record of a bird banded in UK. ✦

Fluttering Shearwater *Puffinus gavia* 31-35cm Large, but one of the smaller shearwaters. Upperparts and upperwing entirely black, with a blunt black half-collar down onto all-white underparts. Underwing white, with broad dark grey margins and distinctive grey patch in 'armpit'. Undertail white, with narrow black terminal band. Legs and feet grey and black. Often gregarious, spending much time on water. Flies close to surface, with rapid whirring wingbeats and brief spells of gliding. Difficult to separate from Hutton's. *Voice:* seldom vocal at sea. *Habitat:* oceanic, breeding on offshore islands in New Zealand and elsewhere. Widespread along southern and southeastern coasts; common and sometimes very numerous. ✦

Hutton's Shearwater *Puffinus huttoni* 35-37cm Large, slightly larger than very similar Fluttering. Upperparts uniformly brownish black, with prominent brown shoulders and collar stretching onto upper breast. Underparts white. Underwing whitish, with broad black trailing edge; variable amounts of grey-brown obscure much of the white, especially in the 'armpits'. Flight similar to Fluttering. Spends much time on the surface, diving frequently. *Voice:* seldom vocal at sea. *Habitat:* oceanic, breeding at high altitudes in New Zealand. Prefers inshore waters; scarce round all coasts in winter months. ✦ ⚑

Little Shearwater *Puffinus assimilis* 26-30cm Medium-large, but the smallest of Australian shearwaters. Uniformly black above, white below, with white face distinctively extending above the eye. Underparts white, including undertail which has narrow black terminal band. Underwing white, bordered black. Beak black, characteristically small and slim. Legs and feet blue. Often on water, frequently gregarious. *Voice:* shrill pipings, varied wheezy croonings on breeding grounds, silent at sea. *Habitat:* oceanic, breeding off southwest coast. Disperses to southern and southeastern coastal waters. Fairly common locally in southwest, scarce elsewhere. ✦ ⚑ ®

Audubon's Shearwater *Puffinus lherminieri* 30cm Medium-large, but small for a shearwater. Broadly similar in appearance to Little, but browner, with an appreciably longer slim pale beak. Underparts white; underwing white with broad black margin. Tail comparatively long with distinctively blackish undertail coverts. Pinkish-yellow feet contrast against tail. Wingbeats fast; glides often and low over the water. *Voice:* seldom vocal at sea. *Habitat:* oceanic, breeding on tropical islands, dispersing widely. Vagrant to southeastern coastal waters. ✦

Manx Shearwater

Fluttering Shearwater

Hutton's Shearwater

Little Shearwater

Audubon's Shearwater

Wilson's Storm-Petrel *Oceanites oceanicus* 18cm Medium. Typical storm-petrel shape and erratic light-weight flight. Dark sooty-black head and body, with conspicuous white patch on rump and down onto flanks. Tail black, rounded. Wings comparatively long, sooty-black with grey diagonal bar across secondary coverts. Beak tiny, black, with paired tubular nostrils. Legs distinctively long; feet protrude beyond tail but are often carried trailing showing yellow webs between toes. Feeding technique characteristic, with bouncing buoyant flight just above the surface, long legs dangling and feet pattering, head down. *Voice:* not vocal at sea. *Habitat:* oceanic, breeding around Antarctic Circle. Disperses northwards to southern Australian coastal seas in autumn and spring; seen off northern coast through the winter. Comparatively widespread and common. ⟋ ⎀

Grey-backed Storm-Petrel *Oceanites nereis* 17cm Medium-sized. Typical storm-petrel shape. Head, nape and breast black; beak small and dark with prominent tubular nostrils. Back and inner halves of wings grey, flight feathers blackish. Rump pale grey; slightly rounded tail grey with distinctive narrow black terminal band. Belly white. Underwing white, with broad black border. Legs long, black. Erratic buoyant flight characterized by periods of hovering, legs dangling. *Voice:* not vocal at sea. *Habitat:* oceanic, breeding in south Indian and South Atlantic oceans and off New Zealand, dispersing as an irregular rare winter visitor to the southeastern seaboard. ⟋

White-faced Storm-Petrel *Pelagodroma marina* 19cm Medium-sized storm-petrel with unique and distinctive face markings. Crown and nape black, forehead white, conspicuous black patch through eye separated from crown by bold white supercilium. Back and inner halves of wings grey, primaries blackish. Tail square, black, contrasting characteristically with pale grey (not white) rump. Underwing white, diffusely bordered dark grey. Beak black and slim, with prominent nostril tube. Fluttering, dipping flight, usually into wind, long black legs with yellow webs to feet trailing conspicuously. Swims frequently, floating high in the water with tail and wingtips up-tilted. *Voice:* not vocal at sea. *Habitat:* oceanic, breeding on many islands off the southeast and southwest. Not uncommon locally in summer along entire south coast; rare in winter. ⟋ ⎀ ⓡ

Black-bellied Storm-Petrel *Fregetta tropica* 20cm Medium-sized storm-petrel, largely black above apart from dark grey inner halves to the wings and bold white rump contrasting with square black tail. Underparts usually distinctive, with faint white patch on black throat, and black breast extending in a narrow central line down white belly. Underwing white, with blackish undersides to flight feathers. Legs usually carried under black tail, protruding distinctly beyond tip. *Voice:* not vocal at sea. *Habitat:* oceanic, breeding on sub-Antarctic islands. Vagrants to southern Australian sea. ⟋ ⎀

White-bellied Storm-Petrel *Fregetta grallaria* 20cm Medium-sized compact storm-petrel, generally difficult to distinguish from Black-bellied but with a sharply defined black throat and upper breast, with no central stripe. Feet do not protrude beyond square-cut black tail. *Voice:* not vocal at sea. *Habitat:* oceanic, breeding on sub-Antarctic islands. Vagrants to eastern Australian seas. ⟋ ⎀

Wilson's Storm-Petrel

Grey-backed Storm-Petrel

White-faced Storm-Petrel

Black-bellied Storm-Petrel

White-bellied Storm-Petrel

Matsudaira's Storm-Petrel *Oceanodroma matsudairae* 24cm
Medium-large slim-built storm-petrel, readily recognizable with a long, deeply forked tail. Plumage entirely sooty brown apart from distinctively bright grey diagonal bar across the secondary coverts, and white quill bases showing like obscure and miniature skua wing-flashes at close range. Strong, rather slow and direct flight. *Voice:* not vocal at sea. *Habitat:* oceanic, breeding on islands south of Japan. Vagrant to northern coastal waters. ≼

Leach's Storm-Petrel *Oceanodroma leucorhoa* 20cm Medium-sized fork-tailed petrel. Sooty brown above and below, with distinctively narrow grey diagonal bars across secondary coverts, white rump usually with a brown central streak, and shallowly but distinctly forked tail. Characteristically resolute bounding flight. *Voice:* not vocal at sea. *Habitat:* oceanic, breeding on remote islands in the Northern Hemisphere. Vagrant to Australian waters. ≼

Common Diving-Petrel *Pelecanoides urinatrix* 20-25cm A distinctively tubby petrel with short stiff wings and distinctive whirring flight low over the sea before plunge diving. Upperparts uniformly dark sooty brown, shading to white below, with a smudgy breast band. Underwing grey. Tail square-ended. Beak short and stubby with broad twin nostrils. Legs quite bright blue. As name suggests, dives frequently using wings for propulsion, often popping up under the bows of approaching boats and shooting off low over the water. *Voice:* not vocal at sea. *Habitat:* oceanic, breeding on islands off Victoria and Tasmania, and elsewhere south into sub-Antarctic. Locally fairly common in Bass Strait area year-round; rare elsewhere. ≼ ⌁ ®

South Georgian Diving-Petrel *Pelecanoides georgicus* 18-20cm A dumpy diving-petrel, closely similar to the Common Diving-Petrel, but with a plumper more rounded beak with flatter nostrils (useful only in the hand). Some have distinctive white longitudinal bars on scapulars at bases of wings. *Voice:* not vocal at sea. *Habitat:* oceanic, breeding on islands off New Zealand and in southern Indian Ocean. Vagrant. ≼

Matsudaira's Storm-Petrel

Leach's Storm-Petrel

Common Diving-Petrel

South Georgian Diving-Petrel

Australian Pelican *Pelecanus conspicillatus* 160-190cm Enormous. Unmistakable. Familiar short-tailed, bulky-bodied appearance, with long neck and short stout legs. Head, neck and body all-white, sometimes washed grey on head. Adult has short rough crest. Tail white, with black terminal band. Wings long and broad, white, with flight feathers producing a broad black trailing edge above and below. Immature dark brown and off-white. Soars frequently. *Voice:* gruff growls and honks in colonies. *Habitat:* breeds colonially on maritime islands or by inland waters; locally common on suitable salt, brackish or fresh waters. ⛱ ⚓ 🦢 △ ®

Australasian Gannet *Morus serrator* 85-95cm Enormous, distinctive seabird. Adult predominantly white, with yellow tinge to head strongest in breeding season. Primaries and secondaries black; tail long and pointed, white with black central feathers. Beak long, dagger-shaped, grey with black lines. Immatures initially greyish, speckled white, becoming steadily whiter. *Voice:* harsh honks at colony. *Habitat:* maritime, breeding on coastal cliffs and rocky islands, feeding in coastal sea. Locally common along southern coasts. ⚓ ❘ ®

Cape Gannet *Morus capensis* 85-90cm Enormous seabird, closely similar in many respects to Australasian Gannet, and immatures are probably indistinguishable. Adult Cape Gannet has all-black tail, a longer black stripe down the throat, and marginally more extensive black fleshy areas on face. *Habitat:* oceanic, breeding Southern Africa. Vagrants have occurred at breeding colonies of Australasian Gannet. ⚓

Red-footed Booby *Sula sula* 68-76cm Very large seabird, gannet-like, with diagnostic bright red feet. Two colour forms: white, with all-white body and wings, and with black primaries and secondaries forming a broad black trailing edge to the wing; dark form, with uniformly brown body and wings. Intermediates occur with whitish rump and tail and sometimes with white on breast and belly. Immatures of all forms are mottled brown, with grey legs. This species nests and sometimes roosts in trees. *Voice:* harsh honks in breeding colonies, silent at sea. *Habitat:* oceanic, nesting on islands including those off the northern Australian coast, normally in vegetation, occasionally on ground. Local, never numerous. ⚓®

Masked Booby *Sula dactylatra* 80-85cm Very large. Lacks yellow head of the gannets, and has yellow or yellowish beak (adult), not steel blue. Bare facial skin blue-black. Feet blue or blue-grey. Gannet-like in its black and white plumage. Immature mottled brown, but with white collar and rump. *Voice:* not vocal at sea. *Habitat:* oceanic, breeding on islands including those off the north Australian coast. Locally quite common, but more pelagic than most of its family and rarely seen inshore. ⚓®

Brown Booby *Sula leucogaster* 72-75cm Large, but a comparatively small, dark booby. Facial skin blue in male, yellow in female. Beak and legs yellow. Adult blackish brown above, with blackish throat and breast cut off sharply from white belly. Underwing white, broadly bordered in blackish brown. Pattern of underparts is diagnostic in flight. Immature similar, but with white areas pale brown. *Voice:* harsh honks on breeding grounds; silent at sea. *Habitat:* oceanic, breeding on islands including those off the north Australian coast, nesting on the ground, often in clearings in scrubby vegetation. Locally quite common along northern seaboard; vagrant farther south. ⚓®

Australian Pelican (adult)

Australasian Gannet (adult)

Cape Gannet (adults)

Red-footed Booby (adult dark form)

Masked Booby (adults)

Brown Booby (adult)

Darter *Anhinga melanogaster* 90cm Very large, distinctively slim cormorant-like bird, with characteristically long sinuous neck. Adult male variable, but usually glossy black with a narrow white streak down side of dark chestnut neck. Female paler and browner, with neck stripe. Immature lacks neck stripe. Swims low, often with only snake-like head and neck out of water, dives frequently. *Voice:* various clicking sounds and cackling. *Habitat:* predominantly freshwater lakes, rivers and swamps; occasionally coastal lagoons and estuaries. Widespread but erratic and rarely numerous. ⏛⏚⏛®

Black-faced Cormorant *Phalacrocorax fuscescens* 62-67cm Very large white-breasted cormorant. Black above, the black crown characteristically stretching down to the bright green eye. Underparts white, legs black. Black thigh patch. In breeding season, adult has short white plumes on nape, rump and thighs. Immature brown above, paler grey-brown below, with dark throat and breast. *Voice:* harsh croaks at breeding colonies. *Habitat:* favours rocky coastal seas. Sedentary and confined to southeastern and southwestern seaboards, where locally quite common. ⏚®

Pied Cormorant *Phalacrocorax varius* 70-75cm Very large, similar to Black-faced but larger and more heavily built. Bare facial skin orange, eye-ring blue. Adult black above, strikingly white below, with white over eye and below crown. Immature browner above, shading to off-white on underparts. *Voice:* coarse grunts on breeding grounds. *Habitat:* larger areas of inland and coastal fresh, brackish or saline waters, estuaries, shallow bays. Widely distributed; locally quite common. ⏛⏚⏛®

Little Pied Cormorant *Phalacrocorax melanoleucos* 55cm Very large, but the smallest Australian cormorant. A miniature, duller edition of the Pied, but adult lacks the large coloured facial skin patches. White face extends above eye. Tufted crest of black feathers on forehead in early breeding season. Lacks the black thigh patch of the two larger pied species. Immature has brown upperparts merging into off-white underparts, and has blackish thigh stripe. *Voice:* brief croaking calls in colony. *Habitat:* almost any water, inland or coastal; fresh, salt or brackish; of any size. Widespread, often common. ⏛⏚⏛®

Great Cormorant *Phalacrocorax carbo* 80-90cm Very large, the largest Australian cormorant and cosmopolitan species. Adult iridescent black, with bare yellow facial skin and throat patch. In breeding season a white chin and thigh patches develop. Immature dark brown, paler below. *Voice:* varied croakings at breeding colonies. *Habitat:* inshore coastal seas, estuaries, larger inland fresh and brackish waters. Widespread except in central and southern regions, irregular inland, rarer along northern coasts. ⏛⏚⏛®

Little Black Cormorant *Phalacrocorax sulcirostris* 60-65cm Very large, but one of the distinctively smaller, slimmer all-black cormorants. Head, body, wings and long tail entirely black, with iridescent green on back, appearing almost bronze in breeding season. Often gregarious, and very active when feeding. *Voice:* calls rarely, occasional grunts at nest. *Habitat:* most types of larger coastal and inland waters and rivers; fresh, salt or brackish. Widespread and generally quite common; nomadic in the interior. ⏛⏚⏛®

Darter (adult ♂)

Black-faced Cormorant (adults)

Pied Cormorant (adults and immature)

Little Pied Cormorant

Great Cormorant (adult)

Little Black Cormorant

Christmas Frigatebird *Fregata andrewsi* 90-100cm Huge and unmistakably a frigatebird, with immensely long, angled wings (spanning over 2m) and very long, deeply forked tail. Adult male largely black, with expandable red throat pouch and a white belly patch. Brownish panels on upper surface of wings. Female resembles Least Frigatebird, but has black throat extending in a V onto upper breast, distinctive in flight. Immature blackish-brown above, paler below, indistinguishable from other immature frigatebirds. *Voice:* not vocal at sea. *Habitat:* oceanic, breeding on Christmas Island. Vagrant. ⬤

Great Frigatebird *Fregata minor* 80-100cm Huge and unmistakably a frigatebird. Male entirely blackish brown, with distinctively long wings and forked tail. Red throat pouch usually indistinct, but inflated over breeding grounds. Brownish patches visible indistinctly on upper surface of wings. Female black above, with black crown and nape, and with grey throat and white breast contrasting with blackish belly. Immatures as other frigatebirds. *Voice:* males make extraordinary warbling and rattling noises over breeding grounds. *Habitat:* oceanic, breeding on tropical islands including outer Great Barrier Reef. Local, otherwise uncommon in northeastern seas. ⬤

Least Frigatebird *Fregata ariel* 70-80cm Huge and unmistakably a frigatebird. Extremely agile in flight. Adult male glossy black, with faint brownish patches on upper wing surfaces, and with diagnostic but rather small white markings in 'armpits'. Reddish throat only really visible over breeding grounds. Female blackish above, but with black throat and white collar (see Greater). Immature brownish, with distinctively ginger-brown head and neck. *Voice:* shrill rattle over breeding grounds. *Habitat:* oceanic, breeding on tropical islands, including several off the northern and northeastern coasts. Locally fairly common along north coasts and over Great Barrier Reef; rare farther south. ⬤ ®

Red-tailed Tropicbird *Phaethon rubricauda* 85cm, including about 40cm of tail. A plump seabird the size of a large gull, with the aerobatic grace and speed of a tern or skua. Body white, flushed pale pink in breeding season, with black patch through eye and blackish marks on scapulars and primary bases. Beak stout and with a serrated edge. Legs black. Diagnostic feature of the adult are the immensely long flexible central tail feathers. Immature delicately grey scaled above, with blackish beak; lacks elongated tail feathers. *Voice:* vocal, frequently with metallic rattling calls. *Habitat:* oceanic, breeding on tropical islands including those off the southwest and northeast coasts. Regular but often rare off much of the Australian coastline. ⬤ ®

White-tailed Tropicbird *Phaethon lepturus* 70-80cm, including long tail. Similar in plumage and behaviour to Red-tailed, but more buoyant on the wing. Black mark through eye; black diagonal bar on inner half of wing (absent in Red-tailed), and substantial blackish patch at base of primaries. Belly sometimes tinged yellow (Indian Ocean race *fulvus*). Beak robust, yellow. Central tail feathers white with black quills at base. Immature lacks tail streamers; white mottled and barred black above (see Red-tailed). *Voice:* high-pitched rattling calls; vocal. *Habitat:* oceanic, breeding on tropical islands. Regular but uncommon visitor to northwestern seas; less common off northeastern coast. ⬤

Christmas Frigatebird (young immature)

Great Frigatebird ♀

Least Frigatebird ♂

Red-tailed Tropicbird (adult)

White-tailed Tropicbird (adult)

Great-billed Heron *Ardea sumatrana* 120cm A huge brownish heron, with a distinctively heavy, long, dark beak. Upperparts brown, underparts paler and greyer. Short crest on nape of breeding adult, which has long slender silver-grey feathers on the mantle and breast. Immature more uniformly brown. Dark coloration and ponderous flight are useful distant features. *Voice:* deep-throated roar, often repeated up to four times in succession. *Habitat:* typically coastal in mangrove swamps, or on estuaries and lagoons, nesting in trees or mangroves. Uncommon along northern coasts. 🌾⚓🦅▦®

Pacific (White-necked) Heron *Ardea pacifica* 80-100cm Very large heron, distinguished by white head and neck, black beak and legs, and iridescent blackish back, with short iridescent maroon plumes in breeding season. Black spots down the front of the neck are more obvious in immature. Belly buffish. In flight, black-and-white appearance is distinctive, as is bold white spot at 'wrist' of dark upper surface of wings. Immature brown above, buff below with darker flecks. *Voice:* guttural croak. *Habitat:* wet pastures, swamps, freshwater lakes and floods. Widespread and fairly common. 🌾🦅△®

White-faced Heron *Ardea novaehollandiae* 70cm Large and familiar heron. Adult distinctively pale grey, with a white face and chin. Breeding adult has fine black and white plumes across the mantle. Underparts buffish. Legs characteristically greenish yellow. Immature drabber and buffer, with white only on chin, and greenish legs. *Voice:* harsh metallic croaks. *Habitat:* shallow waters of all types, fresh, brackish and salt; also moist (sometimes dry) pastures. Nests in trees, not necessarily close to water. Very widespread and often common. 🌾⚓🦅△®

Pied Heron *Ardea picata* 45-50cm Large, but smallish in heron terms, and highly distinctive. Adult has slim dark slate-grey body, contrasting dramatically at one end with a white head and neck capped with a bold black crown and crest, and at the other with bright yellow legs. Immature has browner body, and all-white head and neck, without crest; legs and beak yellowish. In flight, size, dark body and wings, and white neck are useful features. *Voice:* harsh croaks. *Habitat:* usually near coast on swamps, lagoons, estuaries and mangrove swamps - and sewage farms. Nests in trees over water. Largely confined to northern coastal strip. 🌾⚓🦅®

Cattle Egret *Ardea ibis* 45-52cm Large, but the smallest of the egrets. Non-breeding adult white, often rather scruffy, with yellowish beak and legs. Distinctive 'undershot jaw' appearance. Breeding adult unmistakable, with long yellow or ginger plumes on head, neck, back and throat. Often gregarious, frequently feeds among grazing animals, often far from water. Immatures are like non-breeders. *Voice:* coarse croaks. *Habitat:* swamps, open grazing land, often distant from water. Breeds colonially in trees over water. Widespread, locally common. 🐃🌾△®

Great Egret *Ardea alba* 90-100cm Very large egret. Distinctively all-white and slim, with a characteristically kinked long neck, usually held outstretched. Beak long, strong and dagger-shaped, linked by bare yellow facial skin to golden eye; beak is black during the breeding season, when facial skin becomes green. Distinctive heavy flight. *Voice:* deep throaty croak. *Habitat:* larger shallow fresh waters of most types, estuaries and lagoons. Breeds in treetop colonies over water. Widespread but erratic in appearance and rarely numerous. 🌾⚓🦅△®

Great-billed Heron

Pacific (White-necked) Heron

White-faced Heron (adult)

Pied Heron (adult)

Cattle Egret (breeding)

Great Egret

Little Egret *Ardea garzetta* 60cm Large slim white egret, usually seen feeding with neck extended and straight. Beak always dark, slim and dagger-shaped. Bare facial skin orange in breeding season, lemon yellow in non-breeding birds. Legs diagnostically black with yellow soles to feet (beware muddy habitats). *Voice:* harsh croaks. *Habitat:* most types of fresh waters, sewage farms, coastal lagoons and estuaries. Breeds colonially, often with other herons, in treetop colonies over water. Widespread and locally fairly common in north and east; uncommon elsewhere. 🌊🦆🐟❗️△®

Intermediate Egret *Ardea intermedia* 65-70cm Large egret, intermediate in size between Little and Great egrets but more resembling the latter, with a comparatively shorter beak and neck (roughly equal in length to the body), and with a rounder head. Flight appreciably faster and more elegant than Great Egret. Non-breeding birds and immatures have orange beaks, and black legs. Breeding birds have deep orange to pinkish beaks, bluish facial skin, and a dense curtain of fine white plumes on mantle and breast. *Voice:* harsh rattling calls. *Habitat:* most types of shallow wetlands, coastal lagoons, estuaries and sewage farms, and open grazing land, often with Cattle Egrets. Breeds in tree-top colonies over water. Widespread in the north and east, locally fairly common, rarer to the south. 🌊🦆🐟△®

Eastern Reef Egret *Ardea sacra* 60-70cm Large beach or reef heron with two colour phases, and distinctively longer, more robust beak and comparatively shorter legs than other herons of similar size. Grey morph is uniformly slate grey except for a whitish throat; beak and legs yellowish-grey, commoner in south. White morph all-white, with yellow beak and legs, commoner in north. Flight fast and direct, with legs protruding only a short distance beyond tail. Often solitary. *Voice:* hoarse croak. *Habitat:* coasts and islands, including mudflats and mangroves. Breeds in loose colonies, nesting in trees, on cliff ledges or on ground. Widespread except on southeastern coast: rarely numerous. 🦆🐟🏖️®

Striated Heron *Butorides striatus* 50cm Large. A dumpy, comparatively small, heavy-headed heron, often and appropriately called the Mangrove Heron. Plumages vary from region to region, but all share dark crown and drooping crest and pinkish-buff underparts with line of black and white streaks down front of neck. Beak relatively short and stout, blackish; legs yellowish, orange in breeding season. Back plumage iridescent olive (eastern), grey-green (northeast), grey-brown (north), pale grey (northwest), ginger brown (western). Secretive, keeps close to vegetation. *Voice:* various sharp sneezing calls. *Habitat:* estuaries, muddy inlets, especially mangroves. Nests usually in mangroves. Occurs along parts of northwestern, northern and eastern coasts, locally quite regular in north. 🦆🐟🏖️®

Rufous Night Heron *Nycticorax caledonicus* 57-62cm Large, but comparatively dumpy, large-headed small heron. Beak large, deep and black; legs yellowish. Plumage distinctive, bright cinnamon above, with dark crown and white drooping crest in breeding season; underparts buff shading to white. Immature also distinctive, dark brown above with plentiful bold white spots; legs yellowish. Crepuscular or nocturnal. *Voice:* deep frog-like croaks. *Habitat:* estuaries and muddy creeks; rivers, lakes, dams and swamps. Nests high in trees over water. Widespread, locally quite common; erratic inland. 🌊🦆🐟®

Little Egret (breeding)

Intermediate Egret (breeding)

Eastern Reef Egret (dark form)

Striated Heron (adult, eastern form)

Rufous Night Heron (adult)

Rufous Night Heron (immature)

Little Bittern *Ixobrychus minutus* 25-30cm Medium-sized, and easily the smallest of the heron family in Australia – itself a useful feature. Male elegant, with glossy black back, tail and flight feathers contrasting with bold cinnamon wing patches; striking both perched and in flight. Pale chestnut breast (with dark streaks on throat) and white belly with darker streaks on flanks. Female similarly patterned but browner and more streaked. Immature brown and streaked, darker above than below. Very secretive. *Voice:* deep, repetitive, breathy 'hock'. *Habitat:* nests and lives year-round in dense freshwater wetland vegetation. Comparatively widespread but only quite rarely recorded. 🌊®

Yellow Bittern *Ixobrychus sinensis* 30-35cm Medium-sized, but a very small bittern. Male yellowish brown with a blackish cap and short crest. Back yellowish (not black as in Little Bittern). Primaries and tail blackish, in flight giving yellowish pied appearance. Female duller and more streaked. Immature difficult to separate from Little Bittern except by larger size. *Voice:* deep croaks. *Habitat:* essentially as Little Bittern. Vagrant. 🌊

Black Bittern *Ixobrychus flavicollis* 55-60cm Large. A slim and distinctively dark bittern, more like a heron in build. Male has sooty black body and nape to long neck, yellow-buff sides to neck, and streaked black and white front to neck and breast. Female is duller and browner, immature similar but with buff scaly markings. Typically secretive, but may emerge from cover during a long, motionless birdwatch. Very dark in flight, with neck partly folded back and distinctly short tail. *Voice:* deep, segmented 'who-oo-oo-oo', repeated regularly. *Habitat:* nests and lives in dense wetland vegetation, including mangroves. Northern and eastern coastal belt, and isolated population in southwest. Inconspicuous and probably commoner than records suggest. 🌊🐦🗻®

Australasian Bittern *Botaurus poiciloptilus* 65-72cm Large, bulky bittern, with overall finely mottled plumage in buffs, browns, greys and blacks giving excellent camouflage to assist its secretive habits in brownish reedbeds. Crown blackish, throat whitish with narrow black margin. Male, female and immature broadly similar. Legs greenish; beak pale horn. If disturbed, may 'freeze' in slim upright pose, almost invisible against reed stems. *Voice:* characteristic foghorn-like booming 'whumph', repeated monotonously. *Habitat:* nests and lives in dense freshwater marshland vegetation. Generally uncommon, but occasionally more numerous; restricted to southeast and southwest. 🌊🐦®

Little Bittern (adult, ♂)

Little Bittern (immature)

Yellow Bittern (adult, ♀)

Black Bittern

Australasian Bittern

Black-necked Stork *Ephippiorhynchus asiaticus* 130cm Huge, often known as Jabiru. Adult unmistakable, with white body contrasting with black flight feathers, back and tail, and iridescent purplish neck and head. Beak massive, black. Legs long, bright red. Immature brown above paling to whitish below; beak and legs grey. *Voice:* deep booms, beak clappering. *Habitat:* wetlands of most types, inland and coastal, occasionally dry pasture and scrub. Widespread, sometimes fairly common in belt along north and east coasts. ✦✦✦®

Glossy Ibis *Plegadis falcinellus* 48-55cm Large, but small and dark for an ibis. Body iridescent purplish brown, with glossy greenish sheen on wings. Beak yellowish grey; long, slim and downcurved. Immature browner. In flight looks very dark, and carries head and neck outstretched. *Voice:* various deep croaks and grunts at breeding colonies. *Habitat:* freshwater wetlands of most types, sometimes estuaries and creeks, occasionally dry grassland. Though widespread, erratic in distribution and generally uncommon. ✦✦△®

Australian White Ibis *Threskiornis molucca* 70-75cm Large white ibis, often appearing grubby, with a bare-skinned blackish head, black wingtips and, in breeding season, black filamentous plumes from scapulars drooping over yellowish tail. Beak long, downcurved, black. Immature greyer, with feathered head, lacks plumes. Often gregarious. *Voice:* harsh croaks. *Habitat:* most types of wetland, open land in general. Breeds colonially in bushes, in reeds or on ground. Widespread; locally abundant but nomadic. ✦✦△®

Straw-necked Ibis *Threskiornis spinicollis* 65-70cm Large, but detectably smaller than White Ibis, with which it often associates. Head and throat bald, black. Neck greenish black on nape, with short straw-coloured plumes on front of throat and breast. Back and wings metallic black; underparts white, including tail. In flight, white-bodied, black-winged appearance is distinctive. Immature lacks plumes, and is generally duller. *Voice:* harsh grunts. *Habitat:* much as White Ibis, but makes more use of drier grasslands, sometimes far from water. Widespread, often fairly common, but erratic in appearance and numbers. ✦✦△®

Royal Spoonbill *Platalea regia* 75-80cm Large and predominantly white, with spoon-shaped beak obvious at close range. Beak and facial skin black. Legs black. Body and wings white in adults, with ragged crest of sometimes buffish plumes and yellowish wash to breast in breeding season. Immature greyer, with blackish wingtips. Distinctive feeding technique, sweeping beak from side to side through shallows. *Voice:* normally silent. *Habitat:* larger areas of water; fresh, brackish and saline. Widespread; sometimes locally common but erratic in appearance and numbers. ✦✦✦△®

Yellow-billed Spoonbill *Platalea flavipes* 80-90cm Large - the larger of the two spoonbills. Beak characteristically pale yellow, facial skin yellowish grey; legs yellow. Body all-white, but often grubby, with white breeding season plumes on breast and very fine blackish plumes on back. Immature greyer-bodied, with sooty grey wingtips. *Voice:* normally silent. *Habitat:* varied freshwater types including small dams; less often on coastal lagoons than Royal, and rarely on tidal mudflats. Widespread, but very variable in occurrence and numbers. ✦✦✦△®

Black-necked Stork (adult ♂ and juvs)   Glossy Ibis

Australian White Ibis   Straw-necked Ibis

Royal Spoonbill   Yellow-billed Spoonbill

Magpie Goose *Anseranas semipalmata* 75-90cm Very large. A strange, swan-like long-legged goose, with very distinctive pied plumage. Head and neck black, 'shoulders' and back white, rest of wings black, rump white and tail black. Underparts white; underwing white with broad black trailing edge. Head domed; beak and facial skin pinkish yellow. Legs long and yellow. Immature drabber and greyer. Often gregarious; some flocks huge. *Voice:* shrill honking. *Habitat:* well-vegetated wetlands and floodplains. Locally abundant, but erratic, in northern coastal areas; occasional elsewhere. 🌊△®

Wandering Whistling-Duck *Dendrocygna arcuata* 55-60cm Large, long-necked long-legged duck with distinctive upright stance. Adult dark cinnamon-brown, paler on neck, with darker back feathers with chestnut scaly edgings. Conspicuous chestnut-edged white flank plumes. Wings dark in flight, contrasting with bold white rump and black tail (see Plumed Whistling-Duck). Immature paler and duller. *Voice:* distinctive high-pitched twittering whistle. *Habitat:* deep well-vegetated lagoons, flooded grassland. Erratic, but often common in northern areas; less common in southern part of range. 🌊△®

Plumed Whistling-Duck *Dendrocygna eytoni* 45-60cm Large whistling-duck, similar to Wandering, but paler, with barred chestnut sides to breast and diagnostic long white flank plumes. In flight appears uniformly palish grey-brown, with barely discernible paler rump stripe. Immature paler and duller. *Voice:* vociferous, especially in flight, brisk staccato whistles. *Habitat:* swamp and freshwater margins, occasionally estuaries, by day, tending to lush grasslands and stubbles at night. Northern distribution, but more widespread than Wandering, penetrating farther inland and southwards. Erratic, but locally very abundant. 🌊△®

Black Swan *Cygnus atratus* 120-140cm Huge, distinctive, and familiar. Almost all-black apart from yellow-tipped red beak and small white bar on wings. In flight, white primaries and secondaries show as a broad white trailing edge to the entire wing. Immature grey, with greyish wings, beak and legs. *Voice:* loud musical trumpeting. *Habitat:* large open waters of all types including salt, flooded pastures, swamps. Occasionally on the sea. Widespread; uncommon deep inland, generally common elsewhere if erratic; sometimes abundant. 🌊△®

Mute Swan *Cygnus olor* 130-160cm Huge and distinctive. Adult all-white, with a long sinuous neck. Beak orange-red. Immature pale greyish-fawn, becoming whiter with age. *Voice:* normally silent; occasionally hisses or grunts. *Habitat:* larger fresh waters and ornamental lakes. Introduced; now very scarce (now only at Northam, WA). 🌊

Freckled Duck *Stictonetta naevosa* 50-58cm Large, distinctively uniform and drab duck. Neck short, head with slight crest. Beak characteristically wedge-shaped, slightly upturned at tip, that of male becoming bright red over base when breeding. Adult has dark freckled grey-brown plumage, slightly paler below than above. Wings uniformly brown above; pale, almost white leading edge in flight from below. Immature paler and browner. *Voice:* soft piping contact calls; female has harsh 'quack', male a breathy grunt. *Habitat:* breeds beside heavily-vegetated fresh waters; at other times larger inland fresh or saline waters. Erratic in appearance, numbers usually small. 🌊△®

Magpie Goose

Wandering Whistling-Duck

Plumed Whistling-Duck

Black Swan (adult)

Mute Swan (adult)

Freckled Duck (breeding) ♂

Cape Barren Goose *Cereopsis novaehollandiae* 80-90cm Large

goose, unmistakably grey with large distinctive fleshy green cere covering base of beak. Body uniformly grey, with large black spots on wings. In flight shows black trailing edge with pale patch at base of primaries, and black tail. Legs brownish, feet black. Immature has denser spots, rather brownish back and duller cere. Wingbeats distinctively rapid. *Voice:* often noisy, especially in flight; male calls harsh repeated 'ark', female grunts. *Habitat:* breeds on small tussock-grass-covered offshore islands, disperses to pastures, often near lakes or dams. Locally quite common.

Australian Shelduck *Tadorna tadornoides* 55-70cm Large, rather

goose-like duck with distinctive chestnut and blackish plumage. Adult head and neck dark green, usually appearing blackish, separated by narrow white band from chestnut breast and mantle. Distinctive white horizontal line on black closed wing. Underparts largely black. Female has white patches around eye and base of blackish beak. In flight, white forewings contrast with dark flight feathers viewed from above or below. Legs blackish, comparatively long. Immature duller, with white-flecked head. *Voice:* female has various goose-like 'onk' and 'gangk' notes, male a crackling grunt. *Habitat:* breeds in hollow or under cover, sometimes far from water. Otherwise large shallow waters of most types, coastal and inland. Locally common in southeast, scarce elsewhere.

Radjah Shelduck *Tadorna radjah* 49-55cm Large, dark-backed pale-

bellied shelduck, with comparatively long neck and small head. Head and neck white, back and narrow collar band brown, rest of underparts white. Upperwing has white inner half with broad greenish speculum, black primaries. Underwing has white inner half, black primaries. Tail black. Legs and feet pale pink. Immature duller, brown-washed. Gregarious, active and noisy. Sometimes perches in trees. *Voice:* varied rattling and whistling calls. *Habitat:* breeds in tree holes near water; otherwise most types of larger open fresh, brackish or saline waters, inland or coastal. Local, rarely numerous.

Pacific Black Duck *Anas superciliosa* 50-60cm Large, familar and

typical dabbling duck. Male and female broadly similar, predominantly brown, with paler feather margins and distinctive dark stripes on head. Beak grey, legs and feet greenish. In flight shows purplish-green speculum and characteristic broad white underwing linings. Wary. Usually in singles or small groups, mostly dabbling in shallows. *Voice:* female resounding 'quark', male a sharp quacking 'rarb'. *Habitat:* well-vegetated waters of most types, visiting tidal areas. Widespread; in places common.

Mallard *Anas platyrhynchos* 55-65cm Large, now familar and typical

dabbling duck. Adult male has bottle-green head, yellowish beak, narrow white collar, chestnut breast, brownish back and grey-fawn belly. Tail black and white, with distinctive curled feathers. Feet orange. Female browner, lacking bold dark head stripes of Black Duck. Wings have greenish purple speculum, lack white linings. Eclipse male resembles female. *Voice:* female typical loud 'quack', male quiet 'yeeb'. *Habitat:* most types of water, particularly town park lakes, ponds and dams. Introduced; infrequent away from human occupation. Hybridizes with Black Duck.

Cape Barren Goose

Australian Shelduck ♀

Radjah Shelduck

Pacific Black Duck

Mallard (breeding) ♂

Mallard ♀

Grey Teal *Anas gracilis* 36-48cm Medium-large, familiar, rather featureless dabbling duck. Adult pale grey-brown with buff feather margins, crown darker than face, underparts paler than back, particularly pale throat. Lacks head stripes, and is appreciably smaller than Black Duck. Beak lead grey, eye red, legs and feet blackish. In flight, bold white bars in centre of upper and underwing are distinctive. Gregarious, flocks often large. *Voice:* female has laughing cackle; male a sharp 'pip'. *Habitat:* any water type, inland or coastal. Nomadic and erratic, but widespread and often locally common. ≋ ≼ ≽ △ ®

Chestnut Teal *Anas castanea* 38-45cm Medium-large, but small as dabbling ducks go. Adult male distinctive, with dark green head, black-speckled chestnut breast and belly, white between legs, black tail and brown back. Beak grey and normally shaped (see Australasian Shoveler); legs grey-green. Female and eclipse male mottled browns, appreciably darker than Grey Teal. In flight, shows narrow white bar on upperwing, white patch on underwing smaller than on Grey Teal. Fast in flight. *Voice:* female a chuckle, male sharp 'pip', very similar to Grey Teal. *Habitat:* breeds brackish or fresh swamps near coast; otherwise coastal estuaries, saltmarshes. Locally fairly common, most numerous Tasmania and Bass Strait. ≋ ≼ ≽ △ ®

Australasian Shoveler *Anas rhynchotis* 47-53cm Medium-large heavy-beaked dabbling duck. Distinctive head-down low profile on water. Male head iridescent blue-grey, with slim vertical white crescent between eye and beak visible at close range. Back and breast brown, with buff scaly feather margins. Flanks dark chestnut, the feathers with brownish centres. Beak grey, massive, spoon-shaped; legs bright orange. Female mottled brown. Blue-grey forewing and white bar on inner section of wing distinctive in flight, which is fast on whirring wings, large head slightly up, wings characteristically appear set well back on body. *Voice:* male soft 'tonk', female quiet quack. *Habitat:* heavily vegetated swamps, floodwaters, occasionally on coast. Widespread; locally quite common. ≋ △ ®

Northern Shoveler *Anas clypeata* 47-55cm Medium-large heavy-beaked dabbling duck, similar in shape, attitude and flight to Australasian Shoveler. Male has greenish head, with no white crescent; white breast and belly and unmarked chestnut flanks. White markings distinguish from Australasian in flight. Female and immature, and eclipse male, almost impossible to distinguish from Australasian. *Voice:* male has low-pitched double quack 'tuk-tuk', female quiet quack. *Habitat:* reed-fringed lakes, reservoirs, sheltered coastal waters. Vagrant. ≋ ⧘

Grey Teal

Chestnut Teal (breeding) ♂

Chestnut Teal ♀

Australasian Shoveler (breeding) ♂

Australasian Shoveler ♀

Northern Shoveler (breeding) ♂

Garganey *Anas querquedula* 38-40cm Medium-large duck, about the size of Grey Teal. Breeding male (February to June) distinguished readily by brown head with broad white mark curving over eye and down neck, and by long black and white scapular feathers. Back brown, underparts white. Female and nonbreeding male brownish,distinguished from Grey Teal by dark crown and eye-stripe, contrasting with pale supercilium and throat. In flight males show characteristic very pale grey forewing (dull brown in females). *Voice:* distinctive harsh rattle. *Habitat:* well-vegetated fresh waters. Rare but possibly regular straggler from the Northern Hemisphere. ≋ ∤

Pink-eared Duck *Malacorhynchus membranaceus* 38-45cm Medium-large and distinctive dabbling duck. White face, dark brown patch through eye extending into downcurved marking on nape. Tiny pink spot behind eye is origin of name, but visible only at close range. Beak grey, very long, with characteristic drooping skin flaps near tip. Back brown; undertail coverts distinctively yellow. Crown, neck and underparts whitish, barred with brown, finely on neck, boldly on flanks. Flight shoveler-like, but with beak held downwards. Shows white trailing edge to brown wings and crescentic white rump. *Voice:* strange but distinctive continuous chirruping. *Habitat:* shallow fresh or saline inland waters. Widespread but irregular; locally quite common. ≋ △®

Hardhead *Aythya australis* 43-50cm Medium-large, dark, compact, fast-flying diving duck. Adult largely distinctive mahogany-brown, male darker than female, white on belly and with white undertail coverts beneath a darker brown tail. Eye of male white. Beak grey, distinctively long, yellow near tip. Immature duller brown, shorter beaked. In flight, white underwings and bold white bar running the length of the upperwing are very distinctive. Dives frequently. Gregarious, sometimes in large flocks. *Voice:* rarely heard whistle (male); croak (female). *Habitat:* deeper inland waters of all types. Widespread; locally quite numerous. ≋ △®

Australian Wood Duck *Chenonetta jubata* 44-50cm Medium-large: rather long neck and upright posture give appearance of small goose. Male has brown head with substantial drooping crest, chestnut-speckled grey breast, grey body, and black rump, tail and undertail coverts. Beak small, delicate, grey. Female has distinctive white stripes above and below eye on brown head, grey back, brown-barred flanks, black tail with white undertail coverts. Swims distinctly tail-high. In flight, grey forewing and black and white speculum are conspicuous. *Voice:* nasal 'mnow'. *Habitat:* fresh waters and wet pastures, often among scattered trees (often perches in trees). Widespread; locally common. ➹ ≋ ♨ ∤ △®

Garganey (breeding) ♂

Pink-eared Duck

Hardhead ♂

Australian Wood Duck ♂

Australian Wood Duck ♀

Cotton Pygmy-Goose *Nettapus coromandelianus* 34-38cm

Medium-large, but a diminutive duck. Male has white face and neck, dark crown and short neat beak. Back greenish black, with broad blackish collar. Underparts white, buff under tail. Female duller and duskier, with more extensive dark crown and blackish bar through eye. In flight keeps low. Broad white trailing edge extends full length of wing in male; female shows only narrow white trailing edge (see Green Pygmy-Goose). All-dark underwing. *Voice:* male a staccato 'car car car', female a quiet quack. *Habitat:* deeper swamps, dams, lakes, usually with plentiful emergent vegetation. Locally common in northeast Queensland; scarce elsewhere.
⚒ ⌘ ®

Green Pygmy-Goose *Nettapus pulchellus* 30-36cm

Medium-large, but even smaller than Cotton Pygmy-Goose. Male has greenish black crown, neck and back, with distinctive white face patches, grey-barred white flanks and a whitish belly. Female browner above, with a blackish streak through the eye, with a white face, smoky neck and grey-barred flanks. Beak tiny, grey with yellow tip. In flight, both sexes show broad white trailing edge to inner portion of wing only. *Voice:* variations on 'pee-whit' 'pee woo' and an unlikely sounding high-pitched trill. *Habitat:* lagoons, lakes, dams etc, with emergent vegetation. Locally fairly common along northern coastal belt, more so west of Darwin. Scarce farther south. ⚒ ⌘ △ ®

Blue-billed Duck *Oxyura australis* 37-44cm

Medium-large, dark chunky stiff-tailed diving duck. Breeding male body and back rich chestnut with purplish black head and black spiny stiff tail usually carried on the water. Beak rich blue, robust but deeply concave. Female uniformly brown with paler feather fringes. Nonbreeding male similar but with blacker head. Swims low in water, dives frequently. Secretive, often solitary. *Voice:* seldom heard rattle. *Habitat:* breeds beside deep, heavily vegetated fresh waters; in winter on fresh waters of all sorts. Generally uncommon. ⚒ △ ®

Musk Duck *Biziura lobata* 48-70cm

Male appreciably larger than female. Strange large and heavily built duck, long-tailed and floating low in the water, male with a large lobe of skin hanging beneath the beak. Overall sooty brown, with darker brown crown and nape giving pale-faced appearance. Body finely vermiculated with wavy fine pale buff lines. Beak grey, stout and triangular. Tail long, diamond-shaped, usually carried flat on water. Rarely flies–sculls away across water, but will fly after dark, often calling as it goes. *Voice:* extraordinary combined whistle and grunt by male during display, when long tail is held erect and the dewlap is exhibited prominently, beak upraised. *Habitat:* permanent densely vegetated swamps, large lakes, lagoons and bays. Fairly widespread but erratic and only sometimes numerous, especially during autumn and winter. ⚒ ⌘ ⌘ △ ®

Cotton Pygmy-Goose (breeding) ♂

Green Pygmy-Goose (breeding) ♂

Blue-billed Duck (breeding) ♂

Blue-billed Duck ♀

Musk Duck (breeding) ♂

Osprey *Pandion haliaetus* 50-65cm Large 'fish eagle'. Head slightly crested, with white crown, broad brown stripe through eye. Upperparts brown, with buff feather edgings; underparts whitish, faintly brown-streaked, with a characteristic brown collar. Wings long, brown above, whitish below with a dark trailing edge and brown carpal patch, always carried distinctively angled at 'wrist'. Plunge diving for fish characteristic. *Voice:* high-pitched repeated 'fee'. *Habitat:* coastal waters of all types, occasionally well inland on larger rivers and lakes. Irregular. 🌊⚓🦅🏞 ⚓⛰®

Black-shouldered Kite *Elanus axillaris* 33-38cm Medium-large, elegant hawk. Adult has white head with conspicuous black mark round red eye; back pearl grey, tail paler. Shoulders of closed wings distinctively black. Underparts entirely white. In flight, shows broad black leading edge to inner part of upper wing; underwing smoky white with sooty carpal patch and greyish primaries (see Letter-winged). Hovers. Immature similarly patterned but yellowish brown on head, back and breast. *Voice:* repeated 'chee'. *Habitat:* open woodland, grassland. Widespread but erratic; locally reasonably common. 🌾⚓⛺🏞 ⚓⛰®

Letter-winged Kite *Elanus scriptus* 35-38cm Medium-large, elegant hawk. Similar to Black-shouldered, but nape and mantle are darker grey, and legs are pale, not rich, yellow. In flight, underwing pattern is diagnostic, with a long black bar, sometimes broken, forming a V or W along whitish wing. Flight less direct than Black-shouldered, more tern-like. Nocturnal hunter. *Voice:* harsh 'kar' calls and a clear alarm whistle. *Habitat:* open, often arid landscapes, watercourses with trees. Very erratic in numbers and distribution, closely associated with rodent 'plagues'. 🌾⚓⛺🏞⛰®

Pacific Baza *Aviceda subcristata* 40-45cm Medium-large long-tailed round-winged hawk. Head, mantle and upper breast dark grey. Eye pale cream. Upperparts dark grey. Belly barred black and white; undertail coverts pale chestnut. In flight, long tail with black terminal band, barred belly and pale underwings with heavily fingered, brown-barred tips are characteristic. Immature drabber and browner. Buoyant flight, hovers around canopy. *Voice:* repeated shrill double whistle. *Habitat:* forests of all types in coastal belt. Never numerous. 🌲🏕⚓®

Black Kite *Milvus migrans* 48-55cm Large, well-known, long-tailed kite. Uniformly brown, appearing slightly chestnut at close range, black at a distance. Wings long, and comparatively narrow, often held angled. Tail distinctively long, only slightly forked, but characteristically held slightly fanned and flexed to control manoeuvres. *Voice:* plaintive 'see eer'. *Habitat:* very catholic. Widespread; often quite common. 🌲🌾🌊⚓🦅⚓⛰®

Square-tailed Kite *Lophoictinia isura* 50-56cm Large, slim, long-winged kite. Broadly similar to Black Kite, but adult has distinctly whitish face, and appears dark brown above, cinnamon below (not uniformly brown). In flight, harrier-like gliding just above canopy is characteristic. Marked underwing pattern of plain cinnamon forewing with heavily barred grey primaries and secondaries is distinctive, as is the long brownish tail with single black terminal bar. Immature paler, more chestnut and brown, lacks pale face. Often solitary. *Voice:* high-pitched yelp. *Habitat:* open woodland, lightly treed country, rocky hillsides. Widespread but generally rare and little-known. 🌾⚓⛺🏞⛰®

Osprey

Black-shouldered Kite (adult)

Letter-winged Kite (adult)

Pacific Baza (adult)

Black Kite

Square-tailed Kite (adult)

Black-breasted Buzzard *Hamirostra melanosternon* 53-60cm
Large, short-tailed and robustly-built hawk. Adult blackish above, sometimes with golden-chestnut nape, with brown wings and pale brown tail. Underparts usually black, with cinnamon undertail coverts. Pale phase is fawn with darker streaks. Immature mottled brown above, cinnamon below. Flight distinctive with black primary tips contrasting with white 'window' at their base. Tail short and square. *Voice:* short, harsh yelps, whistles. *Habitat:* open plains, lightly timbered grassland. Widespread but generally rare. Slightly more numerous in far north. 🦅 ♦♦ ▦ △®

Brahminy Kite *Milvus indus* 43-51cm
Large distinctive kite. Adult unmistakable, with white head, mantle and breast contrasting with chestnut back, wings and tail; blackish primaries. Immature can be mistaken for Whistling, more nondescript, pale brown with darker streakings. *Voice:* plaintive 'pee-aa-aa-ah'. *Habitat:* usually coastal, mangroves, inlets, harbours. Locally fairly common. 🌊 ♦ 🦅 ⊞ ®

Whistling Kite *Milvus sphenurus* 51-59cm
Large, familiar, pale kite with distinctive call. Adult pale fawn, with faint darker streaks, tail long and pale. Immature richer brown with plentiful darker streaks. In flight, dark primaries and secondaries form broad trailing edge to wing, broken by characteristic pale block of feathers in mid-wing. *Voice:* distinctively vocal, with whistling descending 'see-ooo' leading to shrill staccato chatter. *Habitat:* open landscapes, woodlands and coasts. Widespread but erratic in both distribution and numbers; occasionally common. 🦅 🌊 ♦ ♦♦ ▦ 🐚 ♦♦ ®

Brown Goshawk *Accipiter fasciatus* 40-55cm
Large, powerful, long-tailed hawk. Adult has grey head, separated indistinctly from grey back and tail by pale chestnut collar. Underparts white, finely but densely barred with pale chestnut. Legs yellow, long, with 'baggy trousers'. Immature grey-brown above, white below with broad brown barring and striations. In flight, wings are shortish and broad. Pale ginger wing lining contrasts with lightly barred, pale grey flight feathers. *Voice:* shrill 'ki-ki-ki' chatter, female has mellow whistle. *Habitat:* open forest and woodlands, other landscapes with plentiful trees. Widespread; often quite common. 🦅 🦅 ▦ ♦♦ △®

Collared Sparrowhawk *Accipiter cirrhocephalus* 30-40cm
Medium-large long-tailed hawk, smaller and lighter-built than Brown Goshawk. Adult grey-brown above with a paler head; pale chestnut below, . Immature darker brown above; white heavily barred and streaked darker below. In flight, tail is square-cut, not slightly rounded as in Brown Goshawk. *Voice:* rapid, high-pitched 'kikikiki...' call, faster than Brown. *Habitat:* most types of forest and woodland, well-developed scrub. Widespread, comparatively inconspicuous, probably less common than Brown Goshawk. 🦅 🦅 ▦ ♦♦ ▦ 🐚 △®

Grey (White) Goshawk *Accipiter novaehollandiae* 40-50cm
Large, powerful hawk, with two colour phases. Grey phase adult pale grey above, with blackish flight feathers; paler grey below, very faintly and finely darker barred. White phase entirely white, reminiscent of Sulphur-crested Cockatoo. Immatures grey, with broader brownish-grey barring on underparts. *Voice:* high-pitched chatter, slower deeper 'yook yook'. *Habitat:* forests, woodlands, well timbered landscapes, sometimes hunting over open country. Locally fairly common but generally scarce. 🦅 ▦ ♦♦ ®

Black-breasted Buzzard (adult)

Brahminy Kite (adult)

Whistling Kite

Brown Goshawk (immature)

Collared Sparrowhawk (adult)

Grey (White) Goshawk (white form)

Red Goshawk *Erythrotriorchis radiatus* 50-60cm Large powerful
goshawk. Crown, nape, mantle and breast rusty red with dark brown streaks; face and throat whitish, streaked black. Back and wings dark brown, with broad paler feather margins; flight feathers blackish. Tail grey, with several darker bars. Beak strong but compact; cere grey. Legs pale yellow, noticeably stout. In flight, rather longer-winged than other goshawks, with more fingered wingtips. Cinnamon underwing contrasts with pale undersides to flight feathers with several long slender bars, similar in colour to Square-tailed Kite but with totally different flight characteristics, being a true, fast-moving hawk. *Voice:* slow, deep chattering. *Habitat:* usually open forests, lightly-wooded country, watercourses. Generally rare. 🐾 🦅 ®

White-bellied Sea-Eagle *Haliaeetus leucogaster* 75-85cm Very
large and distinctively pale eagle. Adult has white head and nape, white underparts, white rump and short wedge-shaped tail. Back and wings grey. In flight, upper wing is entirely grey, underwing characteristic with white forewing and 'armpits' contrasting with blackish flight feathers. Wings long and very broad. Immature dark brown, heavily streaked, with paler head. Beak massive, grey with black tip; cere grey. Legs stout, yellowish. Hovers clumsily and low before dropping onto fish - unlike the Osprey's dive. *Voice:* loud, metallic honking, often in duet. *Habitat:* close to larger waters of most types, fresh or saline, coastal. Widespread but erratic, rarely common. 🌊 🐟 🦅 ®

Wedge-tailed Eagle *Aquila audax* 89-110cm Massive, distinctive
dark eagle. Adult black, with tawny feathers on nape and upperwing of older birds. Wings broad (span over 2m), heavily fingered, with whitish line on underside. Tail distinctive, long and diamond-shaped. Head protrudes comparatively short distance in front of wings, but beak massive, grey, with yellow cere. Legs with baggy feather 'trousers', bare tarsus short and strong, pale yellowish. Immature (may take 5 years to adult) browner, with variable paler markings on head, back and wings, but with characteristic tail shape. *Voice:* rarely vocal; feeble yelps near nest. *Habitat:* catholic, from mountains to plains and sub-desert. Widespread but erratic, locally common. 🦅 👣 🏔 ⛰ △ ®

Little Eagle *Hieraaetus morphnoides* 45-51cm Large, but
comparatively small for an eagle, though still powerful. Two colour forms. Dark form: brown above, with black streaks on crown, rough crest and face, paler grey-brown below. Light form: almost white, sparsely streaked below, with brown-streaked yellowish-buff head and mantle. Immature light phase quite yellow. Underwing pattern distinctive, with broad white diagonal bar separating brownish leading edge from blackish secondaries, and linked to white 'window' patch at carpal joint, including the primary bases. Wingtips blackish. Flight style characteristic, often soaring in tight circles, wings flat, tail fanned, head protruding well forward of wings. *Voice:* rapid two or three-note whistle. *Habitat:* open forest, woodland and scrub, usually near water; tree-lined watercourses. Widespread but generally uncommon. 🦅 👣 🏔 △ ®

Red Goshawk

White-bellied Sea-Eagle (adult)

Wedge-tailed Eagle

Little Eagle (pale morph)

Little Eagle (dark morph)

Spotted Harrier *Circus assimilis* 50-60cm Large - and one of the most elegant birds of prey. Owl-like facial disc chestnut; eyes piercing yellow, forward facing. Adult grey above, with fine white speckles on wings; ginger below, spotted and barred with white. Flight feathers blackish, tail grey with several narrow blackish bands. Legs long and slim, yellow. Immature brown, streaked, with chestnut face and shoulders, can be confused with Swamp Harrier. Spotted chestnut underside distinctive in flight, which is typically harrier-like, gliding low on broad wings stiffly-held in a shallow V, quartering the ground. *Voice:* more or less silent. *Habitat:* open plains and scrub, often dry. Builds stick nests in trees - unique in harriers. Widespread; commoner inland and in the north. 🦅🌲🔫△®

Swamp (Marsh) Harrier *Circus approximans* 50-60cm Large, heavy, rather dark harrier; generally brown, rather more rufous on head, paler underparts in male than female. Rump white, conspicuous in flight. Tail long, grey, faintly barred. Wings long, dark above, barred below; held in shallow V as bird sails low, rocking from side to side. Perches upright, with distinctively small owl-like head. Legs long, greenish yellow. *Voice:* 'kee-ow' and various squeals, not often heard outside breeding season. *Habitat:* open country, particularly swamps and marshes, occasionally saltmarshes or crops. Often quite common in suitable wetland areas; rare in arid country. 🦅〰️🔫△®

Eastern Marsh Harrier *Circus spilonotus* 45-55cm Large, but slim, pale, and of medium size for a harrier. Male has black head and grey back, with a distinctive white rump; underparts white with few streaks. Underwing lining white, with only narrow dark margins to wing, primary tips blackish. Female and immature variable, not safely separable from those of Swamp, however females have a combination of strongly barred tail and clear whitish rump. Potential vagrant. 〰️

Black Falcon *Falco subniger* 48-56cm Large, dark, robust falcon, with a distinctively long tail. Plumage largely sooty brown, with very faint paler barring on flanks and tail, and with a paler cheek against which dark falcon 'moustaches' can be detected at close range. Beak strong but compact, steel-grey; cere and eye-ring blue-grey; short legs and talons greyish to yellowish. Very long wings and tail are apparent both perched and in flight. Often soars high, on drooped wings with tail fanned, waiting for prey. Flight leisurely in appearance but lethally fast. *Voice:* chattering 'kakaka' and screeches. *Habitat:* open or lightly-treed landscapes of most sorts. Widespread, but erratic and usually uncommon. 🦅🌾🏘️🌲🔫🔫△®

Peregrine Falcon *Falco peregrinus* 36-50cm Large, robust, world-famous cosmopolitan falcon. Adult has steel-grey back, black hood, white collar and brown-barred buff underparts. Beak grey, robust; cere yellow. Tail and flight feathers blackish. Legs strong, yellow. Immature browner above, mottled and barred; buff, heavily brown-spotted and streaked below. Soars high on broad, triangular wings with usually narrow tail fanned. Half-closes wings and streamlines tail to stoop at great speed on avian prey passing beneath. *Voice:* chattering 'chak-chak-chak'. *Habitat:* open landscapes, often near water, often with gorges or cliffs (or buildings!) offering nesting ledges. Widespread, but generally uncommon. 🦅🌲🔫🔫△®

Spotted Harrier

Swamp (Marsh) Harrier (adult ♀)

Eastern Marsh Harrier (adult ♂)

Black Falcon

Peregrine Falcon (adult)

Australian Hobby (Little Falcon) *Falco longipennis* 30-35cm
Medium-large, slimly-built, long-winged falcon, almost like a giant long-tailed swift in silhouette. Upperparts grey, with darker flight feathers. Underparts whitish shading to chestnut on belly, with black moustachial face patch. Immature browner, with paler feather fringes. Long-winged when perching, but in flight very fast on its long wings, when rufous lower belly and legs can be seen. Beak grey; cere and eye-ring yellow; legs rather short, yellow. Fast hunter, relying on sheer speed to surprise and overtake prey, which ranges from large insects to ducks and small herons! *Voice:* rapid twittering Kestrel-like 'kee-kee-kee...'. *Habitat:* open country, even over built-up areas. Widespread, but generally uncommon. 🦅🦅🐃🏛️🏕️△®

Grey Falcon *Falco hypoleucos* 33-43cm Medium-large, pale long-winged falcon. Adult distinctively grey above, with faint blackish streaks; paler grey, usually unmarked below. Tail long, grey, faintly barred; wings grey with blackish flight feathers. Immature darker above, paler below, more streaked. Legs and talons yellow. Beak grey; cere and eye-ring orange-yellow. Broad-shouldered appearance in flight, and more robustly built than Hobby or Kestrel. Shallow flickering wingbeats; stoops on prey like a Peregrine. *Voice:* harsh 'chak,chak chak...' *Habitat:* varied open habitats, including pasture and semi-arid regions. Widespread, rarely coastal, generally rare. 🦅🐃🏛️🐃🐃△®

Brown Falcon *Falco berigora* 41-51cm Large, variable falcon. Upperparts brown, plain in male, spotted or streaked in female, rather ginger in birds from central Australia. Underparts variable, from off-white to buff with brown streaks, to almost black in some immatures. Conspicuous feature of all plumages is a dark double comma-shaped moustachial streak originating around the eye. Beak grey; cere, eye-ring and legs greyish. Often approachable, perching on posts. Deep wingbeats are distinctive, as is habit of soaring on upswept wings. Will chase small animal prey on foot on the ground. Hovers clumsily. *Voice:* very noisy and in consequence familiar, with screeches and maniacal cackles. *Habitat:* catholic in choice; widespread, often quite common. 🦅🏛️🐃🏕️🐃🐃△®

Australian (Nankeen) Kestrel *Falco cenchroides* 30-35cm
Medium-large, often familiar falcon, with characteristic expert hovering technique. Upperparts distinctive chestnut, sparsely spotted in male, densely so in female and immature. Underparts pale buff, shading to white on lower belly, almost unstreaked in males, streaked in females, heavily streaked in immature. Tail long, grey with a black terminal bar in male; brownish with several darker bars in female and immature. Flight feathers blackish. Hovers, showing pale undersurface or distinctive chestnut and black upperwing pattern. Wings slim and pointed, often angled. *Voice:* shrill 'keekeekeekee...' *Habitat:* catholic, mostly avoiding forests or dense woodlands, often breeds in cities. Widespread, reasonably common in southern areas, becoming appreciably less common to the north. 🦅🦅🏛️🐃🏕️🐃🐃△®

Australian Hobby (Little Falcon)

Grey Falcon (immature)

Brown Falcon (dark morph)

Brown Falcon (pale morph)

Australian (Nankeen) Kestrel

Orange-footed Scrubfowl *Megapodius reinwardt* 45cm Large, bulky-bodied, small-headed chicken-like bird. Head, neck and underparts dark lead-grey; head with small upstanding brownish crest. Back, wings and tail variable dark rufous brown. Usually runs off noisily if disturbed; flight clumsy. Nest an enormous mound of rotting vegetation and sand, 12m in diameter. *Voice:* raucous crow, usually double; chicken-like clucks. *Habitat:* rainforest, woodland, scrub, occasionally mangroves. Locally reasonably common. 🐾 🏚️ ®

Malleefowl *Leipoa ocellata* 55-60cm Large turkey-sized bird with plumage like a bustard. Small head grey with inconspicuous, rarely raised, blackish crest. Longish neck grey, with prominent black frontal streak. Back, wings and tail finely mottled in greys, buffs and browns. Underparts white. Beak short, stout and black; legs strong, greyish. Nest initially an excavation, ultimately a large mound (diameter 5m) of vegetation and sand. *Voice:* usually quiet, male has far-carrying three-note boom, female a crow. *Habitat:* mallee, scrub, open woodlands, often on sandy soils. Local, occasionally fairly common. ♊ ⛰️ ®

Australian Brush-turkey *Alectura lathami* 60-70cm Large turkey-sized and turkey-like bird. Small head and long neck bare-skinned, reddish, bright red in breeding males, ending in yellow collar of loose skin (whitish in Cape York race).. Beak small, strong and black. Body large and black, with pale feather fringes on underparts, and large fan-shaped black tail, folded and flattened vertically. Nest mound up to 4m-diameter. *Voice:* nasal 'kee-ock', chicken-like clucks. *Habitat:* rainforest, woodland and scrub, mostly coastal. Local, occasionally common. 🐾 🏚️ ♊ ®

Stubble Quail *Coturnix pectoralis* 18cm Small, plump, well camouflaged game bird. Upperparts brownish, streaked and flecked with buff, grey and black, with three bold longitudinal stripes along crown and nape. Male has chestnut face and throat; female and immature white. Breast buff, with darker streaks (often almost entirely blackish in male) shading to white belly. *Voice:* sharp 'pippy-wheet', 'titch-whip'. *Habitat:* grassland, weedy ground, low scrub, cereal crops and stubbles. Widespread but erratic; locally quite common. 🌾 ♊ △ ®

Brown Quail *Coturnix ypsilophora* 20cm Small, but the largest quail. Dumpy, variably plumaged but usually quite dark, chestnut or brownish with darker and paler streaks, bars and flecks; paler below, particularly in female and immature. Legs yellowish; beak short and strong. *Voice:* a useful guide, distinctive whistling 'f-weep' and disyllabic 'be-quick, be-quick'. Often vocal early and late, and at night. *Habitat:* marshy rank vegetation, damp paddocks, lush pastures such as clover; rice; scrub, sometimes near coast. Widespread but erratic; sometimes locally common. ♊ ♊ △ ®

King Quail *Coturnix chinensis* 13cm Very small dumpy quail. Secretive, but male distinctive if seen, with blue face, breast and flanks, and rich chestnut belly. Characteristic black-and-white throat patch. Female and immature similar above, but with whitish throat and buff underparts with dense dark barring. Legs yellowish; beak short and strong. *Voice:* two or three high-pitched notes in descending scale. *Habitat:* dense grassland and pastures, usually damp or swampy. Generally scarce. 🌊 ♊ ®

Orange-footed Scrubfowl

Malleefowl

Australian Brush-turkey ♂

Stubble Quail ♂

Brown Quail

King Quail ♂ and ♀

Indian Peafowl *Pavo cristatus* 200-240cm Huge (measurement includes train). Familiar and extremely colourful bird. Male purple with crested head, black-and-white face pattern and black belly; chestnut, green and marbled black-and-white wings. Train (elongated rump feathers) extremely long, sometimes fanned (showing stiff quills of true tail), with familiar eye-spot pattern. Female smaller, crested, brown above, off white below, with simple brown tail. Legs long, male with spurs, greyish. *Voice:* far-carrying wail. *Habitat:* scrub, open woodland, parks and gardens. Introduced, but isolated and scarce. ◢ ♨ ⅏

Red Junglefowl *Gallus gallus* 43-75cm Large, variable but well-known varieties of domestic fowl, some resembling ancestral Jungle Fowl. Male with red comb (or wattles), gold and chestnut back, dark blackish arched tail, and dark underparts, all spectacularly iridescent. Female brown, with darker markings and reduced wattles. Legs strong, spurred in male. *Voice:* familiar farmyard cluckings and crowings. *Habitat:* woodland. Introduced - isolated feral populations survive on islands in the Capricorn Group, Queensland. ◢ ⅏

Common Pheasant *Phasianus colchicus* 55-90cm Large, well-known long-tailed game bird. Male colourful. Head and neck green, slightly crested, usually separated from back and breast by narrow white collar; fleshy red face wattles. Body iridescent chestnut, gold and bronze, with black-and-white crescentic marks. Tail long, particularly central feathers, and brown-barred. Female much duller, well camouflaged, fawn with brown markings; tail rather shorter. Legs strong, blackish, spurred in male. *Voice:* strident 'kork-cock' followed by wing-claps. *Habitat:* scrub, open woodland, grassland, crops. Introduced to various islands; stocks regularly replenished. ◢ ⅏ ⁑

California Quail *Lophortyx californicus* 25cm Small-medium pigeon-like American game bird. Adult male grey and dark brown above, with striking black-and-white face pattern and diagnostic forward-curving slim upright crest. Breast blue, belly barred and flanks chestnut with bold diagonal streaks. Tail blue. Female duller, with pale eye-stripe and smaller crest. Shy, running from danger; explodes into flight if pressed. *Voice:* three-syllable plaintive 'kew-car-cow'. *Habitat:* dense grasslands, scrubby woodland. Introduced, surviving to be quite common on King Island in Bass Strait. ◢ ⁑

Chukar Partridge *Alectoris chukar* 33cm Medium-sized gamebird. Grey-brown above, with distinctive white face and throat bordered broadly in black. Flanks boldly barred black, chestnut and white. Legs pinkish red. Upright, short-necked heavy-bodied stance; runs swiftly, crouches. If pressed whirrs off low on bowed wings, gliding much of the way. *Voice:* clucking notes, also a 'chuck-aar'. *Habitat:* open, dry grassland, rocky hillsides. Introduced; status unstable. ◢ ⁑

Indian Peafowl (breeding) ♂

Red Junglefowl

Common Pheasant ♂

California Quail ♂

Chukar Partridge

Common Turkey *Meleagris gallopavo* 90-110cm Huge, more familiar from butcher's shop. Plumage blackish with pale specklings, iridescent. Male has skin of nape naked, purple and white, with fleshy wrinkled red wattles on throat. Female smaller and duller, with grey head skin. Tail bulky and long, white-tipped, sometimes fanned. Legs strong, spurred in male. *Voice:* gobbling, crowy call. *Habitat:* grassland, scrub and light woodland. Introduced, with surviving feral populations on King and Flinders Islands, Bass Strait. Status unstable. ◢ ᜃ

Helmeted Guinea Fowl *Numida meleagris* 60cm Large, strangely shaped and bulky, with tiny head on longish neck. Plumage grey with fine white spots. Naked skin of face and sides of neck blue. 'Helmet' or casque bony, brownish and roughly triangular. *Voice:* sharp wail, twittering clucks. *Habitat:* scrub and woodland. Introduced, with surviving feral populations on some Great Barrier Reef Islands and Brisbane, Queensland. Status unstable. ◢ ᜃ

Red-backed Button-quail *Turnix maculosa* 14-16cm Small, comparatively long-legged quail. Upperparts brown, finely mottled and streaked with buffs and white, with indistinct broad darker longitudinal bars on head. Slightly larger female has distinctive chestnut face and sides to nape and breast. Underparts buff, boldly spotted and barred blackish on flanks. Legs yellowish. Eye white; beak small, characteristically pale, usually yellowish. Hard to flush, but flies fast and low to cover. *Voice:* penetrating repeated booming 'ooom'. *Habitat:* grassland and scrub, usually moist. Inconspicuous and erratic; sometimes locally common. ᜃ ≛ ®

Painted Button-quail *Turnix varia* 16-19cm Small, dark-backed quail. Crown dark, with suggestion of brown central stripe; face and throat white, speckled with black. Eye brown; beak short but stout, grey. Upperparts brown, finely mottled and streaked with black, buffs and white, with chestnut shoulder patch more conspicuous in female than male. Underparts pale buff, with large whitish scaly markings. Legs comparatively long, rich yellow. When flushed shows distinctively long pointed wings with blackish flight feathers; usually flies for some distance. *Voice:* booming repeated 'oom'. *Habitat:* scrub, woodland and forest, grassland and heaths. Widespread, but erratic and nowhere common. ◢ ≛ ≛ ®

Chestnut-backed Button-quail *Turnix castanota* 17-22cm Small quail, similar to but more chestnut above than Painted. Head dark with brown central crown stripe; face and throat white with black flecks. Beak heavy, blue-grey; eye yellow. Upperparts chestnut brown, with rather bold black, white and buff markings, with an almost clear dull chestnut rump and tail. Underparts pale buff with bold white spots. Legs pale yellow. Usually runs from danger; any flight is of short duration, but shows markedly chestnut back. *Voice:* deep repeated 'oom'. *Habitat:* open woodland, scrub, rocky hillsides. Inconspicuous, erratic, and nowhere common. ≛ ≛ △ ®

Common Turkey (♂♂ and a ♀)

Helmeted Guineafowl

Red-backed Button-quail ♀

Painted Button-quail ♀

Chestnut-backed Button-quail ♀

Buff-breasted Button-quail *Turnix olivei* 18-20cm Small quail,
broadly similar to Chestnut-backed but note distribution. Head dark, with brown central crown stripe; face and throat white, flecked black. Eye yellow. Beak distinctively long and heavier than Chestnut-backed, yellowish. Upperparts chestnut brown, with bold black, white and buff markings, with a clear chestnut-brown rump and tail. Underparts grey-buff, characteristically almost unmarked, yellower on flanks. Legs yellowish. Usually runs from danger, but shows distinctive chestnut back if flushed. *Voice:* deep repeated 'oom'. *Habitat:* grassy woodlands, rocky scrub-covered hillsides. Inconspicuous, nowhere common. 👥 ⬧ ®

Black-breasted Button-quail *Turnix melanogaster* 17-19cm
Small, very dark quail. Head distinctively black in female; flecked black and white in male, with striking white eye and short, stout black beak. Upperparts grey-brown, flecked and streaked with black, buffs and white. Breast almost black with white flecks in female; scaly black and white in male. Hard to flush, usually remains motionless rather than running. *Voice:* deep double 'oo-oom', repeated regularly. *Habitat:* dry forests and thickets, occasionally pasture. Nowhere common. 🦃 ⬧⬧ ▥ ®

Little Button-quail *Turnix velox* 12-14cm Small tawny quail. Female
head, nape and breast distinctively ginger-cinnamon, with white throat and belly. Male has browner, speckled head and grey-buff breast, with black scaly markings. Beak short and stout; eye pale yellowish or whitish. Upperparts brown, slightly chestnut-tinged, with fine black, buff and white mottlings and streaks. Runs like a small rat; flushes with a sharp call, flashing pale rump and underparts on landing. *Voice:* squeaking 'tchek' of alarm. *Habitat:* pastures, grassy plains, open woodlands. The most widespread quail, but erratic in occurrence and numbers; sometimes locally quite common. 👥 ⬧⬧ △ ®

Red-chested Button-quail *Turnix pyrrhothorax* 13-16cm Small
quail, superficially similar to Little but with darker upperparts. Female head dark, with brown crown stripe and marbled black and white face and cheeks. Male head paler, less distinctly marked. Upperparts dark grey-brown, with fine black and buff mottlings and streaks. Female underside distinctive rich orange buff, particularly on upper breast and throat; male paler with white throat and belly, with black markings on breast and flanks. Difficult to flush, makes only short flights before plunging back into cover. *Voice:* sharp rattle when flushed; repeated 'oom' in breeding season. *Habitat:* open grassy woodland, scrub, pastures. Widespread but erratic; usually scarce. ⬧⬧ ®

Plains-wanderer *Pedionomus torquatus* 15-17cm Small, fast-running,
rather courser-like bird of uncertain affinities. Head small, rounded and brown, with paler face, white eye, and chestnut nape. Neck characteristic, black, flecked densely with white, crescentic chestnut patch on upper breast. Body held upright, finely vermiculated browns, buffs and blacks above; paler below with scaly markings on breast and flanks. Often stands on tips of toes. In flight shows black and white carpal patches, with long yellow legs trailing. Male smaller and appreciably paler and duller than female. *Voice:* quail-like repeated 'oom'. *Habitat:* grassland, paddocks, cereals and stubble. Erratic; generally scarce or rare. 🚜 ⬧⬧ ®

Buff-breasted Button-quail

Black-breasted Button-quail ♀

Little Button-quail ♀

Red-chested Button-quail ♀

Plains-wanderer ♀ (left) and probable ♂

Buff-banded Rail *Gallirallus philippensis* 28-33cm Medium-large rail. Head distinctive, with stout sharp brownish beak, dark crown, prominent white supercilium over chestnut cheeks, and grey throat. Upperparts olive brown, flecked with black and white. Breast and belly white, boldly barred black, with a buff half-collar on breast. Undertail coverts buff, barred black. Tail frequently flicked. Legs long and grey. Flies rarely, on rounded wings with legs trailing. Active at dusk. *Voice:* various squeaks, clicks and croaks; raucous bray. *Habitat:* swamps, marshes, moist dense pastures, not always close to water. Widespread coastally, erratic and uncommon farther inland. ♨△®

Lewin's Rail *Dryolimnas pectoralis* 21-23cm Medium-sized dark rail. Beak long and pointed, slightly downcurved, black with reddish base. Crowned nape chestnut with darker flecks; throat and breast dull grey. Upperparts dark olive, flecked with black. Belly black, with white feather fringes. Undertail dark, barred, with white margins. Legs long, pinkish. Shy and inconspicuous. *Voice:* loud stream of clicks, often in unison and at variable tempo. Grunts. *Habitat:* reeds, rushes, rank moist vegetation, saltmarsh. Generally uncommon. ♨🐾®

Chestnut Rail *Eulabeornis castaneoventris* 40-52cm Large: the largest and perhaps most distinctive Australian rail. Body and neck entirely rich chestnut, browner on back and tail. Small head blue-grey, with paler cheek patches. Distinctive long greenish beak. Legs long, greenish yellow. Extremely shy - normally heard rather than seen, despite striking plumage. *Voice:* alternating 'wack, wacka' rapidly repeated, and grunts. *Habitat:* mangroves along north coast. Scarce but possibly under-recorded. ♣🐾🗻®

Red-legged Crake *Rallina fasciata* 19-22cm Medium-sized rare but unmistakable crake, with a small blackish bill. Head and neck distinctively pale chestnut; back and tail dull olive-brown. Underparts boldly and broadly barred black and white, running into underwing linings. Legs bright pink. Immature has duller brown head and neck, sooty and whitish barring on breast, flanks and undertail. Legs pale brownish. *Voice:* a series of loud, nasal 'pek' calls, uttered at half-second intervals; also a descending trill. *Habitat:* densely vegetated wetlands and river margins. Vagrant. ♨

Red-necked Crake *Rallina tricolor* 28cm Medium-large unmistakable crake, with dark sooty-brown body showing sometimes obscure pale buff feather fringes on lower belly and undertail. Head, neck, mantle and breast strikingly bright reddish chestnut; beak lime green; legs yellowish green. *Voice:* often nocturnal; pig-like grunts; metronomic and monotonous 'clock, clock, clock...' sometimes seeming interminable but distinctive. *Habitat:* dense rainforest and scrub, usually near water. Probably under-recorded; locally quite common. ♨🐾®

Corncrake *Crex crex* 26cm Medium-sized cosmopolitan crake. Head brown, with grey cheeks and a rusty bar through eye. Upperparts sandy brown with dark feather centres. Underparts buff, with widely spaced crescentic brownish bars. Wing shoulders rich chestnut, striking in flight. Beak pale with dark tip; legs dull pinkish, trail in flight. Shy, vanishing with ease and speed into vegetation. *Voice:* dry, rasping 'crex', often nocturnal and persistently repeated. *Habitat:* lush paddocks, grassland, cereals and other crops. Vagrant. 🚜♨🟰

Buff-banded Rail

Lewin's Rail

Chestnut Rail

Red-legged Crake

Red-necked Crake

Corncrake

Baillon's Crake *Porzana pusilla* 15cm Small, secretive crake, smaller than Australian (Spotted) but broadly similar in plumage. Upperparts olive-brown, flecked with white, more heavily marked with black. Throat, neck and breast grey; belly boldly barred black and white, extending onto undertail coverts. Beak short, lime-green; legs long, greenish. Immatures much duller and browner. *Voice:* harsh 'krek'; trilling alarm call. *Habitat:* dense marsh and waterside vegetation. Widespread but irregular and probably under-recorded. 🌾△®

Australian (Spotted) Crake *Porzana fluminea* 17-20cm Medium-sized dark crake. Upperparts dark olive-brown, flecked with white and with blackish feather centres. Throat, neck and breast dark lead-blue; belly boldly barred black and white; undertail coverts with prominent white edges conspicuous when tail is flicked. Beak lime-green with red base (see Baillon's); legs green. Less shy than many other rails or crakes, feeding away from cover. *Voice:* vocal and varied, staccato chattering 'kirri-kirri-kirri...'. *Habitat:* freshwater swamps and marshes, saltmarsh and lagoon margins. Widespread, but erratic inland; locally quite common in east, rarer elsewhere. 🌾🌾△®

Spotless Crake *Porzana tabuensis* 20cm Medium-sized dark and distinctive crake. Body entirely sooty black, browner on wings and back, and with soft white barring on black undertail coverts. Eye chestnut, beak short, slim and black. Legs strikingly red. Immature paler, with whitish throat, browner legs. Often swims. Sometimes confiding, feeding unconcerned out in the open. Usually solitary. *Voice:* varied, grebe-like chattering, another like distant motorcycle engine. *Habitat:* shrubby freshwater vegetation, saltmarsh, mangroves. Widespread but scattered and erratic in appearance; generally uncommon. 🌾△®

White-browed Crake *Porzana cinerea* 18cm Small slim crake with a distinctive head pattern: bold white stripes above and below black stripe through eye. Upperparts olive brown with darker markings; underparts pale grey, shading to white on belly and to yellow-buff on undertail coverts. Beak short, greenish-yellow with red base; legs olive-green. Not shy. Often solitary, walking on exposed roots, stems, or floating leaves. *Voice:* characteristic loud 'cutchee, cutchee', sometimes provoking a communal response. *Habitat:* mangroves and other lagoons or lakeside vegetation. Under-recorded, probably reasonably common. 🌾®

Baillon's Crake (adult)

Australian (Spotted) Crake

Spotless Crake

White-browed Crake

Bush-hen *Amaurornis olivacea* 25cm Medium-sized, robust, drab crake. Upperparts sooty olive-brown; tail blackish. Underparts purplish grey, with distinctive rich buff belly and undertail coverts. Beak heavy but pointed, greenish, with comparatively small orange-red frontal shield. Legs and long spidery toes yellowish. *Voice:* vocal during breeding season; several long, harsh 'nee-oo' calls in succession, followed by series of quieter calls. *Habitat:* rainforest margins, wet woodlands, swamps; largely near coast. Local and scarce. 🌊 🦆 ⚊ ®

Tasmanian Native-hen *Gallinula mortierii* 44cm Large, robustly-built, nearly flightless, dull-plumaged crake. Upperparts sooty brown, tail black. Underparts dark sometimes purplish grey, with white bar across flanks. Beak massive, triangular, yellowish green; stout legs grey. Often in small groups, active and frequently argumentative. Runs swiftly, swims well. *Voice:* harshly noisy grunts and screams. *Habitat:* confined to Tasmania: open wet paddocks, swamps, marshes and watersides. Locally not uncommon. 🌊 ⚊ ®

Black-tailed Native-hen *Gallinula ventralis* 32-36cm Medium-large dark crake, moorhen-sized but swamphen shaped. Upperparts olive-brown, with relatively long erect black tail. Underparts blackish, with blue sheen on neck and breast, and bold white spots on sides of breast. Beak green, orange at base. Legs long, conspicuously scarlet. Often gregarious; unconcerned by the presence of man. *Voice:* rarely vocal; metallic cackling rattle. *Habitat:* swamps, lake and river banks, riverine woodland; occasionally parks and gardens. Widespread but erratic; locally common, even abundant. 🌊 △ ®

Dusky Moorhen *Gallinula tenebrosa* 38cm Medium-large, familiar 'waterhen'. Upperparts blackish brown; underparts wholly black except for distinctive white sides to undertail coverts. Tail frequently flicked. Beak red, yellow tipped, with red frontal shield. Legs greenish, becoming reddish when breeding. Flies with legs trailing. *Voice:* shrill cries, resonant 'querk'. *Habitat:* swamps, lakes, ponds, dams, slow-moving rivers. Widespread; quite common in many areas. 🌊 △ ®

Purple Swamphen *Porphyrio porphyrio* 46-48cm Large, cosmopolitan and distinctive. Head, neck and underparts deep purple (some populations blue on breast); back and wings black, with prominent white undertail coverts. Beak stout and triangular, scarlet, with red frontal shield. Legs red and long, disproportionately so, with long toes. *Voice:* loud screeches. *Habitat:* swamps, lake margins, shallow slow-moving rivers. Widespread; locally quite common. 🌊 △ ®

Eurasian Coot *Fulica atra* 38cm Large, appearing distinctively dumpy. Uniformly sooty black body, wings and tail, relieved only by rich brown eye. Beak and frontal shield white; legs blue-grey, with lobed toes. Swims buoyantly, diving frequently. Often gregarious, but also aggressive. *Voice:* characteristically metallic 'kyok' and other twanging notes. *Habitat:* larger and usually deeper fresh waters, including lakes, reservoirs and floods; also swamps, sewage farms and occasionally sheltered seas. Widespread; often common, sometimes abundant. 🌊 △ ®

Bush-hen

Tasmanian Native-hen

Black-tailed Native-hen

Dusky Moorhen (adult)

Purple Swamphen (adult)

Eurasian Coot (adult)

Brolga *Grus rubicundus* 120-140cm Huge and upright, stork-like. Neck and body uniformly grey, with contrasting scarlet bare skin on head and nape limited in extent (see Sarus). Primaries blackish, secondaries long and grey, drooping over tail in 'bustle'. Beak long, comparatively slim, dagger-shaped and pinkish grey. Characteristic dark bristly 'dewlap' of skin on throat. In flight, head and neck held extended; wings broad, heavily fingered, wingbeats powerful. Long grey legs trail. Spectacular dancing display. *Voice:* far-carrying trumpeting whoops, often given in flight, frenzied in display. *Habitat:* shallow swamps, wet pastures, marshes, paddocks and fields. Widespread but generally local and uncommon; occasionally abundant.

Sarus Crane *Grus antigone* 120-150cm Very similar to Brolga. Bare scarlet skin of face and chin extends well down throat; no dewlap (see Brolga). Legs characteristically pink (see Brolga). Immatures of the two crane species are difficult to separate, but have traces of the bare skin pattern, pinkish in Brolga, pale rufous in Sarus. *Voice:* far-carrying, unforgettable trumpeting. *Habitat:* shallow swamps, marshes, wet pastures and grazing land. Restricted, but locally overlooked and sometimes fairly common.

Australian Bustard *Ardeotis australis* 75-150cm Large to huge turkey-like bird, male much bigger than female. Male has dark crown, whitish face and neck finely marked with grey, narrow black breast band and white underparts. Back brown, shoulders of wings chequered black and white. Female with greyer neck and browner crown, less distinct collar. Beak fairly short but robust, grey. Legs long, powerful, yellowish or pale olive. Male has amazing dancing display, with throat feathers arranged like a gigantic chrysanthemum. Shy. *Voice:* silent except for roars during display. *Habitat:* open grassland, light scrub, open woodland, sometimes crops. Widespread but generally scarce; locally common in suitable remote areas.

Comb-crested Jacana *Irediparra gallinacea* 23cm Medium-sized, long-legged, long-toed, crake-like bird. Neck white, tinged yellow, with black crown and nape. Characteristic large reddish fleshy comb from forehead. Rest of upperparts dark brown. Broad black breast band, white belly. Plumage duller and browner outside breeding season. Distinctive habit of walking carefully across floating water plants. Immature duller, lacking breast band, with much reduced pale comb. Active and noisy, moves with head bobbing and tail flicking in time with steps. *Voice:* high-pitched chattering 'pee-pee-pee'. *Habitat:* floating vegetation, lakes, swamps, dams. Generally scarce but locally common.

Pheasant-tailed Jacana *Hydrophasianus chirurgus* 31cm including long tail (breeding plumage only). Most likely to occur in non-breeding plumage, when striking neck pattern a useful distinction from immature Comb-crested. Blackish stripe through eye runs down sides of neck to breast, separating whitish foreneck from buff sides of neck (Comb-crested has whitish head and neck, with black only on hindneck). In flight wings extensively white (concealed when at rest) on both surfaces (wholly dark in Comb-crested). Breeding plumage unmistakable but only worn for short period: very long curving tail, blackish body and striking white wings, head and throat. *Voice:* shrill chatterings. *Habitat:* open waters with plentiful floating vegetation. Vagrant.

Brolga

Australian Bustard

Sarus Crane

Comb-crested Jacana (adult breeding)

Pheasant-tailed Jacana (non-breeding)

Bush Stone-Curlew *Burhinus grallarius* 55-58cm Large, strange, long-legged and long-tailed aberrant wader. Crown and nape grey-buff, streaked with black; curved white stripe above and broad brown mark through staring golden eye. Forehead, chin and throat white, shading into dark streaked sandy-buff breast. Belly white. Rest of upperparts sandy grey-brown, with fine darker streaks. Well camouflaged. Legs long, greenish, with conspicuous knobbly 'knees' (=ankles). Characteristic deliberate, slow-motion movements. In flight (difficult to flush) fies fast and low on stiff wings showing double (one large, one small) white patches at bases of dark primaries. *Voice:* harsh, often nocturnal, wailing. *Habitat:* dry open woodland, sandy scrub, golf courses and plantations. Widespread; locally common in north of range. ⚊◢♨△®

Beach Stone-Curlew *Esacus magnirostris* 56cm Large, strange but unmistakable wader. Upperparts sandy brown with darker streaking on neck. Distinctive curved white stripe above eye running down onto neck, with a broad black eye patch below it following same pattern. Eye staring, golden. Beak diagnostic: disproportionately large and robust, mostly black with yellow base. Throat white, breast pale buff, finely streaked dark brown. Belly white. Closed wings show white-bordered black shoulder patches, which give distinctive flight pattern of a white trailing edge and a white skua-like 'window' in black primaries. Legs long, yellow, with swollen 'knees'. *Voice:* high-pitched shrieking wail. *Habitat:* large open sandy beaches, mudflats, reefs, occasionally among mangroves. Coastal, generally uncommon. ◢®

Painted Snipe *Rostratula benghalensis* 24cm Medium-sized compact wader, female brighter than male. Crown and nape dark olive, with central creamy-buff stripe. 'Spectacle' patch round eye, buff in male, strikingly white in female. Back and wings olive brown, finely vermiculated and streaked with buffs, black and chestnut. Belly white. Beak relatively long, thick-tipped, yellowish. Legs comparatively short, greenish. Tends to remain in concealment. Flight rail-like, not snipe-like. *Voice:* sharp 'kek' if flushed, vibrating 'poo-oo-oo' in display. *Habitat:* densely vegetated wetland margins, sewage farms. Widespread in east, but irregular and uncommon. ♨∥△®

Pied Oystercatcher *Haematopus longirostris* 48-50cm Large, distinctive and conspicuous wader. Head, neck, back and wings black, showing distinctive bold white wingbar and black-and-white rump and tail pattern in flight. Underparts white. Beak straight, stout, laterally flattened, characteristically bright red. Red eye-ring. Legs relatively short, stout, bright pink. Often gregarious. *Voice:* piping succession of 'peepa peepa' calls, distinctive 'kleep' in flight. *Habitat:* most types of shoreline, occasionally on nearby paddocks. Less often on rocky shores. Widespread and generally fairly common. ◢▨∥®

Sooty Oystercatcher *Haematopus fuliginosus* 48-51cm Large distinctive wader. Body entirely dark sooty black, relieved only by red eye-ring, stout, straight scarlet beak, and pink legs. In flight, all-black upperparts (and underparts) are distinctive. Usually solitary or in pairs, sometimes with Pied Oystercatcher. *Voice:* piping 'peepa peepa' calls, 'kleep' in flight. *Habitat:* most types of shoreline but prefers rocky coasts. Widespread but less frequent than Pied. ◢▨®

Bush Stone-Curlew

Beach Stone-Curlew

Painted Snipe ♀

Pied Oystercatcher

Sooty Oystercatcher

Masked Lapwing *Vanellus miles* 35-38cm Large, long-legged, distinctive plover. Crown black, beak creamy-white, face covered by characteristic drooping yellow fleshy wattles. Neck and underparts white. Back sandy brown, rump white, tail black, giving distinctive pied and buff flight pattern, with rounded buff black-tipped wings contrasting with white rump and tail with a broad black terminal band. Horny spur visible at close range on shoulder of closed wing. Legs long, red. Gregarious and aggressive. *Voice:* noisily vocal (colloquially called 'alarmbird'), strident 'kekekekek...' and single shrieking 'kek'. *Habitat:* margins of ponds and dams, grasslands of all types including some in built-up areas; occasionally on the shore. Widespread, familiar, reasonably common. 🏞🌊⚓🦆🔱△®

Banded Lapwing (Plover) *Vanellus tricolor* 25-28cm Medium-large distinctive plover. Black crown and nape, with bold white stripe through eye. Small bright red wattle on forehead. Throat white, sides of throat black, merging into broad black breast band. Belly white. Rump white, tail white with broad black terminal band. In flight shows distinctive pattern of buff forewing with broad white diagonal stripe, black flight feathers, with narrow black trailing edge along secondaries. Legs dark red. *Voice:* strident 'kew-kew-kew', distinctive 'er-chill-churr'. *Habitat:* open bare, stony or short-grass areas, often far from water; occasionally on beaches. Widespread, locally fairly common. 🏞🔱△®

Grey Plover *Pluvialis squatarola* 28-30cm Medium-large, robustly-built, often solitary plover. Breeding adult strikingly handsome: upperparts richly black-flecked silver-grey, separated from black face, throat, breast and belly by broad white margin. Winter adult and immature flecked grey-buff above; white below. In flight, shows faint wingbar and characteristic bold black patches in 'armpits' beneath wings. Beak black, stubby; legs black, long. *Voice:* plaintive fluting 'tee-too-ee'. *Habitat:* sheltered coastal bays and estuaries. Widespread, but local and rarely numerous. ⚓🦆▮

Pacific Golden Plover *Pluvialis fulva* 25-28cm Medium-large, elegant and upright plover. Breeding adult beautifully flecked gold, black and white above, with black throat, breast, belly and undertail coverts, bordered white down sides of neck and breast. Winter birds duller but still with a golden tinge to a pale buff forehead and throat. Upperparts speckled dark brown. Legs comparatively long, black. In flight, fast and long-winged showing darkish grey underwing, with faint paler wingbar on upperside of dark brown wings. *Voice:* fluting 'to-wheet' and melodious, sad 'tlooi'. *Habitat:* estuaries, muddy bays, reefs, occasionally mangroves. Widespread and fairly common. ⚓🦆▮

Eurasian Golden Plover *Pluvialis apricaria* 28cm In all plumages very similar to Pacific Golden, but slightly larger and plumper, with less tapered "rear-end", shows less leg above "knee" and has diagnostic white (not grey) underwing. Breeding adult has whiter (not blotched dusky) undertail coverts. *Voice:* fluting whistle 'tloo-ee'. *Habitat:* coastal marshes and inland on damp fields and grassland. Potential vagrant. ⚓🦆▮

Masked Lapwing (Northern race)

Banded Lapwing (Plover)

Grey Plover (non-breeding)

Pacific Golden Plover (non-breeding)

Eurasian Golden Plover (non-breeding)

Red-kneed Dotterel *Erythrogonys cinctus* 18cm Small, squat, distinctive plover. Adult has black crown and nape joining broad black breast band to surround distinctive bright white throat patch. Back sandy brown. Belly white, chestnut on flanks. Immature uniformly brown above, white below. Beak stubby, red with black tip; legs comparatively long, brownish, pinkish red around the 'knee' (=ankle) joint. Distinctive upperwing pattern in flight, with buff leading edge to inner part of wing, black primaries and broad white bar along trailing edge. Tail buff centrally, with broad white outer margins. *Voice:* trilling song, melodious 'chet chet' call. *Habitat:* surroundings of shallow fresh or brackish lakes, floods, claypans, sewage farms. Widespread but erratic; locally quite common. ♨△®

Hooded Plover *Thinornis rubricollis* 19-21cm Small, neat plover. Adult has black face, crown and throat, white nape separating this 'hood' from black half-collar extending down onto sides of breast. Back sandy buff. Underparts white. Beak stubby, red with black tip; red eye-ring. Legs pink. Immature sandy brown above with white collar; white below. In flight, hooded appearance is distinctive, shows broad white wingbar, and dark centre to tail and rump broadly surrounded by white. *Voice:* deep, gruff 'kew kew'. *Habitat:* extensive sandy beaches, dunes, reefs. Occasionally inland in west. Locally fairly common. ♨ ♣ ♟®

Ringed Plover *Charadrius hiaticula* 20cm Small, fast-running plover. Adult brown above, white below. Black and white facial pattern, lacking white crown band and yellow eye-ring of Little Ringed. Black collar. Beak yellowish with black tip (dark in nonbreeding birds), stubby; legs orange-yellow. White wingbar conspicuous in flight. Immature marking brownish, not black. *Voice:* fluting 'too-lee'. *Habitat:* sandy coasts and saltpans; occasionally inland on river banks and excavations. Breeds Northern Hemisphere. Vagrant. ♨ ♣ ♟ ♦

Little Ringed Plover *Charadrius dubius* 15cm Small, fast-moving wader. Adult brown above, white below. Bold black-and-white head pattern, with white band between black fore crown and sandy rear crown. Black collar band; yellow eye-ring. Beak black, with a little yellow at base of lower mandible, stubby. Legs pinkish. Immature lacks black-and-white pattern, and has incomplete brownish collar. In flight, shows characteristically plain, pale brown wings. Usually single or in pairs. *Voice:* plaintive, piping 'tee-you'. *Habitat:* sandy coasts, saltpans and lagoons; inland on excavations. Rare migrant. ♨ ♣ ♟ ♦

Mongolian Plover *Charadrius mongolus* 20cm Small version of Large Sand Plover, which it often joins in flocks. Upperparts brown, in breeding plumage with black 'mask' through eyes broken by white forehead patch. Throat white, with narrow black border; breast and flanks rich chestnut, belly white. Non-breeding and immature birds have brown backs, with a white forehead and supercilium, darker cheek patch, and a broad brown breast band. Beak distinctively small and slim; legs characteristically blackish. In flight shows slender white wingbar, white-edged tail. *Voice:* dry rolling 'drrit', soft 'tikit'. *Habitat:* mudflats, lagoons, estuaries, beaches, mangroves. Widespread; locally common on coasts. Rare inland. ♣ ♟ ♦

Red-kneed Dotterel (adult)

Hooded Plover (adult)

Ringed Plover (adult)

Little Ringed Plover (adult)

Mongolian Plover (breeding)

Mongolian Plover (non-breeding)

Double-banded Plover *Charadrius bicinctus* 18cm Small, nimble plover. Breeding adults have sandy-brown upperparts, broad white forehead with black margin. White underparts are broken by a black bar across the lower throat, and by a broader chestnut band between breast and belly. Beak short, stubby, black. Legs yellowish or greenish. Non-breeding birds and immatures resemble Mongolian, but with buff forehead and supercilium (not white) and with an indistinct, broken breast band. In flight show comparatively faint white wingbar, sandy white-edged tail with broad white tips. *Voice:* staccato 'pit' or 'chip', usually double. *Habitat:* catholic; mudflats, saltmarshes, beaches, lagoons, lakesides, dams and bare paddocks. Breeds New Zealand. Widespread along south and east coasts, locally common. Occasional inland. 🌊 🦆 🦆 🦆 ⸙

Large Sand Plover *Charadrius leschenaultii* 20-23cm Broadly similar to Mongolian Plover. Breeding adult brown above with black-and-white forehead, white mark over eye. Throat white, lacking black margin; narrower chestnut breast band than Mongolian. Beak characteristically larger, more heavily knobbed (comparison with Mongolian is often possible). Legs greenish, long and extending beyond tail tip in flight. Non-breeding adult and immature similar to Mongolian, but more diffusely coloured and with greenish legs. *Voice:* melodious trill, characteristic mellow 'chweep chweep' (see Mongolian). *Habitat:* extensive sandy beaches, saltmarshes, mudflats, reefs and mangroves. Widespread and regular migrant; more numerous in west and north. 🌊 🦆 🦆 🦆 ⸙

Caspian Plover *Charadrius asiaticus* 21cm Very similar to Oriental Plover, with which vagrants might associate, best separated by usually greener legs and diagnostic white underwing (dark grey in Oriental) which offers little contrast with whitish underparts. Breeding adults have a dark mark through eye and a bolder head pattern than Oriental (lacking plain-headed appearance of latter). Greener legs of nonbreeding birds are a useful feature, additionally Caspian has a wider supercilium and a more complete breast band than Oriental. In flight the difference in underwing colour is the most important and clinching field feature. *Voice:* sharp 'chip chip chip' and 'klink'. *Habitat:* usually inland on open plains, dry grassland and fields. Coastal saltmarshes and flats are less favoured. Vagrant. 🦆 🦆

Oriental Plover *Charadrius veredus* 22-25cm Medium-sized, slim, long-legged and long-winged plover, more upright in stance than the sand plovers. Breeding adult has brown crown and back, with white forehead, face and throat, and a brown smudge through the eye. Broad chestnut breast band (in males, females have brownish breast band), edged with black where it joins white belly. Non-breeding birds are sandy-brown above, with a buffish supercilium; breast grey-buff, throat and underparts white. Legs distinctively yellow or pinkish-yellow. In flight, has dark capped appearance, shows no trace of wingbars and has characteristic dark grey underwing, contrasting with white underparts, and a darker sub-terminal band to white-bordered tail. *Voice:* loud 'chip-chip-chip', trilling calls. *Habitat:* open landscapes from ploughed fields and plains to airfields and saltmarshes. Widespread in north; locally common. 🦆 🦆 ⸙

Double-banded Plover (breeding)

Double-banded Plover (non-breeding)

Large Sand Plover (breeding)

Large Sand Plover (non-breeding)

Caspian Plover (non-breeding)

Oriental Plover (non-breeding)

Red-capped Plover *Charadrius ruficapillus* 15cm Small, fast-moving, dumpy plover. Breeding adult sandy above, with chestnut neck and crown (extending into half-collar), black-edged white forehead and dark smudge through eye. Male rather brighter than female. Legs characteristically black. Non-breeding birds have only a trace of chestnut on sandy nape and crown, with no black bar on forehead. Shows wingbar in flight. *Voice:* sharp 'tick'; rattling trill. *Habitat:* bare sandy or dry mud areas, usually coastal. Widespread, locally common; occasional inland. 🌊🦆🐦△®

Black-fronted Dotterel *Elseyornis melanops* 16cm Small, distinctive, and robust plover. Adult sandy on crown and back, with darker streaks. Distinctive head pattern, with black forehead and short central crown stripe, and black marking through eyes extending down nape and broadening into V-shaped breast band. Bold white 'eyebrows', cheeks and throat. Immature lacks black markings. *Voice:* repeated metallic 'tip', melodious yodelling and trilling in display chases. *Habitat:* margins of lakes, swamps, dams; less often saline lagoons, rarely coastal. Widespread; locally quite common. 🐦🌊△®

Inland Dotterel *Peltohyas australis* 21cm Medium-small very distinctively marked plover of arid habitats. Adult has sandy, almost golden back with darker markings, crown separated from white forehead by most unusual transverse black stripe over crown and vertically down through eyes. Throat and upper breast white, bordered broadly by distinctive black V-shaped mark extending down onto rich buff belly. Non-breeding birds duller. Legs usually dull yellow. *Voice:* rarely vocal; 'kwoik' 'krroot' calls described. *Habitat:* dry stony, sparsely vegetated plains, gibber, rarely near water. Erratic and generally uncommon. 🐦🚜🚜△®

Black-winged Stilt *Himantopus himantopus* 38cm Unmistakable medium-large wader, with extremely long legs. Adult back and wings black; head, neck and underparts white, with varying amounts of grey or black on nape. Beak black, long and very slender. Legs rich pink, almost ridiculously long, enabling it to wade and feed in deeper water than other waders. Immature browner above; legs greyish-pink. *Voice:* noisily vociferous; yelping 'kyip' call. *Habitat:* lakes, saltpans, coastal lagoons and marshes. Widespread, locally fairly common. 🌊🦆🐦△®

Banded Stilt *Cladorhynchus leucocephalus* 42cm Unmistakable large wader, similar to but larger than Black-winged, with diagnostic broad chestnut V marking on breast and belly. Immature lacks breast band, but has all-white head and neck, lacking the smokey-grey nape of immature Black-winged. *Voice:* barking double 'chook' or 'yook'. *Habitat:* salt lakes, saltpans, lagoons, mudflats; occasionally beside fresh water. Erratic in distribution and numbers; usually scarce, but occasionally locally common. 🌊🦆🐦△®

Red-necked Avocet *Recurvirostra novaehollandiae* 40-45cm Large distinctive wader. Head and long neck chestnut, with white eye-ring. Body entirely white, with black-and-white wings. Distinctive long slim upturned black beak. Legs long, blue-grey, feet webbed. In flight, black wingtips and black diagonal bar across inner half of wing produce striking pattern. *Voice:* fluting 'toot', vocal over breeding grounds. *Habitat:* estuaries, mudflats, shallow fresh, brackish and saline waters, coastal and inland. Widespread but erratic; locally common in south. 🌊🦆🐦△®

Red-capped Plover (breeding ♂)

Black-fronted Dotterel (adult)

Inland Dotterel (breeding)

Black-winged Stilt

Banded Stilt (adults)

Red-necked Avocet

Ruddy Turnstone *Arenaria interpres* 23cm Medium-small, cosmopolitan, dumpy harlequin-like wader. Breeding adult back rich pale chestnut; head, neck and underparts white, all boldly patterned with black. Non-breeding adult and immature retain pied parts of plumage, but chestnut is replaced with grey. Feeds among seaweeds on rocky shores; well camouflaged. In flight, white wingbars and pied plumage are unmistakable. Beak dark, short, flattened from top to bottom; used to overturn weed and stones. Legs yellowish. *Voice:* staccato, chattering 'tuk-uk-tuk' call. *Habitat:* rocky coasts; rare inland. Widespread; locally fairly common. ◄ ↑

Eastern Curlew *Numenius madagascariensis* 53-61cm Very large wader with unmistakable beak: black, reddish towards base, extremely long (up to 18cm) and markedly downcurved. Upperparts sandy buff with darker streaks on head and neck; bolder black and brown markings on back and wings. Tail with several dark bars. Underparts grey-buff on breast, paling to whitish on belly. Legs long, grey. In flight shows characteristic dark rump and no wingbar. Often gregarious. Wary. *Voice:* wild 'coo-er-lee', bubbling trill. *Habitat:* coastal mudflats, mangroves, estuaries. Regular, occasionally quite numerous. ◄ ▨ ↑

Whimbrel *Numenius phaeopus* 40cm Large Curlew-like wader but smaller and shorter-beaked. Crown dark brown, with three characteristic yellow-buff longitudinal stripes. Beak grey-brown, long (but not as dramatically as Eastern Curlew) and downcurved. Adult and immature greyish-brown above, with copious white and darker brown flecking. Underparts pale buff with darker brown streaking, shading to white on belly. Legs blue-grey, comparatively long. In flight, shows no striking wing markings, only small whitish rump patch and buff tail with darker bars (see Eastern Curlew.Vagrants of American race *hudsonicus* have occured, such birds lack any white in rump). Rarely gregarious. *Voice:* short, high-pitched, piping whistle, usually repeated several times in quick succession. *Habitat:* usually on coastal marshes. Widespread; rarely numerous, commoner in north. ▨ ◄ ▨ ↑

Little Curlew *Numenius minutus* 30-35cm Medium-sized, but the smallest of the curlews. Central crown stripe buff, stripes over eyes paler and bolder. Upperparts brown with buff or greyish feather margins on back and wings; neck finely streaked brown. Breast buff; streaked brown, belly white, with dark flank markings. Beak medium-long, slightly downcurved. Legs grey. In flight shows dark rump (not white as in Whimbrel), no wingbar but dark primaries contrast with brown forewing. Flight buoyant. Often gregarious. *Voice:* whistling 'tit tit tit tit', harsh Greenshank-like 'tchew tchew tchew'. *Habitat:* open short grasslands, not necessarily close to water, tidal mudflats. Regular; commonest in north where sometimes abundant. ◄ ▨ ▪▪ ↑

Ruddy Turnstone (breeding)

Ruddy Turnstone (non-breeding)

Eastern Curlew

Whimbrel

Little Curlew

Upland Sandpiper *Bartramia longicauda* 28-30cm Medium-sized wader, with a comparatively small head and long neck. Upperparts buffish marked with dark brown streaks and spots. Crown darker brown, with pale buff stripe over and round eye. Superficially resembles Little Curlew, favouring similar habitats, Upland however is even smaller, has yellow (not grey) legs, a longer tail (projecting beyond wingtips), shorter and straighter bill and very plain face (lacking Little Curlew's dark eye-stripe). In flight shows distinctively white-barred underwings. *Voice:* fluting 'kip-ip-ip-ip'. *Habitat:* grassy plains. Vagrant. 🦆 🪶

Wood Sandpiper *Tringa glareola* 20cm Medium-small, slimly built wader.Brownish above, copiously flecked with white; white below with light streaking on neck and sides of breast. Buff-white supercilium below dark cap. Legs characteristically yellow (see Green). In flight, shows whitish underwings, square white rump and white tail with faint dark barring; no wingbars. *Voice:* distinctive 'chiff-if-if' call. *Habitat:* inland and coastal marshes and pools. Regular; rarely numerous, commoner in north. 🦆 🪶

Green Sandpiper *Tringa ochropus* 23cm Medium-small wader, appearing black and white in flight. Crown, nape and back dark greenish-grey. Underparts white, with dark breast. Beak dark, medium length. Legs dark green. Flight jerky and Snipe-like, all-dark wings contrasting characteristically with white rump. Tail white, with black barring. Underwings blackish, not pale as in Wood. *Voice:* whistling 'tee-loo-eet'. *Habitat:* coastal and inland pools, creeks and marshes. Vagrant. 🦆 🪶

Grey-tailed Tattler *Tringa brevipes* 25cm Medium-small, sombre grey wader. Breeding adult greyish above. Pale supercilium; throat whitish. Underparts white, barred with grey. Non-breeding birds lack barring below. Legs yellow. In flight, shows uniformly dark grey upperparts and underwing but no other markings. Flight low over water on flicked wings. *Voice:* 'tloo-eep', 'wheat-eat', harsher double' klee-klee'. *Habitat:* rocky shores, mangroves, mudflats and beaches. Widespread; commoner in north. 🦪 🪶

Wandering Tattler *Tringa incana* 26-28cm Distinguished with difficulty from Grey-tailed. Upperparts in non-breeding plumage are darker than Grey-tailed, with a pale supercilium stretching only from beak to eye, not beyond. Nasal groove on upper mandible extends for three-quarters of the beak length (one-half in Grey-tailed). *Voice:* trilling 'wee-wee-wee....' *Habitat:* predominantly reefs and beaches; less often mudflats. Rare but regular to Great Barrier Reef islands; vagrant elsewhere. 🦪 🪶

Common Sandpiper *Actitis hypoleucos* 20cm Small wader with distinctive flight. Brown above, white below, with brown streaking on throat and on sides of breast forming collar. Beak short and straight. Legs greenish. Flight low over water, with rapid, shallow wingbeats on downcurved wings, shows white wingbar, brown rump and brown tail with barred outer feathers. Bobs incessantly. *Voice:* distinctive, trilling 'twee-wee-wee....'. *Habitat:* fresh and salt marshes; beside lakes, dams, streams, sheltered coasts. Widespread; rarely numerous, commoner in north and east. 🦆 🦪 🪶

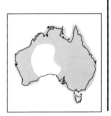

Upland Sandpiper

Wood Sandpiper (non-breeding)

Green Sandpiper (breeding)

Grey-tailed Tattler (non-breeding)

Wandering Tattler (non-breeding)

Common Sandpiper (non-breeding)

Greenshank *Tringa nebularia* 30cm Medium-large wader. Breeding adult grey-brown above, richly flecked with black and silver; strikingly white below. Non-breeding birds paler and drabber grey. Beak greyish, medium-long, and slightly upturned. Legs green, long. In flight, shows all-dark wings with no wingbars, and striking white rump reaching to a point high on back. *Voice:* characteristic, far-carrying, tri-syllabic 'tu-tu-tu'. *Habitat:* coastal lagoons and sheltered sandy or muddy estuaries and bays; on fresh marshes and beside streams, dams and sewage farms, sometimes well inland. Widespread; rather commoner coastally than inland. 🌊🦆🪶❚ △

Spotted Greenshank *Tringa guttifer* 30cm Very similar to Greenshank, but legs distinctly shorter (especially above 'knee') and yellower, and bill relatively longer and thicker, less tapering towards tip. Breeding birds are white beneath, grey above with black markings. Breast has distinct dark brown spots. In flight, underwings are very white, and the feet barely protrude beyond tail. *Voice:* call a loud "ke-you". *Habitat:* lagoons, saltpans, estuaries and muddy coasts. Vagrant. 🌊🦆🪶❚

Redshank *Tringa totanus* 28cm Medium-sized wader. Breeding adult brown, with streaking, shading to white on belly. Non-breeding birds duller greyer-brown. Beak reddish basally, slim, medium-long. Legs bright red. Bold white rear wing distinctive in flight which prevents confusion with Ruff, which often has bright red legs. *Voice:* anxious yelps and piping calls, usually variants of 'tu-lee-lee'. *Habitat:* salt and fresh marshes, muddy estuaries and sandy bays. Very scarce migrant. 🌊🦆🪶❚

Lesser Yellowlegs *Tringa flavipes* 24cm Medium-sized, slim wader. Recalls Wood Sandpiper, but larger and with prominent black wing tips extending beyond tail. Breeding adult back grey-brown, flecked white. Head, neck, breast white, finely streaked grey; belly white. Non-breeding birds greyer, drabber, paler. Legs yellow or yellow-orange, comparatively long. In flight, white rump contrasts with dark back and barred tail. *Voice:* soft 'tew-tew'. *Habitat:* coastal and inland wetlands. Vagrant. 🌊🦆🪶❚

Marsh Sandpiper *Tringa stagnatilis* 23cm Greenshank-like but much smaller, with needle-fine bill and relatively longer, more spindly legs. Legs usually dark greenish, but sometimes yellow (suggesting vagrant Lesser Yellowlegs or Wilson's Phalarope, differing from both in flight by having white rump extending high up back into a point as in Greenshank). Breeding adult back grey-brown, with spotted appearance. Head and neck buff, forehead white; underparts largely white with brown streaks on sides of breast. Non-breeding birds paler and greyer. *Voice:* call a mellow 'tee-oo' with variants. *Habitat:* usually on freshwater marshes, dams, sewage farms, lagoons and saltpans; occasionally on muddy coasts. Regular but scarce. 🌊🦆🪶❚ △

Terek Sandpiper *Xenus cinereus* 24cm Medium-sized, squat wader. Breeding adult has crown, nape and back pale brownish-grey; dark centres to feathers form irregular but conspicuous V-marking across closed wings and onto back. Underparts whitish. Non-breeding birds paler grey. Beak dark, relatively long and stout, and characteristically noticeably upturned. Legs distinctive orange-yellow. In flight, white rump and white trailing edge to dark wings are conspicuous. *Voice:* fluting 'du-du-du-du'. *Habitat:* estuaries, muddy bays, reefs, lagoons and saltpans. Widespread; locally common in north, scarce in south. 🦆🪶❚ △

Greenshank (non-breeding)

Spotted Greenshank (non-breeding)

Redshank (breeding)

Lesser Yellowlegs (non-breeding)

Marsh Sandpiper (non-breeding)

Terek Sandpiper (non-breeding)

Latham's Snipe *Gallinago hardwickii* 27-29cm The 3 snipes are very similar, differing in tail structure (only visible when handled) and breeding ecology. Latham's is the largest, and marginally the longest billed, has obvious rufous and white in tail (which projects well beyond folded wing when at rest) and is the most likely snipe to be encountered, the others are rare but overlooked. All are medum-sized, well-camouflaged, squat, waders with very long beaks. Usually first seen when flushed: they rise suddenly uttering a harsh call, the long bill being the most obvious feature. All have similarly drab, mottled brownish upperwing and densely barred (looks grey) underwing, the only whitish area being the centre of the belly. *Voice:* rasping 'schack'. *Habitat:* muddy freshwater shallows. Widespread, but generally uncommon. 🐾 ▌

Pin-tailed Snipe *Gallinago stenura* 23cm Slightly smaller, shorter-billed and shorter-tailed than the other snipes. On the ground tail hardly projects beyond folded wing (obviously so in the other two), and shows less rufous and white. Critical viewing might reveal presence of buff flecking in blackish crown stripes (typically solidly dark in the other two), plain primary tips do not extend beyond the barred tertials (a feature also shared by Latham's). In flight the toes project beyond tail tip (very difficult to see, but gives impression of a pointed tail); tail appears relatively shorter and browner than in other snipes (especially if fanned when alighting). *Voice:* an abrupt, dry 'scaap' when flushed. *Habitat:* damp fields, sewage farms. Rare, but overlooked. 🐾 ▌

Swinhoe's Snipe *Gallinago megala* 24-26cm Very similar to Latham's but smaller, heavier and longer-billed than Pin-tailed. On the ground tail clearly projects beyond folded wing and shows obvious rufous (like Latham's); the plain primary tips extend slightly beyond barred tertials (unlike the other two). In flight much as Latham's but bill relatively a little shorter, lacks toe projection of Pin-tailed and shows reasonably obvious rufous and white in tail if fanned. Rises more quickly and with more zig-zagging than Latham's. *Voice:* a short, gruff "grep", calling less frequently than Pin-tailed. *Habitat:* fields, sewage farms, usually in north. Rare, but overlooked. 🐾 ▌

Asian Dowitcher *Limnodromus semipalmatus* 25-35cm Long-beaked and godwit-like but bill entirely black, expanding slightly towards the tip (godwit beaks are pinkish towards the base and taper to a sharp tip). Body grey-brown above with darker streaks; whitish below. Crown dark, emphasizing supercilium. Breeding plumage largely rufous. In flight shows whitish tail with narrow dark bars, paler, greyish secondaries contrast with browner forewing. Feet protrude beyond tail. Feeding technique distinctive, like a sewing machine stitching. *Voice:* usually silent. *Habitat:* tidal mudflats, lagoons, muddy lake edges. Vagrant. 🐾 ◄ ⬛ ▌

Black-tailed Godwit *Limosa limosa* 40cm Large long-beaked wader. Breeding adult striking, with back mottled brown and chestnut, head and neck cinnamon brown, underparts whitish, with chestnut barring on flanks. Non-breeding birds grey or grey-brown above, paling to near-white below. In flight, always shows striking broad white bar in blackish wings, and black-tipped tail. Beak pinkish-red, blackish towards the tip, very long and straight. Legs black, long. Gregarious. *Voice:* noisy 'wicka-wicka-wicka'. *Habitat:* estuaries, sheltered sandy or muddy bays; occasionally on freshwater marshes. Widespread; locally common. 🐾 ◄ ⬛ ▌ △

Latham's Snipe

Pin-tailed Snipe

Swinhoe's Snipe

Asian Dowitcher (non-breeding)

Black-tailed Godwit (breeding)

Black-tailed Godwit (non-breeding)

Bar-tailed Godwit *Limosa lapponica* 40cm Large, long-beaked wader. Breeding adult back richly marked brown; head, neck and breast rufous cinnamon brown; belly chestnut. Non-breeding birds mottled grey to grey-brown above, shading to white below. In flight, shows no wingbars; tail pattern is of dense, narrow, dark brown barring across white tail (see Black-tailed). Beak pinkish-red but darker towards the tip, very long, slightly but noticeably upturned. Legs black and long. Gregarious, sometimes in large flocks. *Voice:* rarely vocal, except in breeding season; usually harsh 'kirrick'. *Habitat:* muddy or sandy estuaries, sheltered coastal bays, inland on shallow lakes, sewage farms. Widespread; locally common on coast. ⩵🦆 ▮

Hudsonian Godwit *Limosa haemastica* 40cm Closely similar to Black-tailed but with more upturned beak. Distinctive features best seen in flight. Black-tailed has white underwing, with black margins, whereas Hudsonian has largely black underwing with narrow white central bar. On upperwing, Hudsonian shows less conspicuous, less clearly-defined white wingbar, and slightly smaller white rump. *Voice:* rarely vocal outside breeding season. *Habitat:* estuaries, lagoons and sheltered sandy bays. Vagrant. 🌊⩵🦆

Red Knot *Calidris canutus* 25cm Medium-sized squat wader. Breeding adult brown above, with golden scaly markings; distinctively rusty below. Non-breeding birds nondescript, flecked grey-brown above, whitish below. Beak dark, straight, medium length; legs dark, medium length. Faint white wingbar visible in flight. Gregarious, gathering in close-packed flocks, thousands-strong. *Voice:* occasional grunts. *Habitat:* mostly on sand and mudflats of sheltered coastal bays and estuaries; very occasionally inland on floodwater. Widespread; locally quite common in north, scarce along south coast. ⩵🦆 ▮

Great Knot *Calidris tenuirostris* 28-30cm Medium-large, robust and comparatively short-legged wader. Breeding adult has handsomely marked chestnut upperparts, with white underparts with bold black crescentic marks, dense on breast, scanty on flanks. Belly white. Non-breeding birds grey above, heavily mottled, white below, usually showing darker shoulder patches on closed wing. Shows whitish rump in flight (Red Knot is finely but densely grey-barred). Beak black, medium length. Legs short, greenish. *Voice:* rarely heard disyllabic grunts. *Habitat:* tidal mudflats, sandy beaches, lagoons; occasionally inland on lakes and saltpans. Widespread; locally numerous in north and increasing. ⩵🦆 ▮

Bar-tailed Godwit (non-breeding)

Hudsonian Godwit (non-br. front, br. back)

Red Knot (non-breeding)

Great Knot (worn breeding)

Great Knot (non-breeding)

Sharp-tailed Sandpiper *Calidris acuminata* 18-23cm One of the most widespread small waders. Medium-sized and variably-plumaged, with relatively short bill and green or yellowish-green legs. Juveniles distinctive with combination of chestnut crown and ear-patch, white supercilium and throat and buff-washed weakly marked underparts. Breeding plumaged birds have bright chestnut fringes to feathers of upperparts and crown, and head and underparts heavily mottled with dark chevrons (appearing almost uniformly mottled at longer range). Nonbreeders are drab, greyish waders, best identified by size and structural features. In flight shows relatively long wings with narrow whitish bar, blackish tail and rump centre (with white sides). *Voice:* dry 'tritt tritt'. *Habitat:* wetlands of all types, coastal and inland. Widespread and frequently common migrant. 🌊🏊🦆 ▮ △

Pectoral Sandpiper *Calidris melanotos* 20-24cm Very similar to Sharp-tailed, with which it associates. Differs principally in having strikingly white, unmarked, lower underparts contrasting sharply with densely marked breast band in all plumages. Plumage less variable than Sharp-tailed, however some individuals of latter can show similar contrast, but breast centre invariably unstreaked and there should be some scattered markings on lower underparts. Relatively longer bill and yellower legs are also useful pointers. Flight pattern similar. *Voice:* fluting 'churk'. *Habitat:* shallow fresh waters, usually with grassy margins, floods, sewage farms. Regular but generally scarce migrant. 🌊 ▮ △

Baird's Sandpiper *Calidris bairdii* 18cm Recalls a large juvenile Red-necked Stint, but buffer with relatively shorter legs and longer body giving a somewhat "flattened" appearance. Larger than stints, with distinctive elongated black primary tips extending beyond tertials and tail (like White-rumped) and very scaly pattern to upperparts. Can be very difficult to separate from vagrant White-rumped unless seen in flight (check tail pattern). In flight shows narrow wingbar and wide dark centre to rump. Often solitary. *Voice:* shrill 'kreeep'. *Habitat:* lake edges, wet swampy grassland. Vagrant. 🌊🏊🦆

White-rumped Sandpiper *Calidris fuscicollis* 17cm Larger, shorter-legged and longer-winged than Red-necked Stint, very similar in size and shape to vagrant Baird's. Breeding birds speckled brown, with bronze feather edges on back, nape and crown. Clear, white supercilium. Underparts white, streaked brown on throat, breast and flanks. Non-breeding birds duller; greyish band on upper breast. In flight, appears long-winged, with whitish wingbar and white rump patch above blackish tail. *Voice:* distinctive, high-pitched squeak in flight. *Habitat:* wetlands of all types, coastal and inland. Vagrant. 🌊🏊🦆

Western Sandpiper *Calidris mauri* 15-17cm Broadly similar to Red-necked Stint, but with longer heavier black beak, downcurved at tip. Breeding birds rusty brown above, with bold mottling of black and grey. Non-breeding birds grey-brown above, with white supercilium and rufous feathers on crown and mantle. Legs blackish. In flight shows faint wingbar and white sides to rump and tail. Active, feeds in shallows, plunging head under water. *Voice:* trilling 'chrreeep'. *Habitat:* muddy wetlands of most types, coastal or inland. Vagrant. 🌊🏊🦆

Sharp-tailed Sandpiper (non-breeding)

Pectoral Sandpiper (non-breeding)

Baird's Sandpiper (non-breeding)

White-rumped Sandpiper (non-breeding)

Western Sandpiper (breeding)

Little Stint *Calidris minuta* 14-15cm Very similar to Red-necked, with which it associates, but slightly shorter-bodied and longer-legged. Most plumages show a distinct whitish 'V' on mantle when fresh (least noticeable in nonbreeding and most obvious in juveniles). In breeding plumage has whitish throat, with rufous only on sides of head and breast. Juvenile much brighter and darker-capped than Red-necked, with whitish mantle 'V' and extensive rufous (not grey-buff) feather markings, particularly to scapulars and tertials. Nonbreeding birds are drab greyish little waders, not safely separable from Red-necked. Flight pattern as Red-necked. *Voice:* terse 'chit'. *Habitat:* muddy saline lagoons and creeks; inland freshwater marshy areas. Vagrant. 🌊 ⬅ 🦆

Red-necked Stint *Calidris ruficollis* 15cm Tiny common wader. Breeding adult has black-streaked rufous crown, reddish back with bold black speckling and grey feather fringes. Face, neck and upper breast reddish, faintly streaked white and dark brown. Underparts white. Non-breeding birds sandy grey-brown above with darker mottling and streaking, with some reddish fringes in immatures. Beak short, finely pointed, black. Legs black. In flight shows white wingbar and sides to rump and tail. *Voice:* continuous chattering while feeding, or 'chit' calls. *Habitat:* tidal mudflats, lagoons; freshwater marshes, lakes. Widespread and often common on coast; less numerous inland. 🌊 ⬅ 🦆 ❘ △

Long-toed Stint *Calidris subminuta* 14-16cm Tiny, long-legged stint superficially recalling a miniature Sharp-tailed Sandpiper. Breeding birds have dark mark through eye, with whitish stripes above and below. Back and wings richly mottled chestnut and black. Non-breeding birds dull brown above with darker mottlings and pale feather fringes. Clear whitish supercilium. Distinctive yellowish legs. In flight, shows faint wingbar, white sides to rump and upper tail only. *Voice:* loud ringing trill 'chreeee'. *Habitat:* inland swamps and muddy lakes; sometimes on muddy coasts. Regular but generally scarce. 🌊 ❘ △

Curlew Sandpiper *Calidris ferruginea* 20cm Smallish, lanky wader, with long, slightly downcurving, tapering beak. Breeding adult strikingly chestnut brown above and below, with duller, darker brown wings. Non-breeding birds characteristically pale, mottled grey-brown above; whitish-buff below. In flight shows clear wingbar, and conspicuous characteristic white rump and black tail pattern. *Voice:* distinctive, soft, trilling 'chirrup'. *Habitat:* sheltered bays and estuaries, lagoons, freshwater marshes. Widespread and regular, but in varying numbers. Sometimes very common. 🌊 ⬅ 🦆 ❘ △

Dunlin *Calidris alpina* 18cm Resembles Curlew Sandpiper in size and shape, but has slightly shorter black legs. Breeding plumage birds show rufous upperparts, pale sides of head and breast and a large black belly patch. Juvenile not unlike Pectoral but smaller and shorter-necked, more rusty brown on breast, has some dark streaks on white belly, black legs and longer all black bill. Nonbreeders very similar to Curlew Sandpiper, only safely separable when flushed by black (not white) rump centre (like many other small waders), wing pattern otherwise similar. *Voice:* call nasal 'treeer'; *Habitat:* sheltered coastal bays, estuaries and lagoons. Vagrant. Several records are considered to refer to a bird known as 'Cox's Sandpiper *C. paramelanotos*' (now considered to be a rare hybrid between Sharp-tailed and Curlew Sandpipers). 🌊 ⬅ 🦆

Little Stint (juvenile)

Red-necked Stint (breeding)

Red-necked Stint (non-breeding)

Long-toed Stint (non-breeding)

Curlew Sandpiper (non-breeding)

Dunlin (breeding)

Sanderling *Calidris alba* 20cm Small, distinctively fast-running wader. Breeding adult rufous cinnamon above, with scaly buff markings; white below. Non-breeding birds distinctly pale silver grey above; pure white below. Grey-black smudge mark through eye. Beak dark, short; legs dark. Runs at speed on sand, typically following waves in and out. In flight, white wingbar conspicuous on blackish wings. *Voice:* short 'quick'. *Habitat:* sandy bays and beaches, reefs. Widespread, patchy, but generally scarce.
🦆🪶

Buff-breasted Sandpiper *Tryngites subruficollis* 20cm Small, grassland wader, basically warm buff above and below with upperparts strongly scaled in all plumages (paler lower underparts in first year birds). Recalls a miniature non-breeding Ruff in pattern but Ruff has thicker-based and stronger beak, has a small dark mark behind eye (pale surround in Buff-breasted), lacks patch of black spotting at breast sides and has less projection of dark wingtip beyond tertials. In flight, shows white underwing with narrow carpal bar; upperparts uniform, with no wing or rump markings. *Voice:* sharp 'check check', trilling 'preeeet'. *Habitat:* open grassy or lightly vegetated areas, usually near water. Vagrant. 〰

Broad-billed Sandpiper *Limicola falcinellus* 18cm Recalls a large stint with an oversized bill. Breeding adult dark brown above, heavily streaked and mottled with chestnut and buff. Crown with double supercilium. Non-breeding birds duller and greyer, but retain distinctive head pattern. In flight, shows uniformly dark wings; a narrow wingbar in fresh plumage soon wears away. Tail has dark central stripe. Beak width only visible from some angles and at close range. Legs greenish. *Voice:* a weak 'trrrt' in flight. *Habitat:* inland waters and coastal lagoons, reefs or saltmarsh. Widespread; generally scarce but locally quite common. 〰🦆🪶

Ruff *Philomachus pugnax* 23-27cm Medium-sized wader, long-necked, small-headed, male appreciably larger than female. Male in breeding season unmistakable, with copious ruff of feathers round neck. Smaller female mottled rich buffs and browns above; pale buff below. Non-breeding male and immature similar to female. Beak dark, medium-long. Legs variable in colour, but usually yellow or orange, relatively long. In flight, appears long-winged and leisurely, showing pale wingbar. Tail pattern characteristic, with dark central bar separating large, white, oval patches on each side of rump. *Voice:* rarely vocal. *Habitat:* coastal lagoons and inland muddy pools. Rare but probably regular migrant. 〰🪶

Stilt Sandpiper *Micropalama himantopus* 21cm Medium-small long-legged sandpiper resembling a rather large, 'stretched' Curlew Sandpiper. Non-breeding birds are grey above, with darker feather centres and broad pale fringes. Crown brown with darker streaks. Prominent whitish supercilium over blackish-brown cheek patch. Throat white. Breast grey buff with darker markings; belly white. Legs long and greenish; beak long, black and downcurved near tip. In flight, shows white rump/black tail pattern similar to Curlew Sandpiper, but lacks wingbar. Legs project well beyond tail tip. *Voice:* soft 'too too'. *Habitat:* wetlands, marshes, usually freshwater; rarely coastal. Vagrant. 〰

Sanderling (breeding)

Sanderling (juvenile)

Buff-breasted Sandpiper

Broad-billed Sandpiper (non-breeding)

Ruff (non-breeding)

Stilt Sandpiper (non-breeding)

Red-necked Phalarope *Phalaropus lobatus* 18-19cm Small, slim, aquatic wader. Breeding birds mottled brown and buff above with bold double V markings on back. Head dark brown. Throat and chin white; reddish stripe on side of slim neck. Underparts white. Female brighter than male. Non-breeding birds pale grey-brown above, with dark smudge surrounding eye; white below. Beak dark, very fine. In flight, shows white wingbar and black tail with grey outer feathers (compare Sanderling). Characteristically swims buoyantly, spinning to disturb food. *Voice:* sharp 'prip'. *Habitat:* usually winters at sea, but may occur on inshore waters; occasionally on inland fresh waters. Rare migrant. 🌊 ⪮ 🦐 ⎸

Wilson's Phalarope *Phalaropus tricolor* 23-25cm Medium-small, aquatic wader. Breeding birds distinctive, grey above with bold double chestnut V markings on back. Bold black streak running through eye and down sides of neck onto breast. Throat white, rest of underparts white flushed apricot. Female brighter than male. Beak long, straight and very fine; legs yellowish or greenish. Non-breeding birds uniformly pale grey above, white below, with pale grey smudge through eye (compare Marsh Sandpiper). In flight, rump white, tail grey, lacks wingbar. Feet protrude beyond tail tip. *Voice:* strange deep honk. *Habitat:* maritime, or occasionally on inland fresh waters. Vagrant. 🌊 ⪮ 🦐

Grey Phalarope *Phalaropus fulicarius* 20-22cm Small, dumpy, aquatic wader. Breeding adult unmistakable, with throat, breast and flanks chestnut, paling to white on belly. Back brown with buff markings; head and nape grey, with large white cheek patch. Female brighter than male. Non-breeding birds pale grey above; white below. Bill thicker (not needle-thin) than that of Red-necked. In flight, shows bold wingbar, dark rump and tail with grey outer feathers (compare Sanderling). Characteristically swims buoyantly, spinning to disturb food. *Voice:* sharp 'whit' or 'prip'. *Habitat:* usually well out at sea, but sometimes bays, occasionally inland on fresh waters. Vagrant. 🌊 ⪮ 🦐

Oriental Pratincole *Glareola maldivarum* 23cm Medium-small, short-beaked, long-winged wader, sometimes usefully described as a cross between a swallow or tern and a plover. Upperparts sandy brown, with darker flight feathers. Underparts buff, shading to white on belly, with distinctive black-bordered rich buff throat patch. Legs of medium length, black. Beak short. Non-breeding birds duller. In flight, shows diagnostic white tail with black-bordered V notch at tip, and distinctive chestnut underwing at close range. Characteristic swooping flight catching insects. *Voice:* vocal in flight, 'chick chick' and softer plover-like 'tu-wheet'. *Habitat:* open plains, bare ground near water or claypans. Regular, and in north and west locally abundant. 🌊 ⪮ ⎸ △

Australian Pratincole *Stiltia isabella* 23cm Medium-small wader, longer-legged than Oriental Pratincole. Sandy brown above, with blackish wingtips extending far beyond tail. White throat, buffish breast, broad characteristic chestnut band across belly, white undertail coverts. Immature duller, with speckled brown belly band. Legs comparatively long, grey. In flight, shows distinctive belly pattern, and black (not chestnut) underwing. Tail short, square, broadly edged black and tipped white. *Voice:* shrill 'kirreee-peet'. *Habitat:* open semi-arid plains, claypans, gibber, dry floodplains. Widespread, but erratic in appearance and numbers. 🌊 ⪮ ⎸ △ ®

Red-necked Phalarope (non-breeding)

Wilson's Phalarope (non-breeding)

Grey Phalarope (non-breeding)

Oriental Pratincole (breeding)

Australian Pratincole (breeding)

Great Skua *Catharacta skua* 60cm Large seabird, the size and shape of Pacific Gull. Adult and immature bulky and heavy, but powerful in flight. Adult plumage dark brown, with paler and darker flecking; cheeks slightly paler and crown slightly darker than elsewhere. Adult has central tail feathers slightly but not noticeably elongated. Immature plumage slightly more rufous. In flight, striking bold white flashes in dark wings immediately separate Great Skua from immature large gulls. Pursues other birds up to Gannet-size to pirate food. *Voice:* barking 'tuk' or 'uk-uk-uk', rasping 'skeeer'. *Habitat:* On migration, may pass through coastal waters. Regular, but generally scarce in winter. ≰ ⫯

South Polar Skua *Catharacta maccormicki* 55cm Large seabird, very similar in appearance, behaviour and habits to Great Skua but slimmer and often appreciably smaller. Two colour forms: the darker sometimes almost blackish, sometimes paler on nape; the paler light grey-brown and paler than most Great Skuas, with buffish nape and mantle contrasting in flight with blackish wings. Wings and wing flashes as Great Skua. *Voice:* harsh 'ark'. *Habitat:* oceanic. Vagrant. ≰

Arctic Jaeger *Stercorarius parasiticus* 45cm Large seabird but medium-sized for a skua, occurring in two colour forms. Dark-phase adult uniformly chocolate brown, slightly paler on collar. Pale-phase adult brown above, with blackish cap; neck and belly buffish-white, with brown breast band. Adult tail has slim central feathers noticeably elongated. Immature rich brown, heavily speckled and barred; lacks long central tail feathers. Beak and legs greyish-brown, gull-like. In flight, all stages show striking white patches in long slender wings. Slim silhouette and agile flight help separate from Pomarine. Pursues other birds to steal food. *Voice:* yelping 'tuk tuk'; harsh 'eee-air'. *Habitat:* offshore waters, occasionally coastal. Regular but rarely numerous. ≰ ⫯

Pomarine Jaeger *Stercorarius pomarinus* 50cm Like Arctic occurs in both dark and pale colour morphs. Larger, fatter and rather broader-winged than Arctic but variable bulk of latter makes separation difficult unless tail extensions have developed. Adult tail has central feathers elongated, conspicuously broad and twisted. Immature uniformly rich brown, with darker barring and speckling: double (not single) whitish carpal patches on underwing of immature Pomarine, are helpful in separating from Arctic. At all ages Pomarine has a rather slower and more ponderous wing action than Arctic and is more of a scavenger on carrion. *Voice:* harsh 'which-yoo'. *Habitat:* regular, Australian coastal seas September-April; commoner in east. ≰ ⫯

Long-tailed Jaeger *Stercorarius longicaudus* 38cm, plus tail of up to 12cm The smallest, slimmest and most tern-like of the jaeger family in flight. Adult brown above, with dark crown. Neck and rest of underparts buffish-white. Central tail feathers slim and elongated; may reach 18cm beyond rest of tail. Immature grey-brown, finely barred and streaked with pale grey; others vary from being almost wholly dark, to having whitish head and underparts, lacking rusty tones of larger jaegers and showing almost no white in upperwing (although pale flash evident on underwing). *Voice:* rarely vocal at sea. *Habitat:* rare and usually well offshore in Australian waters. ≰ ⫯

Great Skua

South Polar Skua (dark morphs)

Arctic Jaeger (adult, pale morph)

Arctic Jaeger (adult, dark morph)

Pomarine Jaeger (adult, pale morph)

Long-tailed Jaeger (adult)

Silver Gull *Larus novaehollandiae* 41cm Large seabird, the most familiar of Australian gulls. Adult has white head, neck and body; pale grey wings with black primaries showing white tips at rest. Beak, eye-ring and legs scarlet. Immatures duller, with brown flecks on wings forming a conspicuous bar in flight; tail with broken brown subterminal bar. Beak brownish, legs blackish. Gregarious. *Voice:* short 'karr' and 'kee-ow', harsh 'karr-karr-karr'. *Habitat:* breeds colonially on islands offshore or in larger fresh or saline lakes and lagoons; at other times most types of water, coastal or inland, sewage farms, rubbish tips, playing fields. Widespread; often abundant coastally, less numerous inland and in north. 🐝🐜♨️🦪🦆△®

Pacific Gull *Larus pacificus* 58-66cm Large - one of the largest gulls. Adult has white head, neck and body; jet black wings with characteristically all-black primaries showing well in flight, and a white trailing edge to the secondaries. Tail white with distinctive black subterminal band. Beak massive, yellow with red tip; legs yellow. Immature dark grey-brown, with dark pinkish-grey legs, assuming adult plumage over 3-4 years. Searches tideline on steady wings; plunge-dives in shallow water. *Voice:* loud 'kow kow' or 'ork-ork-ork'. *Habitat:* breeds remote coast and islands; at other times usually in coastal waters, occasionally inland on sewage farms and rubbish tips but rarely far from sea. Widespread; often common. 🦪🦆®

Kelp Gull *Larus dominicanus* 54-59cm Large, almost as large as Pacific Gull but overall lighter in build. Adult has white head, neck and body; jet black wings with a characteristic broad white trailing edge and white spots near tips of primaries conspicuous in flight (see Pacific). Tail entirely white. Beak yellow with red spot near tip, detectably slimmer than Pacific. Legs greenish yellow. Immature mottled coffee-brown on back, paler on head and underparts; beak black, legs pinkish; assumes adult plumage over 3-4 years, when sometimes difficult to separate on plumage alone from Pacific. *Voice:* distinctive laughing 'yo-yo-yo-yo....'. *Habitat:* breeds remote coasts and islands, at other times in coastal seas. Widespread; overall rather scarce but locally more common and increasing. 🦪🦆®

Silver Gull

Silver Gull (immature)

Pacific Gull (adult)

Pacific Gull (immature)

Kelp Gull (adult)

Kelp Gull (immature)

Black-tailed Gull *Larus crassirostris* 47cm Large gull, midway in size between Silver Gull and Kelp Gull. Adult has white head and body, with grey flecking on crown in non-breeding birds. Back and wings slate grey, in flight showing characteristic all-black primaries and white trailing edge on inner section of wing. Tail white, with broad black subterminal band. Beak robust, distinctively yellow with black band and red spot near tip. Legs yellow. Immature grey-brown, paler on head and neck, with all-dark primaries. White only on rump and belly; broad black band on tail. Bill pink with black tip. *Voice:* high-pitched cries. *Habitat:* shallow coastal waters. Vagrant. ◢▨

Franklin's Gull *Larus pipixcan* 35cm Small gull. Breeding adult has black hood and bold white eyelids. Rather small beak, and legs reddish. Wings slate grey, in flight showing white trailing edge, with white spots on black primary tips. Non-breeding adult has white forehead, and mottled crown. Immature similar to non-breeding adult, but with primaries all-blackish and a black subterminal tail-band. *Voice:* harsh high-pitched, laughing calls, shrill yelps. *Habitat:* coastal seas, lagoons, estuaries, harbours. Vagrant. ◢▨

Laughing Gull *Larus atricilla* 42cm Large, hooded gull. Breeding plumage adult with sooty black hood and white eyelids. Beak relatively long, and drooped, scarlet. Body white, with medium-grey back, black primaries showing small white tips only when very fresh. Legs and feet dark red. Non-breeding birds have often blackish beak and legs, have white forehead and smudgy grey ear patch and nape. In flight, adult shows uniformly mid-grey wings with black primaries and a slender white trailing edge, the outer primaries all dark, lacking white tips. Immature similarly uniform, including head and nape, mid-brown, wings with a narrow white trailing edge and white tail with broad black subterminal band. *Voice:* harsh shrill laughing calls. *Habitat:* coastal seas. Vagrant. ◢▨

Sabine's Gull *Xema sabini* 32cm Small oceanic gull, with striking wing pattern. Breeding adult distinctive, with largely white plumage and black-bordered grey hood. Beak short and black with yellow tip. In flight, grey inner portion of wing and black primaries enclose a triangular white patch, creating a striking pattern. Tail white, forked. Immatures have similar pattern, but forewing brown (not grey) as is crown and nape and tail has narrow black terminal band. Flight dipping and tern-like; often feeds on the wing. *Voice:* rasping tern-like 'keeer'. *Habitat:* at sea, rarely close to land. Vagrant. ◢

Whiskered Tern *Chlidonias hybridus* 25cm Medium-sized marsh tern. Black cap contrasts with white cheeks. Breeding adult grey above. Underparts ash grey, paler on belly. Tail pale grey, shallowly forked. Beak red, comparatively small; legs red. Non-breeding adult grey above, white below, with white forecrown. Immature has brownish saddle and is very much like immature White-winged but bulkier, with stouter bill and longer legs. *Voice:* croaks and rasping calls. *Habitat:* breeds colonially on freshwater swamps, marshes, flooded areas, claypans. At other times, usually over freshwater wetland areas; occasionally sheltered salt waters. Widespread, but only locally common. ▨▨△®

Black-tailed Gull (adult)

Franklin's Gull (adult, non-breeding)

Laughing Gull (breeding)

Sabine's Gull (breeding)

Whiskered Tern (breeding)

Whiskered Tern (non-breeding)

White-winged Tern *Chlidonias leucopterus* 22cm Small marsh tern. Breeding adult unmistakable; greyish-white above, with head, breast and belly jet black. Tail pale grey, almost square-ended. Upperside of wings almost white; underside black, except for pale flight feathers. Beak and legs dark red. Non-breeding adult largely greyish-white; crown and wings pale grey, whiter on underside, often with diagnostic scattered black feathers on underwing coverts. Lacks collar marks (see Black). Immature similar, but with blackish mantle. Characteristic flight, dipping down to water surface to feed. *Voice:* rarely vocal; occasional 'kit' or 'kreek'. *Habitat:* over both coastal and inland waters. Regular but erratic migrant; rarely numerous. ≋ ≋ ⫪ △

Black Tern *Chlidonias niger* 23cm Small, dark marsh tern. Breeding adult largely dark sooty grey above and below with whitish underwing. Head, breast and belly slate black. Tail dark grey, shallowly forked. Beak and legs black. Non-breeding adult grey above, white below, with dark crown, white forehead and black 'half-collar' marks on shoulders. Immature similar to winter adult, but browner. *Voice:* occasional 'krit' or 'kreek'. *Habitat:* on migration, over both coastal and inland waters. Vagrant. ≋ ≋ ≋

Caspian Tern *Sterna caspia* 53cm Large - a giant among terns. Breeding adult white with black bristling cap, grey back and wings with dark grey tips. Tail white, shallowly forked. Beak strikingly coral red, large. Winter adult and immature have grey-flecked crowns and brownish-orange beaks. Enormous size (bodily almost as big as Kelp Gull) and heavy gull-like flight are distinctive. *Voice:* deep, harsh, crow-like 'kraaa-uh' and 'kaaah'. *Habitat:* breeds in singles or small colonies on beaches, usually close to salt water. At other times, over lagoons, coastal waters and occasionally but erratically inland. Scarce. Widespread, but nowhere numerous. ≋ ≋ ≋ △ ®

Gull-billed Tern *Sterna nilotica* 38cm Medium-sized tern. Adult in breeding season predominantly white; crown black; back, rump and wings pale grey. Tail greyish-white, shallowly forked. Beak all-black, stout, relatively short. Non-breeding adult lacks dark cap. Immature has back and crown brown-speckled grey; wings with brownish-grey streaks. *Voice:* rasping 'tzar-tzar-tzar' and deep 'kay-wreck'. *Habitat:* breeds colonially on sandy beaches and islands in fresh or saline waters. Hunts over sea, lagoons and saltpans, characteristically also over nearby fields, grassland, plains. Widespread, but erratic year-round. Locally common. ⫪ ≋ ≋ ≋ △ ®

Common Tern *Sterna hirundo* 35cm Medium-sized, slim, sea tern. Breeding adult predominantly white, with black cap and grey wings, with darker wedges in primaries (see Arctic). Tail white, deeply forked. Beak red with black tip, legs reddish black. Non-breeding adult has white forehead and all-black bill. Immature with dusky band along leading edge of wings. Gregarious. *Voice:* harsh 'kee-aarh' with emphasis on second syllable; hurried 'kirri-kirri-kirri'. *Habitat:* coastal lagoons, inshore waters. Widespread and regular; generally uncommon. ≋ ≋ ⫪

White-winged Tern (non-breeding)

Black Tern (non-breeding)

Caspian Tern (breeding)

Gull-billed Tern (breeding)

Common Tern (non-breeding)

Arctic Tern *Sterna paradisaea* 37cm Medium-sized, slim sea tern. Breeding adult white, with black cap. Wings grey with distinctively pale and translucent primaries. Tail white, with long streamers. Beak entirely red (see Roseate). Legs red, extremely short. Non-breeding adult has white forehead, dark beak and legs. Immature similar, but with shorter tail and very white secondaries. *Voice:* short, sharp 'keee-ah', with emphasis on first syllable. *Habitat:* oceanic, occasionally visiting southern coastal waters. Rare. ◢◣ ▮

Antarctic Tern *Sterna vittata* 36cm Medium-sized sea tern, with heavier-build than Arctic or Common. More robust beak than Arctic. Very similar to Arctic in breeding and non-breeding plumages, but plumage stages are usually seasonally opposite to each other. *Voice:* sharp and high-pitched 'kik-kik'. *Habitat:* coastal waters. Difficult to identify positively other than at very close range, so may be under-recorded. Vagrant. ◢◣ ▮

Roseate Tern *Sterna dougallii* 38cm Medium-sized, the slimmest sea tern. Breeding adult white, sometimes flushed pink on breast. Very white wings often show darker outer primaries; latter lack dark tips of Common and Arctic on underside. Forked tail, with extremely long streamers. Crown black. Beak black with blood red patch at base. Non-breeding adult has white forehead. Immature, with dark grey scaly markings. *Voice:* distinctive soft 'chee-vee' or 'chow-ick'. *Habitat:* breeds on sandy or pebbly beaches, or short grass on islands. Feeds offshore, disperses well out to sea. Generally uncommon; locally sometimes quite numerous. ◢◣ ▮ ®

White-fronted Tern *Sterna striata* 40cm Breeding adult white, with bold black cap and characteristic narrow white forehead band. Upperparts pale grey. Beak black, slightly downcurved; legs black or reddish. Non-breeding birds much whiter overall than Common, lacking dark tips to primary undersides. Immature distinctive, with blackish forewing and primaries and a triangle of grey midwing. *Voice:* high-pitched 'keee-eet' and 'kech'. *Habitat:* breeds New Zealand and some Bass Strait islands, dispersing to southeastern seas. Regular, occasionally numerous. ◢◣ ▮ ®

Black-naped Tern *Sterna sumatrana* 32-35cm Very white slim, sea tern. Adult white, with long tail streamers, crown white has bold black mask merging to give black nape. Beak and legs black. Immature has brownish scaling on mantle. Compare Roseate. *Voice:* high-pitched 'see-chee-chee-tip'. *Habitat:* breeds on sandy or coral beaches on islands off northeast coast, dispersing nearby to coastal waters. Locally quite common. ◢◣ ▮ ®

Sooty Tern *Sterna fuscata* 42-46cm Large sea tern. Adult upperparts sooty black with triangular white forehead patch. Tail, blackish with white outer streamers. Beak and legs black. Immature sooty above and below apart from white undertail coverts, and whitish spots on inner sections of wings. Distinctive 'skim and dip' flight pattern when feeding. Gregarious. Compare Bridled. *Voice:* nasal 'ker-wack-wack'. *Habitat:* breeds colonially on remote rocky or sandy island beaches, dispersing to tropical oceanic waters. Widespread except along southern coasts. Locally common. ◢◣ ▮ ®

Arctic Tern (non-breeding)

Antarctic Tern (breeding)

Roseate Tern (breeding)

White-fronted Tern (breeding)

Black-naped Tern (breeding)

Sooty Tern (breeding)

Bridled Tern *Sterna anaethetus* 36-42cm Medium-large dark sea tern very similar to Sooty. Adult has black cap, and narrow white forehead patch extending in stripe to just behind eyes. Wings and tail browner than Sooty; tail with white outer feathers. Beak and legs black. Immature similar, but cap streaked with white; back brown with copious pale scaly markings. Fast in flight, dipping down to snatch food items. *Voice:* shrill yaps. *Habitat:* breeds in loose colonies on islands; dispersing northwards into oceanic waters. Widespread except along south coasts, generally uncommon. ⬥🐟🦅®

Little Tern *Sterna albifrons* 22cm Small sea tern. Adult white, with grey wings showing blackish outer wedge. Crown black; forehead white, more extensive in non-breeding birds. Short, shallowly forked white tail. Beak yellow, usually with black tip. Legs yellow. Immature lacks bold head pattern, has grey-brown marks on back and wings and dark bill and legs. Flight flickering. *Voice:* high-pitched 'kree-ik' and hurried 'kirri-kirri-kirrick'. *Habitat:* breeds on coastal beaches and islands. Feeds in shallow inshore seas and lagoons. Widespread; locally sometimes common. 🌊⬥🐟🦅®

Fairy Tern *Sterna nereis* 22-26cm Dumpier than Little but hard to distinguish. Breeding adult has wider forehead than Little, with white lores. Beak orange rather than yellow, usually without black tip. Legs short, orange-yellow. Wings show dark grey outer primaries in flight. Non-breeding bird has more extensive white on crown than Little. Immature lacks dark shoulder bar. *Voice:* loud, low 'chee-wick' and rattling 'ket, ket, ket....'. *Habitat:* breeds on coastal beaches and islands, disperses to coastal seas, occasionally inland. Widespread along south and western coasts; locally common. ⬥🐟🦅®

Crested Tern *Sterna bergii* 44-48cm Large and familiar tern. Breeding adult grey above, white below, with short, moderately forked tail. Crown black, roughly crested, with narrow white forehead. White collar. Beak long and comparatively slender, distinctively yellow. Non-breeding birds have front half of crown white, liberally flecked black. Immature pale grey, heavily marked with black; crown generally dark (see Lesser Crested). *Voice:* rasping 'karrick'. *Habitat:* breeds colonially on beaches and islands around almost the entire seaboard, dispersing to coastal seas and occasionally inland. Widespread; generally common. ⬥🐟🦅®

Lesser Crested Tern *Sterna bengalensis* 37-42cm Large tern, similar to larger Crested. Breeding adult grey above, white below, with short moderately forked tail. Beak distinctively orange. Crown black with little or no trace of white forehead, shaggily crested at nape. Lacks distinct collar of Crested. Non-breeding birds have clear white forehead; white crown becoming densely black-streaked well behind the eye, appearing much whiter-headed than Crested. Beak yellowish. Immature has paler midwing than Crested, and darker leading edge. *Voice:* similar to Crested 'karrick'. *Habitat:* breeds in small colonies on tropical beaches and islands, dispersing into coastal seas. Widespread north of the Tropic, but generally uncommon. ⬥🐟🦅®

Bridled Tern (breeding)

Little Tern (breeding)

Fairy Tern (breeding)

Crested Tern (breeding)

Lesser Crested Tern (breeding)

Common Noddy *Anous stolidus* 38-41cm Large, the largest noddy, often difficult to identify with certainty. Adult upperparts and underparts sooty brown, with characteristically darker brown flight feathers (at close range) and long, heavy, wedge-shaped tail. Forehead white, shading to grey on nape. Black mark from beak to eye; white eyelids. Beak black, robust; legs and feet blackish. Immature lacks pale cap, and has paler speckling on upperparts. *Voice:* harsh 'kwark', softer 'quwok'. *Habitat:* breeds colonially in trees or on ground, on tropical islands and beaches, dispersing to coastal seas nearby. Widespread except on south coast; locally common. ◄ ✖ 🚶 ®

Lesser Noddy *Anous tenuirostris* 31-34cm Medium-large, appreciably smaller and darker than Common Noddy. Adult upperparts and underparts sooty black, with prominent white forehead and grey crown. Black mark around eye does not stretch to beak. Eyelids white. Beak black, comparatively slender. Comparatively short, broad and slightly forked tail can be a useful guide, as can fast buoyant flght (with experience). *Voice:* soft 'chrrr'. *Habitat:* breeds colonially, usually in trees, often mangroves, on islands off west coast, dispersing into coastal waters and Indian Ocean. Restricted but locally common. ◄ ✖ ®

Black Noddy *Anous minutus* 33-36cm Medium-large - and the darkest of the noddies. Adult uniformly very dark, with contrasting white forehead and pale grey crown. Eyelids white. Beak black, comparatively longer and slimmer than other noddies. Flight buoyant; tail short, broad and slightly forked. *Voice:* grating 'chrrr' and distinctive 'kick-kirrick'. *Habitat:* breeds colonially, usually in trees, on remote tropical islands, dispersing to local seas. Largely restricted to Great Barrier Reef islands and seas, where locally common. Rare elsewhere. ◄ ✖ ®

Grey Ternlet *Procelsterna albivittata* 28-30cm Medium-large distinctive light-weight blue-grey noddy. Adult uniformly pale blue-grey, darker on back and wings, with a whitish cap and white underwings. Eye dark, with black surrounds, looking comparatively large. Tail short, broad, shallowly forked. Beak relatively short and black; legs and feet black with pinkish or yellow webbing. Graceful, like White Tern in flight. *Voice:* purring 'crorr-rr-rr'. *Habitat:* tropical and subtropical islands of South Pacific, straying west to southeastern coastal seas. Vagrant. ◄ ✖ 🚶

White Tern *Gygis alba* 29-33cm Medium-large delicate 'fairy' tern. Adult distinctively all-white, with large dark eye and surrounds. Beak black, dark blue at base (close range); legs and feet black. Dainty in flight, feathers translucent to almost transparent overhead against a blue sky. Immature generally whitish, but has brownish smudge behind eye, grey-flecked crown, and brown flecking on wings. *Voice:* sharp 'keech'. *Habitat:* tropical and subtropical oceans and islands. Vagrant. ◄ ✖ 🚶

Common Noddy (breeding)

Lesser Noddy (breeding)

Black Noddy (breeding)

Grey Ternlet (breeding)

White Tern (breeding)

Banded Fruit-Dove *Ptilinopus cinctus* 23cm Medium-large
distinctive pigeon. Head, neck, nape and breast strikingly white, tinged yellowish. Back black; wings and rump grey; tail black with broad grey terminal band. Underparts blue-grey, separated from white breast by broad black band. Immature has pale grey 'head end'. Shy. Feeds in canopies of fruiting trees, sometimes flapping noisily to keep balance. *Voice:* deep booming, not often heard. *Habitat:* year-round resident in rainforest, montane forest gullies. Local and scarce. 🔛 ♣♣ ®

Superb Fruit-Dove *Ptilinopus superbus* 23cm Medium-sized, but
small and spectacularly coloured. Adult male upperparts rich green, with darker markings; nape golden-chestnut, crown scarlet. Face pale green; breast purple, bounded by broad black band; belly whitish with broad green bars on flanks. Female and immature largely green with white belly. Beak black. Inconspicuous. *Voice:* double 'coo' and steadily repeated booming 'oom'. *Habitat:* year-round resident in tropical and subtropical forests and scrubs, also mangroves. Locally fairly common in north of range, otherwise scarce and erratic. ♣ 🦅 📷 ☷ 🔛 ❗ ®

Rose-crowned Fruit-Dove *Ptilinopus regina* 22cm Medium-sized,
but small and spectacularly coloured. Adult male golden-green above, with yellow-bordered crimson crown. Face, neck and breast iridescent pale lavender; belly rich orange, leg feathering greenish. Female duller. Immature overall green with golden feather fringes. Adult male beak distinctive lime green. Less wary than others in its group. *Voice:* distinctive and loud, initially slow then accelerating to a frenzied 'hook-coo, hook-coo, hook-coo, coocoocoocoo...' *Habitat:* year-round resident in woodland and forest, scrub, parks with fruit-bearing trees or shrubs. Fairly widespread; locally quite common in north, scarcer farther south. 📷 🔛 ♣♣ ❗ ®

Wompoo Fruit-Dove *Ptilinopus magnificus* 36-55cm Large,
spectacularly colourful pigeon: tropical race (north Queensland) substantially smaller than NSW race. Adult has pale lavender head and nape, purple throat and breast, bright yellow belly and undertail. Back and wings emerald green, with diagonal gold bar on closed wing. Tail black. Beak yellow with reddish base; legs lime yellow. Immatures have colours subdued with greenish blotches. Flight swift, revealing bright yellow underwing. *Voice:* turkey-like 'pock-pock-oo' and soft 'wampoo'. *Habitat:* year-round resident in rainforest, woodland and scrub with plentiful fruiting trees. Locally fairly common in north of range, scarce elsewhere. 📷 🔛 ®

Banded Fruit-Dove

Superb Fruit-Dove ♂

Superb Fruit-Dove ♀

Rose-crowned Fruit-Dove ♂

Wompoo Fruit-Dove

Torresian Imperial-Pigeon *Ducula spilorrhoa* 38-44cm Large pigeon, strikingly beautiful despite its simple coloration. Adult largely white, with contrasting black flight feathers and broad terminal bar to tail, and with flanks and undertail boldly black-barred. Pied appearance as distinctive in flight as it is perched. Beak pale, yellowish; legs grey. Male has distinctive 'up, stall, plunge' display flight. Often gregarious, travelling in fast-flying flocks to feeding grounds. *Voice:* deep 'coo-woo', sometimes trisyllabic 'coo-rar-who'. *Habitat:* rainforest, riverine forest, mangroves, where fruit is plentiful. Migrant, breeding more or less colonially Nov-Mar. Widespread; locally quite common along northern coastal belt. 🐦🦅🚗 🐾🎵🕯️®

Black-collared Fruit-Pigeon *Ducula mullerii* 43cm Large colourful pigeon of very restricted distribution. Head pattern distinctive, with purple-brown crown, white chin and face extending to narrow band around edge of crown, black nape and throat band, with a broad white crescentic patch on upper breast. Body deep pink, with grey back and wings and pale grey and black banded tail. Immature duller. *Voice:* not known. *Habitat:* fruiting woodland and riparian trees. Vagrant to islands off northern Queensland. 🐦🦅🎵

Topknot Pigeon *Lopholaimus antarcticus* 40-45cm Large drab grey pigeon with ginger crests. Head characteristic, with white-flecked, slightly crested grey crown, separated from grey face and throat by bristling ginger eyestripe 'crests'. Body largely grey, with some iridescent sheen on breast; wings dark grey, tail blackish with distinctive white subterminal band. Beak and feet reddish. In flight, appears fast and distinctively long-winged, with square-ended banded tail prominent. Noisy when clambering about in the canopy. *Voice:* occasional grunts; quarrelsome screeches. *Habitat:* forest and woodland; isolated fruiting trees. Present year-round but nomadic. Locally common, especially in NSW and southern Queensland. 🐦 🐾🎵🌳®

White-headed Pigeon *Columba leucomela* 38-40cm Large, distinctive, black-and-white pigeon. Male has head, neck, mantle and underparts white or dirty white; wings and tail black with greenish iridescent feather fringes. Beak red with yellow tip; legs pinkish. Female and immature appreciably greyer or buffer, with yellowish brown beak and feet. Occasionally perches conspicuously, often forages early morning or late afternoon, sometimes on ground. Gregarious. *Voice:* loud repeated 'whoo-hoo'. *Habitat:* tropical and subtropical trees and shrubs, occasionally in towns or parks. Favours Camphor Laurel. Locally fairly common but erratic. 🐾🎵🌳🏛️®

Feral Pigeon *Columba livia* 34cm Large and familiar as the town or homing pigeon. Variable in colour from pinkish through browns to near-black, but typically largely grey, often chequered darker on wings, with iridescent sheen particularly on throat and breast, and with darker flight feathers and black-banded grey tail. Wings are usually uniform beneath, and may show a variety of dark barrings on upper surface of inner section. May show conspicuous white rump. Beak grey; legs pink. Display flight with wings held up in V format. *Voice:* 'coorookoo' 'rackety-coo'. *Habitat:* almost any location associated with man and his crops. Widespread; locally common. Introduced. 🏚️🛵®

Torresian Imperial-Pigeon

Black-collared Fruit-Pigeon

Topknot Pigeon

White-headed Pigeon

Feral Pigeon

Spotted Turtle-Dove *Streptopelia chinensis* 31cm Medium-large pigeon. Head, neck and underparts greyish fawn, flushed pink on breast in adults; back and wings yellow-brown with darker mottlings. Distinctive black-and-white chequered neck patches conspicuous in adults, absent in immatures. Tail long, slightly pointed, blackish broadly tipped white. *Voice:* mellow 'coos', linked in various ways; eg 'coo-coo, croo coor'. *Habitat:* city and suburban parks, gardens, farmland. Widespread and well established; locally common. Introduced. ▲ ▲ ®

Laughing Turtle-Dove *Streptopelia senegalensis* 26cm Medium-sized, slightly built reddish dove. Distinctive breast crescent of golden-brown, flecked black, absent in immatures. Back rufous brown; wings with characteristic blue-grey shoulders. Rump grey; tail blackish with white corners. *Voice:* usually a musical laughing 'coo-oo, coo coo'. *Habitat:* city, suburban and surrounding farmland areas in southwest. Locally common. Introduced. ▲ ▲ ®

Brown Cuckoo-Dove *Macropygia amboinensis* 40cm Large, long-tailed brown pigeon. Upperparts distinctively rich cinnamon brown; underparts paler. Immature shows traces of brown barring on underparts, and is mottled buff or rufous on back. *Voice:* mellow 'coo-coo rooork', the last syllable characteristically rising. *Habitat:* forests, woodlands, well-treed country, favouring fruiting trees or the ground beneath them. Generally quite common ▒ ▒ ▲▲ ▒ ®

Peaceful Dove *Geopelia placida* 21-23cm Small for a pigeon. Upperparts sandy grey-brown, with fine black barring, except on pale grey crown, face and throat. Blue-green patch of bare skin round eye. Underparts whitish, densely barred black on upper breast. Tail long and pointed, grey-brown. Immature paler and less clearly marked. In flight, shows chestnut underwings. *Voice:* vocal, high-pitched but musical 'doo-da-loo' or 'coo-coo-coo'. *Habitat:* open woodland, scrub, farmland, city and suburban parks and gardens. Widespread; often common, less so in southeast. ▲ ▲ ▒ ▲▲ ▒ △ ®

Diamond Dove *Geopelia cuneata* 19-21cm Very small for a pigeon. Head, nape, throat and breast plain grey, with deep red eye-ring. Underparts white. Back sandy brown with distinctive fine white spots. Long, rather pointed tail dark grey brown. Immature browner, with buffish barring on back and wings. Flight whirring, but fast and direct, showing chestnut on primaries. *Voice:* mournful four-note cooing. *Habitat:* usually near water in open woodland, riverine woodland and hill country. Widespread but erratic; locally fairly common. ▲ ▲▲ ▒ ▲▲ △ ®

Bar-shouldered Dove *Geopelia humeralis* 28-30cm Medium-large, slim, long-tailed pigeon. Head, throat and upper breast grey, nape golden chestnut, back brown. Nape, back and rump characteristic, boldly marked with fine crescentic black bars. Underparts white, pinkish buff on flanks. Eye pale yellow, eye-ring blue-grey. Flight swift and direct, with head carried distinctively high, showing bronze shoulders and chestnut underwing. White tail tips comparatively inconspicuous. *Voice:* distinctive high-pitched 'coo-lee-coo', strong 'hook-coo'. *Habitat:* tropical and subtropical shrub and scrub, often near water, occasionally gardens. Locally common in undisturbed areas. ▲ ▲ ▒ ▒ ▲▲ ▒ △ ®

Spotted Turtle-Dove

Laughing Turtle-Dove

Brown Cuckoo-Dove

Peaceful Dove

Diamond Dove

Bar-shouldered Dove

Emerald Dove *Chalcophaps indica* 23-25cm Dumpy, dark and unobtrusive pigeon. Adult has lavender pink head, nape and underparts, with a blackish back crossed by two indistinct broad whitish bars. Wings metallic green, with small white patch on shoulder in male. Flight feathers and short tail blackish; wings showing traces of chestnut primary bases in flight. Ground feeder; flies fast and low, normally only a short distance. *Voice:* low-pitched monotonously repeated 'coo'. *Habitat:* forest, woodland, mangroves and scrub with fruiting trees, usually near water. Locally fairly common. ▰ ▭ 🐦 🎵 ®

Common Bronzewing *Phaps chalcoptera* 32-35cm Medium-large, plump forest pigeon. Upperparts brown with broad buff feather fringes giving a scaly appearance to the back; underparts dull pink; wings showing extensive bronze and green iridescence. At close range, pale buff forehead, brown crown and white line below eye are distinctive. Female and immature appreciably duller and greyer, especially about the head, but have the distinctive wings. Ground feeder; very wary, taking off with a dreadful clatter of wings. *Voice:* monotonous and repetitive 'oom'. *Habitat:* forest, woodland and scrub of most types. Widespread and fairly common. ◄ ⁑ ▥ ▨ ▰ △ ®

Brush Bronzewing *Phaps elegans* 28-30cm Medium-large, dark and plump forest pigeon. Upperparts dull brown, shading to deep chestnut on nape, mantle and collar; underparts dull grey. Wings brown with two broad iridescent bronze bars. At close range yellow-buff forehead, grey crown, chestnut throat and chestnut and white stripes through eye are distinctive, the chestnut stripes merging on the nape. Female and immature duller and greyer, especially on head. In flight, chestnut shoulders and rusty flight feathers are distinctive. *Voice:* repetitive booming 'oom'. *Habitat:* forests and woodland, usually with a dense well-developed understorey. Restricted and generally scarce, with pockets where it is more frequent. ⁑ ▥ ▨ △ ®

Flock Bronzewing *Phaps histrionica* 28-30cm Medium-large, distinctive pigeon. Upperparts an unusual sandy-cinnamon; underparts blue-grey. Male has white 'face', black crown, white-outlined black cheek patch, black throat with small white 'bib' above breast. Female and immature are duller, with brown crown and whitish throat patch. Tail brown; wings blackish with obscure pale tips to primaries. Characteristically gregarious and mobile, flocks moving at speed on relatively long, swept-back wings, flighting to water at dawn and dusk. *Voice:* unusually characteristically silent. *Habitat:* dryish open plains, grassland, crops, with nearby water. Very erratic; locally common. ▥ ▰ △ ®

Crested Pigeon *Geophaps lophotes* 31-35cm Medium-large, long-tailed pigeon Head grey, with red eye-ring, and distinctive near-vertical spiky black crest on crown. Upperparts sandy buff, with brownish tail. Wings characteristically barred black on shoulders, with large purplish-bronze iridescent wing patch edged in white. Underparts pinkish-buff. Immature duller, lacking crest and much of the wing iridescence. Fast flying, with frequent glides on flat wings, crest flattened. On landing, characteristically raises tail. *Voice:* explosive 'whoop'. *Habitat:* open, well-watered country, farmland paddocks, occasionally suburban areas. Widespread and expanding range; locally quite common. ◄ ▰ ⁑ ▥ ▰ △ ®

Emerald Dove (adult)

Common Bronzewing ♂

Brush Bronzewing ♂

Flock Bronzewing ♂

Crested Pigeon

Squatter Pigeon *Geophaps scripta* 28-32cm Medium-large, plump, partridge-like pigeon. Head distinctive, with brown crown (sometimes raised as small crest); face and throat patterned in black and white. Greenish-bronze iridescent wingbar. Breast grey-brown, belly white. Ground feeder; partridge-like when flushed, but often running first. In flight, broad dark tips of outer tail feathers show prominently. *Voice:* quiet 'coo's. *Habitat:* grassy open landscapes, lightly treed country, around homesteads. Restricted; generally common. ♨♨ ⚹⚹ ®

Partridge Pigeon *Geophaps smithii* 25-28cm Medium-large, plump, partridge-like pigeon. Head distinctive, with comparatively heavy black beak and prominent large red facial patch (sometimes yellow) black-outlined white throat with dark brown cheek patch. Upperparts dull sandy brown, with small greenish-bronze iridescent patch in wings. Neck and V-shaped breast patch dull brown; belly white. Ground feeder. When flushed, birds whirr off in all directions. *Voice:* soft 'coo-coo'. *Habitat:* grassy woodlands, often landscapes, usually near water. Restricted but locally quite common. ♒ ♨♨ ⚹⚹ ®

White-quilled Rock-Pigeon *Petrophassa albipennis* 28-30cm Medium-large, stocky, dark pigeon. Plumage dark cinnamon-brown, with faint paler scaly markings. Throat blackish with fine white speckling; white lines above and below eye on relatively small head. If flushed, whirrs off low showing diagnostic bold white patches at base of primaries. *Voice:* loud 'coo-corcck' and low 'coo'. *Habitat:* rocky escarpments, gorges, rough rocky country with scrubby vegetation. Restricted, but locally common. ♨♨ ⛰ ®

Chestnut-quilled Rock-Pigeon *Petrophassa rufipennis* 30-32cm Slightly larger and darker than White-quilled. Range important for identification if not seen in flight. Reluctant to fly, but when flushed shows conspicuous chestnut primaries. *Voice:* low 'coo', loud 'coo-carook'. *Habitat:* rocky escarpments, gullies, gorges and hillsides with scattered stunted trees. Restricted, but locally common. ♨♨ ⛰ ®

Spinifex Pigeon *Geophaps plumifera* 21-23cm Medium-small, dumpy terrestrial pigeon. Upperparts sandy buff, marked with broad black and rich buff crescentic bars. Underparts yellowish buff, paling to white on belly, with narrow blackish breast band. Western Australian birds are uniformly richer buff, lacking the white belly in southern populations. Conspicuous red patch around eye, and black-and-white face and throat pattern, are distinctive, as is tall upright sand-buff crest. Usually runs away nimbly. If flushed, whirrs off showing a characteristic rich cinnamon patch in rounded wings and dark outer tail feathers. *Voice:* soft 'coo's, 'ooh-ah' and 'cooloo-coo'. *Habitat:* Spinifex country - hilly or sandy ridges, but near water. Quite widespread but discontinuous; locally fairly common. ♒ ⚹⚹ △ ®

Wonga Pigeon *Leucosarcia melanoleuca* 43cm Large, heavily-built pigeon. Upperparts grey apart from white face and darker mark through eye. Throat and breast grey, with a distinctive white V marking. Beak and legs pink. Terrestrial when feeding early and late in the day. *Voice:* loud whistling 'coo', distinctive repetitive 'wonk'. *Habitat:* damp dense coastal forest, woodland and scrub, occasionally plantations and large gardens. Generally uncommon. 🦃 ⛺ ®

Squatter Pigeon

Partridge Pigeon

White-quilled Rock-Pigeon

Chestnut-quilled Rock-Pigeon

Spinifex Pigeon

Wonga Pigeon

Palm Cockatoo *Probosciger aterrimus* 56-64cm Large and distinctive, the only all-black cockatoo. Uniformly dark sooty black, with long ragged erectile crest. Beak large, hooked; facial skin pink, turning scarlet when excited. Female has smaller beak and facial patch; immature has buffish markings on underwing. In flight, appears broad-winged, with slow, measured and deep wingbeats, beak tucked down. Glides to perch on downcurved wings. Arboreal, occasionally feeding on ground. *Voice:* whistling 'kweet-kweet', harsh screeches and wailing in flight. *Habitat:* tropical rainforest, nearby eucalypt woodland, especially paperbarks. Locally fairly common. 🐦 🎵 ®

Red-tailed Black-Cockatoo *Calyptorhynchus banksii* 60-65cm Large, the most frequently seen 'black cockatoo' inland and in the north. Male uniformly sooty black but with red panels at base of tail, best seen in flight. Beak black, robust. Rounded fluffy crest erected forwards over forehead. Female and immature have duller plumage with yellow speckling, yellowish-orange tail panels and a strikingly white beak. Often terrestrial and often gregarious. In flight, shows long tail and harrier-like long fingered wings. *Voice:* metallic trumpeting 'kreee'. *Habitat:* open forest and woodland. Widespread; fairly common in interior and north, scarce farther south. 🎵 👥 🏚 △®

Glossy Black-Cockatoo *Calyptorhynchus lathami* 46-50cm Large, but the smallest black cockatoo. Male brownish-black on head, breast and belly; dull black on back and tail. Red panels in tail. Beak black, large and rather bulbous. Little trace of crest. Female and immature duller, flecked yellow, with yellowish tail panels; females with a speckled yellow collar. Wings and tail long; flight seems to be an effort. Usually arboreal, typically in *Casuarina*, cracking seeds. *Voice:* feeble whine rather than wail, 'tarr-red'. *Habitat:* coastal forest, woodland, riverine woodland. Generally local and uncommon; declining. 👥 🏚 ®

Yellow-tailed Black-Cockatoo *Calyptorhynchus funereus* 63-68cm Large black cockatoo, with small floppy crest. Round yellowish patch on cheeks; yellow panels in tail. Many feathers have pale fringes, giving scaly appearance, particularly in female and immature. Eye-ring orange in male, grey in female. Beak fairly large and grey in male, whitish in female. Flight characteristically buoyant, with deep slow wingbeats, showing long tail and long, fingered wings. *Voice:* distinctive wierd wailing 'wee-you', 'why-lar', screeches. *Habitat:* rainforest, montane forest, woodlands including non-native conifers. Patchy in distribution and numbers. 🌲 🎵 👥 🏚 ®

Long-billed Black-Cockatoo *Calyptorhynchus baudinii* 53-58cm
Short-billed Black-Cockatoo *Calyptorhynchus latirostris* 57-60cm
These two very similar species both resemble Yellow-tailed but have white, not yellow, in the tail and greyish-white cheek patches. Chief difference is bill shape (Long-billed having more elongated point to upper mandible). *Voice:* contact call is a high-pitched, wailing whistle 'wheela', but Short-billed prolongs the second syllable more than Long-billed. *Habitat:* extreme southwest of Western Australia. Long-billed in wetter marri and mixed marri and jarrah forests of the extreme south of their ranges; more widespread Short-billed feeds on banksias, dryandras and hakeas in drier woodland and scrub zone of coastal belt. Both visit pine plantations; flocks overlap, but do not mix, outside of breeding season. 🌲 🎵 👥 🏚 ®

Palm Cockatoo

Red-tailed Black-Cockatoo ♂

Glossy Black-Cockatoo ♂

Yellow-tailed Black-Cockatoo ♂

Short-billed Black-Cockatoo

Gang-gang Cockatoo *Callocephalon fimbriatum* 34cm Medium-large, slightly owl-like cockatoo. Male slate grey, with pale feather fringes giving scaly appearance. Crown and face scarlet, with curly bristling crest on nape. Beak whitish. Female has grey head and crest; upperparts like male; feathers of breast and belly fringed yellowish-red. Immature duller. Quiet and inconspicuous, usually arboreal. If disturbed, swoops low and up into next tree. Flight distinctly owl-like, with large head, short square tail and moderately long broad wings. *Voice:* distinctive rising creaking growl, like a rusty hinge. *Habitat:* forests and woodlands of most sorts, wintering in more open lowland country including parks and gardens. Restricted, but locally fairly common. ◖ ⨪ ♙ ⓘ ®

Galah *Cacatua roseicapilla* 34-38cm Large, familar and distinctive cockatoo. Back and tail pale grey, with darker wingtips; neck and underparts striking rose-pink, with paler crown and slight crest. Immature has greyer breast. Often gregarious, often noisy, usually feeds terrestrially. Flocks striking in flight as colour changes from pink to grey as the birds wheel and turn. *Voice:* distinctive high-pitched 'chee chee', screeches. *Habitat:* open country with trees, grasslands, crops, always fairly near water. Widespread, often common. ◖ ⨪ ♙ ⦀ ⨪ △ ®

Long-billed Corella *Cacatua tenuirostris* 35-40cm Large, predominantly white, long-beaked cockatoo. Overall white, with pink on face, forehead and throat, often faintly pink on breast and belly. Crest small and inconspicuous, usually held flattened. Blue facial patch round eye. Long white beak. In flight shows yellow bar on undersides of wings, and yellow underside to base of tail. Feeds terrestrially, grubbing for roots with its long white beak. *Voice:* quavering high-pitched 'wuk-wuk-wuk', screeches. *Habitat:* open forest, woodland, grassland with trees, riverine woodland; grazing land, crops. Discontinuous distribution, generally uncommon. ⨪ ♙ ®

Little Corella *Cacatua pastinator* 36-38cm Overall white, often dirty, with a short erectile crest over forehead, blue fleshy patch below eye, and small pink patch in front of eye (see Long-billed Corella). Pink bases of throat feathers can be seen as bird preens. Beak whitish, shorter than Long-billed, except in race *pastinator* of extreme southwest of Western Australia which has recently been accepted as a separate species (Bare-eyed or Western Corella). In flight, shows yellow underwings and yellow below tail. Flight fast, like a pigeon. Often gregarious, sometimes in huge flocks. *Voice:* noisy, high-pitched 'wuk-wuk-wuk' like Long-billed. *Habitat:* open land, watercourses, grassland, crops, bushes and scrub of all descriptions, including mangroves; but always near water. Discontinuously and erratically distributed. Locally common, often abundant. ⨪ ≋ ♙ ⦀ ≋ ⨪ △ ®

Gang-gang Cockatoo ♂

Gang-gang Cockatoo ♀

Galah

Long-billed Corella

Little Corella

Pink Cockatoo *Cacatua leadbeateri* 33-36cm Large handsome cockatoo. Body pale pink; wings, back and tail white. Head pink, with reddish forehead and upswept crest, white when folded, long and banded with pink and yellow when erect. In flight, rich underwings contrast with white flight feathers; wingbeats rapid, shallow and irregular. Gregarious but only in small groups; often terrestrial, often with Galahs and corellas. *Voice:* shrill quavering calls, harsh screeches. *Habitat:* open land, scrub, mallee and mulga, saltbush, riverine woodland. Widespread but erratic; normally not numerous. ▦ △ ®

Sulphur-crested Cockatoo *Cacatua galerita* 46-50cm Large, conspicuous, familiar, pure-white cockatoo. Body almost entirely white, with indistinct yellow mark behind eye and long, sulphur-yellow crest, slightly upcurved when folded. Beak comparatively compact and black. In flight, shows yellow wash on underwing and at base of tail. Flight distinctive on stiff, rather rounded wings, usually to a flap-flap-glide format. *Voice:* raucous screeches and squawks. *Habitat:* catholic in taste: many types of wooded, scrub and open country. Widespread; generally common, sometimes abundant. ◢ ⬤ ⬛ ⬛ ▦ ⬛ △ ®

Eclectus Parrot *Eclectus roratus* 42cm Large, unmistakable, short-tailed parrot with striking sexual dimorphism. Male bright green, with large orange beak. Flanks scarlet. In flight, blue flight feathers are conspicuous on upperside of wing. Scarlet underwing contrasts with black undersides to flight feathers and tail. Female largely scarlet, with purplish breast and belly, and with large black beak. Wing linings blue; underside of tail orange-scarlet. Immature resembles dull version of adult, with brownish beak. Gregarious and noisy, usually arboreal and conspicuous. *Voice:* harsh screech, often disyllabic. *Habitat:* tropical rainforest and adjacent eucalypt woodland. Restricted, but locally common. ⬛ ▦ ®

Red-cheeked Parrot *Geoffroyus geoffroyi* 22-25cm Medium-sized, compact green parrot. Male has body and short tail bright green; green wings with blue linings visible in flight; purplish-blue crown and striking red face. Beak compact, red above, black below. Female bright green, but with brown head and grey beak. Immature as female but duller: may show traces of adult colour on head. Inconspicuous but noisy canopy feeder, agile, often hanging upside-down off branches or fruits. *Voice:* metallic 'hank', screeches and chatterings. *Habitat:* dense tropical forest and woodland. Restricted, locally quite common. ⬛ ®

Pink Cockatoo

Sulphur-crested Cockatoo

Eclectus Parrot ♂

Eclectus Parrot ♀

Red-cheeked Parrot ♂

Red-cheeked Parrot ♀

Rainbow Lorikeet *Trichoglossus haematodus* 25-30cm Medium-large, long-tailed, colourful and familiar. Back and long tail bright green; nape yellow; crown and face blue, with compact scarlet beak. Breast reddish orange, shading to yellow on flanks; belly blue, undertail coverts yellowish green. Immature duller with blackish beak. In flight, fast-flying with rapid shallow wingbeats; shows red wing lining and narrow yellow wingbar on underside of wing. *Voice:* almost continuous screeching and chattering. *Habitat:* rainforest, eucalypt forest and woodland; sometimes scrub, gardens. Widespread but discontinuous; generally fairly common.
🦆 🦆 🏞 🏕 ⚘ 🌲 🏖 Ⓡ

Red-collared Lorikeet *Trichoglossus rubritorquis* 27-30cm Often regarded as a subspecies of Rainbow, which it replaces in the north. Back and tail bright green, mantle blue; nape, collar and breast orange; crown and face blue, with compact red beak. Belly band black; undertail coverts golden yellow. Immature duller, with blackish beak. Flight fast, with shallow wingbeats; shows broad yellow bar on underside (see Rainbow). *Voice:* continuous screeching and chattering. *Habitat:* forests of most types. Replaces Rainbow in central northern areas; generally fairly common.
⚘ 🌲 △ Ⓡ

Scaly-breasted Lorikeet *Trichoglossus chlorolepidotus* 23cm Medium-sized, green-headed lorikeet. Predominantly bright green plumage, with scaly yellow markings on collar and sides of breast and flanks. Beak compact, red. Immature has less yellow in duller green plumage; beak brown. In flight, shows orange-red underwings. *Voice:* high-pitched continuous screeching and chattering. *Habitat:* usually coastal forests and woodland, occasionally in cities and suburbs. Discontinuous distribution; generally common, sometimes abundant. 🦆 🦆 ⚘ 🌲 Ⓡ

Varied Lorikeet *Psitteuteles versicolor* 18cm Medium-small, colourful lorikeet. Most of upperparts green, flecked with yellow. Head softly colourful, with scarlet cap, blue nape, yellow cheek patch, green throat and pinkish breast, all subdued by fine white, yellow or green streaks. Distinctive white eye-ring. Flight fast; shows green wing linings contrasting with blackish flight feathers. *Voice:* thin screeches, less strident than other lorikeets. *Habitat:* basically eucalypt and other woodland, but forays some distance in search of suitable trees in bloom. Northern and erratic; locally fairly common.
🏞 ⚘ 🌲 △ Ⓡ

Musk Lorikeet *Glossopsitta concinna* 20-22cm Medium-small, predominantly green, sturdily-built lorikeet. Back and tail rich green, underparts bright green, yellow on sides of breast. Forehead red, crown blue-green. Red cheek patch, leading to distinctive brownish nape and mantle. Beak red above, black below. Female duller; immature appreciably so. Gregarious, associating with various other parrots. In flight, shows comparatively stumpy wedge-shaped tail, pale green underwing and some red on underside of tail feathers. *Voice:* metallic, high-pitched screeches and chattering. *Habitat:* woodland and forest, often hilly, shelter belts, riverine woodland. Widely distributed; erratic in both numbers and location, but sometimes locally common. 🦆 🦆 ⚘ Ⓡ

Rainbow Lorikeet

Red-collared Lorikeet

Scaly-breasted Lorikeet

Varied Lorikeet ♂

Musk Lorikeet

Purple-crowned Lorikeet *Glossopsitta porphyrocephala* 16cm

Small, blue-breasted lorikeet. Nape, mantle, back, wings and tail bright green. Forehead orange; small purple crown patch. Orange-yellow spot on cheeks. Beak compact, all black. Throat, breast and upper belly pale blue, rest of belly and undertail coverts pale green. Often with other lorikeets. Comparatively quiet and inconspicuous moving about in the canopy. In flight, shows unexpected crimson flanks and underwings, and relatively stubby wedge-shaped tail. *Voice:* characteristic thin 'zit' or 'zit-zit', calls often in flight. *Habitat:* woodland and scrub, particularly mallee. Discontinuous distribution; erratic, generally fairly common but locally abundant. ♨ ⅷ ®

Little Lorikeet *Glossopsitta pusilla* 16cm

Small, red-faced lorikeet. Body generally bright green, yellow on underparts. Nape and mantle brown. Face red, beak compact and black. Immature appreciably duller, with less red on face. Inconspicuous in foliage, often feeding with other lorikeets. If disturbed, flight fast ('bullet-like') showing pale green underwings. *Voice:* thin, high-pitched, repetitive 'zit' calls, harsher than Purple-crowned. *Habitat:* tall open forests, woodland, plantations; isolated big trees in flower, occasionally suburban street trees. Widespread; generally fairly common but scarcer in southern areas. ♠ ♦ ♨ ®

Double-eyed Fig-Parrot *Cyclopsitta diophthalma* 14cm

Small, plump, spiky-tailed, blue-winged parrot, the smallest of the Australian parrots. Body generally bright green, darker on the back, with yellow flanks and distinctive deep-blue primaries. Large-headed and short-tailed, with a robust pale grey beak with blackish tip. Face patterns are distinctive, but vary with race and sex. Farthest north is *marshalli*: the male has a red forehead and cheeks, with a thin blue lower border; female a blue forehead and blue-bordered white cheeks. Next southwards is *macleayana*: male with red and blue forehead, and red cheeks with a broad blue border; female with red and blue forehead, and blue-bordered grey-brown cheeks. Farthest south is *coxeni*: male with a predominantly blue forehead and small red cheek patch; female with duller cheeks. Quiet and inconspicuous in canopy. *Voice:* thin 'zeet-zeet'. *Habitat:* rainforest and other stands of timber. Generally uncommon and local. ⅷ ⅷ ®

Australian King Parrot *Alisterus scapularis* 42cm

Large, distinctive, broad-tailed parrot with striking sexual dimorphism. Male diagnostically has plain scarlet head and body. Wings dark green with paler band; rump dark blue; distinctive long broad tail bluish black. Beak compact, red above, black below. Female predominantly green, with scarlet belly and undertail coverts. Wary. Flight strong but erratic, long 'heavy' tail prominent. *Voice:* metallic 'chack chack' or 'carrack carrack'. *Habitat:* forest and woodland of most sorts, especially if damp, and surrounding plantations, farmland, gardens. Fairly widespread, but erratic in distribution and numbers; only locally common. ♠ ♦ ♨ ⅼ ®

Purple-crowned Lorikeet

Little Lorikeet

Double-eyed Fig-Parrot (race *macleayana*) ♂

Australian King Parrot ♂

Australian King Parrot ♀

Red-winged Parrot *Aprosmictus erythropterus* 32cm Medium-large parrot. Strikingly coloured male has bright green head and underparts, with black back, purple and yellow rump, and longish green tail with yellow tip. Wings greenish, with distinctive large scarlet shoulder patch. Female predominantly green, with blue rump and yellow-tipped tail and prominent broad scarlet stripe on wing. Beak compact, reddish. Wary. Distinctive erratic and laboured flight. Noisy. *Voice:* metallic 'ching ching' or 'crilling, crilling', screeches. *Habitat:* open woodland of many types, mulga, mangroves, plantations. Widespread; in places erratic, but quite common in main range. ♨♨ ⁞⁞⁞⁞ △®

Superb Parrot *Polytelis swainsonii* 38cm Large, graceful, long-tailed green parrot. Most of body brilliant green, duller in female. Male has striking yellow forehead and throat, with a scarlet band across the lower throat. Female head all-green. Beak compact, pinkish red. Immature as female. Flight distinctive, fast, with long slender tail and swept-back, falcon-like wings. *Voice:* 'currack, currack', not harsh. *Habitat:* open forest and woodland, riverine or on flood plains, adjacent farmland. Note restricted distribution; erratic but locally quite common. Beware aviary escapes. ↬ ♨♨ ®

Regent Parrot *Polytelis anthopeplus* 40cm Large, slim, distinctive golden yellow and green, long-tailed parrot. Male very distinctive, predominantly golden canary yellow, with deep blue-black flight feathers and long tail. Wings have golden shoulders and narrow red bar. Female largely yellowish green; wings and tail similar to male but less bright. Immature duller still. Beak compact, reddish. Feeds on ground or in foliage. Flight fast, falcon-like, with distinctive long tail. *Voice:* harsh 'currack, currack'. *Habitat:* varied woodlands (especially red river gum and black box) and nearby farmland and plantations. Split distribution: occasional in southeast; more widespread and often common in southwest. ↬ ♨♨ ⁞⁞⁞⁞ △®

Alexandra's Parrot *Polytelis alexandrae* 35-45cm Large, subtly pastel-coloured long-tailed parrot of arid habitats. Male substantially larger than female. Upperparts soft olive-green, with bluish lavender crown, blue rump and green tail shading to blue at tip. Wings green, with bright golden shoulders. Throat pink; breast and belly grey-buff delicately shaded blue. Undertail black, feathers with distinctive pink margins. Compact pink beak. Female and immature rather duller. Flight distinctive and undulating, unhurried, long tail prominent. Feeds on ground and in foliage. *Voice:* described as a prolonged rolling chatter, 'queet' in alarm. *Habitat:* arid shrublands, especially mulga, *Spinifex* country with desert oaks. Often far from water. Range poorly known: erratic in distribution and numbers; generally rare. ⁞⁞⁞⁞ ♨♨ ▭▭ △®

Cockatiel *Leptolophus hollandicus* 32cm Medium-sized grey and white long-tailed parrot, sadly familiar as a cage bird. Male has dark-grey body contrasting with broad white shoulder patch and with bright yellow face and throat with a scarlet cheek patch. Distinctive long yellowish-grey crest. Female much duller, with little yellow on head and fainter cheek patch. Beak small, compact, blackish. Feeds largely on the ground, often gregarious and often with other parrots. *Voice:* gives warning of presence; rolling 'weeron, weeron', sharp 'queel'. *Habitat:* open land, scrub, farmland, usually basically semi-arid but with nearby water. Widespread; erratic, occasionally locally abundant. ↬ ♨♨ ⁞⁞⁞⁞ ▭▭ △®

Red-winged Parrot ♂

Superb Parrot ♂

Regent Parrot ♂

Alexandra's Parrot ♂

Cockatiel ♂

Ground Parrot *Pezoporus wallicus* 30cm Medium-sized, green, long-tailed and secretive, largely terrestrial parrot. Upperparts rich green, streaked black; underparts yellower green, with soft blackish barring. Tail long, green, faintly barred yellower. Forehead red, but inconspicuous. Beak small and dark. Spends much time in cover. Flight is distinctive: fast and low, with glides on downcurved wings, and sudden jinks in direction like a snipe. Shows yellowish wingbar. *Voice:* at dawn and dusk, three or four bell-like 'tee' notes in measured time, sometimes accelerating and ascending in pitch. *Habitat:* coastal heaths, densely vegetated swampy areas, button-grass plains in Tasmania. Poorly known discontinuous distribution; local, generally scarce or rare, threatened. ▥ ▦ ▰▰ ®

Night Parrot *Pezoporus occidentalis* 23cm Medium-small, dumpy, large-headed terrestrial parrot. Upperparts green, streaked black, with medium-long dark-barred green tail. Underparts yellower, black-barred on breast but brighter and clearer on belly. Lacks red forehead. Terrestrial, secretive and largely nocturnal. *Voice:* reported as strange croak of alarm and a harsh double note. *Habitat:* arid interior plains with saltbush or *Triodea*. Range and distribution imperfectly known; certainly very rare, in all probability threatened. Several reliable and possible sightings in recent years, including a road-killed specimen. ▥ ▰▰ ▱▱ △ ®

Budgerigar *Melopsittacus undulatus* 18cm Small, slim, most familiar of the world's parrots; a common cage and aviary bird. Upperparts yellowish brown, densely marked and speckled blackish; underparts bright green. Tail long, slim and blackish. Head and throat distinctively yellow, finely barred with black on crown and nape, with blue moustachial patch and 'necklace' of black spots. Male has blue cere, female brown. Immature duller, shorter-tailed, more heavily barred. Gregarious. Flight fast, undulating. *Voice:* musical chirruping, highly vocal. *Habitat:* often arid or semi-arid open plains, farmland, open woodland and light scrub. Widespread; but erratic in numbers and distribution. Often very common. ▰▰ ▥ ▰▰ ▱▱ △ ®

Swift Parrot *Lathamus discolor* 24cm Medium-sized, slim and lorikeet-like. Upperparts bright green; underparts yellower; tail distinctively long and slim, dark red. Wings dark green, with red tips to secondaries showing in closed wing. Head pattern characteristic, with red forehead, blue crown, red throat edged yellow. Beak small, brownish; eye bright yellow. Flocks fly fast through woodland, calling characteristically and showing striking red wing linings contrasting with blackish undersides to flight feathers. *Voice:* high-pitched chattering 'clink clink...', repeated piping 'pee-pit'. *Habitat:* open forest and woodland, plantations, parks and gardens. Breeds Tasmania, migrates to southeast. Often common. ▰ ▰ ▰▰ ▥ ▮ ®

Red-capped Parrot *Purpureicephalus spurius* 36cm Large, rather gaudy parrot with long, relatively broad tail. Back and tail bright emerald green; rump lime-yellow; wings green with dark bluish flight feathers. Breast and belly purple; undertail coverts scarlet. Head with dark red crown and nape, with distinctive yellow face and throat. Beak grey, comparatively long and curved. Female duller than male. Immature has brownish-grey breast, and yellow margins to feathers beneath tail. Flight undulating, relatively weak and fluttery. *Voice:* grating 'checkacheck' or 'shrek'. *Habitat:* forest and woodlands, orchards, parks and gardens. Restricted, but locally common. ▰ ▰ ▰▰ ®

Ground Parrot

Night Parrot

Budgerigar

Swift Parrot

Red-capped Parrot ♂

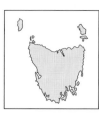

Green Rosella *Platycercus caledonicus* 36cm Large broad-tailed parrot, restricted to Tasmania and the Bass Strait islands. Adult has crown, nape, breast, belly and undertail coverts rich yellow, with a red forehead and grey-blue throat patch. Upperparts dark, green mottled black, with dark blue shoulders and edges to the closed wing. Tail dark green with pale blue margins. Female slightly smaller and duller than male; immature appreciably duller and more olive above and below. Often in groups. Flight fast and direct, often high overhead when yellow underparts are conspicuous. *Voice:* characteristic loud 'cussick, cussick' flight calls, softer bell-like calls when perched. *Habitat:* catholic, from gardens and farmlands to dense montane forest. Widespread, often common. ▲ ▲ 🚜 ®

Crimson Rosella *Platycercus elegans* 36cm Large broad-tailed parrot, conspicuous and familiar in the east and southeast. Adult predominantly deep crimson, heavily mottled black on back, with blue throat/cheek patch, blue shoulder to the wing and blue-green tail. Southeast Australian immature strikingly different, with golden-olive body, crimson forehead, breast and undertail; elsewhere, immature similar to adult but duller. Race *flaveolus* adults (Murray/Darling basin) have crimson replaced with golden yellow, with a red forehead; immature plumage golden-olive. Races *subadelaidae* and *adelaidae* ('Adelaide Rosella') have orange-yellow in place of crimson in both adult and immature. Often seen in groups. Flight fast and swooping, often with deep 'slow motion' wingbeats. *Voice:* bell-like 'klee klee-klee', metallic repeated 'klee' in flight. *Habitat:* catholic, from gardens and farmlands to forest and watercourse *Eucalyptus* stands. Widespread, often common. ▲ ▲ 🚜 ⚎ ®

Eastern Rosella *Platycercus eximius* 31cm Medium-sized, distinctively colourful, broad-tailed parrot. Adult has crimson head and upper breast, white throat and cheeks, and bright greenish-yellow underparts. Back gold, heavily mottled black; rump greenish yellow, a good flight characteristic; wings blue with black shoulders. Female slightly less colourful than male; immature appreciably drabber but with the same basic colours. Often in groups. Flight deeply undulating. *Voice:* high-pitched 'pink pink' in flight, slow mellow piping 'pee-peeee' elsewhere. *Habitat:* often associated with man; gardens, parks, crops and open woodlands. Widespread, often common. ▲ ▲ ⚎ ®

Pale-headed Rosella *Platycercus adscitus* 30cm Medium-sized broad-tailed parrot with a characteristic pale-headed appearance. Adult variable, but usually with white or pale yellow head, small blue-grey bib, yellow breast, pale blue belly and red undertail coverts. Southern birds may lack blue bib and have all-blue-grey underparts. Back yellowish, heavily mottled black; rump blue-grey. Immature duller. Female and immature may show some red patches on body. Often in groups. Flight deeply undulating. *Voice:* sharp 'krik krik' in flight, high-pitched 'pee pee pee' elsewhere. *Habitat:* farmland, open woodlands, scrublands. Widespread, often common. ▲ ⚎ 🏭 ®

Green Rosella ♂

Crimson Rosella (race *elegans*) ♂

Crimson Rosella (race *flaveolus*) ♂

Crimson Rosella (race *adelaidae*) ♂

Eastern Rosella ♂

Pale-headed Rosella ♂

Northern Rosella *Platycercus venustus* 29cm Medium-large, distinctively black-hooded, rosella. Back black with broad yellow feather margins giving scaly appearance; breast, belly and rump yellow, finely barred with grey. Wings predominantly blue. Tail long, broad, greenish-blue; undertail coverts scarlet. Hood conspicuous, extending below eye, black with red flecks. Throat white. Beak comparatively small, whitish. Immature duller, with more red flecks. Usually in small flocks, feeds on ground and in trees. *Voice:* quick-fire high-pitched chattering. *Habitat:* open woodland, scrub, clearings, riverine woodland, usually near water. Restricted, and generally not common. 🚜 🚶 ®

Western Rosella *Platycercus icterotis* 26cm Smallest rosella, and distinctive. Adult male scarlet, with diagnostic yellow cheek patches; back heavily mottled black. Wings greenish with blue shoulders. Female dark olive green above, with obscure yellow cheek patch; forehead red. Underparts reddish, with green or gold feather fringes. Immature brighter green, but with less red on underparts. Often in pairs or small groups, comparatively quiet and tame. Flight direct, but at gentle speeds; immature and female show faint wingbar. *Voice:* soft 'chink chink'. *Habitat:* farmland, open woodlands, gardens. Sometimes quite common. 🚜 🚶 ®

Mallee Ringneck *Barnardius barnardi* 33cm Large, colourful, bulky-tailed parrot. Now officially merged with Ringneck. Pale green body and blue shoulders contrast with distinctive dark blue-grey mantle. Reddish patch in centre of belly. Head shows red forehead, green crown and characteristic ringneck bright yellow collar mark. Female and immature duller. Beak compact but robust, whitish. Northern race *macgillivrayi* is smaller, yellower, and lacks red forehead. *Voice:* metallic 'kling kling kling', and repeated 'put-kleep'. *Habitat:* semi-arid scrub including mallee and mulga and woodland of varied types, farmlands. Widespread; often quite common. 🚜 🚶 🚜 △®

Ringneck *Barnardius zonarius* 36cm Large, robust and distinctive parrot. Generally similar to Mallee Ringneck: green above and below, but with a yellow belly (not reddish patch) and with a characteristic black hood, bluish on cheeks contrasting with yellow collar. Race *semitorquatus* from Western Australia has small red forehead patch, all-green belly and distinctive 'twenty-eight' call. Beak comparatively robust, whitish. Immature has duller plumage, browner head. Flight strong, sometimes with exaggerated deep 'slow-motion' wingbeats. Often visits crops, can be damaging. *Voice:* usually ringing repeated 'kling'. *Habitat:* catholic in choice, ranging from forest through scrub to farmland, including semi-arid areas but usually near water. Widespread, sometimes fairly common. 🚜 🚶 🚜 △®

Northern Rosella ♂

Western Rosella ♂

Western Rosella ♀

Mallee Ringneck ♂

Ringneck (race *semitorquatus*) ♂

Red-rumped Parrot *Psephotus haematonotus* 27cm Medium-small

long-tailed parrot. Male has upperparts bright green, with green breast and bright yellow belly. Long tail green above, grey below. Wings green, with yellow shoulder mark and dark blue flight feathers. Brick-red lower back and rump prominent and distinctive in flight. Female more olive-green, with green rump. Immature duller. Usually feeds on ground. Flight fast and undulating. *Voice:* warbling song, unusual among parrots; in flight disyllabic whistling 'chee-chlip'. *Habitat:* open woodland, scrub, farmland, usually not far from water. Quite widespread; generally quite common and perhaps increasing in numbers and extending range. 🐦 ♙♙ ⵊⵊⵊ ♙♙ ®

Mulga Parrot *Psephotus varius* 28cm Medium-small, brilliantly

coloured, lorikeet-like parrot. Male slim, largely emerald green, with scarlet thighs and lower belly. Wings green with bright yellow bar; flight feathers dark blue. Forehead distinctively yellow. Small reddish patch on nape, and on rump (best seen in flight). Female duller green, with obscure head markings. Lacks scarlet on thighs but has dark crimson shoulder stripe on wing. Immature drabber still. Usually in small groups, feeding on ground or in trees. Flight fast, with bursts of wingbeats preceding deep swoops with wings closed. *Voice:* characteristic repeated 'swit', various rather fluty calls. *Habitat:* arid and semi-arid shrubland, including mallee and mulga, saltbush, but rarely far from water. Widespread, but erratic, only locally fairly common. ⵊⵊⵊ △®

Golden-shouldered Parrot *Psephotus chrysopterygius* 26cm

Medium-small, slim, turquoise parrot. Male has brown back and wings with striking golden shoulder patches and dark flight feathers. Rump turquoise-green; tail dark grey. Forehead pale yellow; crown and nape characteristically black. Face green, shading into turquoise throat, breast and belly. Lower belly, thighs and undertail coverts reddish, with yellow feather fringes. Female generally dull yellow-green, lacking golden shoulder, and shaded browner on crown and nape. Rump and underparts pale blue or greenish blue, with traces of red on lower belly. Immature similar, but with darker brownish crown. Usually as pairs or small groups, feeding on ground. *Voice:* various chirrups and soft fluting whistles. *Habitat:* open woodland and scrub, characteristically with termite mounds; occasionally mangroves. Restricted, only locally common, perhaps threatened. ♙♙ ⵊⵊⵊ ®

Hooded Parrot *Psephotus dissimilis* 26cm Medium-small, rather

similar to Golden-shouldered. Male has brown back and nape, with black limited to crown (see Golden-shouldered). Wings brown, with darker flight feathers and extensive striking golden shoulder patches. Rump bluish; tail blue-green. Face, breast and belly turquoise; lower belly, thighs and undertail coverts brick red with pale scalloping. Female as female Golden-shouldered, but with salmon-pink lower belly and undertail coverts. Usually feeds on ground. Flight fast and undulating, shows distinctive contrast between dark head and back and golden forewings. *Voice:* sharp 'chissick'. *Habitat:* dry open woodland, *Spinifex* scrub, rocky grassland, often with termite mounds and usually near water. Restricted and rare. ♙♙ ⵊⵊⵊ ®

Red-rumped Parrot ♂

Mulga Parrot ♂

Golden-shouldered Parrot ♂

Hooded Parrot ♂

Hooded Parrot ♀

Paradise Parrot *Psephotus pulcherrimus* 28cm Medium-sized, beautifully coloured, long-tailed parrot. Male has scarlet forehead, black crown and nape, brown wings with scarlet shoulder patches and deep blue flight feathers, blue rump and blue-green tail. Face green, shading to turquoise on breast,=; bluer on belly, with scarlet lower belly and undertail coverts. Female duller and paler, but generally similarly coloured. Immature even duller. *Voice:* recorded as repeated sharp musical whistling 'queek'. *Habitat:* grassy open eucalypt woodland, usually with termite mounds. Distribution was restricted, now at least extremely rare, sadly but perhaps probably extinct. ♨♨ ⦿ ®

Blue Bonnet *Northiella haematogaster* 28cm Medium-large and distinctively coloured parrot. Upperparts characteristically pale grey-brown, with a blue or purplish blue face and forehead. Breast pale grey brown; belly yellow with scarlet patch between legs; undertail coverts golden yellow. Wings vary with race, from brown with blue shoulders to brown with large red and green shoulder patches, always with dark blue flight feathers. Tail long, slim, pale grey. Fast erratic flight on whirring, shallow-beating wings. Usually feeds on ground. *Voice:* harsh 'jack, jacka-jack', piping whistles. *Habitat:* open woodlands and scrub of many types, saltbush, crops, grassland. Discontinuous but quite widespread; locally fairly common. ♨♨ ⦿ △ ®

Bourke's Parrot *Neopsephotus* 19cm Medium-small, unusually-coloured, long-tailed parrot. Body distinctively pinkish brown with scaly markings, becoming reddish-pink on belly. Lower belly, thighs and undertail coverts deep blue. Forehead blue (lacking in female), with white marks above and below eye. Wings blue, with bold yellowish feather fringes giving a marked scaly impression. Immature duller, lacking pink on upper breast. In flight, shows pale blue underwing and flashes of white in outer tail feathers. *Voice:* mellow 'choo-ee' in flight, various twittering calls. *Habitat:* inland semi-arid to arid scrub, particularly mulga. Widespread but erratic across the interior; locally fairly common. ♨♨ ⦿ △ ®

Blue-winged Parrot *Neophema chrysostoma* 22cm Medium-small, often terrestrial, long-tailed grass-parrot. Male olive-green above, and on throat and upper breast. Small yellowish face patch and thin blue forehead line running to eyes. Rest of breast and belly, and undertail coverts, bright yellow. Wings entirely deep royal blue. Tail long, pointed, greenish-blue with yellow outer feathers. Female and immature duller, lacking blue forehead. *Voice:* 'tinkling' double trill 'brrt brrrt', low chattering when feeding. *Habitat:* varied, from open forest and woodland, through heath and scrub communities to coastal dunes and saltmarshes, including grassy paddocks, farmland, gardens. Generally common coastally and in Tasmania, local, usually scarce elsewhere. ♨♨ ⦿ ⛱ ♨ △ ®

Elegant Parrot *Neophema elegans* 22cm Medium-small, long-tailed grass-parrot, easily confused with Blue-winged. Male yellowish green above, with greenish breast and yellower belly. Distinct yellow face patch and blue forehead stripe extending over and past eye. Wing coverts green, with pale blue shoulder; only flight feathers deep blue. Tail bluish, with yellow outer tail feathers. Beak small and dark. Shows golden rump in flight. *Voice:* single brief 'tssit'. Conversational twittering when feeding. *Habitat:* as catholic as Blue-winged. Discontinuous distribution; erratic but sometimes fairly common. ♨♨ ⦿ ®

Paradise Parrot

Blue Bonnet ♂

Bourke's Parrot

Blue-winged Parrot ♂

Elegant Parrot ♂

Rock Parrot *Neophema petrophila* 22cm Medium-small, comparatively dull grass-parrot. Male olive to olive-brown above, and on breast, with deep blue forehead band and dusky indistinct blue face patch. Wing coverts olive, with blue on shoulder and deep blue flight feathers. Long tail blue-green with yellow outer feathers. Beak small and black. Female duller; immature similar but with pinkish beak. Often feeds on ground, flitting along like a finch. If alarmed, lands in upright posture, often on a rock. *Voice:* 'tssit' calls. *Habitat:* rocky islands and coasts, dunes, coastal sands and grassland. Locally quite common. ®

Orange-bellied Parrot *Neophema chrysogaster* 21cm Medium-small, brilliant green, grass-parrot. Male rich bright green above and on breast. Blue forehead band just reaches eye. Yellow face patch indistinctly demarcated. Belly and undertail coverts yellow, with orange central patch and on flanks. Wing coverts green; flight feathers dark blue. Tail green with yellow outer feathers. Beak small and black. Female and immature duller, showing only traces of orange. Looks comparatively dark and heavy in flight. *Voice:* diagnostic metallic buzzing 'zizizizizizi....'. *Habitat:* coastal grass, low scrub, saltmarsh. Breeds Tasmania, migrating north. Restricted, local, and very rare. Probably threatened. ®

Turquoise Parrot *Neophema pulchella* 20cm Medium-small, distinctive grass-parrot. Male bright green above, with blue crown, face and throat. Wing coverts green with characteristic reddish shoulder bar (see Scarlet-chested). Flight feathers deep blue. Rest of underparts rich yellow. Female paler, with white around eye; lacks reddish shoulder to wing; upper breast green, shading to yellow on belly. Immature duller. Long green tail with yellow outer feathers. *Voice:* tinkling double call 'brrrt brrrt' like Blue-winged. *Habitat:* open woodland and scrub of many types. Note distribution compared with Blue-winged. Generally rather rare and local; very occasionally locally common. ®

Scarlet-chested Parrot *Neophema splendida* 20cm Medium-small, the brightest coloured grass-parrot. Male bright green from back of crown to tip of tail, with deep blue face patch, forehead and throat. Wing coverts green with pale blue shoulder; flight feathers dark blue. Upper breast scarlet, shading into bright yellow on belly. Tail long, green with yellow outer feathers. Female and immature duller, with green, not scarlet, breast. Quiet and inconspicuous, flitting along like a finch. *Voice:* quiet twittering. *Habitat:* open eucalypt woodland, mallee, mulga with reasonable herbaceous storey. Relatively widespread but erratic; generally scarce, occasionally locally common. ®

Rock Parrot ♂

Orange-bellied Parrot ♂

Scarlet-chested Parrot ♂

Turquoise Parrot ♂

Scarlet-chested Parrot ♀

Oriental Cuckoo *Cuculus saturatus* 32cm Medium-large, long-tailed, short-legged and rather hawk-like. Adult has grey head, nape, mantle and breast, with long pointed dark-grey wings and long straight-sided tail showing conspicuous white spots on the underside. Belly and undertail coverts white, boldly barred blackish. Eye white, with conspicuous yellow eye-ring. Beak short, pointed and slightly downcurved, blackish yellow at base. Immature brown above with chestnut barring; whitish below with black barring. Legs short, yellow. Distinctive falcon-like flight (see Australian Hobby) but note slightly spoon-ended tail. *Voice:* generally quiet. *Habitat:* open woodland and forests, paddocks with trees. Generally uncommon.
🐾 🐜 ⸙

Pallid Cuckoo *Cuculus pallidus* 33cm Medium-large, pale, slender-tailed cuckoo. Adult pale grey above, with darker wings and tail. Distinctive black mark through eye; pale yellow eye-ring. Underparts white, suffused pale grey, faintly barred blackish on undertail coverts. Tail long, tapered, boldly barred black and white on underside. Legs short, olive-grey. Beak black, downcurved and pointed. On the wing, flight feathers show white spots. Juvenile brown above, heavily barred; pale below. Immature distinctively chequered black-and-white. Flight falcon-like but undulating. *Voice:* familiar accelerating and rising series of notes. Maniacal 'crook-yer' when pursuing female. *Habitat:* open woodland of most types, scrub, paddocks with trees, gardens. Widespread, but in variable numbers, often common. 🦅 🐜 ⸙ 🔺®

Brush Cuckoo *Cacomantis variolosus* 23cm Medium-sized drab cuckoo with distinctive voice. Adult has pale grey head, back, wings and tail, with a greyish throat and pale buffish-grey underparts, richer buff on undertail coverts. Long tail has faint barring and small terminal white spots visible on underside. Immatures rufous and barred. Falcon-like flight, usually between trees. *Voice:* loud, plaintive descending series of 'fear, fear fear....' often seven or eight notes long; mournful 'ther-er-wee' becoming maniacal in courtship chases. *Habitat:* open damp forest and woodland, mangroves, farmland. Regular but in varying numbers; sometimes common.
🐾 🐜 ⸙ ⸙ ⸙ ®

Oriental Cuckoo (adult)

Pallid Cuckoo (adult)

Pallid Cuckoo (immature)

Pallid Cuckoo (juvenile)

Brush Cuckoo (adult)

Chestnut-breasted Cuckoo *Cacomantis castaneiventris* 24cm Medium-sized, dark, distinctive cuckoo. Upperparts dark slate grey, with grey extending below eye. Conspicuous yellow eye-ring. Wings blackish, showing indistinct white wingbar in flight. Tail long, rounded, and barred beneath. Underparts distinctive deep chestnut. Immature brown above; buff below with darker barring. *Voice:* descending weak trill. *Habitat:* rainforest, scrub, mangroves. Restricted and uncommon.

Fan-tailed Cuckoo *Cacomantis flabelliformis* 26cm Medium-large, slim, rather dull-coloured cuckoo. Upperparts darkish grey, with white on shoulder of wing. Tail grey, with white barring, striking on underside. Throat grey-buff, breast and belly richer cinnamon-buff. Eye-ring yellow; beak black, pointed, downcurved and yellow at base. Legs yellow. Immature dark chestnut brown with scaly ginger feather edges, paler beneath tail. Tail brown, heavily barred. Flight undulating, showing white wingbar and white notches on outer tail feathers. *Voice:* plaintive descending trilling 'peeeeer', disyllabic 'ket-urk'. *Habitat:* dense forests and woodlands, sometimes open country with plentiful trees. Reasonably widespread and locally fairly common.

Black-eared Cuckoo *Chrysococcyx osculans* 20cm Medium-small, inconspicuous, but elegantly marked bronze-cuckoo with comparatively short tail. Head pattern characteristic, with brown crown, white stripe over eye, broad curving black patch through eye and onto side of neck, white throat. Beak small, black, slim and pointed, barely downcurved. Upperparts sandy brown with faint iridescent sheen, and with darker flight feathers and tail, distinctly barred white on underside. Underparts fawn to pale apricot, highly barred on undertail coverts. Flight swift and direct, short tail and pale rump prominent. *Voice:* long-drawn-out, mournful, descending 'peeeeeer'. *Habitat:* arid and semi-arid woodland and scrub, including mallee and mulga. Widespread but erratic; generally rare.

Horsfield's Bronze-Cuckoo *Chrysococcyx basalis* 16cm Small, comparatively dull bronze-cuckoo. Upperparts brown or bronze, with greenish metallic lustre rather than gloss. Tail short, greenish, with distinctive rufous-brown outer feathers with white notches. Curving white stripe over eye and down sides of neck; greenish cheek patch. Underparts white, sporadically and incompletely barred brown, with pale central patch. Immature duller and browner above, with fewer bars on greyish underparts. *Voice:* insistent descending 'tsseee-eeuw', repeated often. *Habitat:* open country, light woodland and scrub of most types. Widespread and regular; migrant in south, resident in north.

Shining Bronze-Cuckoo *Chrysococcyx lucidus* 16cm Small, bright, bronze-cuckoo. Most Australian birds are bright metallic green on back, wings and tail, with a copper crown and nape, separated from the eye by a slim, indistinct white supercilium. Underparts white, with relatively broad, regularly arranged and complete bronze bars. Tail short and square, outer feathers broadly barred white on undersides. Immature duller and browner, underpart barring often incomplete. Inconspicuous except when calling. *Voice:* high-pitched firm whistle 'peee, peee, peee', each distinctly rising in tone at end. *Habitat:* forest, denser woodlands and tall dense scrub. Widespread but rather erratic; scarce to locally fairly common.

Chestnut-breasted Cuckoo (adult)

Fan-tailed Cuckoo (adult)

Fan-tailed Cuckoo (immature)

Black-eared Cuckoo (adult)

Horsfield's Bronze-Cuckoo (adult)

Shining Bronze-Cuckoo (adult)

Little Bronze-Cuckoo *Chrysococcyx minutillus* 15cm Small bronze-cuckoo. Generally resembles slightly smaller version of Shining Bronze-Cuckoo, but dark blue-green head contrasts to form almost a cap against back. Shows bold white spotting on undersides of outer tail feathers, and rufous central feathers. Usually shows white face and clear white stripes above and below greenish eye patch. Male has red eye-ring; brown in female. Underparts white, closely and finely marked with brownish-bronze bars, often interrupted. *Voice:* high-pitched descending and accelerating 'see-see-see'. *Habitat:* rainforest, open forest and woodland, sometimes mangroves. Widespread but erratic across the north; locally fairly common. ◣▬ 🦜🏠⚎🎋 ⃒ ®

Gould's Bronze-Cuckoo *Chrysococcyx russatus* 15cm Small, distinctively copper-coloured bronze-cuckoo. Upperparts green, with characteristic coppery or rufous tinge, more marked on back, wings and tail. Flight feathers blackish. Underparts white, washed rich buff on breast, finely and comparatively palely barred bronzy brown. Little evidence of white supercilium. Male has red eye-ring. Immature browner. *Voice:* distinctive descending bubbling trill. *Habitat:* open forests and woodlands, scrub, mangroves, gardens and orchards. Restricted but locally common. ◣▬ 🦜⚎ ®

Common Koel *Eudynamys scolopacea* 42-46cm Large cuckoo with distinctive voice and plumage. Adult male wholly glossy black, with long slightly fanned tail. Eye strikingly red; beak usually blue-grey. Female quite different, equally distinctive, with black cap (and red eye), densely white-spotted brown back, closely barred tail, and rich yellow-buff underparts with small dark bars. Immature as female but duller and greyer. Shy when feeding in canopy but noisy, easily seen in breeding season. *Voice:* unmistakable far-carrying 'ko-eeel', shrill maniacal 'quodel quodel quodel'. *Habitat:* forest, woodlands, well-treed areas of most types. Relatively widespread; locally common. ◢◣ 🦜⚎⚎ ⃒ ®

Channel-billed Cuckoo *Scythrops novaehollandiae* 59-65cm Unmistakable, but hardly cuckoo-like. Generally large and grey, with darker grey faintly barred wings, paler grey underparts faintly barred beneath tail, and a long straight-sided conspicuously dark-barred white-tipped tail. Red fleshy patch at base of beak and round eye. Most striking is the large whitish beak, built on crow or currawong-like proportions. *Voice:* distinctive raucous, shouting 'oik' or 'awk'. *Habitat:* open forests, woodlands, scrub, usually with tall trees. Fairly widespread but generally uncommon except in humid coastal Queensland and NSW. 🦜⚎⚎ ⃒ ®

Pheasant Coucal *Centropus phasianinus* 55-75cm Large, but skulking, more often heard than seen. Head and underparts black (brown when not breeding), with red eye and short, strong, black beak. Long, slightly fanned tail, small head and stubby beak give the appearance of a dark, short-legged pheasant. Back and wings finely mottled and streaked chestnut, black, buff and white. Tail blackish, faintly barred. Female appreciably larger than male. Immature brown, pale fawn below. Runs swiftly but not gracefully; flight heavy and uncertain, flopping noisily into nearest cover. *Voice:* accelerating bass 'poop-poop-poop-poop-bubble' like liquid flowing from a bottle. *Habitat:* thick, usually damp undergrowth, swamps, crops. Fairly widespread; locally quite common. ◢⚎🎋⚎ ®

Little Bronze-Cuckoo (adult)

Gould's Bronze-Cuckoo (adult)

Common Koel ♂

Common Koel ♀

Channel-billed Cuckoo

Pheasant Coucal (adult breeding)

Rufous Owl *Ninox rufa* 44-50cm Large, flat-headed, rich-cinnamon owl. Face brown, as 'spectacle' patches round eyes rather than clearly demarcated facial disc. Eyes yellowish. Upperparts dark reddish brown with indistinct paler barring; underparts rich cinnamon, with dense fine reddish-brown barring. Tail medium length, broadly barred grey and whitish. Female darker than male. Immature has paler underparts. Habits not well known. *Voice:* deep, slow 'hoo-hoo' double hoot. *Habitat:* tropical rainforest, scrub. Restricted and discontinuous distribution; generally local and uncommon. 🐾 ᴍ ®

Powerful Owl *Ninox strenua* 60-66cm A very large greyish owl. Faint double darker facial disc; eyes golden. Upperparts dark brownish grey, with whitish barring and mottling; buffish white below with copious dark brown bold V markings. Tail medium but broad, grey with paler bands. Tarsus unfeathered, yellowish. Immature paler, more heavily barred above, with whitish underparts and crown and dark face. Regular in habits; uses same roosts intermittently for months, even years. Approachable. In flight, wings massive and broad. *Voice:* penetrating deep 'whoo-whoo'. *Habitat:* densely forested hillsides, gullies. Generally uncommon. ᴍ ⁑ ®

Southern Boobook *Ninox novaeseelandiae* 30-36cm Large, variable, but relatively familiar owl, with distinctive racoon-like eye-patches. Face whitish, with double dark patches like spectacles around yellow eyes. Back brown (sandy in some areas) with bold white spots down junction of wing and across shoulders of wing. Breast and belly whitish, varying from lightly to boldly streaked brown or dark brown, often simply whitish in immature. Tends to feed at dusk, round homesteads or in towns, taking insects attracted to lights, using a prominent perch. *Voice:* characteristic and well-known high-pitched 'boo-book' repeated at intervals. *Habitat:* catholic in choice of forest, woodland, farmland, parks, scrub. Widespread; often quite common. 🐾 ᴍ ⁑ ®

Barking Owl *Ninox connivens* 38-43cm Large, robust owl. Face dull brown, with little evidence of facial disc or spectacles, eyes yellow. Adult brown above, with white spots on secondary coverts in wing. Tail medium length with dark barring. Underparts whitish, boldly marked with broad linear brown streaks. Immature paler, more spotted, with pale face giving more emphasis to brown spectacle patches round eyes. Sometimes hunts in daylight. *Voice:* distinctive dog-like 'wook-wook', gradually increasing in tempo and volume. Tremulus scream. *Habitat:* catholic: open forest, woodland, scrub. Fairly widespread but generally uncommon except in northeast and northwest, where more numerous. 🐾 ᴍ ⁑ ®

Rufous Owl

Powerful Owl (adult)

Powerful Owl (immature)

Southern Boobook

Barking Owl

Barn Owl *Tyto alba* 30-36cm Large, cosmopolitan, very pale owl. Facial disc characteristically heart-shaped, white, surrounding large black eyes. Upperparts sandy, beautifully and delicately mottled with pale greys, buffs and browns. Underparts white, with a few sparse darker spots. Legs long; distinctive knock-kneed stance when perching upright on a branch or post. Relatively long-winged when hunting; often 'quarters' the ground, gliding and rocking from side to side like a harrier. Carries legs dangling. *Voice:* thin but penetrating scream. *Habitat:* favours open forests, woodlands, and particularly farmland and grasslands. Widespread, but numbers fluctuate greatly. 🏍️ 👥 👥 △ ®

Masked Owl *Tyto novaehollandiae* 35-50cm The largest *Tyto* owl, typically *Tyto* in shape. Facial disc heart-shaped, usually cinnamon brown, distinctively outlined in black, surrounding dark eyes. Variable, but usually appreciably darker brown above than Barn, but equally finely marked. Underparts also darker, often cinnamon, with faint brown spotting. Birds from the northwest (race *kimberleyi*) may be as pale as Barn. *Voice:* rarely vocal, deep rasping screech. *Habitat:* forest, woodland clearings. Some roost in caves. Widespread except in arid interior; generally scarce but commoner in Tasmania. 👥 👥 👥 ®

Grass Owl *Tyto capensis* 34-37cm Large, slim, *Tyto* owl with terrestrial habits when roosting and nesting. Heart-shaped facial disc buff, with black marks running down from eyes, which are distinctively small. Usually rather darker than Barn Owl with heavy silvery-grey marbling on upperparts, and with noticeably longer legs with the tarsus almost unfeathered and grey. Underparts pale, flushed orange-buff and highly spotted. Perches tall and upright, even more knock-kneed than Barn. Legs dangle and extend well beyond tail in flight. *Voice:* quavering thin whistling screech. *Habitat:* grassy plains, grassy swamps, heaths, sedge and reed beds. Limited by suitable habitat; generally very rare. 👥 👥 △ ®

Sooty Owl *Tyto tenebricosa* 40-47cm Large, dark, greyish *Tyto* owl; rather short-tailed. Facial disc pale grey, heart-shaped, outlined in black, with sooty black areas round each dark eye. Upperparts dark sooty-grey with sparse white or silver speckling, and fine barring on nape and crown. Underparts grey and spotted on breast, becoming plain white on lower belly. Legs long, knock-kneed, white-feathered down to talons. Secretive. *Voice:* descending whistling wheeze; sometimes piercing whistle, strange chirruping calls. *Habitat:* dense rainforest, forests and woodlands, often with gullies. Behaviour little-known. Restricted and scarce generally; perhaps under-recorded. 👥 👥 ®

Lesser Sooty Owl *Tyto multipunctata* 33-37cm Large and dark greyish *Tyto* owl, but appreciably smaller than Sooty. Facial disc heart-shaped, grey; distinctively white near outer rim. Eyes dark, set in sooty patches. Plumage closely similar to Sooty, but heavily speckled on upperparts and more densely dark-barred on lower breast. Appears dumpier than Sooty, often in crouched rather than typical upright *Tyto* posture. Behaviour little-known. *Voice:* high-pitched whistles and chirrups. *Habitat:* dense forests and woodlands. Note range to north of Sooty. Restricted, scarce, perhaps under-recorded. 👥 👥 👥 ®

Barn Owl

Masked Owl (pale form)

Grass Owl

Sooty Owl

Lesser Sooty Owl

Tawny Frogmouth *Podargus strigoides* 35-45cm Large, strangely big-headed, well camouflaged, rather nightjar-like bird. Head large, with a tuft of bristles on forehead. Beak large, opening to an enormous gape. Eyes large and yellow, but often closed in daylight. Plumage usually grey, sometimes rufous on shoulders, finely mottled and streaked with white, buff and black providing excellent camouflage against a branch: often perches upright and motionless, like a broken-off branch. Tail long, rounded. Northern birds are appreciably smaller, and reddish- or chestnut-plumaged forms are sometimes seen. Active at dusk and after. *Voice:* strange persistent 'oom-oom-oom...', often extended. *Habitat:* forests, woodlands, well-treed land, suburban parks and gardens. Widespread; locally common, scarcer in arid habitats. 🐾 ﷽ ⚎ △®

Papuan Frogmouth *Podargus papuensis* 45-56cm Very large frogmouth with long pointed tail. Plumage greyish, richly mottled and streaked with blacks, buffs and white; paler with more rufous markings on underparts. Sometimes shows buff shoulder bar; individuals with more-rufous plumage occur. Beak large, surrounded by feathery bristles, eye red (but often closed in daylight). Habits as Tawny. *Voice:* repeated 'ooms', a ghostly laughing owl-like hoot also reported. *Habitat:* open forest and woodland, riverine woodland, occasionally mangroves. Restricted, generally scarce. 🐾 ﷽®

Marbled Frogmouth *Podargus ocellatus* 40-48cm Large, slim frogmouth with long wedge-shaped tail. Usually rufous-brown above, finely mottled and streaked in buffs, blacks, greys and white and excellently camouflaged. Underparts paler and buffer, equally intricately marked. Beak large, with conspicuous tufts of plume-like bristly feathers. Eye orange, set in dark facial streak with characteristic long buffish-white supercilium above. Some individuals are greyer, some females darker and more rufous, heavily marked. Typical frogmouth habits. *Voice:* monotonous 'coo-loo coo-loo coo-loo...'and 'wok-wok-waddle-waddle-waddle-waddle' *Habitat:* rainforests. Restricted and discontinuous distribution; generally uncommon. 🐾 ﷽®

Australian Owlet-nightjar *Aegotheles cristatus* 21-24cm Medium-sized, looking like a cross between a small owl and a nightjar. Plumage usually darkish grey above, with fine darker markings, and with paler rufous-grey areas in stripe over eye, as cheek patch and as collar marking on nape. Underparts paler, finely barred on breast, almost white on lower belly. Immature browner overall. A rufous form exists with more clearly marked head striping. Beak looks weak and small, but gape large, surrounded by fine bristles. Legs short and feeble, pink. Eyes large and brown. Perches crossways on branches like nightjar. Flight swift and direct, showing long, slightly fanned, tail. *Voice:* penetrating, hard, high-pitched and repetitive 'churr, churr...' *Habitat:* forests, woodlands and scrub, favouring areas with old trees. Widespread, and fairly common in appropriate habitat. 🐾 ﷽ ⚎ △®

Tawny Frogmouth (pale morph) with young

Papuan Frogmouth

Marbled Frogmouth

Australian Owlet-nightjar

White-throated Nightjar *Eurostopodus mystacalis* 33cm Medium-large, the largest and darkest nightjar, typically well camouflaged. Upperparts grey-brown, finely and beautifully mottled and streaked with greys, buffs, browns and black. Greyish stripe over large eye; buffish, speckled, moustachial streak. Two white crescentic marks on throat, usually obscure despite its name. Wings long, dark, rather pointed. Tail long, finely vermiculated above. In flight, looks dark and characteristically shows no white on tail, and only inconspicuous small white tips to the middle primaries. Immature duller and more rufous. Difficult to flush; best seen at dusk. *Voice:* laughing, accelerating series of 'kook' calls, rising in pitch. *Habitat:* open forests and woodlands with rocky ridges and clearings. Eastern, generally scarce but locally commoner in middle of range. 🐾 🐜 🐾®

Spotted Nightjar *Eurostopodus argus* 30cm Medium-large, the most widespread and numerous nightjar. Crown brown, back grey; wings grey brown, finely spotted and streaked grey, black and yellow-buff, giving a grey-backed, buff-winged appearance. Row of bolder spots along closed wing. Underparts grey-brown, equally finely vermiculated. Crescentic white throat patch. In flight, shows clear white patches on undersides of wings at base of primaries, but no white in tail (see Large-tailed). Hunts at dusk; difficult to see at other times. Remains motionless, relying on camouflage, unless almost trodden on. *Voice:* series of 'caw' notes breaking into an accelerating gobbling. *Habitat:* dry forest and woodland with clearings or open ridges; mallee, mulga and semi-desert scrub with stony clearings. Widespread except in extreme east; locally fairly common. 🐾 🏚 🐜 🐾 △®

Large-tailed Nightjar *Caprimulgus macrurus* 27cm Medium-large nightjar with white in tail. Plumage grey-brown, marked and camouflaged much as other nightjars but with grey stripe along scapulars and rows of bold golden-buff spots on wing. Yellowish moustachial streaks, and yellowish crescent on breast below obscure white throat patch. In flight, from beneath shows bold white patches at base of wing primaries, and diagnostic and conspicuous white blocks on either side of tail tip. Hunts at dusk, otherwise difficult to see. *Voice:* distinctive and strange extended series of hollow chopping notes. *Habitat:* tropical forest and woodland clearings and margins. Discontinuous northerly distribution; locally quite common. 🐾 🐜 🐾®

Glossy Swiftlet *Collocalia esculenta* 11cm Small, dark swift with white underside. Typical swift flight silhouette, with long, slim, swept-back wings and fast flight. Upperparts distinctively entirely glossy blue-black; tail only very slightly forked. Throat and breast black; belly distinctively white, becoming flecked black close to dark undertail coverts. *Voice:* soft, twittering calls. *Habitat:* in Australia over coastal hills and offshore islands in northeast. Vagrant. 🕊 🐾 🐜 ❢

White-rumped Swiftlet *Aerodramus spodiopygius* 11cm Small, dark, grey-rumped swift. Typical swift outline in flight, showing sickle-shaped wings, comparatively broad at the base, and shallowly forked tail. Upperparts dull black, with characteristic grey rump, sometimes difficult to see; underparts sooty grey. Gregarious. In flight, swoops and dips more than many swifts, with sudden and erratic changes in direction. *Voice:* high-pitched 'cheer'; in nesting caves clicks characteristically. *Habitat:* breeds in caves in craggy hill and mountain country; in flight over coastal belt of forest, woodland and scrub. Restricted but locally common. 🕊 🐾 🐜 ❢®

White-throated Nightjar

Spotted Nightjar

Large-tailed Nightjar

Glossy Swiftlet

White-rumped Swiftlet

Uniform Swiftlet *Aerodramus vanikorensis* 12cm Small, sooty-brown swift. Uniformly dully plumaged, with rather broad-based wings and a slightly forked tail. Upperparts sooty-brown, with a faint metallic sheen sometimes visible at close range, as may be a slightly paler grey rump and darker tail. Beneath, throat and upper breast look slightly paler than the remainder, given a good view and good light. Other all-dark swiftlets may stray from southeast Asia, so detailed field notes are necessary. *Voice:* quiet twittering. *Habitat:* mountainous, rocky coastal ranges and islands. Vagrant. 🐾🐦🎵

White-throated Needletail *Hirundapus caudacutus* 20cm
Medium-sized, the largest Australian swift. Bulky but as effectively streamlined as a bullet. Wings swept back, broad and long; flight powerful and exceptionally fast on stiff flickering wings, with frequent swooping glides. Upperparts dull brown, darker on crown, with tiny white forehead. Distinctive square-ended tail. Wings show traces of metallic green at close range. Underparts distinctive, with conspicuous white throat and undertail coverts contrasting with dark brown belly. *Voice:* high-pitched chattering. *Habitat:* almost inevitably in the air, over most habitats except desert, but most often over hillsides. Regular migrant; most numerous in southeast. 🐾🐦🎵

Little Swift *Apus affinis* 15cm Small, square-tailed, white-rumped swift. Wings comparatively shorter and broader than most swifts. Upperparts blackish with distinctive rectangular white rump patch. Tail short, slightly notched, black. Underparts blackish. Body appears plumper than Fork-tailed. *Voice:* rattling trill. *Habitat:* aerial, over most habitats. Vagrant. 🐾🎵

Fork-tailed Swift *Apus pacificus* 17cm Medium-small, slim, long-tailed swift with long slim swept-back wings and distinctive long forked tail. Fork may be closed in flight, giving pointed-tail appearance, then fanned open into a clear V when manoeuvring. Overall dark grey-brown (looks blackish) with white rump and whitish throat patch. *Voice:* high-pitched drawn-out vibrating 'dzeeee'. *Habitat:* aerial, over many habitats. Regular; common in places. 🐾🎵

Uniform Swiftlet

White-throated Needletail

Little Swift

Fork-tailed Swift

Azure Kingfisher *Alcedo azurea* 18cm Small and brightly coloured wetland kingfisher. Upperparts deep bright azure blue, with blackish flight feathers. Small white mark on each side of neck, and small usually chestnut patch on forehead. Underparts whitish on throat; rich orange-buff on breast and belly, with smokey shading on flanks. Beak long and black; feet tiny and red. Perches on branches low over water. *Voice:* distinctive shrill 'peet peet', usually in direct, fast whirring flight. *Habitat:* tree-lined rivers, creeks and swamps. Occasionally coastal creeks, mangroves. Easterly distribution; locally common. 🌊 🐟 🦐 🏞 ®

Little Kingfisher *Alcedo pusilla* 12cm Tiny blue-and-white wetland kingfisher. Upperparts metallic deep blue above, with paired buffish forehead spots and white or buff collar marks. Underparts largely white, with variable amounts of blue on flanks. Beak black, looks slightly upturned. Feet minute, black. Young birds duller, with scaly crown. Size, white underparts and habitat are distinguishing features. *Voice:* high-pitched whistle. *Habitat:* coastal creeks with overhanging vegetation, mangroves. Restricted and erratic; only locally quite common. 🌊 🐟 🦐 🏞 ®

Laughing Kookaburra *Dacelo novaeguineae* 45cm Large - the most massive of Australian kingfishers, and the best known. Crown white, smudged and streaked brown, with distinctive dark patch through eye. Back and wings brown, with bluish feather-edges on shoulders. Rump and tail chestnut, barred black. Tail often cocked. Collar and entire underparts white, sometimes faintly barred grey on flanks. Beak long and strong; black above, yellowish below. Flight heavy and direct, showing white patch at base of primaries. *Voice:* famous raucous accelerating laugh, increasing in volume then fading. *Habitat:* open forests and woodland. Eastern and southwestern discontinuous distribution; widespread; locally common. 🌿 🏕 ®

Blue-winged Kookaburra *Dacelo leachii* 40-45cm Large, but slightly smaller than Laughing. Crown white, densely flecked brown; smudgy brown cheek patches. Back brown, with copious blue in wings apart from blackish primaries. Rump and tail azure blue in male; tail chestnut barred black in female. Underparts white, faintly but copiously buff-barred. Beak long and strong, grey above, yellowish below. Immature paler, feathers with buff fringes. *Voice:* noisy, poorly-formed cacophony of harsh cackles and screeches. *Habitat:* open woodland, forest, swamps. Northerly discontinuous distribution; locally fairly common. 🌿 🌊 🏕 ®

Azure Kingfisher

Little Kingfisher

Laughing Kookaburra

Blue-winged Kookaburra ♀

Forest Kingfisher *Todiramphus macleayii* 20cm Medium-sized, blue-and-white forest kingfisher. Back greenish blue; wings and tail metallic dark blue; male has white collar and dark blue crown, merging into black eye-patch; female has blue nape. Paired white spots on forehead. Underparts white. Wings show bold white patches at base of primaries in flight. Beak long, with upturned lower mandible, brownish-grey, paler at base. Immature duller, with pale feather fringes. *Voice:* harsh, high-pitched rattling trill; metallic 'kree kree kree'. *Habitat:* open forest and woodland, wooded swamps, mangroves. Northeastern distribution; widespread, generally scarce. 🌊🦅🐟🐦🏞️🦎🕯️®

Red-backed Kingfisher *Todiramphus pyrrhopygius* 20cm Medium-sized, green-backed forest kingfisher. Back and tail pale greenish-blue, rump distinctively chestnut. Crown white, densely streaked green and black. Broad black stripes through eye extend to meet on nape. Underparts entirely white. Beak grey at tip, paler at base. Female duller than male. Perches conspicuously, often on wires, often in surprisingly open country. *Voice:* mournful whistling 'peel', noisy chattering. *Habitat:* inland open woodlands, scrub, plains, even arid *Spinifex* regions. Widespread, but erratic and generally uncommon. 🦎🏞️△®

Sacred Kingfisher *Todiramphus sanctus* 22cm Medium-sized, dark-capped, green and yellow forest kingfisher. Crown blue-green, with broad black bands through eyes meeting on nape, and creamy white collar. Small paired buff patches on forehead. Back and rump metallic greenish blue; wings and tail bluer. Throat white, rest of underparts yellow-buff. Female duller and greener than male. Immature markedly scaly. *Voice:* distinctive and familiar loud four-note 'dek dek dek dek'; musical rising trill. *Habitat:* open forest and woodland, often near water; streamsides, occasionally coastal creeks and mangroves. Widespread and regular, except in arid interior. 🦅🐟🐦🦎🏞️🕯️△®

Collared Kingfisher *Todiramphus chloris* 27-29cm Medium-large wetland kingfisher, a larger, greener version of Sacred, often appropriately called Mangrove Kingfisher. Crown green, with paired white forehead patches. Broad black bands through eyes meet on nape to emphasize capped appearance. Collar and underparts white. Beak long and distinctively heavy, dark above, yellowish at base of lower mandible. Back, wings and rump metallic emerald green, with bluer tail and blue-black flight feathers. Immature paler and scaly. *Voice:* measured, repetitive 'kek kek' rising on second note; also loud 'pewkee pewkee'. *Habitat:* mangroves, tidal creeks, harbours and jetties. Strictly coastal distribution, mostly north of Tropic, but usually common in appropriate habitat. 🦅🐟🐦🕯️®

Forest Kingfisher

Red-backed Kingfisher ♂

Sacred Kingfisher ♂

Collared Kingfisher ♂

Yellow-billed Kingfisher *Syma torotoro* 19cm Medium-sized, green and ginger, yellow-beaked forest kingfisher. Crown crested, pale ginger in male, ginger with black central stripe in female. Black patch on nape. Upperparts and wings soft greenish-blue, with rich blue tail. Throat white, rest of underparts ginger or cinnamon-buff, paler and yellower on belly. Legs and feet tiny and yellow; beak yellow, with black line on ridge of upper mandible. *Voice:* rising trilling but mournful whistle. *Habitat:* tropical forest and woodland margins and clearings. Restricted to extreme northeast on Cape York Peninsula; locally common. 🐾 ®

Buff-breasted Paradise-Kingfisher *Tanysiptera sylvia* 30-35cm including very long tail. Distinctive, medium-sized and beautiful forest kingfisher. Cap purple, bordered by broad black stripes through eyes, meeting on nape. Back white, with black margins. Wings black and purplish blue on shoulders; flight feathers black. Underparts entirely striking rich orange-yellow; beak characteristically scarlet. Rump and immensely long filamentous central tail feathers white. Remaining tail feathers greenish blue. Tends to raise tail vertically on returning to perch. Immature duller, with short tail and all-black beak. *Voice:* ascending rattling trill. *Habitat:* rainforest with clearings and termite mounds suitable for nest burrows. Restricted range; only locally common. 🐾 🌿 ®

Common Paradise-Kingfisher *Tanysiptera galatea* 38cm Distinctive, medium-sized, blue and white forest kingfisher with a very long tail. Crown glossy metallic blue with black cheeks; back deep blue, rump white; central tail feathers elongated, blue with spatulate white tips. Wings metallic blue and black on shoulders, secondaries rich metallic blue, primaries black. Underparts entirely white. Beak pinkish-red, black in immatures, which also lack elongated tail feathers. *Voice:* noisy rattling slow-speed trill. *Habitat:* tropical forests. Potential vagrant. 🐾

Rainbow Bee-eater *Merops ornatus* 27cm including tail. Medium-sized, slim and colourful, appropriately known as 'rainbow bird'. Upperparts show green forehead, golden crown, green back; blue, green and chestnut wings. Tail black with elongated blob-ended wire-like central pair of feathers, shorter in female than male, lacking in immature. Underparts greenish turquoise, bluer beneath tail. Throat yellow, bordered black; broad black eye-stripe. Beak relatively long, slim, downcurved. Flight like a large swallow, wings harlequin above, golden beneath. *Voice:* distinctive metallic 'pirr', often repeated, usually in flight. *Habitat:* widespread in open country; needs sandy banks or cuttings to excavate nest burrows. Generally quite common. 🪨🌊🦎🦅🏕️🏛️🚜🚃 🌿 △®

Dollarbird *Eurystomus orientalis* 28-30cm Medium-large, stocky and sombre, often using prominent perches. Head dull brownish; back greenish-blue; tail blue-green with broad but obscure dark terminal band. Wings turquoise green on shoulders; flight feathers dark blue, with conspicuous and distinctive white spot (the 'dollar') at base of primaries. Throat blue with lilac streaks; rest of underparts greenish-blue. Beak short but strong, slightly hooked, broad and bright red. Legs red. Immature generally brownish-grey, with wingspot; beak and legs grey. Flight swooping and floppy. *Voice:* rasping, harsh and accelerating 'kak kak kak....'. *Habitat:* open forest and woodland, riverine woodland, suburbs with large trees. Widespread and regular migrant to east and north, but usually in small numbers. 🪨🚜🏛️ 🌿 △®

Yellow-billed Kingfisher ♂

Buff-breasted Paradise-Kingfisher

Common Paradise-Kingfisher

Rainbow Bee-eater

Dollarbird

Red-bellied Pitta *Pitta erythrogaster* 18cm Medium-small, colourful, long-legged, dumpy and 'tail-less'. Crown and face deep purplish brown; nape dull red, back green. Wings green with blue flight feathers. Underparts characteristic, with black-bordered metallic blue breast band and red lower breast and belly. Beak short and pointed. In flight, dark underwing shows small white patch at base of primaries. Immature appreciably duller. Secretive, but noisy. *Voice:* harsh 'craah', mournful whistle. *Habitat:* dense tropical forests and scrub. Restricted to Cape York Peninsula: probably uncommon but poorly known. 🐾 🌿 ⑂ ®

Blue-winged Pitta *Pitta moluccensis* 18cm Medium-small, colourful pitta. Typical long-legged, 'tail-less' appearance. Head distinctive: boldly marked with white throat, black eye-stripe and black and buff striped crown. Back and wings emerald green, with bright blue shoulders and blackish flight feathers. Stumpy tail blue-green. Underparts rich buff, reddish under tail. Said to fly more readily than other pittas, but still difficult to see. *Voice:* terse three-note whistle. *Habitat:* rainforest. Vagrant. 🌿

Noisy Pitta *Pitta versicolor* 20cm Medium-small, dark-headed, pale-breasted pitta. Hood black, with dark chestnut crown. Back brilliant green, yellower on rump. Wings green with bright metallic pale blue shoulder bar. Underparts rather mustard-yellow, reddish below tail with black patch between legs. Noisy mover through leaf litter, standing upright on long legs, flicking stubby tail. White patches prominent in wings in flight. Uses regular 'anvil' stones to smash open snail shells. *Voice:* three-note whistle (quoted as 'walk-to-work'). *Habitat:* rainforest and other dense tropical woodland and scrub. Most widely distributed Australian pitta by far; locally fairly common. 🐾 🌿 〰 ®

Rainbow Pitta *Pitta iris* 17cm Medium-small, dark-fronted pitta. Hood, breast and belly black, with dark chestnut stripes on crown. Undertail coverts contrastingly red. Back brilliant green; wings green with bright pale blue bar on shoulder. White spot on underwing visible in flight. *Voice:* double or triple plain soft whistle. *Habitat:* dense forest and scrub, usually near coast, occasionally mangroves. Note distribution. Locally common. 🐾 🌿 〰 ®

Albert's Lyrebird *Menura alberti* 65-90cm, male with much longer tail than female. Unmistakable long-legged chicken-like bird, with dark brown back and brownish chestnut wings. Underparts pale grey-brown. Female tail long and broad, male long, broad and drooping, amazing when fanned in display, feathers mostly long, lacey and filamentous, the two central feathers broad and brown. Spectacular display on regularly used, twiggy mound. *Voice:* powerful and ringingly musical, full of mimicry. *Habitat:* dense subtropical forest and scrub. Restricted, but locally common. 🐾 🌿 ®

Superb Lyrebird *Menura novaehollandiae* 75-100cm, male with much longer tail than female. More often heard than seen, but unmistakable, chicken-like and long-legged, dark brown above, paler grey beneath. Female tail long, drooping and rather pointed. Male bird with mass of long filamentous plumes, with two broad lyre-shaped feathers, silvery white with pale brown notches on webs. Striking dancing display on regularly used cleared arena is one of the most fabulous of any bird. *Voice:* musical, mellow and far-carrying, containing much mimicry of a wide range of forest birds. Other than in display, uses characteristic 'bilick, bilick' calls. *Habitat:* dense forested slopes and gullies, including ferns. Wider distribution than Albert's; locally common. 🐾 🌿 ®

Red-bellied Pitta

Blue-winged Pitta

Noisy Pitta

Rainbow Pitta

Albert's Lyrebird ♂

Superb Lyrebird ♂

Rufous Scrub-bird *Atrichornis rufescens* 17-19cm Small, dull, extremely elusive babbler-like bird. Upperparts rufous-brown with fine darker barring, including on longish, wedge-shaped tail. Throat white, sides of breast and flanks mottled black in male, pale rufous-brown in female; undertail pale rufous-brown. Beak comparatively strong, pointed, giving distinctive wedge-shaped profile with low forehead. Flight feeble, usually sneaks away on foot. *Voice:* loud and far-carrying, characteristically accelerating series of 'cheep' notes of descending pitch. *Habitat:* dense fern or tussock undergrowth in temperate rainforest. Restricted, local and uncommon. ®

Noisy Scrub-bird *Atrichornis clamosus* 22-25cm Medium-small, dull, normally heard not seen. Upperparts, including comparatively long tail, brown finely barred black. Sides of throat white, with central patch black in male, forming triangular bib. Female and immature lack the black bib. Breast pale buff, becoming more rufous on undertail coverts. Wings short and rounded, flight low and feeble. Legs long and strong, indicative of a largely terrestrial life-style. *Voice:* amazing, powerful and ventriloquial. Varied, often melodious, characteristically a falling series of 'chip chip chip' calls, increasing in volume and ending in a 'chip-ip-ip-ip', the final notes like the crack of a rifle. *Habitat:* dense, damp coastal and watercourse scrub. Restricted, local, and rare. ®

Singing Bushlark *Mirafra javanica* 12-15cm Very small, stocky, variably coloured lark. Upperparts brown, varying from sandy or greyish to rufous, boldly marked with darker browns, buffs and blacks. Underparts paler but of the same basic tone; breast and throat with heavy dark streaks. Legs pale; beak short and stout, blackish. Chestnut patch just visible in closed wing, distinctive in flight. Flight short, fluttering, soon dropping back into cover. Distinctive song flight, high and hovering, in breeding season. *Voice:* call a 'chirrup', song musical and varied, with mimicry of other local birds. *Habitat:* long, rank grasslands, open woodland, scrub, crops. Widespread; generally uncommon but in places numerous. ®

Skylark *Alauda arvensis* 18cm Small lark. Head with dark streaks; short crest raised when excited. Pale buff throat extending as pale margin to cheek patch. Brown above, all feathers with dark centres. Underparts pale, heavily streaked on breast. Wings brown, flight feathers blackish. Tail blackish, with white sides visible in flight. Beak pale, stout; legs pinkish brown. See Richard's Pipit. *Voice:* call liquid 'chirrup'; song characteristic, produced in song-flight hovering or circling high above ground; musical, varied and extended, containing much mimicry of other birds. *Habitat:* open farmland, pastures, grassland, coastal dunes. Locally quite common in southeast. Introduced. ®

Rufous Scrub-bird

Noisy Scrub-bird

Singing Bushlark

Skylark

White-backed Swallow *Cheramoeca leucosternum* 14cm Robust but elegant and distinctive swallow. Crown, throat and back white, contrasting with black nape, eye-stripes, wings and rest of body. Tail deeply forked. Flight fluttering and hesitant, showing characteristic white throat and back. *Voice:* single or double clicking call in flight, twittering but melodious song. *Habitat:* open country, usually near exposed sandy or gravelly banks. Widespread; locally fairly common. 🐾 ♨ ⠿ ⠿ ⠿ △®

Barn Swallow *Hirundo rustica* 20cm Small, similar to Welcome but with distinctive black breast band. Adult and immature glossy blue-black above, with dark chestnut face patch edged with black band, and white spots on tail conspicuous in flight. Underparts white. In flight, shows curved wings, slim silhouette and long, deeply forked tail with narrow streamers. Tail longer in adult than immature, and longer in male than female. Flight swift, swooping; feeds on wing. *Voice:* prolonged, musical twittering; call sharp 'chirrup'. *Habitat:* coastal, wetland and urban areas; feeds over most habitats. Irregular, usually scarce, migrant. 🐾 🐾 ♨ ⠿ ⠿ ⠿ ♩

Welcome Swallow *Hirundo neoxena* 15cm Small; the familiar hirundine. Adult and immature dark glossy blue-black over much of upperparts, with white spots around margin of deeply-forked tail conspicuous in flight. Underparts white, with face, throat and upper breast rich chestnut (see Barn Swallow). Tail streamers very long in male, shorter in female and immature, which are also generally duller. Fast, swooping flight. *Voice:* call a sharp 'chep'; shrill 'seet' in alarm (often indicates oncoming bird of prey), strong twittering song. *Habitat:* catholic, but avoids densest forests and most arid parts of interior. Widespread; locally common. 🐾 🐾 ♨ ⠿ ⠿ ⠿ ♩ △®

Red-rumped Swallow *Hirundo daurica* 18cm Small, typical hirundine. Upperparts characteristic with crown, back, wings and tail dark blackish-blue, interrupted by chestnut-buff nape and diagnostic large pale chestnut rump patch. Tail long, deeply forked. Underparts whitish, tinged buff, finely but usually copiously streaked brown. Looks like a Welcome Swallow but flies more like a Tree Martin. *Voice:* scolding alarm chatter; twittering song. *Habitat:* open, usually arid and rocky country, occasionally over woodland. Vagrant. 🐾 ⠿ ⠿ ⠿

Tree Martin *Hirundo nigricans* 15cm Small, dark-headed martin. Upperparts glossy blue black, with black wings and square blackish tail, contrasting with 'dirty-white' rump, conspicuous in flight. Small chestnut patch on forehead of adult visible only at close range. Underparts white, with grey cheek patches and smokey-grey streaks and smudges on throat. Wings relatively shorter and broader at base than swallows. Flight swooping, but stiff-winged and fluttering compared with the swallows. *Voice:* brief dry rattling call, twittering musical song. *Habitat:* breeds and feeds in open woodland trees, often near water, occasionally in urban areas. Widespread; generally common. ♨ ⠿ ⠿ ♩ △®

Fairy Martin *Hirundo ariel* 13cm Small, red-headed martin. Head chestnut, with blue-black streaks on nape visible at close range and with darker patch through eye. Upperparts blue-black, sometimes looking browner than Tree Martin, with clear white rump and blackish, almost square-ended tail. Underparts white, faintly rufous-tinged on throat. *Voice:* dry, short trill, longer 'dzeee dzeee', melodious twittering song. *Habitat:* open country, usually fairly close to water, nesting in caves, hollow trees and increasingly in man-made structures. Widespread; generally common. 🐾 ⠿ ⠿ ⠿ ♩ △®

White-backed Swallow

Barn Swallow

Welcome Swallow

Red-rumped Swallow

Tree Martin

Fairy Martin

Richard's Pipit *Anthus novaeseelandiae* 18cm Small; brown, streaked, long-legged and familiar. Upperparts brown, broadly streaked with black. Head darker brown, with pale stripe over eye. Underparts buffish-white, breast boldly streaked with black, with moustachial streaks on sides of throat. Tail long, often wagged up and down, dark, with whitish outer feathers visible in flight. See Skylark. *Voice:* distinctive harsh 'chip' or 'pith'. *Habitat:* most types of open land with scant or no vegetation. Widespread; often common. ◣ ◿ ⚏ ▦ ◿ ◢ △®

Yellow Wagtail *Motacilla flava* 17cm Two or three races of this complex reach Australia. Breeding male largely olive above, yellow below with bold yellow (race *taivana*) or white (race *simillima* and others) supercilium. Crown colour may be olive, grey or black, usually with greyish or brownish ear coverts. Tail black, with white edges. Female and immature brownish above, with buff on sides of breast and flanks; much paler yellow below. Non-breeding adults duller, resembling immature; grey-brown above, with whitish supercilium, very pale (often whitish) below, with yellowish only on undertail coverts or even absent (race *simillima*). *Voice:* call rich 'tsweep'; song musical twittering. *Habitat:* damp meadows, farmland and marsh areas. Vagrant. ◣ ◿ ◢ ⌠

Yellow-headed (Citrine) Wagtail *Motacilla citreola* 17cm Waterside wagtail, very similar in shape to Yellow. Breeding male with bright yellow head (obscured by greyish crown and ear-coverts when non-breeding), black nape patch and grey mantle; wings blackish, with broad white bars; tail black, with white outer feathers, frequently wagged. Head and underparts sulphur yellow. Female and immatures similar to Yellow, but have broader supercilium which curves behind rear of earcoverts to join throat, wider white wingbars (if plumage fresh) and narrowly pale forehead. Yellow or whitish throat and supercilium but undertail coverts typically whitish on pale birds. *Voice:* call resembles Yellow, but a more rasping "tzzeep". *Habitat:* grassland and marsh. Vagrant. ◣ ◿ ◢ ⌠

Grey Wagtail *Motacilla cinerea* 18cm The longest-tailed of the wagtails, and the only one with pinkish (not black) legs. In all plumages grey above, with deep yellow upper and undertail coverts and yellowish breast; the very long tail shows obvious white at the corners even when closed. In flight the deep yellow rear body and white outertail are very striking. Much longer tailed and sleeker than Yellow-headed (Citrine) with only a very thin supercilium, and quite different call. *Voice:* call a sharp, "chip"; also a thinner "chit-it". *Habitat:* fast-moving watercourses – streams, rapids, sluices. Vagrant. ◿ ⌠

White Wagtail *Motacilla alba* and **Black-backed Wagtail** *Motacilla lugens* 18cm These wagtails were considered conspecific until recently. Both lack yellow in plumage, have much white on face and underparts and in the wing (males appear white-winged in flight). Adults of both have black crown and nape, eye-stripe and breast patch and are either grey (White) or blackish (Black-backed) above. Immatures are drabber and have less white in wing; separating the two then tricky. Some races of White lack black eye-stripe and are also potential vagrants. *Voice:* usual call a disyllabic 'chizzik'. *Habitat:* watersides and farmland. Vagrant. ◣ ◣ ◿

Richard's Pipit

Yellow Wagtail (race *simillima*)(non-breeding)

Yellow-headed (Citrine) Wagtail(non-breeding)

Grey Wagtail

White Wagtail (non-breeding)

Black-faced Cuckoo-shrike *Coracina novaehollandiae* 32-35cm

Large, slim and familiar cuckoo-shrike. Grey crown, nape, back and tail. Wing shoulders pale grey; flight feathers blackish. Characteristic 'mask' of black forehead, cheeks, throat and upper breast. Breast pale grey, shading to white on belly and undertail coverts. Beak black, medium length but robust. Legs short and grey. Immature lacks black mask, replaced by blackish mark through eye; head and upper breast with fine crescentic barring. Flight deeply undulating. When perched, has distinctive habit of 'shuffling' or refolding wings. *Voice:* musical churring, harsher 'kreeer' and 'skair'. *Habitat:* open woodland, well-treed grassland, orchards, parks, gardens. Widespread; locally common. ⌁ ⛫ ⅏ ⁘ △ ®

Yellow-eyed Cuckoo-shrike *Coracina lineata* 25cm

Medium-small distinctive cuckoo-shrike. Black streak through striking bright whitish or pale yellow eye. Upperparts dark grey, with blackish flight feathers and tail. Throat and upper breast dull grey, rest of underparts white, closely and distinctly barred blackish. Immature paler grey, darker above than below, with smudgy black mark through eye. Beak black, medium length but robust. Legs short and dark grey. Active mover, seeking fruit in foliage, often in small flocks. Looks rather like a small cuckoo in flight. *Voice:* chattering 'aw-loo-lack', repeated and wheezily metallic. *Habitat:* open forests and woodlands, scrub, plantations, gardens. Generally uncommon. ⛫ ⅏ ⁘ ®

White-bellied Cuckoo-shrike *Coracina papuensis* 27cm

Medium-sized pale cuckoo-shrike. Upperparts pale grey, with darker grey tail and black flight feathers. Underparts white, with black mark between base of beak and eye. Southern birds are slightly greyer beneath. Immature duller and browner, with scaly markings on upper breast and back. Beak medium, black and relatively strong. Legs short and black. Occasionally hovers. *Voice:* plaintive 'kissick', kissick' or 'quiz-eek'. *Habitat:* woodland, scrub, riverine trees; occasionally mangroves, gardens. Fairly widespread, but generally not common. ⌁ ⛫ ⅏ ⁘ ®

Cicadabird *Coracina tenuirostris* 27cm

Medium-sized cuckoo-shrike showing marked sexual dimorphism, with dark grey male and brown female. Male uniformly dark blue-grey, with darker flight feathers and a black mark through eye. Female and immature uniform grey-brown above, with a white throat and finely brown-barred buff underparts. Beak comparatively slender, blackish. Quick-moving, restless bird, usually feeding high in canopy. *Voice:* usefully distinctive staccato buzzing, like a warming-up cicada. *Habitat:* forests and woodlands, scrub, occasionally mangroves. Relatively widespread, but generally uncommon. ⛫ ⅏ ⁘ ®

Black-faced Cuckoo-shrike

Yellow-eyed Cuckoo-shrike

White-bellied Cuckoo-shrike (eastern race)

White-bellied Cuckoo-shrike (northern race)

Cicadabird ♂

Ground Cuckoo-shrike *Coracina maxima* 34cm Medium-large, often terrestrial cuckoo-shrike. Adult has grey head, nape, mantle and breast, with strikingly contrasting black wings and tail. Tail slightly forked. Blackish patch from beak to cheek, emphasizing whitish eye. Lower breast, belly and rump white, very finely barred in brownish black; undertail coverts white. Immature duller, with lightly barred head and back. Walks and runs with head jerking back and forth. *Voice:* loud 'pee-oo, pee-oo' in flight, also metallic 'kee-lick'. *Habitat:* open country with sparse tree-cover, usually rather dry, generally inland. Widespread, but erratic and generally uncommon. ♨♨ ⵯ △®

White-winged Triller *Lalage tricolor* 18cm Small, slim, graceful cuckoo-shrike. Breeding male has black crown and mantle, grey back and rump, black and white wings with a striking white shoulder patch, all-white underparts, and a white-tipped black tail. Beak fine and black; legs comparatively slender, black. Non-breeding male brown above, white below, with striking white supercilium and brown, white and black wings. Female and immature similar, but white areas heavily tinged buff except for white undertail coverts. Fast undulating flight, except in display when wings and tail are fanned in flight maximizing black-and-white impression. *Voice:* characteristic song, a loud, varied and musical liquid trill rather on the pattern of a canary. *Habitat:* breeds open woodlands, scrub; on migration favours more open country with trees. Widespread, erratic, but often common. ▰ ♨♨ ⵯ ⎮ △®

Varied Triller *Lalage leucomela* 18cm Small, slim cuckoo-shrike. Male rather similar to breeding male White-winged, but shows striking white stripe over eye, and chestnut undertail coverts. Wing lacks white shoulder but has two bold white bars. Female and immature as female White-winged, but with brown-barred buff underparts and double white bars on wing shoulders, less pronounced than male but still striking. *Voice:* characteristically loud, rolling 'breeeer' repeated several times, the volume increasing then fading on each call. Once one calls, others may answer to produce a widespread chorus. *Habitat:* rainforests, forests and woodlands, scrubs and thickets, occasionally mangroves. Commoner in north, rare in south. ⵯ ⵯ ♨♨ ⎮®

Red-whiskered Bulbul *Pycnonotus jocosus* 23cm Medium-sized, upright and conspicuous. Head, nape and collar black, with a conspicuous pointed crest. Cheeks and throat white, crossed by narrow black line. Small red patch behind eye. Back and tail brown, tail with a white tip; breast and belly fawn; undertail coverts distinctively red, often clearly visible as bulbuls choose prominent perches. Immature has smaller crest, lacks red patch behind eye. Beak black, fine and pointed. Legs black. *Voice:* disjointed melodious fluid whistles. *Habitat:* predominantly gardens and parks. Locally common round Sydney and Coffs Harbour. Introduced. ▰ ▰ ♨♨ ⵯ®

Ground Cuckoo-shrike

White-winged Triller (breeding) ♂

White-winged Triller (non-breeding) ♂

Varied Triller ♂

Red-whiskered Bulbul

Bassian Thrush *Zoothera lunulata* 26cm Medium-large, scaly thrush. Face buff, with paler stripes indistinctly outlining cheek patch; small white patch before eye merging with white eye-ring. Upperparts rich brown with blackish feather fringes; wings brown, tail dark brown. Throat buff, paling to white on belly, all copiously marked with characteristic crescentic bars, reduced in density on lower belly. Legs strong, brown; beak blackish, comparatively long and slim. Spends much time on ground, typically running a few paces, then pausing to locate food. In flight, shows diagnostic broad black diagonal bar across white underside to wing. *Voice:* melodious, pleasant warble. *Habitat:* breeds damp forested gullies in southern Australia north to NSW/Queensland border, and also the Atherton Tablelands, dispersing to drier woodlands of several types. Uncommon. The taxonomy and distribution of the *Zoothera* group of thrushes is currently in a state of considerable flux.  ®

Russet-tailed Thrush *Zoothera heinii* 25cm Medium-large, but the smaller of the Australian scaly thrushes. Closely similar to Bassian, but with shorter and more chestnut (russet) tail and more russety wing shoulders. Shows typical underwing pattern. *Voice:* musical two-note whistling 'theeaa. thooaa'. *Habitat:* wetter forests and gullies of northern NSW to central Queensland. Uncommon. ®

Blackbird *Turdus merula* 25cm Medium-large thrush. Adult male distinctive: jet black with orange-yellow beak and eye-ring. Female and immature dark brown, paler and more rufous on underparts, with brownish yellow beak. Female often shows dark-bordered whitish throat. *Voice:* calls loud 'chink' and 'chack; melodious, attractive fluting song. *Habitat:* open woodlands, woodland with dense undergrowth, scrub, parks and gardens. Widespread across Victoria and Tasmania in particular; often common. Introduced. ®

Song Thrush *Turdus philomelos* 23cm Medium-small, sandy-backed thrush with spotted breast. Upperparts sandy or olive brown, with cheek patch outlined darker brown and faint buffish supercilium. Throat and breast buffish, belly white, all with copious large brown spots. Uses regular rocks or 'anvils' to smash snail shells. *Voice:* noted for its simple but musical phrases, repeated two, three or four times in succession. Thin 'seep' in flight. *Habitat:* damp woodland and forest parks and gardens. Largely confined to Melbourne area, where local and rare. Introduced. ®

Bassian Thrush

Russet-Tailed Thrush

Blackbird ♂

Song Thrush

Northern Scrub-robin *Drymodes superciliaris* 21cm Small, slim, long-tailed thrush-like bird. Face pattern unusual, with vertical black line through eye and down side of throat. Face greyish, rest of underparts pale warm buff. Upperparts rich brown, chestnut on rump and tail. Outer tail feathers tipped white. Wings black with distinctive double white wingbars. Legs long, pale pinkish and slender. Spends most of time on ground, hopping quietly through leaf litter. Inconspicuous but approachable. *Voice:* drawn-out whistle; short descending series of high-pitched notes. *Habitat:* floor of tropical forests and scrub, forest margins. Now only in Northern Queensland, where local, nowhere common. 🐾 🐦 ®

Southern Scrub-robin *Drymodes brunneopygia* 23cm Medium-small, dark, thrush-like bird. Upperparts darkish olive-brown, deep chestnut on rump; tail dark brown narrowly tipped white. Wings blackish with pale edges to coverts and secondaries conspicuous. Underparts grey. Faint white eye-ring. Dark vertical sooty bar through eye. Legs long, slim and blackish. Unobtrusive, runs off if alarmed, scolding, but not far. *Voice:* loud musical 'chee-too-quee' and 'chip chip, paree'. *Habitat:* mallee and other semi-arid scrub, coastal heath, tea-tree scrub. Discontinuous southern distribution; generally uncommon. 🐦 🏔 ®

Rose Robin *Petroica rosea* 11cm Tiny, comparatively slim, long-tailed robin. Male has small white forehead patch, otherwise hood, back, wings and tail uniformly plain sooty grey. Tail long, with white outer feathers. Breast rose-pink; belly and undertail white. Beak black, slim and finely pointed; legs relatively long, slender and blackish. Female and immature olive-brown above, with paler forehead; grey-buff shading to white below. Wings brown, with interrupted whitish-buff bars. Catches insects in agile flight, often high in canopy; the most arboreal of the robins. *Voice:* song a trilling 'tick-tick-ticket-deer-deer'; usual call 'tick'. *Habitat:* breeds in dense, usually damp, forests with thick undergrowth; at other times drier open forest and woodland. Locally quite common. 🐦 🐦 ⚑ ®

Pink Robin *Petroica rodinogaster* 12cm Tiny blackish robin. Male uniformly black above, with vestigial white forehead patch; lacking white bar in wing and diagnostically lacking white outer tail feathers. Throat black. Breast and belly deep rose-pink; white confined to undertail coverts. Female and immature dark buffish-brown above, paler below with buff band across breast. Wings brown with double buff wingbars. Feeds in low undergrowth and on the ground. *Voice:* not vocal, quiet fragmentary warbling song; call a sharp 'tick'. *Habitat:* breeds in densely vegetated forest gullies; at other times more open forest and woodland. Widespread and occasionally fairly common in Tasmania; generally uncommon elsewhere. 🐦 🐦 ⚑ ®

Northern Scrub-robin

Southern Scrub-robin

Rose Robin ♂

Rose Robin ♀

Pink Robin ♂

Pink Robin ♀

Flame Robin *Petroica phoenicea* 14cm Small, but the largest *Petroica* robin, and distinctive. Male dark grey above, with white outer tail feathers and striking white bars in wing. Small white forehead patch. Underparts from throat (the only male robin with a coloured throat) to lower belly characteristically scarlet; undertail coverts white. Female and immature dark olive above; grey-buff below with blackish wings showing distinctive wingbars. Often gregarious outside breeding season. *Voice:* high-pitched tinkling but tuneful song. Call a short 'peep'. *Habitat:* breeds open forest and woodland, including montane, dispersing to open country including grassy plains, golf courses, farmland. Widespread but erratic; locally quite common. ⚲ ⁂ ▥ ⌷ ®

Scarlet Robin *Petroica multicolor* 13cm Small, plump and elegant robin. Male has jet-black hood, back, wings and tail, with broad white forehead patch; bold white wingbar; white edges to tail. Breast and belly scarlet; undertail coverts white. Female and immature brown above, with white forehead patch and buffish white wingbar. On underside, grey throat merges into breast patch of orange-red of varying intensity; belly and undertail white. Sometimes gregarious with Flame Robins in winter. *Voice:* ringing repetitive but tuneful 'wee-deedlidee-dalee'; call a quiet 'tick'. *Habitat:* breeds montane forest and woodland, dispersing to open grassland or scrub, including golf courses, gardens. Widespread but discontinuous distribution; locally fairly common. ⁂ ⁂ ▥ ⌷ ®

Red-capped Robin *Petroica goodenovii* 12cm Tiny, plump and striking robin. Male has black upperparts contrasting with distinctive scarlet cap from beak to behind eye. Tail black, with white tips to outer feathers; wings black with bold white wingbar. Breast and central belly scarlet, edged striking white; belly and undertail white. Female and immature olive above, with indistinct white eye-ring and chestnut forehead patch. Wings blackish with bold white bar, white below. Often approachable, feeding on ground and in flight. *Voice:* insect-like rattling trill; call 'tick'. *Habitat:* dry scrub and woodland, dispersing to more open areas but usually with trees. Widespread south of the Tropic; frequently quite common. ⁂ ▥ ⌷ △ ®

Flame Robin ♂

Flame Robin ♀

Scarlet Robin ♂

Scarlet Robin ♀

Red-capped Robin ♂

Red-capped Robin ♀

Hooded Robin *Melanodryas cucullata* 16cm Small robin, male with distinctively pied plumage. Male has black hood and upper breast, black back, and black tail with white bases to outer feathers distinctive in flight. Wings black with bold white bar. White of breast extends onto back to form distinctive narrow white 'braces'. Female and immature olive above, with faint paler supercilium; whitish below. Both show characteristic wing and tail patterns, but against brownish-black feathers. *Voice:* normally quiet, but breeding season song distinctive pre-dawn 'wee-whoo, wee-whoo, wee-whoo'. *Habitat:* dry open woodland and scrub, mallee, rough paddocks. Widespread but erratic; locally fairly common. 🏍🐜🐛🎋🕴️△®

Dusky Robin *Melanodryas vittata* 16cm Small, plain robin. Upperparts uniform olive brown, with rather darker wings and tail. At close range narrow white shoulder to closed wing can be seen, together with an indistinct buff wingbar rather clearer in flight. Throat white, breast rich buff, lower breast and belly pale buff. Beak dark, more robust than the *Petroica* species, with stiff bristles at gape. Legs dark brown. Uses prominent perches to watch for prey, usually darting to the ground to secure it. *Voice:* low but penetrating 'choo-wee', repeated often. *Habitat:* forest tracks, clearings and margins, felled areas and scrub. Restricted, but locally common. 🏍🐛🎋®

Mangrove Robin *Eopsaltria pulverulenta* 16cm Small, distinctively blue-grey robin. Crown, nape, back and rump characteristic slaty blue-grey, with darker eye and cheek patch and black wings. Tail distinctive, blackish with white patches at the bases of the outer feathers, appearing as two white blocks in flight. Underparts white, faintly shaded buff on breast. Beak short, comparatively strong; legs black. Immature browner and mottled. Approachable, but in dense vegetation difficult to observe. *Voice:* soft churring, mournful double whistle. *Habitat:* typically mangroves. Locally common. 🍃🌿🎋®

White-breasted Robin *Eopsaltria georgiana* 16cm Small grey-and-white robin. Upperparts grey to blue-grey, slightly darker on cheeks. Wings and tail darker grey, outer tail feathers tipped white. Underparts white, washed pale grey on breast. Beak black, strong, with conspicuous bristles at gape. At close range, a white mark can be seen along bend of wing, but in flight shows distinct white wingbar. Immature browner and mottled. *Voice:* whistling 'whee-oh', various 'zip' and 'chit' calls; fast, jangling brief song. *Habitat:* dense undergrowth, usually near streams, coastally in damp scrub or thickets. Restricted, but locally quite common. 🍃🐛🎋🌾®

Hooded Robin ♂

Hooded Robin ♀

Dusky Robin

Mangrove Robin

White-breasted Robin

Eastern Yellow Robin *Eopsaltria australis* 16cm Small, the familiar 'yellow robin'. Head, cheeks and nape grey, with faint paler grey supercilium. Back grey washed green; rump greenish (southern) to almost golden (northern birds). Wings and tail dark grey. Chin white; throat, breast, belly and undertail coverts distinctively bright yellow. Beak broad and strong, conspicuous bristles at base. Legs blackish. Immature brownish yellow and mottled. Confiding, cocks tail and flicks wings if alarmed. *Voice:* at dawn and dusk, powerful and repeated 'chop chop'; monotonous piping. *Habitat:* shaded undergrowth in forest and woodland, occasionally mallee, mulga and other scrub. Orchards, parks, gardens. Widespread in eastern coastal region; often common. 𝄢 ♣♣ ⬚ ®

Western Yellow Robin *Eopsaltria griseogularis* 15cm Small - the western version of the yellow robin, but with a greyish breast. Upperparts grey, tinged olive, with a faint paler supercilium; rump greenish to golden. Wings and tail grey-brown. Cheeks grey; throat white; breast white suffused with grey and shading into yellow belly and undertail coverts. *Voice:* explosive 'chip, chip' harsher than Eastern. *Habitat:* catholic, woodland and scrub of various sorts, mallee, coastal scrub; but avoids swampy thickets favoured by White-breasted. Restricted, but locally common. 𝄢 ♣♣ ⬚ ®

Yellow-legged Flycatcher *Microeca griseoceps* 12cm Tiny, pale-legged version of yellow robin. Upperparts grey, washed olive on back and wings, with brownish tail. Slim white eye-ring, broad flat beak with bristles at base. Throat white; breast pale yellow. Legs diagnostically yellow-brown. Often solitary, usually feeding high in canopy, often difficult to see. *Voice:* penetrating 'zzzt zzzt' calls and musical high-pitched trilling song. *Habitat:* tropical rainforest with dense understorey. Local and scarce.. 🐾 ®

Lemon-bellied Flycatcher *Microeca flavigaster* 13cm Tiny flycatcher. Upperparts olive-brown with darker wings and tail. Cheeks greyer, with relatively faint white supercilium. Beak broad, with bristles at base. Throat white; rest of underparts dull yellow. Immature whitish below, cream-spotted brown on upperparts. Populations inhabiting mangroves of northern Western Australia lack yellow in plumage. Perches prominently, dashing out for insects. Distinctive circling, soaring song-flight. *Voice:* melodious varied song, lacking repetition: 'sue-sue sure-we so-we choo'. *Habitat:* open woodland, forest and woodland margins, occasionally parks and gardens, usually near water. Restricted to the north but locally quite common. ⬓ ⬚ ♣♣ ⬚ ®

Jacky Winter *Microeca fascinans* 13cm Tiny, plain, but attractive flycatcher. Upperparts grey-brown, with distinct white supercilia meeting on forehead and slender dark stripe through eye. Cheeks greyer. Underparts white shaded buffish-grey on breast. Wings dark brown, showing pale edges on secondaries and tertials forming a panel in closed wing. Tail distinctive, blackish with white outer feathers, characteristically wagged side to side, flashing white. Perches prominently, dashing out, sometimes hovering, to catch insects. Immature streaked on underparts, whitish speckled above. *Voice:* clear and melodious, often at dawn, variations on 'peter-peter-peter' or 'jacky-jacky-jacky-winter-winter-winter'. *Habitat:* dry forests, woodland, mallee, scrub and farmland. Widespread, but patchy; normally scarce or absent from settled areas, locally quite common elsewhere. ⬓ ♣♣ ⬚ △ ®

Eastern Yellow Robin

Western Yellow Robin

Yellow-legged Flycatcher

Lemon-bellied Flycatcher

Jacky Winter

Pale-yellow Robin *Tregellasia capito* 13cm Tiny, can be confused with Eastern Yellow Robin. Upperparts greenish olive, darker grey on forehead, with distinctive yellowish or whitish patch between beak and large eye. Throat white; breast yellow, paler than Yellow Robin. Beak stubby and strong; legs characteristically yellowish-flesh coloured, not black. Usually found in deep shaded undergrowth. *Voice:* double 'cheep', various simple whistles, scolding churr. *Habitat:* tropical and subtropical rainforests with dense understorey, densely vegetated riverine forest. Discontinuous and restricted distribution, patchy and nowhere common but more frequent in north. 🐾 🎵 ®

White-faced Robin *Tregellasia leucops* 12cm Tiny, distinctive, rotund robin. Upperparts greenish-olive, washed yellow or gold, with characteristic white face and chin patch extending behind eye and margined with smokey black. Throat and remainder of underparts rich yellow. Beak black, flat and broad, with bristles at base. Legs strong and distinctively pale yellow. Typical yellow robin in behaviour, often tame and approachable. *Voice:* grating, repeated 'chee-chee', brief rarely-heard more musical song. *Habitat:* tropical rainforest. Very restricted distribution, but there common. 🐾 ®

White-browed Robin *Poecilodryas superciliosa* 15cm Small, distinctive, brown-and-white robin. Upperparts dark brown, with striking white supercilium over brown cheek flecked with white. Bold white bar in brown wing, with flight feathers tipped white, broadly on tertials. Tail brown, white-tipped. Underparts white, sometimes washed buff on breast and flanks. Often terrestrial. When perched, slowly raises and lowers tail, often droops wings. *Voice:* loud piping four-fold whistle. *Habitat:* rainforest, woodland, riverine forest, mangroves. Patchy and generally scarce. 🌿 🍃 🏛 🐾 🎵 ⚘ ❘ ®

Grey-headed Robin *Poecilodryas albispecularis* 16cm Small, plump, sombre but attractive robin. Crown and nape grey; mantle subdued golden-olive; rump pale chestnut, tail rufous brown. Wings blackish brown with white bar across primary bases and a lesser white bar across tips of secondary coverts. White lower eye-ring. Characteristic black and olive cheek patch. Underparts white, tinged rich buff on flanks. Beak black, relatively long and robust. Legs flesh-pink. Often perches sideways on trunks, darting to ground for prey. Hops swiftly on the ground. *Voice:* characteristic (if monotonous) loud shrill whistle followed by three briefer lower whistles. *Habitat:* rainforests, woodland margins, usually above 250m. Restricted, but locally common. 🐾 ®

Crested Shrike-tit *Falcunculus frontatus* 15-19cm Small but robust, with a distinctively patterned, large head. Three races differ slightly, but all share characteristic black crown, with steep white forehead and conspicuous black crest from crown to nape. Bold white stripe above eye, narrower black stripe through eye, and broad white stripe below eye and across cheek. Broad triangular bib black in male, greenish in female. Beak black, strong, rounded and deep, slightly hooked at tip for bark-tearing. Mantle, back and wings golden in northern birds; mantle green and wings blackish in others. Underparts bright yellow, white on belly in western birds. *Voice:* sad, low slow whistle, usually repeated several times; also 'knock-at-the-door'. *Habitat:* open forests, woodland, scrub, sometimes orchards, parks and gardens. Widespread but discontinuous; generally uncommon. ⚘ ❘ 🎵 ❘ ®

Pale-yellow Robin

White-faced Robin

White-browed Robin (Cape York race)

Grey-headed Robin

Crested Shrike-tit ♂

Olive Whistler *Pachycephala olivacea* 21cm Medium-small, rather drab whistler. Upperparts dull olive brown, dark grey on head. Throat characteristic white, with faint crescentic barring, margined pale grey and shading into darkish buff underparts. Beak black, comparatively short and strong; legs blackish. Female and immature paler, with pale lower mandible. Often solitary, usually inconspicuous, even elusive. Terrestrial, flies off low and silently. *Voice:* various two- and three-tone whistles, sweetly melodious but difficult to locate. Stronger 'jo-jo-jo' territorial call. *Habitat:* dense, often damp, forests and woodlands in breeding season, more open land in winter. Restricted distribution; scarce in north, commoner in south. 🦜 🎵 🦅 ®

Red-lored Whistler *Pachycephala rufogularis* 21cm Medium-small, drab whistler, male showing chestnut underparts. Upperparts dull grey, tinged greenish on wings. Face and throat chestnut in male, pale buff in female and immature. Greyish band across breast and grey flanks common to both sexes; belly and undertail pale cinnamon in male, buff washed chestnut in female. Beak black, long and slender compared with Gilbert's. Often solitary, usually timid and elusive. *Voice:* unmistakably a sad whistler-whistle, an indrawn 'seee-saw' or 'see-saw-sik' falling on middle syllable, rising on last. *Habitat:* mallee/*Spinifex* associations, other scrubs. Restricted; local and rare. 🎵 ®

Golden Whistler *Pachycephala pectoralis* 17cm Medium-sized, golden whistler. Adult male distinctive, with black crown and collar band contrasting with white throat. Nape and underparts rich golden yellow; back greenish olive; wings and tail grey or blackish. Faint grey-green wingbar. Female variable, pale olive grey, darker above than below, northern birds showing a more greenish tinge. Immature drab olive brown, with pale chestnut fringes to wing feathers. Beak short, stout and slightly hooked. Often in company with other species. Conspicuous and vociferous at start of breeding season. *Voice:* range of melodious whistling notes, often with 'whip-crack' ending to a rising phrase 'whee-whee-whee-*whit*', various soft whistles. *Habitat:* usually closed canopy, ranging from rainforest to woodland and mallee. Widespread and fairly common. 🦜 🎵 🦅 🎵 🌿 ®

Mangrove Golden Whistler *Pachycephala melanura* 16cm Medium-sized golden whistler. Adult male slightly smaller than Golden Whistler, but similar in plumage, with a broader golden nape, more orange-tinged underparts, blacker wings and tail and frequently with a yellowish rump. Beak medium, fairly stout and hooked; longer and slimmer than Golden. Female variable, greenish-grey above, paler and greyer below, with yellow undertail coverts. Northern birds may have extensive yellow on breast. *Voice:* similar in quality and range of notes to Golden Whistler. *Habitat:* mangroves, and coastal forests or thickets. Note range compared with Golden. Often fairly common. 🦅 🌿 🦜 🎵 🎵 ®

Olive Whistler ♂

Red-lored Whistler ♂

Golden Whistler ♂

Golden Whistler ♀

Mangrove Golden Whistler ♀

Mangrove Golden Whistler ♂

Grey Whistler *Pachycephala simplex* 15cm Small, dull, northern whistler. Upperparts grey-brown, tinged olive. Underparts show white throat, scarcely distinct from whitish breast with buff wash and buffish sides in Arnhem Land birds; clear white throat with buff margin and pale yellow breast and belly in north Queensland. Narrow white margin visible on bend of closed brownish wings. Beak black, comparatively long and slightly hooked. Tends to feed in canopy, fluttering in front of leaves like a flycatcher. *Voice:* rich melodious song, lacking the terminal 'snap' of some whistlers, melodious 'tum-tum-tee-ta-tum' whistle. *Habitat:* coastal forests, usually damp and dense, mangroves. Erratic, locally quite common to hear but usually difficult to see. ⬦ ▦ 👁 ▩ ▦ ®

Rufous Whistler *Pachycephala rufiventris* 17cm Medium-sized whistler. Adult male has grey crown, back, wings and tail. Distinctive black band extends from beak through eye to surround white throat patch. Rest of breast and belly variable, cinnamon (interior regions) to chestnut (coastal regions). Female and immature olive brown above, buff below with a whitish throat with sparse narrow dark streaks. Beak medium, fairly stout and hooked. Southern birds slightly larger than northern. *Voice:* vocal and melodious, especially in breeding season, with loud melodious passages following an explosive 'ee-chong', and a repetitive 'joey-joey-joey'. *Habitat:* open forests and woodland, mallee and mulga, often in drier areas. Widespread; often fairly common. ♙ ▦ ®

Gilbert's Whistler *Pachycephala inornata* 20cm Medium-large, comparatively plain, greyish whistler. Adult male has dark brownish-grey upperparts, sooty black around the eye. Underparts grey, with chestnut-orange throat. Wings and longish tail dark grey. Female and immature dull plain grey above, paler below, with whitish-grey throat. Adults have deep reddish eyes. Beak short, stout and slightly hooked. Legs blackish. Shy and inconspicuous feeding in canopy or on ground. Flight deeply undulating. *Voice:* richly musical far-carrying whistling calls, particularly vocal in breeding season, variants of 'poo-whee' strengthening on second syllable, a series of 'pew' calls steadily increasing in volume towards an explosively wheezy climax, various soft whistles, and an explosive series of 'jock' calls. *Habitat:* dry scrubs and open woodlands with good shrub layer. Sparsely distributed; usually rare. ♙ ▦ ®

White-breasted Whistler *Pachycephala lanioides* 20cm Medium-sized, robust whistler with a heavy beak. Male distinctive, with black cap and striking white throat outlined in black, surrounded by chestnut nape and collar band. Rest of upperparts blue-grey; underparts pale buff. Tail blackish. Eye prominent and red; beak black, comparatively long and strong, slightly hooked. Female and immature duller, sombre grey-brown above, buff streaked brown below. Usually in pairs. Often feeds on mud, taking small fish and even crabs. *Voice:* rich, melodious, fast-moving song. Four to six note whistling call. *Habitat:* mangroves, occasionally coastal forest. Restricted discontinuous distribution, but locally common. ⬦ ▦ ▦ ®

Grey Whistler

Rufous Whistler ♂

Gilbert's Whistler ♂

White-breasted Whistler ♂

White-breasted Whistler ♀

Little Shrike-thrush *Colluricincla megarhyncha* 19cm Medium-small, rufous, ground-feeding 'thrush'. Upperparts olive-brown, faintly rufous-tinged. Underparts rich rufous-cinnamon, paler almost whitish on throat. Beak distinctively long, reasonably strong, pale in eastern and northern races, blackish in western and central northern populations. Searches noisily through leaf litter. *Voice:* sweet and low 'too-ee, what-what-what', sometimes by pair in unison. Loud chirrup of alarm, and a quiet thrush-like 'wheeze'. *Habitat:* tropical and subtropical rainforest and dense riverine forest, occasionally swampy thickets and mangroves. Locally common in north; scarce in southern part of range. ⬤▨▨ ▨▨▨ ▥ ®

Bower's Shrike-thrush *Colluricincla boweri* 21cm Medium-sized, grey-and-russet, large-headed shrike-thrush. Head looks oversized, emphasized by long stout black beak. Upperparts grey, with distinctly brown wings and comparatively short tail. Underparts rich cinnamon buff, slightly paler on throat, with faint brown streaks on throat and breast. Perches in concealment, dropping down to grab prey. Usually single or pairs. *Voice:* comparatively quiet: various clicking chirps, loud 'chuck', soft brief melodious song. *Habitat:* montane rainforest, usually over 400m altitude. Restricted, but locally quite common. ▨ ®

Sandstone Shrike-thrush *Colluricincla woodwardi* 26cm Medium-sized but large for a shrike-thrush, sombrely plumaged. Upperparts grey-brown; greyer on head and mantle, browner on wings, browner with rufous tinge on tail. Pale patch between eye and beak; throat pale buff. Underparts dull darkish cinnamon, with faint blackish streaking on throat and breast. Beak relatively long and strong, black and hooked. Active but secretive, usually singles or pairs. Largely terrestrial, hopping swiftly, flying low only short distances. Usually heard before (and often rather than) seen. *Voice:* loud richly melodious song, echoes off rocks; call a strident 'peeter'. *Habitat:* sandstone escarpments and similar rocky areas. Restricted, but locally fairly common. ▨▨ ▥ ®

Grey Shrike-thrush *Colluricincla harmonica* 24cm Medium-sized, softly-coloured, familiar shrike-thrush. Crown grey, mantle bronze, wings and tail darker brownish-grey. Male white patch between eye and beak. Throat white, rest of underparts white washed pale grey. Northwestern birds are more olive-brown above, buffer below. Beak black, relatively long and pointed, thrush-like. Female may show faint streaking on throat, greyish ear-patches and a pale eye-ring at close range. *Voice:* rich, beautiful song - often written as variations on 'pip-pip-pip-hoo-eee'; call a distinctive harsh 'yorrick'. *Habitat:* catholic: woodland, forest and scrub, usually open; homesteads, parks, gardens. Widespread; often quite common. ▨▨▨ ▨▨ ▥ ▯ △®

Crested Bellbird *Oreoica gutturalis* 22cm Medium-sized, usually noticed by its call. Upperparts generally olive-brown, with narrow black erectile crest. Forehead, face and throat white, characteristically broadly bordered in black, especially broad on breast. Eye golden, set in black. Underparts white, washed buff on flanks. Female olive-brown above, with a grey head and black central crown streak. Breast grey, belly buff. Eye brown. Beak strong, rounded and stubby. *Voice:* melodious and distinctive, 'did-did-did diddee-dit' the last note loud, mellow and bell-like, at a distance the only note heard, hence the name bellbird. *Habitat:* dryish scrub and woodland. Widespread but erratic; locally common. ▨▨ ▥ △®

Little Shrike-thrush (eastern races)

Bower's Shrike-thrush

Sandstone Shrike-thrush

Grey Shrike-thrush (adult ♂)

Crested Bellbird (adult ♂)

Yellow-breasted Boatbill *Machaerirhynchus flaviventer* 11cm

Tiny and unmistakable flycatcher. Male jet black above, with prominent golden eye-stripe, double white wingbars and white-tipped round-ended tail. Throat bright white, rest of underparts brilliant yellow. Female olive-grey above, with yellowish supercilium and blackish cheek patch. Wings and tail as male but duller. Underparts paler than male, with faint crescentic marks on breast. Beak comparatively large, strangely, even grotesquely wide if viewed from an appropriate angle. Active in canopy, darting out to seize prey. Usually in pairs. *Voice:* trilling, fast 'pee-dee-dee-dee-dwit'. *Habitat:* rainforest, dense waterside vegetation. Restricted, generally uncommon with a few locally common areas. 🐾 ®

Black-faced Monarch *Monarcha melanopsis* 18cm

Small but robust blue-grey and cinnamon flycatcher. Forehead and throat black; head and upper breast distinctive blue-grey. Mantle blue-grey; wings and tail blackish grey. Underparts rich cinnamon. Immature lacks black face, generally duller. Beak black, flattened and broad. Sedately active in canopy - dashing out to snap up insects. Usually in ones or twos. *Voice:* clear 'which-yoo, why-yoo' and mixtures of these phrases. Harsher slurred calls. *Habitat:* forests and woodlands, often damp, when breeding; otherwise open forest or woodland. Locally common in north, scarcer elsewhere. 🐾 ₥ ®

Black-winged Monarch *Monarcha frater* 18cm

Small monarch, similar to Black-faced apart from wings. Blue-grey hood, back and rump; black face, wings and tail. Underparts rich cinnamon. Immature drabber, lacks black face patch. Beak flattened and broad, grey-black. *Voice:* similar to Black-faced. *Habitat:* rainforest and adjacent woodlands. Restricted range; only locally fairly common. 🐾 ₥ ⑂ ®

Spectacled Monarch *Monarcha trivirgatus* 15cm

Small monarch flycatcher with distinctive face pattern. Adult has black forehead, ear-patch and bib. Rest of face, neck, upper breast and flanks pale chestnut. Belly white. Crown, mantle and wings dark grey; tail dark grey with white tips to outer feathers particularly noticeable on underside and in flight. Immature similar but appreciably paler, with whitish patch in front of eye. Very active, fluttering about foliage, and approachable, often fanning longish tail to help keep balance as it perches on trunks and branches. *Voice:* clear 'zwee-ee zwee-ee zwee-ee' call, each phrase rising, buzzing insect-like scolding call, soft scratchy song. *Habitat:* rainforest and woodlands with dense understorey, mangroves. Locally common in north, scarcer elsewhere.
🔺 ⬚ 🐾 ₥ ⅏ ®

Yellow-breasted Boatbill ♂

Black-faced Monarch (adult)

Black-winged Monarch (adult)

Spectacled Monarch (adult)

White-eared Monarch *Monarcha leucotis* 14cm Small, distinctive, pied monarch. Head pattern complex but characteristic: black overall with white collar mark, white supercilium and white cheeks. Upperparts black, with white rump distinctive in flight. Double white wingbar, white-tipped black tail. White bib outlined in black; rest of underparts white washed grey. Slight bristly crest on forehead. Active and vocal pursuing insects in canopy. *Voice:* repetitive drawn out 'few-few-few' or 'ee-ooo, ee-ooo' whistling musical 'you-get-awaaay'. *Habitat:* rainforest, dense coastal woodland and scrub, mangroves. Restricted, locally fairly common in mid-range. 🐾 𝍡 ®

Frilled Monarch *Arses lorealis* 15cm Small monarch, closely similar to Pied. Crown and cheeks black, eye-ring blue, nape white and slightly crested. Back, wings and tail black with bold crescentic 'collar' mark across closed wings and middle of back. Male has small patch of black on chin; rest of underparts white. Immature greyer and speckled. *Voice:* harsh scolding calls, trilling song. *Habitat:* middle storey of rainforest. Very restricted, but locally common. 🐾 𝍡 ®

Pied Monarch *Arses kaupi* 15cm Small, distinctively pied monarch, subtly different from Frilled. Forehead, crown and ear-patch black, eye-ring blue. Crested nape and throat white; mantle and collar across breast black. Wings and tail black, with broad white crescentic patch across back and wing coverts. Female has crown linked to collar by black streak, isolating a barred white nape patch. Creeps on trunks, wings half-open, jerking tail. *Voice:* unexpected soft quacking calls; multiple soft high-pitched whistles. *Habitat:* restricted (see Frilled). Rainforest, adjacent woodland, usually near streams. Locally fairly common. 🐾 𝍡 ®

Broad-billed Flycatcher *Myiagra ruficollis* 16cm Small distinctive flycatcher. Adult (sexes similar) blue-grey, slightly iridescent above, with darker grey cheeks, and a characteristically white-edged blackish tail (see Satin and Leaden females). Chin, throat and upper breast pale chestnut; rest of underparts white. Immature paler. Beak black, unusually broad (rarely visible) with conspicuous bristles at gape. Feeds quietly in canopy. *Voice:* soft churring, clear whinnying, harsh 'shwek' call. *Habitat:* mangroves, swampy woodland. Restricted to northern coastal belt but locally quite common. 🏊 ▬ 🐾 𝍡 𝍡 ⫯ ®

White-eared Monarch

Frilled Monarch ♂

Pied Monarch ♀

Broad-billed Flycatcher (adult)

Leaden Flycatcher *Myiagra rubecula* 16cm Small and distinctive, sexes dissimilar. Male dark blue-grey above, with peaked crown and dark blue-grey wings and tail. Throat and upper breast blue-grey, rest of underparts white. Beak and legs black. Female has dark-grey peaked crown, blackish ear-patch, dark blackish-brown wings and tail. Throat and breast pale chestnut, rest of underparts white. Immature as female, but with broad pale feather edges forming whitish wingbars. Perches in strikingly upright posture. Quivers tail up and down or sideways. *Voice:* guttural croaks, insect-like buzzing, clear 'see-heer, see-heer'; brief tuneful song. *Habitat:* varied, from densely wooded gullies to open woodland and scrub, occasionally swampy coastal woodland and mangroves. Often locally quite common in north of range, scarcer elsewhere. 🐾 ♏ ♨ ⅼ ®

Satin Flycatcher *Myiagra cyanoleuca* 16cm Small flycatcher, with dissimilar sexes, superficially similar to Leaden. Male glossy purplish black above, with peaked crown; wings and tail entirely black. Throat and much of breast (see Leaden) black, rest of underparts white. Female very similar to female Leaden but glossier blue-grey on upperparts. Like Leaden, frequently quivers tail up and down, or sometimes from side to side. Active in top of canopy, darting out to catch prey. *Voice:* varied, more strident than Leaden, guttural croaks, strong 'woo-*chee*, woo-*chee*' and 'chelly chelly chelly'. *Habitat:* dense forests, woodland and scrub, occasionally swampy woodland and mangroves. Distribution overlaps Leaden, but commonest in south (especially Tasmania) and scarce in north. 🐾 ♏ ♨ ⅼ ®

Shining Flycatcher *Myiagra alecto* 18cm Small, unmistakable flycatcher with striking extreme sexual dimorphism. Male uniformly glossy jet black, with characteristic peaked crown. Female has high-peaked blue-black crown; black nape; white throat and underparts, and rich bright pale-chestnut back, wings and tail. Immature like female but duller. Fast moving and shy, picking food off leaves or mud. *Voice:* varied whistling phrases, some penetrating, others melodious; harsh croaking calls. *Habitat:* mangroves and waterside forests. Locally common along northern coast, scarce south of Herbert River, Queensland. ⚓ ⸗ 🐾 ♏ ♨ ⫴ ®

Restless Flycatcher *Myiagra inquieta* 17-21cm Medium-sized, distinctive flycatcher. Upperparts glossy black or blue-black from forehead to rump, with long, broad dull-black tail. Short crest produces shallowly peaked crown. Entire underparts white, often with buff wash on breast, especially in female. Feeds in foliage, hovers. Distinctive swooping flight. *Voice:* characteristic extended churring while hovering; whistling 'zoo-wee zoo-wee'. *Habitat:* open forests and woodlands, often near water. Out of breeding season, also in quite dry scrub. Widespread, locally fairly common. 🐾 ♏ ♨ ⫴ ⅼ ®

Leaden Flycatcher ♂

Leaden Flycatcher ♀

Satin Flycatcher ♀

Shining Flycatcher ♂

Shining Flycatcher ♀

Restless Flycatcher

Rufous Fantail *Rhipidura rufifrons* 16cm Small, red-rumped fantail.
Adult has reddish forehead; brown crown, nape, mantle and wings. Lower back, rump and base of tail fiery orange-red. Rest of long, often-waved, often-fanned tail brown with greyish tip. Throat white, with black gorget; rest of underparts whitish. Immature basically similar but duller and more rufous on breast. Secretive and active, often low in dense undergrowth, darting after insects with flame-coloured rump and tail prominent. *Voice:* high-pitched squeaky call, accelerating twittering song. *Habitat:* dense unergrowth in woodland or forest, usually damp or beside rivers, occasionally mangroves. Widespread but erratic; locally regular but nowhere numerous. 🐾 ♏ ♊ ®

Grey Fantail *Rhipidura fuliginosa* 16cm Small grey fantail with
distinctive tail pattern. Upperparts grey, with short white stripe in front of eye, and separate short stripe behind eye. Wings grey, with paler covert fringes showing as obscure double wingbar. Tail grey, often fanned and waved, showing dark central feathers; broad white tips and white shafts to the others; outer webs of outer primaries distinctively white. Throat white, with black border merging into greyish-buff breast. Immature browner, white areas tinged rufous. *Voice:* loud, rich ascending series of whistling notes; call a sharp 'deck'. *Habitat:* forests, woodland and scrub of varied types. Widespread but erratic; commoner in damper coastal belt. 🐾 ♏ ♊ ®

Mangrove Fantail *Rhipidura phasiana* 16cm Small grey fantail,
considered by many to be merely a pale race of Grey. Upperparts as Grey, but paler, and tail though similarly patterned, appreciably shorter. Throat white, with faint black bordering necklace; rest of underparts distinctively cream. Grey has characteristically short fine beak; Mangrove is distinctively long-beaked. *Voice:* soft, short, twittering whistles. *Habitat:* mangroves. Restricted and discontinuous distribution, but locally not uncommon. 🐟 ▦ ﷯ ®

Northern Fantail *Rhipidura rufiventris* 17cm Small - a browner,
more flycatcher-like version of the Grey Fantail. Upperparts darkish brown, with small white stripe between eye and relatively long, broadly flattened beak. Tail dark brown, white-edged and tipped but lacking white feather shafts. Wings brown with obscure double paler wingbars. Throat white, bordered by dark brown gorget, shading to whitish breast and belly shaded buff on flanks. Immature paler brown, more speckled. Moves more sedately than other fantails. *Voice:* soft metallic 'chip', tinkling musical song. *Habitat:* rainforest margins, open forest and woodland, occasionally mangroves. Locally fairly common. 🐾 ♏ ♊ ﷯ ®

Willie Wagtail *Rhipidura leucophrys* 20cm Medium-small, fantail
flycatcher. Distinctive and well-known: adult black above, white below apart from black throat. Bold white stripe over eye; less distinct white moustachial streaks. Tail black, long, frequently cocked, fanned and flicked. Immature duller and browner, with pale feather fringes giving mottled appearance. Catches insects from favoured perches in flight or on the ground. Aggressive in defence of its feeding area. Usually in ones or twos, or family parties. *Voice:* scolding 'ricka-ticka-ticka-tick'; varied brief but melodious phrases often transcribed as 'sweet-pretty-creature'. *Habitat:* catholic, avoiding dense forests but including mangroves, surburban parks and gardens and even semi-desert. Widespread; in many areas common and sedentary. ▰ ▱ 🐾 ♏ ♊ ﷯ △ ®

Rufous Fantail

Grey Fantail

Mangrove Fantail

Northern Fantail

Willie Wagtail

Logrunner *Orthonyx temminckii* 20cm Medium-sized, terrestrial, stiff-tailed songbird. Crown brown with finer streaks; sides of face grey. Beak medium length, slimmer than thrushes or babblers. Upperparts sombre buffish brown with broad black longitudinal streaking. Throat and breast white in male, orange-buff in female, with broad black lateral margins. Lower belly pale buff. Tail dark brown, quills projecting as fine spines at tip. *Voice:* distinctive and useful strident 'weet' or 'quick' and resonant 'be-quick-queek-queek-queek'. *Habitat:* leafy floors of open subtropical rainforest. Restricted range, but locally common in north. 💢 🎵 ®

Chowchilla *Orthonyx spaldingii* 26-28cm Medium-large and distinctive forest bird. Adults dark brown to blackish above, with dark brown, relatively short tail ending in inconspicuous spines. Head darker, with contrasting pale grey or whitish eye-ring; beak relatively slim. Throat and breast white in male, shading to grey-buff on flanks and under tail; throat distinctive orange in female, with clear-cut divide from white breast. Immature paler brown and more mottled. Terrestrial. *Voice:* loud and dominant in dawn chorus, characteristic 'chow, chowchilla' and varied harsh notes. *Habitat:* leafy floor of montane tropical rainforest. Restricted, but locally common. 💢 ®

Eastern Whipbird *Psophodes olivaceus* 25-30cm Medium-large, distinctively long-tailed and crested. Larger male blackish above, with characteristic erectile crest and long, white-tipped tail. Chin, throat and breast black, with broad and distinctive white moustachial stripes. Belly white, undertail and flanks grey-brown. Female smaller, paler and more olive-brown with smaller white moustachial streaks. Immature similar, lacks white moustaches. *Voice:* familiar whip-crack call of male usually answered by female 'choo-choo'. *Habitat:* dense undergrowth in forest, woodland and scrub of eastern coastal belt. Locally common. 💢 🎵 🎵 ®

Western Whipbird *Psophodes nigrogularis* 20-25cm Medium-sized. Upperparts olive-brown with erectile crest and long, white-tipped tail. Black throat patch edged by slim but distinct white moustachial streaks; rest of underparts grey-buff. Beak relatively long but slim; legs long and strong. Secretive but noisy. *Voice:* distinctive creaking calls, often four-fold and described as 'lets-scratch-*tea*-cher', followed by female response 'pick-it-up'. *Habitat:* dense coastal heath, scrub including mallee. Restricted: note discontinuity. Local, only fairly common in South Australia. 🎵 🎵 ®

Chirruping Wedgebill *Psophodes cristatus* 20cm Medium-sized, long-tailed, wedgebill. Pale sandy-brown, sometimes tinged olive above, with slender spiky upright crest. Long brown tail fan-shaped, boldly white-tipped. Underparts whitish. Beak short and deep (hence wedgebill). White outer webs to central primaries form faint streak in closed wing. *Voice:* duetting calls 'sootzy-sherree' answered by rolling 'eeeet-cheer'. *Habitat:* semi-arid scrub of varied types, savannah. Locally quite common. 🎵 🎵 🎵 🎵 △®

Chiming Wedgebill *Psophodes occidentalis* 20cm Medium-sized, almost inseparable from Chirruping except by voice and distribution. Pale sandy-brown above, with narrowly pointed upright crest; whitish below. Tail long, brown, distinctly white-tipped. *Voice:* monotonous metallic 'when-did-you-get-drunk'. *Habitat:* dense thickets of tea-tree, *Acacia* and *Melaleuca*. Erratic, locally common. 🎵 🎵 🎵 🎵 △®

Logrunner ♀

Chowchilla ♀

Eastern Whipbird (adult)

Western Whipbird (adult)

Chirruping Wedgebill

Chiming Wedgebill

Spotted Quail-thrush *Cinclosoma punctatum* 25-28cm Medium-large. As its name suggests, looking like a cross between a quail and a thrush. Male: crown brown, flecked black; back bronzy-brown, rump dull brown, liberally black-streaked. Tail wedge-shaped, relatively long, dark olive brown. Wings show black shoulders, chestnut patch on tertials. Distinctive long white supercilium; face and breast blue-grey, with black and white throat patch; belly white, buff on flanks, boldly brown-spotted. Female and immature paler, broadly similar but with a white and pale chestnut throat. Largely terrestrial, in pairs or family groups; shy and elusive. *Voice:* high-pitched drawn-out 'seeeep', low harsh chattering, song a soft fluting series of double whistles. *Habitat:* dry forest, woodland and scrub, preferring rocky ridges with deep leaf litter and tussock grass. The southeastern quail-thrush, local and generally scarce. 🐾 🐜 ⚤ 🏕 ®

Chestnut Quail-thrush *Cinclosoma castanotum* 23-25cm Medium-large, dark quail-thrush. Head pattern distinctive, with bold white supercilium and moustachial streak on either side of blackish cheek. Male has olive-brown crown, lightly flecked black; brown mantle, with dark chestnut patch on shoulders and back. Rump brown; tail long and wedge-shaped, dark brown. Throat and breast black; belly and undertail coverts white with heavy blackish spots on flanks and beneath tail. Female and immature rather paler overall, with pale grey throat and breast, not black. Legs strong, dark grey. Wary, usually sneaks off on foot if disturbed. *Voice:* repeated high-pitched 'tseep', piping whistling song from high perch. *Habitat:* mallee and mulga, sandy heaths, arid woodland, saltbush and other dry scrub. Widespread but patchy; only locally at all common. ⚤ 🏕 ⚱ △ ®

Chestnut-breasted Quail-thrush *Cinclosoma castaneothorax* 20-24cm Medium-sized quail-thrush with chestnut breast band. Male resembles male Cinnamon, with browner head (and mantle in eastern birds) and has similar striking head pattern. Black breast separated from black upper belly by diagnostic chestnut band extending down flanks, darker in eastern birds. Female and immature like Cinnamon, but faintly washed chestnut on breast. *Voice:* high-pitched 'tsee', far-carrying whistles. *Habitat:* arid scrub-covered ridges (usually *Acacia*). Discontinuous distribution; uncommon in east, locally quite common in west. ⚤ 🏕 △ ®

Cinnamon Quail-thrush *Cinclosoma cinnamomeum* 18-20cm Medium-sized, variably but distinctively cinnamon-backed quail-thrush. Distinctive head pattern of white supercilium and black-edged white moustachial streak on either side of brown cheek patch. Male cinnamon brown above, sometimes browner on crown. Throat black; breast broadly banded black and white; flanks cinnamon in birds from gibber deserts of east-central regions; breast all-black, flanks black in birds from western south coast. Rest of underparts white. Female and immature duller, with white throat and pale grey breast. *Voice:* insect-like 'see'; 'see-whit'. *Habitat:* gibber plains (race *cinnamomeum*) and Nullabor limestone scrub (race *alisteri*). Discontinuous distribution. Locally fairly common. 🏕 ⚤ ⚱ △ ®

Spotted Quail-thrush ♂

Chestnut Quail-thrush ♂

Chestnut-breasted Quail-thrush ♂

Cinnamon Quail-thrush ♂

Grey-crowned Babbler *Pomatostomus temporalis* 29cm Medium-large, the largest Australian babbler, with distinctive pale crown. Head characteristic, with bold broad creamy white supercilia almost meeting on pale brown crown. Stripe through eye blackish; eye staring, pale yellow. Beak black, conspicuously long, robust but pointed and downcurved. Nape and back brown; tail long, dark brown with small but conspicuous white tip. Throat white, breast dull chestnut (western race *rubecula*) or light grey (eastern birds), rest of underparts brown. Immature has brown eye, paler back, chestnut on wing shoulder. Gregarious, communal, noisy and clumsy; often cocks tail. *Voice:* boisterous 'yahoo' and 'go-ahee', strident 'peeeoo'; groups chatter incessantly. *Habitat:* open forest and woodland, scrub. Widespread; locally common away from settled areas. 🚜 ⚏ ⚏ ®

White-browed Babbler *Pomatostomus superciliosus* 18-20cm Medium-sized, plain brown-and-white babbler, with typical babbler habits. Dark crown with bold white supercilia, with blackish stripes through eyes. Upperparts uniformly dull brown; tail long and fanned, with white tips, extensive on outer tail feathers. Throat and breast white. Flanks and lower belly grey-brown. Legs relatively long and strong; beak comparatively short, pointed and downcurved. Gregarious. *Voice:* strange high-pitched, cat-like miaows; incessant chatter; brisk 'wit-wit' of alarm. *Habitat:* mallee, mulga, and other scrub and open woodland, generally dry. Widespread but erratic; locally common. ⚏ ⚏ △ ®

Hall's Babbler *Pomatostomus halli* 23cm Medium-sized, dark babbler with small white bib. Upperparts dark brown, with broad white supercilium. Tail long, dark brown, fanned and uniformly white-tipped (see White-browed). Chin and throat white; breast, flanks and belly dull brown. Beak comparatively short, pointed and downcurved. Legs strong. Typical babbler habits. Gregarious. *Voice:* excited high-pitched chattering; liquid whistles on 'pee-oo' format. *Habitat:* mulga and other arid *Acacia* scrubs, dry scrubby open woodland. Restricted but locally quite common. ⚏ ⚏ ®

Chestnut-crowned Babbler *Pomatostomus ruficeps* 22cm Medium-sized, brown-and-white babbler with distinctive wingbars. Characteristic head pattern with broad chestnut crown stripe, narrowly black-edged, over long slender white supercilium. Cheek brown. Much of upperparts dull olive-brown, with long white-tipped darker brown tail. Throat and breast white, narrowly edged black; rest of underparts brown with white feathers beneath tail. Wing diagnostic; dark brown with white covert tips forming two bold wingbars, together with a shorter less distinct bar near shoulder. Habits typically babbler-like, gregarious and noisy but relatively shy. *Voice:* call 'wee-chee chee chee', harsh but quite melodious song, often in paired phrases like Song Thrush. *Habitat:* dry to arid inland scrub of several types. Restricted and erratic; only locally fairly common. ⚏ ⚏ △ ®

White-browed Babbler

Grey-crowned Babbler (eastern race)

Hall's Babbler

Chestnut-crowned Babbler

Clamorous Reed-warbler *Acrocephalus stentoreus* 16cm Small,
but large for a warbler. Unstreaked and dull, with a powerful (stentorian) song. Upperparts pale olive-brown, with darker wings and long, slightly rounded tail. Faint supercilium, crown often slightly raised, but peaked rather than as a crest. Throat white, breast and belly white, washed buff. Beak comparatively heavy for a warbler. Shows yellow gape in full-throated song. Legs black. Perches sideways on reed stems. Flight usually low and brief, shows tawny yellow rump. *Voice:* the best reedbed singer: richly varied and sweet, with notes often repeated in groups of three. Harsh 'tic' of alarm. *Habitat:* dense waterside vegetation, particularly bamboos and reeds. Widespread; often common in appropriate habitat. ♨ 🍴 △ ®

Great Reed-warbler *Acrocephalus arundinaceus* 19cm Large for a
warbler. Larger than Clamorous; perhaps more reddish brown, with longer, heavier bill and longer primary projection beyond tertials of folded wing, but otherwise difficult to distinguish other than by wing detail in the hand. *Voice:* distinctively different, loud and grating, with repeated metallic phrases like 'qurk qurk qurk', ' karrang karrang karrang'. *Habitat:* prefers extensive areas of wetland vegetation, favouring reeds. Vagrant. ♨ 🍴

Tawny Grassbird *Megalurus timoriensis* 19cm Medium-sized, but
tail accounts for half length. Crown and nape rather ginger brown, over buff supercilium, dark mark through eye, and smudgy cheek patch. Back brown, with heavy blackish feather centres. Wings and tail rather more rufous. Tail long and broadly pointed. Wings short, flight whirring. Underparts whitish, buff on flanks. Beak comparatively large, grey and pointed; legs grey. Male has fluttering, parachute-descent song flight in breeding season. *Voice:* song light and melodious, reminiscent of Superb Blue Wren. Call a tapping 'chack'. *Habitat:* swampy vegetation, wet coastal heaths, occasionally crops. Fairly widespread; generally scarce and only locally at all common. ♨ ≈ 🍴 ®

Little Grassbird *Megalurus gramineus* 14cm Small, and over one-
third of its length is tail. Dull brown and streaked; skulking. Upperparts brown; head, nape and back with longitudinal blackish streaks. Faint pale supercilium. Back and wings dark blackish-brown, feathers with paler fringes. Underparts pale buff, lightly streaked. Tail long, slim and brown, pointed at tip, often held part-cocked. Wings short; flight whirring, showing yellowish-olive rump, but usually creeps away through vegetation. *Voice:* three-note whistle, the first note short, the others drawn-out 'pe-peee-peee'; dry scolding trill. *Habitat:* dense swamp vegetation, reeds, rank grass, occasionally saltmarsh and mangroves. Widespread but patchy; locally common. ♨ △ ®

Spinifexbird *Eremiornis carteri* 15cm Small and undistinguished,
often first identified by habitat. Crown rufous, rest of upperparts unstreaked brown. Grey-buff supercilium. Cheeks and underparts whitish, palest on throat and breast, grey-buff beneath tail. Tail long, wedge-tipped, dark brown, about half overall length and often carried cocked. Peers at intruders from tussocks before sneaking away. Usually runs. In flight, tail bounces up and down. *Voice:* song a pleasant warbling 'cheery-wheet', with 'cheer-it' and 'chee-roo' variants. Alarm call a sharp 'tchack' like pebbles clicking together. *Habitat:* spinifex and other dense grasses. Fairly widespread; locally common in appropriate vegetation. ≈ ®

Great Reed-warbler

Clamorous Reed-warbler

Tawny Grassbird

Little Grassbird

Spinifexbird

Zitting Cisticola *Cisticola juncidis* 10cm Tiny, perky, streaked warbler. Upperparts rufous buff, lightly streaked on head. Nape unstreaked, back heavily black-streaked. Underparts whitish, washed orange-buff on flanks. Legs pinkish brown. Wings short; flight whirring, usually for short distances before diving into cover. Tail often cocked, has obscure whitish tip visible at close range. *Voice:* usually in song flight, yo-yo-like, with plaintive 'zee-eek' characteristic. *Habitat:* coastal rank grassland, saltflats. Discontinuous distribution; local and scarce. 🌊 ⚌ ®

Golden-headed Cisticola *Cisticola exilis* 10cm Tiny, perky, golden-brown warbler. Breeding male has distinctive golden head and nape; cinnamon back with bold black stripes, and comparatively short buff-tipped blackish tail. Underparts white, washed buff on throat, gold on flanks. Non-breeding male, female and immature duller, more cinnamon-brown, with finely streaked crown. Jerky song flights with tail fanned are frequent, or sings from wires or grass stems. *Voice:* almost incessantly vocal, producing an insect-like buzz, or 'churr, lick-lick'. *Habitat:* long grassland, rushes, rank vegetation often close to water. Widespread; locally common. ⚌ ®

Arctic Warbler *Phylloscopus borealis* 12cm Tiny leaf warbler. Upperparts olive. Wings and tail darker, with yellow-green feather fringes and slim but distinct white wingbar formed by pale covert tips. Long pale supercilium over greenish-grey cheek patch. Underparts white, washed pale yellow beneath tail. Beak blackish, with pinkish lower mandible; legs yellowish brown. *Voice:* typical call a sharp "zik". *Habitat:* wooded areas. Vagrant. ⚌

Rufous Songlark *Cinclorhamphus mathewsi* 16-19cm Pipit-like warbler, male substantially larger than female. Upperparts dull brown, with darker diffuse streaks and blotches, shading to chestnut on rump, distinctive perched and particularly in flight. Tail brown, relatively short, with pointed tip. Slim but distinct whitish supercilium over grey-brown cheek patch. Underparts whitish, buff-washed on breast and beneath tail, occasionally with a gorget of brownish specklings. Sometimes in groups. Conspicuous in song, otherwise rather secretive. *Voice:* melodious song given on the wing or perched, a sustained trilling ending in a flourish. Call a sharp 'tick'. *Habitat:* tall grasses, reeds, rank herbage near water, overgrown crops, hedges. Widespread but erratic; locally common. 🪶 ⚌ ⚌ △ ®

Brown Songlark *Cinclorhamphus cruralis* 18-25cm Medium-sized, dull but distinctive vocalist. Male largely dark brown over all underparts, with a distinctive brown head and fawn crown. Back brown, with paler feather fringes giving scaly appearance. Tail blackish, slightly fanned, long and often held cocked. Legs distinctively long. Female appreciably smaller, a dull brown version of Rufous Songlark. Conspicuous on perches; noisy, song-flights with legs dangling. *Voice:* metallic and memorable, transcribed as 'skit-skot-a-wheeler'. *Habitat:* open country: pastures, short crops, grassland, scrub. Widespread but erratic; locally common. 🪶 ⚌ △ ®

Zitting Cisticola

Golden-headed Cisticola (♀ or non-breeding)

Arctic Warbler

Rufous Songlark ♀

Brown Songlark (adult ♂)

Purple-crowned Fairy-wren *Malurus coronatus* 16cm including

long tail. Blue-tailed, brown-bodied wren, each sex with distinctive head pattern. Breeding male very distinctive, with black-centred lilac-purple crown bordered by black stripe through eyes and around nape. Female and non-breeding male head also distinctive: crown and nape blue, with slim white supercilium over chestnut cheek patch, and white eye-ring. Body pale brown above, pale buff below, white on throat. Tail long, azure blue in both sexes. *Voice:* high-pitched reeling 'cheaper-cheaper-cheaper....'; short chirrup. *Habitat:* mangroves, cane grass and *Pandanus* near water. Note distribution: local, rarely common. 🌊 ⌷ ♦♦ ⫞⫞⫞ ♦♦ ®

Superb Fairy-wren *Malurus cyaneus* 14cm Tiny, the familiar blue

wren of the southeast. Breeding male has pale blue crown, ear coverts and mantle, bordered by black eye-stripe, nape and rump. Throat and breast iridescent dark blue-black. Beak black. Wings brown, belly white, tail dark blue. Female and non-breeding male uniformly brown above, with faint blue-green cast to brown tail. Underparts pale fawn. Beak reddish brown (note feathers from beak to eye-ring reddish brown). *Voice:* loud accelerating trill; 'tsee' of alarm; sharp 'prrip-prrip' contact call. *Habitat:* almost any dense low cover from saltmarsh to gardens. Widespread; often common. ♦♦ ♦♦ 🌊 ♦♦ ⫞⫞⫞ ®

Splendid Fairy-wren *Malurus splendens* 14cm Tiny, the familar

blue wren of the southwest. Breeding male spectacular and unmistakable, entirely rich blue, with paler iridescent blue crown and cheeks, blackish eye-stripes and nape, and black-bordered purplish-iridescent throat and breast. Non-breeding male and female brown above, pale fawn below; male with black legs and beak, female with reddish legs and beak and red patch round eye. Some east-west variation in the amount of pale blue and black. *Voice:* song an accelerating trill, thin 'see' of alarm and soft 'prip' contact calls. *Habitat:* wide range of undergrowth and scrub from woodland margins to mallee, mulga, saltbush and *Spinifex* associations, to orchards and gardens. Widespread but erratic; locally quite common. ♦♦ ♦♦ ⫞⫞⫞ ♦♦ △ ®

Variegated Fairy-wren *Malurus lamberti* 14cm Tiny, the most

widespread red-shouldered wren. Breeding male has iridescent pale blue crown and ear coverts; black throat, upper breast and collar; blue back and rump. Characteristic broad chestnut band across shoulder of brown wing. Tail long, blue, slightly fanned and white-tipped. Non-breeding male and female of eastern birds brown above, pale fawn below, with white-tipped bluish tail, female with dark reddish feathers round eye. Non-breeding male and female from northwest have bluish crowns and backs, whiter undersides. *Voice:* song a high-pitched, metallic monotonous trill; alarm 'tsee', contact 'pringp'. *Habitat:* wide range of shrub/scrub/heath types, and parks and gardens. Widespread but erratic; locally fairly common. ♦♦ ♦♦ ⫞⫞⫞ 🌊 △ ®

Purple-crowned Fairy-wren (breeding) ♂

Purple-crowned Fairy-wren (breeding) ♀

Superb Fairy-wren (breeding) ♂

Splendid Fairy-wren (breeding) ♂

Splendid Fairy-wren (breeding) ♀

Variegated Fairy-wren (breeding) ♂

Lovely Fairy-wren *Malurus amabilis* 14cm Tiny, red-shouldered wren from Cape York Peninsula, closely similar to Variegated. Breeding male has bright blue crown and cheeks; black throat, breast and collar. Wings brown with characteristic rich red shoulder patches. Purple patch on flanks. Underparts white. Tail distinctive, relatively short, dark blue with prominent white tips. Non-breeding male and female mid-blue on crown and back, with pale blue ear coverts and distinctive white eye-ring. Underparts white. *Voice:* song a high-pitched rather monotonous trill; 'see' of alarm, 'pring' contact call. *Habitat:* rainforest and woodland margins. Restricted to far northeast; locally fairly common. 🐦 ♨️ ®

Blue-breasted Fairy-wren *Malurus pulcherrimus* 15cm Small, dark-breasted, red-shouldered wren. Breeding male has iridescent purplish-blue crown and nape, pale blue ear coverts, black patch on each side of nape, and characteristic chestnut shoulders. Wings brown; rump blackish; tail long, dull dark blue, inconspicuously white-tipped. Throat and breast distinctive, dark grey to blackish; rest of underparts pale fawn. Non-breeding male and female similar to Variegated (race *lamberti*), with greyish-brown head, dull red patch round eye, dull brown back, greenish-blue tail but with obscure, not clear, white tips. Underparts pale fawn. *Voice:* song a high-pitched rather metallic and monotonous trill; alarm 'tsee', contact call 'prip-prip'. *Habitat:* undergrowth and scrub, thickets, including sand plains, heath, mallee, mulga and jarrah. Discontinuous distribution; uncommon in South Australia, common to abundant in places in the southwest. ♨️ ⛢ ♨️ ♨️ ®

Red-winged Fairy-wren *Malurus elegans* 14cm Tiny, red-winged, marshland wren. Breeding male has pale iridescent blue crown, cheeks, nape and rump, with black patches on sides of nape and characteristic dull red shoulders. Wing brown, tail grey-blue with obscure white tips. Throat and breast black, belly pale fawn. Non-breeding male and female dark brown above, with grey crown, red round eye, dull bluish tail and fawn underparts. Note black beak (yellow-brown in Blue-breasted). *Voice:* similar to Splendid. *Habitat:* scrub and dense vegetation close to water or swamps. Restricted, but locally common in appropriate habitat. ♨️ ®

White-winged Fairy-wren *Malurus leucopterus* 12cm Tiny, unmistakable, blue-and-white (or black-and-white) wren. Breeding males over most of range (race *leuconotus*) distinctively all bright deep blue, with white wings and brown primaries. Tail long and blue. Races of Dirk Hartog and Barrow Islands off Western Australia are black and white with dull blue tail. Females and non-breeding males are sandy-brown above, white below, buffer beneath long blue tail, lacking eye-patch. *Voice:* thin, high-pitched wavering musical trill (like a fishing reel), call 'prip-prip'. *Habitat:* scrub, rank grass, thickets of low bushes on treeless open landscapes of varied types, including arid central areas. Widespread but erratic; often locally common. ⛢ ♨️ ♨️ △ ®

Red-backed Fairy-wren *Malurus melanocephalus* 13cm Tiny, unmistakable, black-and-red wren. Breeding male sooty black, with rather browner primaries, with strikingly contrasting crimson to orange-scarlet shoulders, back and rump. Female and non-breeding male sandy brown above, male sometimes showing traces of red, with long characteristically sandy-brown tail; paler fawn below. *Voice:* Strong reeling trill, varied in pitch and tempo. Call harsh 'prip, prip'. *Habitat:* varied - open woodland and forest, grasslands, *Spinifex*, swamps. Widespread; often common. ♨️ ♒ ♨️ ♨️ ®

Lovely Fairy-wren ♀

Blue-breasted Fairy-wren (breeding) ♂

Red-winged Fairy-wren (breeding) ♂

White-winged Fairy-wren (breeding) ♂

Red-backed Fairy-wren (breeding) ♂

Rufous-crowned Emu-wren *Stipiturus ruficeps* 15cm Small, but has distinctively tiny body and long tail. Male crown and nape chestnut, back and wings brown streaked with black. Face, throat and breast blue, belly and flanks rich buff. Tail characteristic of emu-wrens, with only six long, dark brown, feebly filamentous feathers. Female and immature lack blue face. *Voice:* call fragile 'prip-prip', squeaking 'seeet' of alarm. High-pitched trilling song. *Habitat:* spinifex, among rocky gullies and ridges. Widespread, the only emu-wren of the interior, but erratic. ⚏ ®

Mallee Emu-wren *Stipiturus mallee* 15cm Small, but tail accounts for half the length. Adult male has chestnut forehead; dark dull chestnut crown; dark brown nape and back streaked black. Face, throat and breast grey-blue; rest of underparts rich buff. Tail fragile-looking, normally held cocked. Female and immature lack blue-grey face and throat. *Voice:* high-pitched trilling song; calls delicate 'prip-prip' and squeaking 'seeet' of alarm. *Habitat:* spinifex/mallee associations and mallee in Murray area. Restricted but inconspicuous and elusive, perhaps overlooked. ⪽ ®

Southern Emu-wren *Stipiturus malachurus* 19cm Medium-small, but tail accounts for half. Upperparts yellowish-brown, with blackish streaks. Male has blue-grey eyebrow, white-flecked buff cheeks and a blue-grey bib, lacking in female. Rest of underparts rich buff. Tail long, fragile and filamentous. *Voice:* high-pitched descending trill; soft chirrups in contact, short sharp alarm 'tsee'. *Habitat:* swampy heaths, wetlands, scrub, subalpine grassland and button-grass plains in Tasmania. Discontinuous distribution along coasts south of the Tropic. Uncommon. ⪻ ⪽ ⩇ ®

Black Grasswren *Amytornis housei* 23cm Medium-sized, heavily built, terrestrial bird. Male has black hood and breast; liberally streaked with white. Rest of underparts and relatively long, rounded tail black. Back, rump and wings rich chestnut; flight feathers blackish with chestnut fringes. Female similar, but with chestnut, not black, belly. Often in groups, running like rats around the rocks. *Voice:* harsh rattling trill, various ticking and metallic contact and alarm calls. *Habitat:* rough sandstone crag and gully country, with occasional spinifex and stunted scrub. Remote and local in Kimberleys; status unclear, but may be locally quite common. ⚏ ®

White-throated Grasswren *Amytornis woodwardi* 21cm Medium-sized grasswren. Head and nape black, finely streaked with white; back rufous-brown, white-streaked; tail long, rounded, dark brown. Conspicuous white throat and breast patch bordered by black moustachial streaks and belt of black, streaked white, across breast, belly rusty (darker in male). *Voice:* rich, rising and falling trilling song, chirruping contact calls, 'zzitt' of alarm. *Habitat:* sandstone crags and gullies. Note distribution. Confined to west Arnhem Land, locally fairly common. ⚏ ®

Carpentarian Grasswren *Amytornis dorotheae* 17cm Medium-small grasswren. Distinctive ginger-brown crown and back, finely streaked with white. Beak short, rounded and robust. Black moustachial stripe. Underparts white, rufous (darker in male) on lower belly and beneath tail. Tail long, slim and rounded, pale brown. *Voice:* variable trilling song, sharp 'zzzit' calls. *Habitat:* sandstone escarpments with sparse spinifex and stunted shrubs. Note distribution relative to other grasswrens. Confined to the north of the Barkly Tableland and western Queensland: rarely seen. ⚏ ®

Rufous-crowned Emu-wren ♂

Mallee Emu-wren ♂

Southern Emu-wren ♂

Black Grasswren

White-throated Grasswren

Carpentarian Grasswren

Striated Grasswren *Amytornis striatus* 16cm, of which almost half is tail. Small, secretive and inconspicuous. Upperparts rufous brown with copious white streaks. Underparts buff or light rufous (depending on race) with faint darker streaking, washed chestnut on flanks of female. Diagnostic black moustachial streaks visible at close range. Tail long, dark brown, frequently cocked. Wings short, rich brown, white streaked; flight whirring. Often terrestrial in behaviour on comparatively strong brown legs and feet. Usually in pairs or small (family?) groups. *Voice:* varied melodious song with repeated 'tu tu tu' phrases. Chattering alarm calls. *Habitat:* spinifex grasslands near mallee or other scrub. Widely but patchily distributed as is its habitat; sedentary, sometimes locally quite common. ▦ ▪▪ ®

Eyrean Grasswren *Amytornis goyderi* 14cm Tiny, pale grasswren with large beak. Upperparts pale ginger, profusely streaked white. Ear coverts greyish. Tail long, narrow, brown and rather pointed. Beak short, rounded, deep and robust. Underparts white, flanks washed rufous in female, shading to buff on flanks and lower belly and beneath tail. Scurries mouse-like between grass tussocks. *Voice:* very quiet trills 'swee-eee-ee', a high 'zeet' and a thin song. *Habitat:* dense canegrass tussocks, usually on sandy soils or dunes. Note restricted distribution north of Lake Eyre. Rarely seen. ▪▪ ▬ ®

Grey Grasswren *Amytornis barbatus* 18-20cm Medium-small grasswren with distinctive head pattern. Black crown, and pale brown nape, back and rump all finely streaked with black and white. Black-bridled face pattern is quite distinctive. Gorget of fine black streaks across lower breast. Rest of underparts pale buff. Beak short, black. Female similar but duller. Often in small groups, scampering through cover. Flies low and fast, more frequently than most grasswrens. *Voice:* high-pitched 'tsi-tsi-tseek' and a 'seep' of alarm. *Habitat:* swamps, canegrass. Restricted distribution (see Thick-billed); uncommon. ▦ ▪▪ ®

Thick-billed Grasswren *Amytornis textilis* 16-18cm Small, dark, plump grasswren. Upperparts brown, copiously streaked with black and white. Beak black and stout. Underparts pale buff with white streaks, pinkish-chestnut on flanks in female. Race *modestus* of central Australia is relatively longer tailed, with paler, almost unstreaked breast. Secretive and elusive, flies more often than most grasswrens. *Voice:* quiet high-pitched song, also an alarm squeak. *Habitat:* sandy plains, gibber, usually in saltbush or bluebush, sometimes in canegrass clumps. Discontinuous distribution: generally uncommon, but may be overlooked.
▦ ▦ ▪▪ ®

Dusky Grasswren *Amytornis purnelli* 17cm Small grasswren, darker than Thick-billed. Upperparts dark rufous-brown with copious black-and-white streaking. Underparts brown in male, rufous-buff in female, in both sexes finely streaked whitish on throat and breast. Race *ballarae* of Selwyn Range, western Queensland, has paler buff breast and grey wash on belly. Small red patch in front of eye visible at close range. Beak short, black and quite robust (but less so than Thick-billed). Shy, usually scampering over rocky ground, tail cocked when at ease, lowered if running away. *Voice:* whispering, reeling trill 'sree-sree-sree-tew-tew', harsh 'chip chip' of alarm, high-pitched 'seeet'. *Habitat:* rocky country, gorges, usually with spinifex or stunted shrubs. Discontinuous distribution; elusive but locally fairly common. ▪▪ ▬ ®

Striated Grasswren

Eyrean Grasswren

Grey Grasswren

Thick-billed Grasswren (race *modestus*)

Dusky Grasswren (race *purnelli*)

Eastern Bristlebird *Dasyornis brachypterus* 21cm Medium-sized, long-tailed, thrush-like terrestrial bird with 'untidy' tail. Upperparts dull brown, with faint paler supercilium. Tail long, round-ended, with bristly, unkempt edges to outer feathers. Wings chestnut, blackish on tertials. Throat white; breast and belly grey-buff, darker on flanks, with faint brownish marks. Beak pointed, relatively short and thrush-like; legs strong and grey. Secretive. *Voice:* loud and far-carrying four-note call - the last rather whipcrack-like. *Habitat:* coastal scrub, heath, reedbeds and dense thickets. Discontinuous and restricted distribution; generally rare, heard more often than seen. 🌊🔥🏞️🗻Ⓡ

Western Bristlebird *Dasyornis longirostris* 18cm Medium-small. Upperparts dark grey-brown, paler feather centres giving mottled appearance. Rump and tail plain dark olive-brown, tail fringed with bristly outer feathers. Wings short, rich chestnut. Underparts pale grey-fawn, with fine crescentic blackish barring. Beak dark grey, short, pointed and slightly downcurved. Terrestrial. *Voice:* song described as 'chip-pee-tee-peetle-pet'; female a 'tink', high-pitched 'seeeet' of alarm. *Habitat:* dense, often damp, coastal scrub. Restricted and rare. 🌊🔥🏞️🗻Ⓡ

Rufous Bristlebird *Dasyornis broadbenti* 23-26cm Medium-sized, built like a miniature pheasant. Head chestnut-capped, paler on nape. Upperparts olive, with plainer brown rump and wings (not chestnut). Tail long, brown, fringed. Underparts pale greyish buff, subtly marked with 'half-moon' spots (see Western). *Voice:* three or four paired clear musical notes, ending with a double whip-crack. *Habitat:* dense coastal scrub, thickets, woodland undergrowth. Note restricted range (overlaps with Western); locally fairly common. 🔥🏞️🏞️🗻Ⓡ

Pilotbird *Pycnoptilus floccosus* 17cm Small, plump, terrestrial bird. Face, throat, breast and belly rich chestnut buff, with yellow eye-ring. Crown, nape, back and wings olive brown. Tail brown, long, wedge-ended. Associates with lyrebirds as a pilotfish with a shark. *Voice:* male penetrating 'eee-see-a-week' answered by female's 'whit-aa, whit-ee'. *Habitat:* forest and woodland floors with copious leaf litter. Restricted but locally fairly common. 🦶🏞️Ⓡ

Origma *Origma solitaria* 13cm Small, dark scrubwren-like bird. Upperparts dark olive-brown, rather blacker on wings and tail, paler on head, with buff patch before and around eye. Throat white, contrasting with rich cinnamon rest of underparts. Largely terrestrial, always active, waves tail side to side and also flicks it up and down. *Voice:* repeated piercing melancholy 'good-bye', harsh scolding calls. *Habitat:* rocky hillsides, gullies and crags, usually near water. restricted range but locally common. 🏔️Ⓡ

Fernwren *Oreoscopus gutturalis* 13cm Small, distinctively dark, forest bird with striking head markings: clear white stripe over dark cheek; white throat and broad moustaches above black triangular bib. Juvenile has grey supercilium, paler grey-buff throat. Whole body dark greyish olive-brown, with comparatively short wings and tail. *Voice:* piercing high-pitched whistle; descending run of chattering notes ending in 'chip chip chip'. *Habitat:* forest floor and undergrowth, often over 500m. Restricted but locally fairly common. 🦶Ⓡ

Eastern Bristlebird

Western Bristlebird

Rufous Bristlebird

Pilotbird

Origma

Fernwren (adult)

Atherton Scrubwren *Sericornis keri* 14cm Tiny forest bird. Dark
olive-brown above, with faint supercilium. Wings brown, tail reddish-brown,
comparatively short. Underparts fawn with browner flanks. Legs pinkish
brown; beak black, relatively slim and pointed. Often feeds on ground as well
as in foliage (see Large-billed). *Voice:* scolding calls. *Habitat:* forest floor and
understorey. Restricted to rainforests above 600m on Atherton Tableland;
uncommon. 🐾 ®

Large-billed Scrubwren *Sericornis magnirostris* 13cm Tiny buff
forest bird. Upperparts buffish-brown; underparts pale. Tail short, rufous-
brown. Characteristic pale buff face emphasizes large dark eye and strikingly
long dagger-like black beak. Usually feeds like a thornbill, fluttering high in
foliage, rarely on the ground. *Voice:* sharp chattering; penetrating ongoing 's-
cheer, s-cheer...' *Habitat:* forests and woodlands, usually dense, often damp
up to 1500m. Comparatively widespread; rather commoner in north of range,
scarce in south. 🐾 🎵 ®

Yellow-throated Scrubwren *Sericornis citreogularis* 13cm Tiny,
smart scrubwren. Head pattern striking: forehead and large cheek patch
black, with bold white (yellow behind eye) supercilium and characteristic
bright yellow throat, shading to buffish white on breast and belly. Crown,
nape and back brown, rufous on tertials, with short reddish-brown tail. Short
wings blackish, with outer webs of primaries golden yellow, producing yellow
patch in closed wing. Female and immature duller and greyer. *Voice:* superb
songster and expert mimic, with fluid melodious notes. Sharp 'tack' contact
call. *Habitat:* leaf litter of dense woodland and forest, often near water.
Discontinuous distribution; locally fairly common. 🐾 🎵 ®

Tropical Scrubwren *Sericornis beccarii* 11cm Tiny scrubwren with
double white wingbar. Head pattern of blackish forehead and face broken by
faint white supercilium and moustachial streak, not prominent but clearer in
male than female. Upperparts brown, slightly more rufous on short wings,
rump and tail. Underparts buff. Distinctive bold double white bar on wing
formed by pale whitish covert tips. Active, sometimes in parties, scratching in
leaf litter. *Voice:* soft, quite musical 'seeer' or 'tsee-chew' notes in series;
harsh scolding calls. *Habitat:* rainforest, monsoon forest, riverine woodland,
usually dense. Restricted, but locally common. 🐾 🎵 ®

White-browed Scrubwren *Sericornis frontalis* 11-13cm Tiny, and
probably the most familiar scrubwren, occurring as several races. Head
pattern distinctive, with brown crown, blackish forehead, white supercilium
above and white moustachial streak below grey-brown cheek patch.
Upperparts brown. Underparts usually buff, yellowish (northeast), or spotted
(south and southwest). Tasmanian form cinnamon below, rufous brown above
is considered a separate species by some, Tasmanian Scrubwren *S. humilis.*
Voice: far-carrying 'see-chew' and 'tsseer' notes; harsh scolding calls.
Habitat: dense undergrowth in forests, woodland and tall scrub, heath,
mangroves, gardens. Widespread; locally common.
🏔️ 🦅 🌊 🐦 🎵 🎶 🎵 🏞️ ®

Scrubtit *Acanthornis magnus* 11cm Tiny scrubwren, with diffuse
whitish surround to brown eye, and distinctive grey cheek patch. Upperparts
rufous-brown, with a slim white wingbar. Tail chestnut, with black subterminal
band and pale tip. Throat white, shading to buff on belly and flanks. *Voice:*
call clear 'too-wee-too', pleasant whistling. *Habitat:* dense forest undergrowth,
fern gullies. Restricted to Tasmania; locally fairly common. 🎵 ®

Atherton Scrubwren

Large-billed Scrubwren

Yellow-throated Scrubwren

Tropical Scrubwren

White-browed Scrubwren

Scrubtit

Chestnut-rumped Heathwren *Hylacola pyrrhopygia* 14cm Small, terrestrial bird with colourful cocked tail. Upperparts dull olive-brown, greyer on head with faint pale supercilium. Throat, breast and belly whitish, with pale but conspicuous brown streaks, buffer under tail. Rump and base of tail bright chestnut, rest of tail browner, shading to black subterminal band and conspicuous broad white tip. Tail often held cocked and slightly fanned. Beak blackish, short and finely pointed. Legs grey, strong. Secretive and shy, swiftly hops into cover if disturbed - heard more often than seen. *Voice:* swells from quiet beginnings to full-throated canary-like melody with mimicry. Call a harsh 'zweeet'. *Habitat:* forest and woodland undergrowth, heath and dense scrub. Generally uncommon. 🐾 ♨ ®

Shy Heathwren *Hylacola cauta* 11-13cm Tiny, perky, 'groundwren' with conspicuous supercilium. Upperparts olive-brown, with bold white supercilium. Wings short, with striking white bar across base of primaries visible as patch in closed wing. More conspicuous in flight when black carpal patch also shows. Underparts whitish, boldly streaked dark brown, undertail pale buff. Rump and base of tail chestnut, rest of tail brown with darker subterminal band and conspicuous white tip. Tail relatively long, usually held cocked. Largely terrestrial, and shy. *Voice:* song rich and sweet, with mimicry; call 'chee-chee chickadee'. *Habitat:* shrubby woodland, mallee and other scrub, often on rocky hillsides. Discontinuous distribution; generally uncommon.
▥ ♨ ®

Redthroat *Pyrrholaemus brunneus* 12cm Tiny, generally inconspicuous, soberly-plumaged but melodious scrubwren. Upperparts pale olive-brown, with distinctive whitish patch between eye and beak. Throat pale chestnut in male, white in female; rest of underparts pale grey, washed buff on flanks. Tail dark brown, with broad white tip. Terrestrial and secretive. *Voice:* rich canary-like melodious song, likened to a melodious Clamorous Reed Warbler, often from high perches, containing much mimicry. *Habitat:* dense scrub: mulga, mallee, tea-tree, saltbush etc, often arid. Generally uncommon. ▥ ♨ ♨ ®

Striated Fieldwren *Calamanthus fuliginosus* 13cm Small, active, fieldwren, conspicuous in song. Upperparts olive brown, boldly streaked blackish, with distinct white supercilium tinged chestnut near beak. Underparts whitish on throat and upper breast, buffer elsewhere, liberally streaked dark brown. Tail usually held cocked, olive, darker near tip with conspicuous white terminal bar. Sings from tops of low scrub. *Voice:* extended, sharp musical twittering song, transcribed as 'wurr-wurr, chick-chick-wurr-ree-ree'. Often the only bird singing. *Habitat:* wide range of open areas with low scrub from inland saltbush to coastal dunes. Restricted to southeast, erratic, occasionally locally quite common. ♨ ▥ ♨ ♨ ♨ ®

Rufous Fieldwren *Calamanthus campestris* 13cm Small, active, streaky fieldwren, conspicuous in song. Upperparts reddish brown, sometimes only faintly streaked or unstreaked; otherwise features as Striated Fieldwren, including white supercilium and cocked tail with blackish and white tip. *Voice:* conspicuous song posts in low scrub, song as Striated Fieldwren. *Habitat:* arid inland low scrubs, sometimes venturing into gibber, sometimes coastal. Discontinuous, erratic; occasionally locally quite common. ▥ ♨ ®

Chestnut-rumped Heathwren

Shy Heathwren

Redthroat ♂

Striated Fieldwren

Rufous Fieldwren

Speckled Warbler *Chthonicola sagittata* 12cm Tiny, streaky-brown, terrestrial fieldwren. Upperparts brown, with darker mottling. Long curved supercilium, dipping behind cheek patch, yellowish in male, whitish in female. Throat and breast white, belly yellow-buff, all copiously dark-streaked. Legs strong, grey. Tail comparatively short, dark brown with a blackish subterminal band and conspicuous white tip; contrasts with plain yellowish-brown rump in flight. Often associates with other ground-feeding birds, comparatively approachable. *Voice:* short, sweet song with some mimicry, grating scolding call. *Habitat:* open forest, woodland and scrub, with bare ground, rocks and leaf-litter. Local; occasionally fairly common. ▥ ▨ ®

Weebill *Smicrornis brevirostris* 9cm Very tiny, stubby-beaked bird, active in foliage. Probably the smallest Australian bird. Upperparts range from olive-green to yellowish green (inland birds); underparts from creamy to bright pale yellow (interior and north). Pale, usually yellowish, stripe over eye; small blackish patch through eye accentuates white iris. Beak stubby, pale pinkish brown; legs long and slim, greyish. Tail comparatively short, blackish, with characteristic white tip. Flutters in and around canopy. *Voice:* noisy for its size, often heard before seen. Deep 'tee-did' with emphasis on first syllable, far-carrying 'willy-wheat'. *Habitat:* wide range of forests and woodlands; scrub, parks and gardens. Widespread; often common. ▥ ▨ ▥ △ ®

Brown Gerygone *Gerygone mouki* 10cm Tiny brownish warbler with whitish tail spots. Upperparts rich brown, tinged rufous on crown. Greyish-white stripe from beak to just behind eye. Eye reddish, set in black streak. Cheeks pale grey (brownish in north Queensland form). Throat whitish, underparts pale buff, tinged russet on flanks. Tail dark brown, all but central feathers broadly tipped white on underside, with broad blackish subterminal band, usefully characteristic. Active and vocal, often in groups. *Voice:* distinctive repetitive 'which-is-it' and 'deedle-it'. *Habitat:* rainforest, dense riverine woodland, occasionally mangroves. Discontinuous along east coast; locally fairly common in northern parts, often scarce towards the south. ▧ ▥ ▨ ®

Large-billed Gerygone *Gerygone magnirostris* 11cm Tiny, brownish warbler with an eye-ring. Upperparts slightly reddish brown; underparts clear white, shaded buff on flanks. Broken thin white eye-ring round reddish eye; lacks supercilium. Tail dark brown, with broad blackish subterminal band and indistinct grey tips. In ones or twos, fluttering around canopy. *Voice:* descending brief soft trill, repeated incessantly; sometimes simple extended series of double notes followed by descending trill. *Habitat:* rainforest near water, stream-side vegetation, swamps with trees, mangroves, occasionally gardens. Northern and discontinuous distribution; locally quite common. ▥ ▰ ▰ ▧ ▨ ▥ ®

Dusky Gerygone *Gerygone tenebrosa* 12cm The only gerygone with whitish eyes. Upperparts pale grey-brown, with buffish patch on forehead and slim white stripe over, and extending just behind, whitish eye. Dark eye patch, greyish cheek patch. Underparts whitish, suffused greyer on flanks. Beak slim and black. Legs slender, black. Tail brownish, with indistinct darker bar, lacking pale spots. Juvenile has grey-brown eyes. Active in foliage. *Voice:* repeated descending trills; slower 'chew-chew-chew whee' or 'chew-wheat'. *Habitat:* usually mangroves and adjacent swampy shrubs and woods; densely vegetated creeks and gorges. Inconspicuous and difficult to observe; probably locally fairly common. ▰ ▰ ▨ ▥ ®

Speckled Warbler ♀

Weebill (yellowish form)

Brown Gerygone (Southern form)

Large-billed Gerygone

Dusky Gerygone (adult)

Mangrove Gerygone *Gerygone levigaster* 11cm Tiny, brown warbler with whitish supercilium and tail spots. Upperparts pale grey-brown, with a clear white stripe extending over and just behind reddish eye, and with a black patch between eye and beak. Cheeks diffusely pale buff; underparts white, buffish on flanks. Tail brown, with a blackish subterminal band and subterminal white spots on the undersides of all but the central feathers. Beak and legs, slender, blackish. Usually feeds within the canopy, often obscured by leaves. *Voice:* sustained frail descending trilling song, with frequently repeated phrases. *Habitat:* usually mangroves and adjacent scrubby woodland. Discontinuous, but generally fairly common. ◢◣⚓ ♨ ⛆ ®

Western Gerygone *Gerygone fusca* 10cm Tiny, brown warbler with black-and-white tail. Upperparts brown, with obscure fawn supercilium; faint, interrupted whitish eye-ring; blackish line through red eye. Underparts whitish, suffused pale grey on breast. Tail characteristic, brown with white patch on outer feathers near the base, and another white patch on outer feathers near tip, which has broad black terminal bar. Tail wagged side to side. *Voice:* vocal, sustained frail trilling, rising and falling in pitch and volume. *Habitat:* catholic in choice of bush or tree cover, even in arid regions, feeding in foliage. Widespread, erratic; generally scarce but locally common in southwest. ♨ ⛆ △ ®

Green-backed Gerygone *Gerygone chloronota* 10cm Tiny, greenish-backed warbler. Upperparts greenish, including cheek patch. Underparts white, suffused yellow on flanks and beneath tail. Tail blackish with indistinct blackish subterminal band. Often solitary, usually shy and secretive. *Voice:* fragile trilling song. *Habitat:* dense vegetation - thickets, forest and woodland margins, mangroves, usually near water. Restricted to far north but often quite common near coast. ≋⚓ ♨ ⛆ ®

Fairy Gerygone *Gerygone palpebrosa* 11cm Tiny, brown-and-yellow warbler. Two races in Australia. Male *flavida* olive-buff above, with white forehead. Underparts pale lemon-yellow apart from small, inconspicuous black bib and white moustachial streaks. Male *personata* greenish above, darker on head, with small white forehead patch, substantial blackish throat with distinctive white moustachial streaks; rest of underparts lemon yellow. Tail blackish, with faint darker subterminal bar, no white tip. Females of two races similar: olive green above, lemon yellow below, with white forehead and throat. *Voice:* extended warble, varying in pitch and volume. *Habitat:* rainforest, dense scrub, mangroves. Northern distribution, *flavida* south of Atherton Tableland, *personata* north. Local, occasionally fairly common. ◢▭ 🐦 ♨ ⛆ ®

White-throated Gerygone *Gerygone olivacea* 11cm Tiny, green-and-yellow warbler. Upperparts olive-brown, tail blackish with broad white tips and with some white near base. Forehead white; black mark through reddish eye; throat white, rest of underparts yellow. Some northern birds lack white in tail. Immature lacks white forehead, and has entirely yellow underparts. Active in canopy foliage, hovers frequently. *Voice:* delicate and beautiful tinkling descending trill. *Habitat:* open forests and woodland, riverine woodland, open land with trees. Erratic in distribution and numbers; only locally common. ♨ ⛆ ®

Mangrove Gerygone (adult)

Western Gerygone (adult)

Green-backed Gerygone

Fairy Gerygone ♂ (race *personata*)

White-throated Gerygone (adult)

Mountain Thornbill *Acanthiza katherina* 10cm Tiny brown and whitish thornbill with white eyes. The only thornbill in its restricted range. Upperparts greenish brown, flecked yellowish about face. Eye strikingly white. Underparts whitish on throat and breast; rest of underparts pale yellowish buff, faintly streaked, darker olive-buff on flanks. Feeds high in canopy. *Voice:* resembles that of Brown. *Habitat:* upland rainforests in far northeast. Restricted, but locally quite common. 🐾 ®

Brown Thornbill *Acanthiza pusilla* 10cm Tiny: the typical 'small brown bird'. Upperparts olive-brown, flecked paler on forehead, shading to cinnamon on rump and base of tail. Tail has broad black subterminal band and obscure white tips. Throat and upper breast whitish, with brown streaks; belly whitish, washed yellow, shading to ginger on flanks. Eye reddish. Active and agile in and around canopy - fans tail in flight. *Voice:* deep 'peee-oar', musical but brief warbling song, with mimicry. Squeaking and buzzing contact calls. *Habitat:* rainforest, damp woodlands, riverine forest with dense understorey, scrub, gardens. Locally common. 🐾 ⚏ 🐾 ⚏ ®

Inland Thornbill *Acanthiza apicalis* 10cm Tiny, reddish-rumped thornbill. Often considered conspecific with Brown. Has distinctive habit of cocking tail as it moves through the foliage. Upperparts olive brown, whitish about face. Throat white, densely streaked brown; belly white, shading to yellow on flanks and beneath tail. Rump and base of tail reddish, contrasting with black terminal band and white tips to feathers. Various races, generally paler inland. *Voice:* deep buzzing and squeaking calls, harsh alarm note, melodious but brief song. *Habitat:* dry scrub and open woodland in east, wetter scrub, heath, mangroves in southwest. Widespread; locally common. ⚏ ⚏ △ ®

Tasmanian Thornbill *Acanthiza ewingii* 10cm Restricted to Tasmania. Chestnut on crown and wings. Upperparts brown with a reddish tinge. Throat whitish, streaked grey; rest of underparts whitish, yellower on flanks. Tail with slender blackish subterminal band and conspicuous whitish tips. Prefers denser, damper undergrowth than Brown. *Voice:* buzzing calls, transcribed as 'zit-zit-zit-whoorl', brief melodious song. *Habitat:* damp forest, woodland and tall scrub. Often common. 🐾 ⚏ ⚏ ®

Chestnut-rumped Thornbill *Acanthiza uropygialis* 10cm Tiny, pale, grey thornbill. Upperparts grey-brown, with faint white markings on forehead. Rump pale chestnut, clearly demarcated from grey back and black, white-tipped tail. Cheeks pale with greyish flecks. Eye white. Underparts whitish, unstreaked. Undulating flight. *Voice:* distinctive 'see' or 'see-see' calls, scolding 'tchick' notes; song based on 'see' notes, a musical jingle 'see-tit-tit-see....' often from bush-top songpost. *Habitat:* dry open woodland, scrub, saltbush, semi-arid grasslands. Widespread inland; often common. 🐾 ⚏ △ ®

Slaty-backed Thornbill *Acanthiza robustirostris* 10cm Tiny, dark-grey inland thornbill. Upperparts dark grey, faintly darker-streaked on crown. Eye reddish. Cheek white, flecked grey. Underparts white, flushed pale grey, unstreaked. Rump pale chestnut, tail largely blackish with white tips. *Voice:* 'see' contact calls, 'thrip' or 'thrrup' of alarm. Brief twittering song. *Habitat:* dense inland scrub, usually mulga, occasionally saltpan vegetation in west. Restricted to arid and semi-arid areas; fairly widespread but generally uncommon. ⚏ △ ®

Mountain Thornbill

Brown Thornbill

Inland Thornbill

Tasmanian Thornbill

Chestnut-rumped Thornbill

Slaty-backed Thornbill

Western Thornbill *Acanthiza inornata* 10cm Tiny and, nondescript.
Upperparts plain brown, characteristically yellowish-olive on rump, barely distinct from back and wings in flight. Tail brown, with blackish subterminal band and white tip. Underparts pale buff, yellower on flanks, unstreaked. Eye pale or whitish. *Voice:* various 'see' calls; quiet tinkling twittering song but with some mimicry. *Habitat:* open woodlands and scrub. Restricted, but locally common. 🦶🦶 ⬛ 🎋 ®

Buff-rumped Thornbill *Acanthiza reguloides* 11cm Tiny.

Upperparts generally olive green; forehead tinged chestnut, crown greyer, lacking supercilium. Cheeks pale cream, lightly darker-flecked. Rump yellow, conspicuous against white-tipped blackish tail in flight. Underparts yellowish (brightest in northern race *squamata*, but almost whitish in southern form), lightly flecked brown on throat. Feeds in parties on ground or bases of trees. *Voice:* rapid metallic 'pit-pit-pit-pitta-pitta' or variations on 'zizzi' notes. *Habitat:* open decrepit forest, woodland or scrub. Widespread, but erratic and not common. 🌿🦶🦶 ®

Slender-billed Thornbill *Acanthiza iredalei* 9cm Also called

Samphire Thornbill. Upperparts dull olive, flecked white on forehead, with faint whitish stripe extending to eye or just behind. Eye white, set in darker patch. Cheek and throat whitish, flecked grey. Breast and belly dull pale yellow. Rump pale yellowish buff, varying in width according to race, but contrasting in flight with white-tipped blackish tail. *Voice:* metallic 'tssip' notes, musical but metallic twittering. *Habitat:* saltbush, samphire, occasionally mangroves and coastal heath. Discontinuous. Local, and generally uncommon. ⬛ 🦬 🦐 ®

Yellow-rumped Thornbill *Acanthiza chrysorrhoa* 11cm Small,

but the largest and boldest-marked thornbill. Upperparts greyish-olive, with a distinctive black forehead flecked with white; a black-streaked white cheek patch; blackish line through eye, and whitish supercilium. Rump yellow, in flight giving a striking contrast with the white-tipped black tail. Underparts pale. Feeds in parties on ground or bases of trees. *Voice:* cheerful tinkling with repeated phrases, flight call a distinctive, repeated 'tcheck'. *Habitat:* open land with trees or scrub, including gardens. Widespread; often quite common. 🌿🦶🦶 ⬛ ®

Yellow Thornbill *Acanthiza nana* 10cm Tiny, yellowish thornbill.

Upperparts olive, tinged yellowish, with obscure paler forehead and black-flecked whitish cheeks. No supercilium. Underparts yellow. No distinct rump patch. Tail brown with black subterminal band and pale tip. Compare Weebill. Hovers in canopy showing uniform back and rump and dark tail. *Voice:* continued 'tizz' calls, rather harsh, sometimes linked in 'chidid-tis-tizz'. *Habitat:* dryish forest and woodland, often of *Acacia* and gardens, occasionally mangroves. Widespread but erratic; locally common. 🌿🦶🦶 ⬛ ®

Striated Thornbill *Acanthiza lineata* 10cm Tiny, can be confused

with Brown Thornbill, but more patterned. Upperparts greenish with brown crown and nape finely streaked with white. Whitish line over grey-brown eye; cheek patch whitish, finely streaked with black. Throat, white, streaked dark brown; rest of underparts white, yellowish on flanks. Tail brown, with black subterminal band and pale tip. Hovers in front of foliage and bark, picking off food items. *Voice:* buzzing 'tizziz', brief sharp insect-like notes. *Habitat:* dry forests and woodland, occasionally gardens, even mangroves. Reasonably widespread; sometimes common. ⬛ 🦶🦶 ®

Western Thornbill

Buff-rumped Thornbill

Slender-billed Thornbill

Yellow-rumped Thornbill

Yellow Thornbill

Striated Thornbill

Southern Whiteface *Aphelocephala leucopsis* 10cm Tiny, robust, brown-and-white, and the most simply marked of the whitefaces. Upperparts grey-brown, paler on head, with black-bordered white forehead patch. Tail dark brown, with white tips particularly conspicuous on outer feathers. Underparts whitish, shading to pale chestnut (darker in western birds) on flanks. Eye white. Beak short, black and characteristically stout. Feeds on or near ground, methodically searching every crack for food. *Voice:* fragile tuneful high-pitched song; continuous twittering 'tweeter' when feeding, flight call 'wit, wit-a-wit'. *Habitat:* open, usually dryish country with dead trees, from open woodland to scrub and grassy plains. Widespread but erratic; locally quite common. ⬛ 🔲 🔲 🔲 △ ®

Chestnut-breasted Whiteface *Aphelocephala pectoralis* 10cm Tiny, rare, desert whiteface. Forehead white, bordered in black; crown grey with black flecks and a short obscure white stripe behind eye. Mantle rich bronzy-brown; wings dark brown with pale feather fringes; tail blackish, white-tipped . Eye white . Underparts white, with characteristic chestnut breast band and chestnut on flanks. Beak black, stubby. *Voice:* song a silvery tinkling trill, bell-like calls. *Habitat:* arid or semi-arid plains, gibber, sparse scrub. Restricted; little known, probably rare. 🔲 🔲 △ ®

Banded Whiteface *Aphelocephala nigricincta* 10cm Tiny, with a distinctive black breast band. Head grey-brown, with black-bordered white forehead; sparse black speckling on crown. Mantle chestnut, rump sandy-brown; wings dark grey with conspicuous pale feather fringes especially on coverts. Tail black, relatively short and broad, tipped white. Underparts white, with characteristic narrow black band across breast; chestnut on flanks. Eye white; beak black, short and strong. Often in groups, sometimes with thornbills. Usually terrestrial and active. *Voice:* male has parachuting song-flight, rising steeply, singing, then dropping back into cover. Song brief, musical and high-pitched; insect-like buzzing calls. *Habitat:* stony plains with mulga and other scrub, gibber, saltbush and bluebush, grasslands. Widespread but erratic; locally fairly common. ⬛ 🔲 🔲 △ ®

Varied Sittella *Daphoenositta chrysoptera* 12cm Small, and as its name suggests, variably plumaged. Shape and habits are immediately diagnostic, more like a nuthatch of Eurasia than a whiteface, with a short soft tail and able to cling to bark head-up, head-down or sideways-on. Head ranges from whitish, through grey, to black. Upperparts generally grey-brown, with white (northern) or chestnut bar in wing, broad and distinctive in flight. Underparts white, ranging from scarcely marked to heavily streaked. Legs distinctively short, yellow and with powerful toes. Beak characteristically yellow with black tip, looks uptilted at tip. *Voice:* distinctive 'see-whit, see-whee', incessant 'chip' notes, song transcribed as 'zeer, zit-zit, zeer-zit-zat-zat'. *Habitat:* forest, woodland, scrub of most types, open land with trees, orchards, parks and large gardens. Widespread; rather erratic but often quite common. ⬛ 🔲 ®

Southern Whiteface (eastern form)

Chestnut-breasted Whiteface

Banded Whiteface

Varied Sittella (race *chrysoptera*) ♂

Varied Sittella (race *pileata*) ♀

White-throated Treecreeper *Cormobates leucophaeus* 14cm
Small, distinctively white-throated. Upperparts dull olive-tinged grey-brown, with white or cinnamon bar in wing and broad black subterminal blocks in tail. Female has small chestnut cheek spot. Throat white; breast and flanks heavily spotted and streaked in black and white. Immature shows striking chestnut rump. Northern race *minor* is smaller and darker. *Voice:* noisy high-pitched monotonous piping; song a mellow warbling trill. *Habitat:* rainforest, damp forest and woodland, tall scrub, riverine woodland. Relatively widespread; locally common. 🐾 ♫ ®

Red-browed Treecreeper *Climacteris erythrops* 14cm Small.
Upperparts grey-brown, with red eye-ring and broad supercilium. Conspicuous white throat; upper breast white, barred chestnut in female, grey in male. Rest of underparts covered in black-edged white streaks. Pale cinnamon-buff wingbar, conspicuous in fast, undulating flight. *Voice:* descending piping chatter, often of double notes. Brief mellow song. *Habitat:* dense rainforest and eucalypt forest, often in highlands. Southeastern; nowhere common. 🐾 ♫ ®

White-browed Treecreeper *Climacteris affinis* 14cm Small. Crown
and nape grey, with characteristic black-and-white striped ear coverts and white eyebrow, with chestnut stripe between eye and beak in female. Back grey-brown, with cinnamon bar in wings conspicuous in flight. Throat grey, rest of underparts white, densely streaked blackish. Undertail coverts barred blackish. Immature greyer, lacking streaks. Often feeds on the ground. *Voice:* thin 'peep, peep' calls, also 'peter-peter', feeble disjointed song. *Habitat:* semi-arid open woodland and scrub. Widespread but erratic and generally uncommon. ♫ 🐾 ®

Brown Treecreeper *Climacteris picumnus* 17cm Small. Head and
nape grey-brown, buffish supercilium and dark-streaked buff ear-coverts. Back brown, blackish in northern birds. Throat white. Breast grey with obscure black marks in male, obscure pale chestnut marks in female. Rest of underparts white, densely dark-streaked, barred on undertail coverts. Often feeds on the ground. *Voice:* loud repeated 'spink', gradually slowing and deepening. Sparrow-like chattering. *Habitat:* drier open forest and woodland clearings, riverine woodland. Widespread; locally quite common. ♫ 🐾 ⫴ ®

Rufous Treecreeper *Climacteris rufa* 16cm Small, colourful
treecreeper. Face cinnamon, with dark line through eye between supercilium and ear coverts. Upperparts olive-brown, with cinnamon bar in wing conspicuous in flight. Rump cinnamon. Breast-patch of male streaked black and white; female rufous and white. Lower breast, belly and undertail rich cinnamon, with darker barring. Immature paler, with rufous rump. *Voice:* single monotonous 'peep', scolding churring; descending, slowing staccato song. *Habitat:* forest, woodland, scrub or open land with trees. Locally common. ♫ ®

Black-tailed Treecreeper *Climacteris melanura* 18-20cm Medium-
small, but the largest, treecreeper. Upperparts dark sooty-brown. Underparts sooty brown (reddish brown in western race *wellsi*), with white throat with sparse chestnut streaks in female, densely black-streaked in male. Wingbar distinctive, pale yellowish fawn. Lacks supercilium. *Voice:* strident, piping 'pee, peepeepeepeepeepee, pee, pee'. *Habitat:* open forests and woodlands, open country with trees, riverine woodland. Discontinuous northern distribution; locally common. ♫ 🐾 ®

White-throated Treecreeper

Red-browed Treecreeper

White-browed Treecreeper

Brown Treecreeper

Rufous Treecreeper

Black-tailed Treecreeper (race *wellsi*) ♂

Red Wattlebird *Anthochaera carunculata* 34-36cm Large, slim, honeyeater. Head, nape and back dark grey-brown, streaked white. Wings and rump grey-brown, and scaly. Cheeks silvery white, with drooping red fleshy wattle at rear becoming larger with age. Throat and breast brown, streaked white; belly yellow, undertail white barred brown. Tail long and graduated, brown, with white tips to feathers visible from below. Long tail and short, rounded white-tipped wings distinctive in flight. *Voice:* one or more 'cough's in succession, 'yak' or 'yakyak', also ringing 'tew-tew-tew-tew', 'chock' of alarm. *Habitat:* open forest, woodland, most types of open area with trees. Widespread; erratic and mobile, sometimes quite common.
🐦🐦🎵🎵🎵🎵 ®

Yellow Wattlebird *Anthochaera paradoxa* 38-48cm The largest honeyeater, but confined to Tasmania. Overall a large but slim grey-brown bird with a bright yellow belly. Brown feathers pale-fringed above, giving scaly appearance; paler below with broad dark streaks. Long yellow fleshy wattles hang from behind eye, absent in immatures. *Voice:* harsh raucous croaking 'kuk' or 'kuk-kuk'. *Habitat:* montane forest and scrub to coastal heath, orchards, gardens. Restricted to Tasmania; common in central and eastern areas. 🐦🎵🎵🎵 ®

Little Wattlebird *Anthochaera chrysoptera* 26-30cm Large, slim, dull honeyeater. Upperparts dark brownish-grey, streaked with white on head, neck and mantle. Wings grey-brown, with paler feather edges giving scaly appearance. In flight, shows dull chestnut patch in midwing. Underparts grey-brown, streaked with white, lacking yellow belly. Tail long, graduated. At least three races: southwestern birds have distinctively paler cheeks than others and a red eye; *Voice:* vocal, often musical but raucous, 'cockay-cock', 'kwok', 'yekop' and one transcribed as 'fetch-the-gun'. *Habitat:* woodland, heath, scrub, favouring *Lantana* and *Banksia*, gardens. Discontinuous distribution; rather erratic, locally common. 🐦🎵🎵🎵 ®

Spiny-cheeked Honeyeater *Acanthagenys rufogularis* 22-27cm Medium-large, yellow-throated honeyeater. Upperparts brownish, with long blackish white-tipped tail. Beak short, black at tip, red at base. Red extends to fleshy patch from beak back around the eye. Characteristic face pattern consists of long black stripe though eye, white cheeks with spiny feathers, slim black moustachial streak and deep yellow throat and breast. Rest of underparts whitish, boldly spotted dark brown. *Voice:* strange strong repetitive calls like 'widit', 'peer', 'chonk', metallic but musical. *Habitat:* drier, often inland, woodland and scrub, saltbush, tea-tree. Widespread but irregular and highly nomadic; locally common. 🐦🎵🎵🎵🔺®

Striped Honeyeater *Plectorhyncha lanceolata* 22cm Medium-sized, brown-and-white honeyeater. Crown and nape white, with dark longitudinal streaks; white stripe over eye; black-streaked whitish cheek patch. Mantle brown, with darker feather centres. Wings and long, square-ended tail grey-brown. Throat white, bordered by black moustachial streaks; rest of underparts white, sparsely streaked dark brown. Beak short, finely pointed. Legs and feet distinctive blue-grey. *Voice:* mellow and melodious 'churr-churr, cherry-cherry', 'cherry-cherry-chew'. Rambling song, often produced flying above canopy. *Habitat:* drier open forest, woodland and scrub, usually inland, including mallee and mulga. Widespread but erratic and nomadic; sometimes locally fairly common. 🎵🎵🎵 ®

Red Wattlebird

Yellow Wattlebird

Little Wattlebird (eastern form)

Spiny-cheeked Honeyeater

Striped Honeyeater

Helmeted Friarbird *Philemon buceroides* 33-35cm Large. Beak long, black and knife-like, with a low 'rhinoceros horn' on the ridge (lacking in juveniles and race *ammiticola* of Arnhem Land NT). Facial patch of bare skin black. Distinctive short, tufted grey crest on nape. Upperparts plain grey-brown; tail long, pale grey-brown. *Voice:* loud and remarkably varied, metallic, commonly 'poor-devil' 'watch-out'. *Habitat:* rainforest, forest and woodland, shrubby habitats, gardens. Restricted; scarcer in west, locally quite common in east of range. 🐦 🌿 ♨ ⁝⁝⁝ ®

Silver-crowned Friarbird *Philemon argenticeps* 27-30cm Medium-large, similar to Helmeted Friarbird but smaller and paler-headed. Beak long, black and knife-like, with a 'rhinoceros horn' knob, sloping at front, rounded at rear. *Voice:* transcribed as 'more tobacco, uh-more tobacco-uh', nasal rather cat-like calls. *Habitat:* open forest, woodland and scrub, often on hillsides; riverine woodland, gardens, occasionally mangroves. Restricted; erratic and nomadic, but locally common. 🌿 ♨ ⁝⁝⁝ ®

Noisy Friarbird *Philemon corniculatus* 32-36cm Large, white-throated friarbird. Head and neck characteristic: largely bare black skin with white throat feathers and line of short buff feathers as 'eyebrow' over red eye. Beak knife-like, with a steep-sided 'rhinoceros horn' knob on ridge. Upperparts olive-brown; tail pale brown with narrow white terminal band. *Voice:* raucous, varied, 'keyholekeyhole', 'four-o-clock', harsh 'yakob' and other ringing, calls. *Habitat:* open forest, woodland and scrub, parks and gardens. Widespread; erratic, nomadic or migratory, but often regular and common. 🌿 ♨ ⁝⁝⁝ ®

Little Friarbird *Philemon citreogularis* 25-28cm Medium-large. Crown and central nape pale brown; sides of neck whitish. Bare facial skin patch distinctively blue-black, with blackish eye. Beak black, knife-like, lacking knob. Upperparts pale brown. Juvenile has yellowish throat. *Voice:* varied, mellow 'gee-wit', song a collection of 'cherweep cherwip chew-will' phrases. *Habitat:* open forest, woodland and scrub, riverine woodland, mangroves, orchards and vineyards (can be a pest), parks and gardens. Widespread and erratic, but generally quite common. 🌿 ♨ ⁝⁝⁝ ®

Regent Honeyeater *Xanthomyza phrygia* 20-23cm Medium-sized, distinctively black-and-yellow honeyeater. Head, nape, throat and upper breast black, with conspicuous, pinkish bare facial skin patch. Upperparts black, mantle and covert feathers with yellow margins. Underparts white, feathers with broad black margins giving a regular scaly appearance. Wings black with prominent yellow wingbar and yellow patch in primaries. Tail long and black, outlined in yellow, broader at tip. *Voice:* metallic 'chink' and 'quip' notes, mellow 'cloop'. *Habitat:* open forest and woodland, *Banksia* and mallee scrub, occasionally gardens. Erratic; becoming scarcer. 🌿 ♨ ⁝⁝⁝ ®

Blue-faced Honeyeater *Entomyzon cyanotis* 31cm Large. Crown and nape black, with small white line between the two. Face and cheek bare, characteristically bright to dark blue (yellowish in immatures), contrasting with white eye. Prominent black bib and white moustachial streaks joining white breast. Back and longish white-tipped tail striking golden olive. *Voice:* strident, distinctive 'woik!', wavering 'queet' notes. *Habitat:* open woodland, any areas with trees or shrubs. Widespread but erratic; locally common in north, scarcer in south. ♨ ®

Helmeted Friarbird (Queensland race)

Silver-crowned Friarbird

Noisy Friarbird

Little Friarbird

Regent Honeyeater

Blue-faced Honeyeater (adult)

Bell Miner *Manorina melanophrys* 19cm Medium-small, olive-green honeyeater. Distinctive at close range are black forehead, short black stripe before eye, short black moustachial streak, and small bare patch of orange skin behind eye. Characteristic olive green, washed golden on back and belly. *Voice:* high-pitched 'ting' closely resembling a bell. Scolding 'jack' notes and churring alarm call. *Habitat:* forest and woodland, usually damp with a dense understorey, suburbs and gardens. Locally quite common.
🐦 ♒♒ ♪♪ ⛫ ®

Noisy Miner *Manorina melanocephala* 24-27cm Medium-sized, mid-greyish honeyeater with distinctive head pattern consisting of pale greyish face, and black crown extending down through eye to link with slim black moustachial streak. Distinctively rich yellow beak and legs. Pale grey rump shows distinctively in flight. *Voice:* distinctive high-pitched 'pwee-pwee-pwee' and 'yoi-yoi-yoi'. *Habitat:* open forest and woodland, scrub. Catholic, often on farmland, in parks and gardens. Widespread but patchy; locally quite common. ▲ ♒♒ ♪♪ ⛫ ®

Yellow-throated Miner *Manorina flavigula* 25-27cm Medium-sized, distinctively pale-grey honeyeater, with black cheek patch, and small patch of bare yellow skin behind eye. Legs yellow. Underparts white, with yellowish tinge to throat. Race *obscura* of southwest Western Australia resembles Black-eared but has less black on face. Gregarious. *Voice:* strident 'pwee' and 'yoi' notes; churring alarm calls. *Habitat:* drier open woodland and scrub of most types, also parks, orchards and gardens. Widespread; patchy, but locally very common. ♪♪ ⛫ ®

Black-eared Miner *Manorina melanotis* 25cm Medium-sized honeyeater, a darker-backed version of Yellow-throated (of which some consider it to be a race). Distinctive black cheek patch with yellow patch of bare skin behind eye. Upperparts characteristically uniformly dull grey with faint darker mottling. Rump grey not pale. Underparts whitish, with dense mottling of pale grey-brown on breast. Lacks yellow on collar and throat. Characteristically shy - not a normal miner feature. *Voice:* similar to Noisy, with 'pwee', 'pee' and 'yoi' notes; churring alarm call. *Habitat:* mallee, occasionally other scrub. Restricted; very local, in scattered colonies but decreasing through hybridisation with spreading Yellow-throated. ⛫ ®

Macleay's Honeyeater *Xanthotis macleayana* 20cm Medium-sized, plump, dark honeyeater. Crown black; nape black flecked with white; mantle brownish black with buff mottling. Cheek patch of bare, yellowish skin round eye; white tuft of feathers on side of nape. Wings brown with distinctive bold arrowhead-shaped white spots. Throat and breast blackish-brown, margined with yellowish-chestnut; belly grey-brown with bold whitish spots. *Voice:* musical 'too-whit, too-whee-whit' but not often used. *Habitat:* rainforest, riverine woodland, swamp woodland, occasionally gardens. Restricted; locally quite common. ▲ 🐦 ♒♒ ®

Tawny-breasted Honeyeater *Xanthotis flaviventer* 19-21cm Medium-sized, dark, but characteristically unstreaked (see Macleay's) honeyeater. Crown dark brown; rest of upperparts dull olive-brown, faintly streaked grey on nape. Eye-ring and small patch of bare skin behind eye yellow. Cheek patch blackish, at close range outlined in yellow. Throat and breast grey. *Voice:* loud whistles; whistling song; one call transcribed as 'which-witch-is-which'. *Habitat:* scrub, woodland and forest edges, mangroves. Restricted; only locally common. 🐦 ♒♒ ⛫ ®

Bell Miner

Noisy Miner

Yellow-throated Miner

Black-eared Miner

Macleay's Honeyeater

Tawny-breasted Honeyeater

Lewin's Honeyeater *Meliphaga lewinii* 22cm Medium-sized, the
largest of four *Meliphaga* honeyeaters, all of which are generally brown with white or yellow cheek spots. Distribution maps are a useful additional aid to these four species. Lewin's is uniform darkish brown above, slightly paler below. Facial pattern characteristic, with narrow whitish line from beak to below eye (but not beyond); broad whitish half-moon cheek patch. *Voice:* familiar long loud staccato rattling. *Habitat:* most widespread and southerly of the group, catholic in habitat choice: woods, scrub, orchards, gardens. Often common in north, scarce farther south. 🦤 🐝 ♨ ⛰ ®

Yellow-spotted Honeyeater *Meliphaga notata* 18cm Medium-
small *Meliphaga* honeyeater, rather greener-washed on upperparts than Lewin's. Note northeast range. Upperparts greenish olive-brown; underparts paler and greyer. Triangular creamy cheek patch. Swooping flight; takes insects on the wing almost like a bee-eater. *Voice:* melodious 'chip', shrill 'ee-you', rattling song like Lewin's but delivery slower. *Habitat:* rainforest, other damp forest and riverine woodland, mangroves, plantations (especially bananas), gardens. Restricted distribution; locally common. 🦤 🐝 ®

Graceful Honeyeater *Meliphaga gracilis* 14-16cm Smallest of the
Meliphaga group, slim and pale. Upperparts palish olive-green; underparts characteristic, pale brownish-grey. Roughly diamond-shaped pale yellowish cheek patch. Most easily identified by voice. *Voice:* distinctive sharp 'plick', 'tick' or 'tuck'. *Habitat:* lowland forest and woodland with dense undergrowth, citrus orchards, gardens. Range similar to Yellow-spotted; locally fairly common. 🦤 🐝 ®

White-lined Honeyeater *Meliphaga albilineata* 19cm Medium-
small, robust, *Meliphaga* honeyeater with a whitish belly. Characteristic face pattern of small white crescent on cheek, and white line dipping below eye. Upperparts uniformly darkish grey-brown, breast grey with faint diffuse browner markings; belly whitish. *Voice:* fluting 'too-wheer, too-whit', sometimes in an accelerating series. *Habitat:* scrub in sandstone escarpment gorges. Note discontinuous northern and northwestern distribution. Locally quite common. 🐝 ♨ ⛰ ®

Eungella Honeyeater *Lichenostomus hindwoodi* 16-18cm Small,
localized honeyeater. Head pattern distinctive at close range, with pale yellow stripe running from beak, below eye, turning upward behind eye. Small white spot over eye; larger white patch at rear of cheek. Crown and mantle grey-brown. Underparts grey-brown. *Voice:* Far carrying, distinctive, up-and-down tinkling phrase: "pee-pee-pip-pip-pip...." Like an organ grinder. *Habitat:* restricted to rainforests and bordering open forests in the Clarke Range, Mackay, Queensland; status uncertain. 🦤 ®

Yellow-faced Honeyeater *Lichenostomus chrysops* 16cm Small,
plain honeyeater with distinctive yellow stripe from beak, below eye then widening to ear-coverts, distinctively bordered in black, with whitish tufts behind eye and ear. Upperparts olive-grey, underparts grey-buff with faint darker streaking. *Voice:* cheerful 'chick-up', fluting descending 'kalip kalip kalip...', 'dip' or 'tip' in flight. *Habitat:* catholic in selection of forest, woodland, scrub and cultivated land; also alpine heaths to over 1800m. Relatively widespread; often quite common. 🦤 🐝 ♨ ®

Lewin's Honeyeater

Yellow-spotted Honeyeater

Graceful Honeyeater

White-lined Honeyeater

Eungella Honeyeater

Yellow-faced Honeyeater

Bridled Honeyeater *Lichenostomus frenatus* 20cm Medium-small, large-beaked, dark-faced honeyeater. Head distinctive, with dark-brown crown, pale buffish nape, black forehead, chin and throat. Characteristic yellow line ('bridle') runs from beak to below eye, curving upwards behind eye. White tuft over eye. Ear-coverts black, faintly outlined by yellow line running from 'bridle'. Upperparts dark grey-brown; underparts brown. *Voice:* tuneful 'wee-aar' and 'watchitta'; rattling song. *Habitat:* highland rainforests when breeding, at other times also lowland woods of varied nature. Restricted, but locally common. 🐾 ®

Singing Honeyeater *Lichenostomus virescens* 18-22cm Medium-sized honeyeater. Head distinctive (see Varied), with long black stripe through eye and down nape over shorter yellow stripe from eye to ear-coverts. Below this runs a less conspicuous pale grey stripe, widening as it reaches nape. Upperparts grey-brown, underparts pale buff, with pale, brownish streaks. *Voice:* despite name, not a prime songster, with rather harsh 'scree', 'prritt' and 'crick-cricket' calls, rattling song. *Habitat:* scrub and woodland from coast to semi-arid interior, cultivated land and gardens. Widespread; locally fairly common.
🪶 ⚓ ♨ 🌾 △ ®

Varied Honeyeater *Lichenostomus versicolor* 20cm Medium-sized, noisy, yellowish honeyeater. Head characteristic, with broad black stripe over plain yellow moustachial area, through the eye, and curving well down sides of nape. Bold white patch below the black from ear-coverts down side of nape. Upperparts olive-brown, underparts yellow, with brownish streaks on breast. *Voice:* boisterous, repetitive, described as 'go-bidger-roo', 'which-way, which-way-you-go'. *Habitat:* coastal scrubs, especially mangroves. Restricted but locally common. ⚓ 🌾 ®

Mangrove Honeyeater *Lichenostomus fasciogularis* 20cm Medium-sized, dark honeyeater, often considered a race of Varied with distinctive throat. Black streak through eye and black-and-white stripe on sides of nape similar to Varied, but throat and upper breast characteristically yellow, bordered by blackish breast band. Upperparts dark olive brown, underparts buff, streaked brown. *Voice:* musical and varied collection of calls, broadly similar to but more tuneful than Varied. *Habitat:* mangroves and adjacent coastal woodland along central east coast. Common in north, scarce in south. ⚓ 🌾 ®

White-gaped Honeyeater *Lichenostomus unicolor* 18-22cm Medium-sized, dull honeyeater, noisily conspicuous. Upperparts plain grey-brown, underparts uniformly dull grey. Diagnostic small white wedge at base of beak. *Voice:* varied and loud, 'whit-oh-wee' or 'whit-ah-whit', sharp 'chop', melodious whistles and trills. *Habitat:* usually near water, mangroves, riverine woodland, swamp woodland, occasionally suburban areas. Locally common in north of range, scarcer to the east. ⚓ ♨ 🌾 ®

Yellow Honeyeater *Lichenostomus flavus* 16-19cm Small, plump and distinctive, like a long-tailed, slim-beaked canary. Upperparts yellow green, golden on wings, with faint dark line through eye and olive cheek patch. Underparts rich yellow. *Voice:* loud whistles, sharp 'whee' or 'whee-ah-whee' calls, trills, and an abrupt 'tutt'. *Habitat:* coastal and riverine forests and woods, mangroves, swamp woods, orchards and gardens. Northeastern, rather patchy, but locally common. 🪶 ⚓ ♨ ♨ 🌾 ®

Bridled Honeyeater

Singing Honeyeater

Varied Honeyeater

Mangrove Honeyeater

White-gaped Honeyeater

Yellow Honeyeater

White-eared Honeyeater *Lichenostomus leucotis* 20cm Medium-small. Upperparts greenish, underparts pale yellowish olive. Head dark, with a characteristic comma-shaped bold white cheek patch. *Voice:* loud and varied, 'chock-up', metallic 'chung-chung-chung', whistling 'beer-brick' and melodious 'cherrywheat'. *Habitat:* varied woodland, forest and scrub. Discontinuous distribution; erratic but locally common, scarce in north of range. 🐝 ♨ ⫴⫴ ®

Yellow-throated Honeyeater *Lichenostomus flavicollis* 20cm Medium-small. Upperparts olive-green. Crown dark grey; ear coverts pale blue-grey, with small yellow spot behind 'ear'. Black moustachial streaks enclose bright yellow chin and throat. Upper breast blackish, shading to pale grey. *Voice:* metallic 'tonk, tonk, tonk', plus 'chook' and 'cher-uk' and a call transcribed 'pick-em-up'. *Habitat:* catholic selection of woodland, forest, farmland and suburban environments. Confined to Tasmania and adjacent islands, where widespread and often common. 🐝 ♨ ⫴⫴ 🌿 ®

Yellow-tufted Honeyeater *Lichenostomus melanops* 19-22cm Medium-sized and striking honeyeater with gold and black head. Crown dull to bright yellow, black patch extending from beak to eye, and with golden ear tufts. Upperparts greenish-olive, underparts generally yellow, blotched greenish-olive. Race *cassidix* (Helmeted Honeyeater) very rare (one area in south-east Victoria) has shortly tufted bright yellow crown contrasting strongly with blackish-olive mantle. *Voice:* varied; sharp and metallic 'yip', 'yeeow' and 'querk', with soft more musical whistling notes. *Habitat:* eucalypt forest, woodland, usually with dense understorey, inland in mallee and brigalow. Widespread in southeast, but erratic, only locally common. 🐝 ♨ ⫴⫴ ®

Purple-gaped Honeyeater *Lichenostomus cratitius* 17-19cm Medium-small, slim, honeyeater. Characteristic yellowish chin and throat, and purplish line (yellow in immature) of bare skin along gape from beak to below eye. Black patch around eye, with a pale yellowish plume on ear coverts. Head grey, rest of upperparts greyish-olive; underparts pale grey, faintly washed yellow. Secretive. *Voice:* noisy and varied; clicks, whistles, whip-cracks, harsh chirps and softer warbling. *Habitat:* often mallee; in southwest, open grassy woodland and scrub. Discontinuous distribution; erratic in numbers and appearance. 🐝 ♨ ⫴⫴ ®

Grey-headed Honeyeater *Lichenostomus keartlandi* 15-17cm Small. Crown distinctive pale grey, merging into grey-green mantle and back. Characteristic sooty face patch, with black and yellow bar over ear. Throat, breast and belly distinctive lemon yellow, faintly streaked pale brown. *Voice:* less strident than White-plumed but otherwise similar; 'chee-toit, chee-toit'; mellow 'chickohwee'; weak trill of alarm. *Habitat:* rocky hillsides, gorges; mallee and mulga. Widespread but erratic distribution; rarely common. ♨ ⫴⫴ ®

Yellow-plumed Honeyeater *Lichenostomus ornatus* 13-16cm Small. Upperparts olive-green, with dark smudge through eye, and another dark smudge over ear, in front of a distinctive yellow half-collar neck plume. Underparts whitish, streaked with brown. *Voice:* sharp 'jo-jo hick', 'chick widideee' or 'chickoweee'; song flight 'hit jo-jo, hit jo-jo, hit'. *Habitat:* semi-arid scrub including mallee. Widespread; erratic, sometimes locally common. ♨ ⫴⫴ ®

White-eared Honeyeater

Yellow-throated Honeyeater

Yellow-tufted Honeyeater

Purple-gaped Honeyeater

Grey-headed Honeyeater

Yellow-plumed Honeyeater

Grey-fronted Honeyeater *Lichenostomus plumulus* 13-16cm
Small. Head pale grey-brown; upperparts olive-fawn, underparts grey-buff,
faintly streaked. Black mark in front of eye; narrow black margin to lower
edge of olive-brown ear-coverts. Characteristic broad yellow neck plume.
Voice: call 'it-wert, it-wert wert wert', sharp metallic 'boink' of alarm. *Habitat:*
semi-arid scrub including mallee and mulga, scrub along dry watercourses,
sparse trees and scrub on rocky hillsides. Relatively widespread across
interior, but patchy and erratic in appearance, local. ♨ ▦ △ ℞

Fuscous Honeyeater *Lichenostomus fuscus* 15cm Small, plain,
honeyeater. Upperparts grey-brown, underparts pale beige-brown. Small
black and yellow neck plume. Characteristic blackish smudge around eye.
Voice: transcribed as 'arig, arig-a-taw-taw' but very variable, to 'pit-quoll, pit-
quoll'. Song flight metallic 'tew-tew-tew-tew'. *Habitat:* variety of open forest
and woodland, riverine forest, scrub and gardens. Relatively widespread in
east and southeast; erratic in places, generally common except in south.
♨♨ ♨ ▦ ℞

Yellow-tinted Honeyeater *Lichenostomus flavescens* 15cm Small,
nondescript. Upperparts sandy-brown, underparts yellowish, with faint
streaking. Characteristic sigmoid black-and-yellow neck plume. Immature
has black-tipped yellow beak. *Voice:* 'jer' or 'jer-jer', descending 'tew-tew-
tew', often incessant. Song high and clear whistling and fluting. *Habitat:*
watercourse vegetation, woodland, occasionally mangroves. Generally fairly
common. ♨♨ ♨ ▦ ℞

White-plumed Honeyeater *Lichenostomus penicillatus* 15-17cm
Small, plain honeyeater. Upperparts pale olive-green. Face yellower and
paler. Underparts pale yellowish grey-buff. Characteristic narrowly black-
bordered, long, white neck plume. Immature has distinctive all-yellow beak.
Voice: brisk 'chickowee' or 'chick-abiddy', rapid sharp chatterings, strident
high-pitched trilling alarm call (likened to an alarm clock). Male in song flight
produces repeated 'chickowee' or 'chick-wert' notes. *Habitat:* usually close to
water in eucalypt woodland or forest, occasionally in open woodland or
scrub, including mallee. Widespread; often quite common. ♨ ▦ △ ℞

Black-chinned Honeyeater *Melithreptus gularis* 17cm Small,
drab honeyeater, with a black forehead and crown, white bar across upper
nape, and black patches through eyes and over cheeks extending and
meeting across back of nape in a black bar. Small black throat patch, with
white moustachial streaks broadening below eye. Bare blue skin over eye.
Upperparts brown, tinged olive. Northern and western birds are golden on
mantle and wings (sometimes treated as a full species, *M laetior* (Golden-
backed Honeyeater)). Underparts pale grey-buff. *Voice:* distinctive high-
pitched grating, croaking and churring, extended into a 'song'. Contact call a
bee-eater-like 'chrrip'. *Habitat:* open woodland, often eucalypt, tall scrub,
riverine woodland. Widespread but erratic in interior; locally quite common.
♨♨ ♨ ▦ △ ℞

Strong-billed Honeyeater *Melithreptus validirostris* 16cm The
Tasmanian equivalent of the Black-chinned. Upperparts dull olive-brown,
underparts dark grey-buff. Head pattern like Black-chinned, but chin patch
less conspicuous. *Voice:* as Black-chinned. *Habitat:* heavily timbered areas,
usually with dense understorey. Restricted to Tasmania and islands nearby;
locally common. ♨ ♨♨ ♨ ℞

Grey-fronted Honeyeater

Fuscous Honeyeater

Yellow-tinted Honeyeater

White-plumed Honeyeater

Black-chinned Honeyeater

Strong-billed Honeyeater

Brown-headed Honeyeater *Melithreptus brevirostris* 11-14cm

Small, dull honeyeater. Upperparts brown, olive on mantle; underparts fawn. Forehead and crown characteristically rich brown, with narrow white band from eye to eye across nape. Brown cheek patches extend behind eye and meet in a broad bar below white on nape. White moustachial streaks. Distinctive yellow fleshy eye-ring. *Voice:* loud 'chip' calls extended and linked into rattling song, accelerating then slowing. Hard trill of alarm. *Habitat:* several types of forest, woodland and scrub. Discontinuous distribution; erratic inland but generally locally common. 🐾 🔆 ▥ ®

White-throated Honeyeater *Melithreptus albogularis* 14cm

Small. Crown and nape black, nape crossed by a narrow white bar which almost reaches the eye. Half-ring over eye white or pale blue. Black extends below eye and through ear coverts, finishing as a broad pointed streak down onto breast. Upperparts olive-brown; underparts pure white. *Voice:* sharp 'pseee', monotonously repetitive 'tt-tee tt-tee...' or 'gorgee', and 'tserp-tserp'. *Habitat:* catholic in choice of forest, woodland, open areas with plentiful trees. Widespread across north; erratic in places but locally common. 🐾 🔆 ®

White-naped Honeyeater *Melithreptus lunatus* 14cm

Small, pink-legged honeyeater with ragged black collar. Upperparts olive; underparts pure white. Forehead and crown black; black nape interrupted by horizontal white bar, stopping well behind eye (see White-throated). Skin over eye pale whitish (western) or orange (eastern birds). Black sides to head, expanding on ear coverts and stretching in jagged half-collar down onto sides of breast. *Voice:* scratchy 'shirp', high-pitched 'cheep', characteristic mellow 'tsew' calls all repeated frequently; alarm a repeated quiet 'pew'. *Habitat:* several forest and woodland types, often eucalypt. Discontinuous; erratic but locally common, sometimes abundant on migration. 🐾 🔆 ®

Black-headed Honeyeater *Melithreptus affinis* 13cm

Small Tasmanian honeyeater, distinguished by all-black hood and small blue-grey skin patch over eye. Black nape extends as half-collar down onto sides of breast. Upperparts olive-brown; underparts white, greenish on flanks. *Voice:* sharp whistle, various 'sherp' and 'cheep' calls. *Habitat:* forests and woodlands, orchards, parks and gardens. Confined to Tasmania and adjacent islands; widespread and locally common. 🪨 🔆 🐾 🔆 ®

Green-backed Honeyeater *Glycichaera fallax* 12cm

Small, nondescript, warbler-like honeyeater. Upperparts greenish, browner on wings and tail. Head greenish-olive with faint whitish eye-ring. Underparts characteristic with white throat, rest pale yellow. Beak long and curved; legs distinctive, blue-grey. Active and acrobatic in foliage. *Voice:* reported as a warbler-like 'peeep', twittering calls, 'twee-twee-twit-twit' gradually rising in pitch. *Habitat:* rainforest and adjacent woodland and scrub. Restricted distribution, but locally quite common. 🐾 ®

Brown Honeyeater *Lichmera indistincta* 14cm

Small, dull long-beaked honeyeater. Upperparts brown, with distinctive whitish triangle behind eye. Breast grey-buff; belly paler. Beak long and slim, strongly downcurved, giving a bee-eater-like appearance. *Voice:* characteristic powerful melodious song (like Clamorous Reed Warbler), harsh alarm calls. *Habitat:* catholic, from forests and woodlands to arid scrubs and suburban gardens. Widespread; scarce inland, generally common, if patchy, elsewhere. 🪨 🪨 🔆 🐾 🔆 ▥ ▥ △ ®

Brown-headed Honeyeater

White-throated Honeyeater

White-naped Honeyeater

Black-headed Honeyeater

Green-backed Honeyeater

Brown Honeyeater

White-streaked Honeyeater *Trichodere cockerelli* 16cm Small.
Upperparts dark brown, feathers of wing conspicuously yellow-fringed. Ear-coverts brown, white streaked, with characteristic golden ear-tufts. Throat and breast brown, with broad white feather centres producing scaly appearance. *Voice:* varied, noisy, often scolding calls, melodious 'sweet-sweet-quarty-quarty' song. *Habitat:* scrub and woodland, often moist. Restricted range, but locally fairly common. 🦅 🎋 ♠ ®

Tawny-crowned Honeyeater *Phylidonyris melanops* 15-18cm
Medium-small. Upperparts pale olive-brown. Stripe over eye white, with black mark from beak through eye, ending in black-and-white ear tufts. Distinctive broad 'moustachial' streaks down sides of breast. *Voice:* quiet high-pitched fluting 'a-peer-peer-pee-pee-pee'. *Habitat:* heaths, occasionally in gardens. Discontinuous and erratic; generally uncommon but sometimes abundant. 🎋 🦅 ®

Crescent Honeyeater *Phylidonyris pyrrhoptera* 15cm Small.
Upperparts dark grey, with a bright golden patch in the wing. Short white stripe behind the eye. Throat whitish, finely streaked, bordered by horseshoe-shaped blackish collar, the 'crescent' of its name. *Voice:* high-pitched sharp 'egypt' or 'juk'; brief melodious warble of song. *Habitat:* woodland, forest, scrub and heath, gardens. Erratic and patchy; locally fairly common on mainland, often common in Tasmania. ♠ ♠ 🎋 🦅 ®

New Holland Honeyeater *Phylidonyris novaehollandiae* 18cm
Medium-small. Upperparts blackish; wings black with bold bright yellow panel. Tail long, blackish with a white terminal band. Distinctive face pattern, with white eye surrounded by a triangular black patch contained by white rear supercilium, moustachial streak and small (see White-cheeked) cheek patch. Throat black, streaked white; belly white with bold black spots. *Voice:* sharp 'tjit' and 'tzeeet', varied piping and chattering calls. *Habitat:* scrub, woodlands, heath and semi-arid mallee associations. Widespread but discontinuous distribution; locally common, scarcer in Queensland. 🐟 ♠ ♠ 🎋 ®

White-cheeked Honeyeater *Phylidonyris nigra* 16-18cm Small.
Characteristic head pattern of black crown, with narrow white stripe over black mask patch. Upperparts sooty black, with bright yellow patch in wing, distinctive when perched and in flight. Throat black. Large white cheek patch. Underparts white, boldly streaked blackish. *Voice:* squeaky 'chip-tew, chippey-chew', brief 'chip', song repetitive 'twee-eee, twee-eee', usually on the wing. *Habitat:* varied, from rainforest edges to coastal heath, eucalypt woodland with dense undergrowth to swamp woodland. Discontinuous; ranging high into the hills, locally quite common. 🐟 ♠ ♠ 🎋 🦅 ®

White-fronted Honeyeater *Phylidonyris albifrons* 16-18cm Small.
Upperparts brown, darker on crown. Throat and breast black, rest of underparts white with heavy black streaks. Forehead and patch round eye white, with small fleshy pinkish spot behind eye. White moustachial streak. Beak heavy, forehead sloping and head disproportionately large, giving top-heavy appearance. *Voice:* metallic 'pert-pertoo-wheet', more melodic 'peter-peet-peet' with varied emphasis on syllables. *Habitat:* more arid scrub, woodland, forest; including mallee and mulga. Widespread, but erratic and generally uncommon. ♠ ♠ 🎋 △ ®

White-streaked Honeyeater

Tawny-crowned Honeyeater

Crescent Honeyeater

New Holland Honeyeater

White-cheeked Honeyeater

White-fronted Honeyeater

Painted Honeyeater *Grantiella picta* 16cm Small black, white and yellow honeyeater. Upperparts blackish, with pale feather fringes especially on wing coverts. Bold yellow bar in wing. Tail short, with striking yellow panels. Small white tuft at rear of ear coverts. Underparts white flecked brownish black on sides of breast and flanks. Beak distinctively pink. Feeds on mistletoe. *Voice:* noisy, disyllabic 'geor-gie' or 'et-tee', 'pretty-pretty' - strung together in loud and quite melodious song. *Habitat:* open woodland and forest, trees usually carrying mistletoes; scrub including mallee and mulga. Widespread but patchy and erratic. 🚜 ♎ △ ®

Brown-backed Honeyeater *Ramsayornis modestus* 11cm Small, slim honeyeater. Upperparts olive-brown, ear-coverts darker and greyish; slim short white moustachial streak. Throat white; breast white with faint brownish crescentic barring; belly white tinged buff. *Voice:* characteristic chattering 'shee-shee-shee', sharp 'chit'; 'mick-mick-mick' distinctive in flight. *Habitat:* waterside trees and scrub (and adjacent flowering trees); mangroves. Restricted; often common near northeast coast. 🌊 ♎ 🏚 ®

Bar-breasted Honeyeater *Ramsayornis fasciatus* 12-15cm Small, dark honeyeater. Upperparts brown, tinged olive by paler feather fringes on wings and by greyish mottling and streaking on crown and mantle. White narrow stripe over eye. Cheeks white; narrow moustachial streak black. Underparts white, boldly barred dark brown on breast and flanks. *Voice:* repeated quiet 'mew', piping trill. *Habitat:* northerly, patchy and erratic; locally quite common. 🌊 ‡‡ 🏚 ↑ ®

Rufous-banded Honeyeater *Conopophila albogularis* 12cm Small, plump, short-tailed honeyeater. Head dull grey; nape, mantle and back brown; characteristically short tail and wings dark brown with yellow feather fringes. Throat distinctively white above a broad, dull, pale-chestnut breast band (lacking in juveniles). Rest of underparts whitish, buffer on flanks. *Voice:* repetitive 'tzeeep', plaintive and rising in tone. Musical high-pitched twittering 'sweetah-zwee, sweeta-zwee' song. *Habitat:* scrub vegetation near water, swamp woodland, mangroves, occasionally cultivated areas and gardens. Northerly; locally fairly common. 🏚 △ ®

Rufous-throated Honeyeater *Conopophila rufogularis* 13cm Small. Upperparts brown, greyer on head, with dark brown wings and tail showing yellow feather fringes. Underparts generally pale buff, but with characteristic rufous throat patch (absent in juveniles) bordered by whiter moustachial areas. Active and acrobatic; conspicuous noisy, fluttering display in breeding season. *Voice:* rasping sparrow-like chatter, sometimes sweeter in tone; sharp 'tzit-tzit' calls. *Habitat:* often close to water: mangroves; occasionally drier scrub and gardens. Quite widespread in north; locally common in west of range, scarce in east. ⚏ ‡‡ 🏚 ↑ ®

Grey Honeyeater *Conopophila whitei* 11cm Small, almost tiny. Upperparts plain brownish-grey with darker wings faintly washed yellow and dark brown; underparts whitish, washed pale buff on breast. Behaves more like a white-eye or a *Gerygone* warbler. *Voice:* silvery run of lisping notes like a white-eye. *Habitat:* semi-arid mulga and other scrub, occasionally round homesteads. A little-known species, quite widespread in the arid interior of the west, but generally rare. 🏚 △ ®

Painted Honeyeater

Brown-backed Honeyeater

Bar-breasted Honeyeater

Rufous-banded Honeyeater (adult)

Rufous-throated Honeyeater (adult)

Grey Honeyeater

Eastern Spinebill *Acanthorhynchus tenuirostris* 16cm Small and colourful. Male has black hood, extending as half-collars down either side of white throat and breast, which has a characteristic rufous and black central spot. Mantle bronze; wings dark blue-grey; tail blue-black with conspicuous white tips to outer feathers. Belly pale cinnamon-buff. Female duller with faint crescent; immature olive-grey above, pale fawn below. *Voice:* high-pitched, high-speed piping, often extended and with fluctuations in volume, pace and tone. *Habitat:* varied forest and woodland, occasionally gardens. Relatively widespread but patchy and irregular; only locally common. 🐦 ♣♣ ⪾ ⪾ ®

Western Spinebill *Acanthorhynchus superciliosus* 16cm Small. Male has grey crown; short white stripe over eye; thick black band through eye and over ear coverts; white chin, and moustachial streaks above striking chestnut throat and breast. Double collar of white and black bands separates breast from pale buff belly. Rest of upperparts olive-brown; tail dark grey-brown with conspicuous white tips to outer feathers. Female brown above with distinctive chestnut nape. White stripe over eye and white moustachial area, otherwise unmarked pale buff below. *Voice:* staccato high-pitched piping, transcribed 'kleet-kleet'. *Habitat:* forest and woodland with good undergrowth, coastal thickets of *Banksia* and *Dryandra*. Confined to southwestern corner; erratic but locally common. 🐦 ♣♣ ⪾ ⪾ ®

Banded Honeyeater *Certhionyx pectoralis* 12-13cm Small. Adult has black crown, back, wings and tail contrasting with white rump, conspicuous in flight. Underparts white with distinctive black breast band. Immature has brown replacing black pattern of adult, with chestnut mottling on mantle; intermediate stages are patchy. *Voice:* clear tinkling twitter of song, various short 'tip' 'tweet', 'jap' calls, single or double. *Habitat:* woodland, swamp woodland, scrub, riverine shrubs, mangroves, occasionally distant from water round flowering trees. Fairly widespread in north, but erratic; locally common. 🐦 ♣♣ ⪾ ⪾ ®

Black Honeyeater *Certhionyx niger* 10-12cm Tiny, long-beaked honeyeater. Male strikingly black and white. Upperparts, face, throat and line down centre of breast black; tail relatively short, black and shallowly notched. Underparts clear white. Female and immature inconspicuous: mottled brown above, with faint paler stripe behind eye; whitish below with buff speckled band across breast. *Voice:* thin 'seeep', 'seee-seee' or 'peee' frequently repeated in song flight. Other sparrow-like chattering calls. *Habitat:* arid or semi-arid inland scrub, often in burnt or regenerating areas. Widespread across interior but very erratic; locally common. ⪾ △ ®

Pied Honeyeater *Certhionyx variegatus* 15-17cm Small, but largest in this group of honeyeaters; male strikingly pied, female brown. Male has black hood and mantle, contrasting with white shoulder and white bar in otherwise black wings; white rump and white base to tail. Underparts white. Female and immature mottled brown above with paler rump; pale buff below, faintly darker-streaked on breast and flanks. Both sexes have small blue-grey fleshy patch below eye visible at close range. *Voice:* comparatively quiet extended 'tee-titty-tee-tee'. *Habitat:* semi-arid to arid savannah country, dry thin scrubland with flowering shrubs. Widespread across interior but very erratic; locally common. ⪾ ♣♣ △ ®

Eastern Spinebill ♂

Eastern Spinebill (adult ♂)

Western Spinebill (adult ♂)

Banded Honeyeater (adult)

Black Honeyeater ♂

Pied Honeyeater ♂

Dusky Honeyeater *Myzomela obscura* 13cm Small, slim, uniformly coppery-brown honeyeater. Upperparts coppery-grey-brown; underparts only slightly paler with suggestion of dark mark in front of eye and on chin. Some may be appreciably paler, others reddish on head. Beak relatively long, black and slim, slightly downcurved. Active, noisy and sometimes inquisitive; hovers and flycatches around blossoms. *Voice:* soft squeaking 'see-see-see', fluting whistle and chattering trill. *Habitat:* coastal rainforest, woodland and scrub, mangroves; swamp woodland and riverine growth, occasionally gardens. Discontinuous but reasonably sedentary; locally common except in south of range. ⚓ 🐦 🌳 ⛰ ⛰ ⫿⫿⫿ ®

Red-headed Honeyeater *Myzomela erythrocephala* 12cm Small, male distinctively red and black. Male has characteristic red hood, contrasting with black eye-patch, black mantle and wings. Red rump conspicuous in flight, contrasting with relatively short black tail. Underparts sooty brown, paler on belly. Female and immature pale grey-brown above; darker olive-brown on wings and tail, with patches of scarlet around face and throat. Beak relatively long and strongly downcurved. Often in pairs, usually active and fast moving. Despite bright colour difficult to see well in foliage. *Voice:* harsh whistling 'chee-ewe-chee-ewe-chee-ewe'. *Habitat:* mainly mangroves, adjacent scrub and woodland areas, swamp woodland, occasionally gardens. Locally quite common. ⚓ 🌿 ⫿⫿⫿ ®

Scarlet Honeyeater *Myzomela sanguinolenta* 11cm Tiny; male distinctively red, black and white. Male has scarlet hood, breast, back and rump, contrasting with black wings (coverts and primaries showing faint white fringes) and short black tail. Rest of underparts white. Female and immature plain brown above; buffish on breast, often with a pink flush on face and throat. Whiter on belly and beneath tail. Active and darting, with bouncing flight. *Voice:* silvery descending tinkling trill, fading in volume; various high-pitched squeaks and twitters. *Habitat:* rainforest, other forest and woodland, riverine vegetation, occasionally gardens. Locally fairly common but erratic along east coast; scarce south of Sydney. ⚓ 🌿 🌳 ⛰ ⫿⫿⫿ ®

Dusky Honeyeater

Red-headed Honeyeater ♂

Scarlet Honeyeater ♂

Crimson Chat *Epthianura tricolor* 11cm Small, plump and upright chat. Adult male has striking crimson crown and breast, contrasting with white throat patch and broad black stripe through eye and onto nape. Back and wings dark brown; short tail blackish with obscure white tips to feathers. Crimson rump patch distinctive in flight, which is characteristically strong and undulating. Female sandy brown above; whitish tinged buff on underparts; often showing traces of crimson on crown, flanks and breast, and particularly on rump. Immature lacks pink on breast and flanks. Eye white. Beak medium length, slim but strong, black; legs comparatively long and slender. Runs actively, often feeds on ground, frequently in small flocks. *Voice:* high-pitched, drawn-out 'see-eee', disyllabic 'tick-it' in flight; fluting whistles and harsh 'tcheck' alarm calls. *Habitat:* open land with sparse low scrub or saltbush. Widespread; sometimes numerous. ▦ ▨ ▬ ▬ △ ®

Orange Chat *Epthianura aurifrons* 11cm Small, plump and upright chat. Adult male has striking orange-yellow head and underparts, contrasting with black throat. Back mottled brownish; rump rich yellow; short tail blackish, with obscure pale tips to feathers. Female and immature streaked pale sandy brown on crown, cheeks and back; pale yellow below; often greyish in immature. Yellow rump patch distinctive in undulating flight. Eye dark chestnut. Beak black, medium length, slim but strong. Legs comparatively long and slender, blackish. Usually feeds on ground, often in small flocks perching prominently on bushes. *Voice:* metallic calls and melodious 'chee-chee-chee' in flight. *Habitat:* open land, often with sparse succulents, grasses or scrub cover. Widespread; normally quite scarce but occasionally numerous. ▦ ▨ ▬ ▬ △ ®

Yellow Chat *Epthianura crocea* 11cm Small chat. Adult male has forehead and underparts bright golden-yellow, with a narrow blackish crescentic breast band. Crown and nape greyish-olive, with thin blackish line joining eye to beak. Back yellowish-brown; rump striking in flight, clear yellow. Tail blackish with obscure yellow tips to feathers. Female paler and drabber, lacking breast band; immature greyer. Beak medium length, black, slim but strong. Eye whitish. Legs comparatively long, black. Often in small groups, feeding in dense wetland vegetation. *Voice:* metallic 'tang', high-pitched tuneful 'pee-eep' and various harsh churring calls. *Habitat:* well-vegetated swamplands, distinct from other chats. Irregularly distributed; apparently sedentary but nowhere common. ▨ ▨ ▬ △ ®

White-fronted Chat *Epthianura albifrons* 12cm Small plump chat. Adult male distinctive, with white forehead, face and throat contrasting with black collar band. Back and rump grey; wings and short tail blackish, with white tips to tail feathers striking in flight. Female pale grey-brown above; whitish below with narrow blackish breast band. Immature even paler and greyer, with obscure brownish-grey breast band. Beak medium length, blackish, slim but strong. Eye whitish to golden. Legs comparatively long, black; runs actively. Flight strong, bouncing. Often in groups or flocks, usually on ground or in low cover. Perches prominently. *Voice:* soft metallic 'tang' and other notes, frequently repeated. *Habitat:* open land, often damp or salty, both coastal and inland, with good cover of ground vegetation such as samphire and saltbush. Widespread, fairly common and usually sedentary. � ▦ ▨ ▬ △ ®

Crimson Chat ♂

Crimson Chat ♀

Orange Chat ♂

Orange Chat ♀

Yellow Chat ♂

White-fronted Chat ♂

Gibberbird *Ashbyia lovensis* 13cm Small, sandy-coloured desert chat. Upperparts pale sandy brown with darker mottling. Tail short, blackish with narrow white terminal band, wagged frequently up and down. Faint yellowish stripe over eye; ear coverts yellowish-fawn. Underparts dull yellow, extending up onto sides of rump and sometimes visible in flight. Breast and flanks obscurely blotched; belly paler. Female paler and duller than male. Legs long, runs swiftly like a pipit, perching on rocks with noticeably upright posture. Often flutters only a short distance. *Voice:* squeaky 'dip-dip'; 'weet-weet-weet' in flight. *Habitat:* characteristically open arid gibber with scanty vegetation. Restricted, erratic and uncommon. ☲△®

Yellow-bellied Sunbird *Nectarinia jugularis* 11cm Tiny flying jewel with extremely long downcurved beak. Upperparts olive-green, including rump; wings and tail blackish with white tips to outer feathers. Thin yellow stripe over eye; olive cheek patch. Male has faint yellow moustachial streak over iridescent blue-black throat and breast. Belly rich yellow. Female and immature have wholly yellow underparts, paler and duller in immature. Black beak relatively very long, slim, pointed and downcurved. Often in ones or twos, flits about, hovering frequently in front of flowers to feed, also catching insects and spiders. *Voice:* distinctive high-pitched 'dzit-dzit' or 'zeet-zeet'; hissing whistles, staccato trilling song. *Habitat:* woodland and forest margins, riverine vegetation, mangroves, cultivated land and not infrequently gardens. Restricted to northeast, but there generally common. 🐦〰️‼️®

Mistletoebird *Dicaeum hirundinaceum* 10-11cm Tiny, stubby-beaked; male unmistakably colourful. Male upperparts uniformly glossy blue-black. Throat and breast bright scarlet; belly whitish with broad black central stripe; undertail coverts dull scarlet. Female grey above with blackish tail. Paler grey below, lightly mottled on breast; undertail mottled with pale red. Beak short, triangular and blackish in male, dark grey in female. Often solitary except in breeding season. Active and agile but often difficult to see in foliage. Wings relatively long and distinctively pointed in flight. *Voice:* brittle 'tzee' or 'tzew', song a characteristic 'kinsey-kinsey-kinsey', 'wait-a-bit' or 'sweezit sweezit weet-weet-sweezit'. *Habitat:* any form of vegetation supporting its prime food source, mistletoes. Widespread but erratic; dependent on fruiting mistletoes; locally common. ▲◢🐦〰️‼️▥△®

Gibberbird

Yellow-bellied Sunbird ♂

Mistletoebird ♂

Mistletoebird ♀

Spotted Pardalote *Pardalotus punctatus* 8-9cm Tiny. Male's crown, mantle and wings black, with a white stripe over eye and white spots on crown. Mantle has buff feather centres giving scaly appearance. Wing coverts and flight feathers have terminal white spots. Rump scarlet; tail short and black with white panels near tip. Cheeks scaly grey; throat orange; belly buff, richening to orange beneath tail. Female similar but duller, with a whitish throat. *Voice:* often loud and clear, transcribed as 'sleep-may-be' or 'maybe', with plaintive 'wee-wee' calls. *Habitat:* forest, woodland and scrub, cultivated land, gardens. Discontinuous; less common in southwest, more common in southeast. 🎵 ♨ ▦ ®

Yellow-rumped Pardalote *Pardalotus xanthopygus* 9-10cm Often treated as a race of Spotted. Male very similar to Spotted, but slightly paler with a yellow throat patch and distinctive yellow rump with a red margin above black tail with double white panels. Back black with white streaks, lacking buff scaly pattern. Female paler and duller, lacking any clear throat patch, and with extensive mottled grey area on cheeks and sides of nape. *Voice:* slow mournful 'wee-wee' in descending pitch, soft whistles. *Habitat:* primarily in mallee, occasionally mulga or woodland. Widespread but erratic; locally common in mallee. 🎵 ♨ ▦ ®

Forty-spotted Pardalote *Pardalotus quadragintus* 9-10cm Tiny, dull, greenish and black Tasmanian pardalote. Crown, nape and mantle olive-green with faint brownish markings. Wings typically pardalote, with black-and-white tips to coverts and flight feathers. Obscure yellow supercilium; yellow cheek patches shading to pale buff belly. Rump and undertail coverts yellow, conspicuous in flight. Inconspicuous and difficult to watch in canopy. *Voice:* harsh and soft double-note calls. *Habitat:* forest. Confined to Tasmanian coastal forest and Bass Strait islands. Local and scarce. ◄ 🎵 ®

Red-browed Pardalote *Pardalotus rubricatus* 12cm Small, but large and pale for a pardalote. Crown black with white spots, over yellow eyebrow with red tuft just before eye. Nape and mantle pale sandy-brown with darker flecks. Wings black, with distinctive orange-buff wingbar. Rump olive, washed golden. Underparts whitish, with an indistinct area of yellow in mid-breast. Sexes similar; immature duller and greyer. *Voice:* distinctive and worth learning, five parrot-like whistles, rising in tone and accelerating. *Habitat:* dryish woodland, scrub and mulga. Widespread; in places erratic, but generally fairly common except in east. 🎵 ♨ ▦ △ ®

Striated Pardalote *Pardalotus striatus* 11cm Small. A complex group of races spead across Australia. Generally mantle, back and rump greyish-olive; tail short and black with obscure white tips. Wings black, with white or brownish-white feather edges and wingbar. Most races have red spot at base of primaries; yellow in *substriatus*, the most widespread race, but inconspicuous except at close range. Underparts whitish with variable amounts of yellow on throat, breast and flanks. Head pattern variable, always with bold supercilium, yellow in front of eye, white behind. Cheeks black flecked grey except in *melanocephalus* (when all-black) from northeast, and crown black, finely streaked white, again all-black in *melanocephalus*. *Voice:* crisp double 'chip-chip' or 'pick-pick', with louder trisyllabic 'wee-diddup'. *Habitat:* varied forests, woodlands and scrub, including mallee and mulga; *melanocephalus* in mangroves. All visit cultivated land and gardens. Widespread overall; in places patchy or erratic, elsewhere locally common. 🎵 ♨ ▦ △ ®

Spotted Pardalote (adult ♂)

Yellow-rumped Pardalote (adult ♂)

Forty-spotted Pardalote

Red-browed Pardalote (adult)

Striated Pardalote (adult, race *striatus*)

Pale White-eye *Zosterops citrinellus* 12cm Small, warbler-like, with characteristic eye-ring and relatively robust beak. Upperparts olive-green, yellower on head and rump. Faint yellowish forehead; conspicuous white eye-ring. Throat yellow; breast and belly white; undertail yellow. *Voice:* peevish but characteristic 'tsee', tremulous 'wee-ee-ee-ee', melodious song. *Habitat:* restricted to wooded islands off east coast of Cape York. Scarce. 🐾 ⴲ ♦♦ ®

Yellow White-eye *Zosterops luteus* 10-12cm Small olive-and-yellow white-eye. Upperparts yellowish olive, paler and greener on head, with small indistinct yellow forehead patch. Wings brown, brightly washed greenish; tail brown, washed greenish at base. Underparts rich yellow. Eye-ring clear and white. *Voice:* shrill 'tsee', wavering 'wee-ee-ee-ee'; melodious song. *Habitat:* primarily mangroves, occasionally adjacent woodland or scrub. Discontinuous coastal distribution; generally quite common. ⬟ ⴲ ♦♦ ⵌ ®

Silvereye *Zosterops lateralis* 10-12cm Small: the widespread familiar white-eye of the southwest, south and east. Plumage variable, but all races have green head; typical white eye-ring reinforced with thin black outer ring, and characteristically pointed but robust white-eye beak. All races have blackish wings with green to golden-green fringes to primary coverts and flight feathers; green to yellow-green rump, and a blackish tail with green fringes near the base. Mantle colours vary from green in southwest to grey (southeast and east). Underparts are basically whitish or pale grey, all races having a yellow throat (sometimes quite pale) and yellow undertail coverts. Grey wash on breast of variable density, and flank colours ranging from pale buff in southwest to near-chestnut (Tasmania and southeast). Despite this plumage complexity, still readily identifiable as Australia's only small grey and olive-green bird with a bold white eye-ring. *Voice:* incessant and usefully characteristic 'psee' and 'tee-oow', both high-pitched. Pleasantly warbling song. *Habitat:* catholic in the extreme, may be found in almost all habitats outside the arid and semi-arid centre. Widespread; often common. ⬟ ⵌ 🐾 ⴲ ♦♦ ⵌ ®

Pale White-eye (juveniles)

Yellow White-eye

Silvereye (eastern race)

Silvereye (western race)

European Goldfinch *Carduelis carduelis* 13cm Small finch. Face
red, surrounded by white, with a black crown patch descending to sides of
mantle. Back rich brown; rump white, contrasting with white-tipped black tail
in flight. Underparts whitish, buff on breast. Wings characteristic, black with
white tips to flight feathers and bold golden bar. Immature duller, has
wingbars but has buff head lacking characteristic pattern. *Voice:* fluid 'tu-
leep', drawn-out 'twee-eet'; tinkling metallic but attractive song 'twiddle-eee-
twiddle-eee-dee'. *Habitat:* cultivated land, scrubby wastes, weedy areas.
Discontinuous and patchy distribution; locally common. Introduced. ▟ ➤ ®

European Greenfinch *Carduelis chloris* 15cm Small, robust finch.
Upperparts olive-green, washed golden. Underparts yellowish, richer in male.
Wings blackish, with grey shoulders conspicuous in males and bold yellow
outer webs to primaries. Tail black, with characteristic yellow patches at
either side of base. Immature duller, more olive overall, with faint streaking.
Voice: distinctive purring song flight; calls nasal 'twee-ee-eet' and 'chip-chip-
chip'. *Habitat:* cultivated land, weedy wasteland, coastal scrub, parks,
orchards and gardens. Restricted to southeast; widespread but patchy, only
locally common. Introduced. ▟ ➤ ®

House Sparrow *Passer domesticus* 15cm Small. Male has distinctive
grey crown, with black face and bib. Chestnut-brown stripe over eye links to
brown nape. Back and wings richly mottled chestnut, black and white; rump
grey-buff. Underparts greyish-white. Female and immature have buff stripe
over eye, upperparts mottled brown, underparts plain fawn. *Voice:* persistent
'cheep', 'chirrp' and harsh 'squedge' calls. *Habitat:* generally close to
settlements or within towns, occasionally in remote mallee, mulga and other
scrubs. Widespread; often common in southeast. Introduced. ▟ ➤ ®

Eurasian Tree Sparrow *Passer montanus* 14cm Small. Sexes similar
in plumage. Crown and nape rich brown, with characteristic white cheek
patch with black central spot. Forehead and bib black; rest of underparts
pale grey-buff. Back and wings richly mottled chestnut, black, buff and white.
Flight feathers and notched tail dark brown. *Voice:* distinctively chirping fluid
'tek', 'choik' or 'tchup'. *Habitat:* suburban areas, occasionally around remote
settlements. Restricted to southeast but patchy; locally fairly common.
Introduced. ▟ ➤ ®

White-winged Wydah *Euplectes albonotatus* 15-18cm Small. Male
conspicuously black in breeding plumage, with distinctively long rounded tail
and short bristling crest on nape. Wings characteristically black with yellow
shoulders and fringes to coverts and a bold white wingbar. Female, non-
breeding male and immature buffish brown, streaked above, with a pale
supercilium over a dark cheek patch. *Voice:* trilling calls, rarely vocal.
Habitat: open grassy or weedy areas. Introduced NSW, but now extinct
there. ➤ ≋ ≈ ®

Red Bishop *Euplectes orix* 13cm Small, usually dull, weaver. Breeding
male with spectacular scarlet-and-black plumage. Female, non-breeding
male and immature brown and sparrow-like, streaked and mottled above,
paler below with a whitish throat and faintly streaked breast. *Voice:* wheezy
calls, sharp 'zik-zik-zik' song. *Habitat:* usually reedbeds. Introduced Murray
River, but now extinct there. ≋

European Goldfinch

European Greenfinch (adult ♂)

House Sparrow (breeding) ♂

Eurasian Tree Sparrow

White-winged Wydah (breeding) ♂

Red Bishop (breeding) ♂

Red-browed Finch *Neochmia temporalis* 10-11cm Tiny. Crown and nape grey; face rather paler, with broad scarlet stripe extending from deep red conical beak through eye and above ear-coverts. Back and wings olive-green; rump scarlet, contrasting with pointed black tail. Underparts entirely pale grey. Immature duller and darker, lacking eye-stripe. *Voice:* high-pitched 'seee' squeak. *Habitat:* primarily undergrowth at forest and woodland margins, grassy areas with scrub, farmland, gardens. Fairly widespread; erratic in places but often generally common. 🐦 ♨ 🏠 ⛺ ✹✹ ®

Beautiful Firetail *Stagonopleura bella* 11-12cm Small, plump, grass-finch. Upperparts dark olive-brown, covered in fine darker-brown barring. Rump crimson; tail brown with widely spaced darker bars. Distinctive black face mask from eye to dark red conical beak; obscure pale-blue eye-ring. Underparts distinctive: finely and closely barred in black and white, black beneath tail. Sexes broadly similar, female with less black on belly; immature duller blackish-brown. *Voice:* soulful piping 'weee', drawn-out 'pee-oooo', song a short series of high notes followed by a descending trill. *Habitat:* dense undergrowth or scrub, often damp, frequents tea-tree and *Casuarina* thickets. Southeastern; patchy and rare overall but locally quite common. ✹✹✹ 🏠 ®

Red-eared Firetail *Stagonopleura oculata* 11-12cm Small, dark grass-finch. Upperparts dark olive-brown, covered in fine blackish barring; rump red; tail brown with widely spaced darker bars. Distinctive face mask (see Beautiful), with broad black band from conical red beak to just behind eye, followed by a broad crimson band along ear-coverts. Blue eye-ring. Throat brown, paler under chin, densely but finely barred blackish. Rest of underparts characteristic, black boldly spotted white. Female has orange, not red, ear-coverts. Immature greyer and duller, lacking mask and with blackish beak. *Voice:* sad 'wee-eee' or 'oooweee'. *Habitat:* clearings and undergrowth in dense forests. Restricted distribution (see Beautiful); generally local and uncommon. ✹✹✹ 🏠 ®

Painted Finch *Emblema pictum* 11cm Tiny. Upperparts brown; rump red; tail black. Much of underparts black, boldly spotted white on sides of breast and flanks, with irregular scarlet belly stripe. Male has red forehead, face and chin, lacking in female. Eye strikingly white. Immature duller, dusky red on rump. Gregarious, often terrestrial. *Voice:* chattering calls in flight, harsh 'drut' or 'check'; song 'che-che-che-che-che wereee-oweeee'. *Habitat:* primarily *Spinifex* in arid rocky areas, but usually near water, occasionally in more open *Spinifex* areas. Relatively widespread but discontinuous, patchy and erratic; locally common. 🏠 ✹✹ ✹✹ △ ®

Diamond Firetail *Stagonopleura guttata* 12cm Small. Adult has grey head and mantle; brown back and wings, and red rump. Tail black. Distinctive facial pattern of bright crimson beak, black mask and red eye-ring. Throat white; breast crossed by broad black band extending down flanks, boldly white-spotted on flanks. Rest of underparts white. Immature paler above, lacking face patch; white below, faintly marked with grey breast band and flanks. *Voice:* sad 'pai-rr', rising in tone; double syllable 'too-hee' falling then rising in pitch. *Habitat:* open forests, woodlands and well-treed grassland, orchards, parks and gardens. Widespread, but patchy and generally scarce. 🐦 ♨ 🏠 ✹✹ ®

Red-browed Finch (adult)

Beautiful Firetail (adult)

Red-eared Firetail (adults)

Painted Finch (adult ♂)

Diamond Firetail (adult)

Star Finch *Neochmia ruficauda* 11cm Tiny. Upperparts olive-green; rump and tail dull purplish-red, with white spots on rump. Face mask scarlet, with faint white speckling; beak scarlet. Underparts pale green, shading to yellow on belly; breast and flanks boldly spotted white. Female duller; immature drab brown above, with reddish tail. *Voice:* piercing 'ssit' or 'sseet', 'chipt' call in flight. *Habitat:* swamp vegetation, open grassland with sparse tree cover, cultivated land. Discontinuous northerly distribution; erratic and patchy, but locally common. 🐦🦆🐤®

Crimson Finch *Neochmia phaeton* 12-14cm Small, unmistakable. Male has grey head; rusty-brown back and wings; scarlet rump, and distinctively long, pointed tail. Face scarlet, with crimson beak and faint grey eye-ring round white eye. Breast and flanks crimson, sparsely spotted white on flanks; belly and undertail black (northwest) or white (Cape York Peninsula). Female brown but with crimson beak, face patch, rump and tail. Immatures, are browner, lack face patch. *Voice:* 'clup' of alarm, shrill 'che-che-che', low, quiet, but fairly tuneful rasping song 'ra-ra-ra-ra-reee'. *Habitat:* usually beside water in tall grasses, canegrass, *Pandanus*, cane fields, crops, gardens. Discontinuous northerly distribution; erratic, rare in east, locally common elsewhere. 🐦🦆🐤®

Black-throated Finch *Poephila cincta* 10cm Tiny. Head dove-grey, with black mask from beak to eye and large black bib. Back and underparts pinkish-brown, paler below, with wasp-like black band round rump and lower belly. Lower rump black in northern birds; white in southern. Tail black, comparatively short and wedge-tipped. Wedge-shaped beak characteristically black. Immature similar but paler. *Voice:* hoarse whistle, soft 'teff', quiet warbling song. *Habitat:* open grassy woodlands and scrub. Northeastern distribution; patchy, but locally fairly common. 🐤🥀🌿®

Blue-faced Parrot Finch *Erythrura trichroa* 12cm Small. Whole body distinctively emerald green, with olive flight feathers, and with yellower underparts. Face cobalt-blue. Tail wedge-ended, brown, washed rufous. Female duller with smaller blue face; immature dull olive green, lacking blue face. *Voice:* reported as 'tseet-tseet'. *Habitat:* rainforest margins and clearings, also mangroves. Restricted to northeast Queensland; extremely rare. 🦜🌿®

Gouldian Finch *Erythrura gouldiae* 13cm Small and unmistakable. Upperparts emerald-green, yellower on nape, with a bright pale-blue rump and base to the tail. Tail long, blue with a black terminal band and elongated central feathers. Wings green with dark-blue flight feathers. Breast lilac; belly yellow; undertail white. Face variable, either all-black bordered in blue (commonest); scarlet bordered by black and pale blue; or orange bordered by black and pale blue (very rare). Females duller and paler; immatures grey-headed, with olive upperparts and pale grey-brown underparts. *Voice:* lisping 'ssitt', sometimes drawn out. *Habitat:* open woodland, grassland, waterside tall grasses. Widespread and once common across the north; sadly now generally scarce. 🐤🥀🐤®

Plum-headed Finch *Neochmia modesta* 10-11cm Tiny. Upperparts brown, with front of crown purplish-brown; obscure black mask. Wings boldly spotted white; rump white closely barred with brown. Underparts characteristic, white barred with brown. *Voice:* drawn-out metallic 'ti-ing', 'tip' and 'tleep'. Quiet high-pitched warbling song. *Habitat:* taller grassland beside water, swamps, grassy scrubland, open woodland and pastures. Fairly widespread in east but erratic; generally scarce. 🦆🐤🥀®

Star Finch (adult)

Crimson Finch (adult ♂, western race)

Black-throated Finch (adult, Cape York race)

Blue-faced Parrot Finch (adult)

Gouldian Finch (adult ♂, black-faced form)

Plum-headed Finch (adult ♀)

Zebra Finch *Taeniopygia guttata* 10cm Tiny, stocky, multicoloured grass-finch with distinctive banded tail. Male has head and nape grey; mantle and wings olive; rump white; tail striking, broadly banded in black and white. Black and white vertical stripes at base of orange-red beak; pale chestnut cheek patch. Throat and breast finely barred black and white; underparts largely white with white-spotted chestnut flanks. Female paler, lacking distinctive markings on underparts and chestnut cheeks; immature similar to female but with a blackish beak. Often gregarious, often terrestrial, often perches in long rows on fence wires. *Voice:* metallic 'teeaah', and chattering trills; noisy. *Habitat:* open country and scrub of most sorts, even in the arid interior usually close to water. Widespread but erratic and patchy; locally sometimes abundant. ⚫ ♨ ⋙ 🚜 ⋙ △ ®

Double-barred Finch *Taeniopygia bichenovii* 10-11cm Tiny grass-finch with an owl-like facial pattern. Forehead black, rest of upperparts brown; rump white, tail black (eastern birds) or rump black (western race). Wings blackish, characteristically finely chequered with white. White face patch bounded by narrow black band running across throat; breast and belly whitish, crossed by second distinctive black band at base of breast. Undertail black. Beak conical, blue-grey. Immatures paler and browner, with indistinct bars. Often terrestrial or in grass. Often gregarious. Flight bouncing on fluttering wings. *Voice:* high-pitched drawn-out 'teee-aat', chattering calls. *Habitat:* fairly dry open landscapes with occasional trees or shrubs, usually close to water. Farmland, parks and gardens. Reasonably widespread; generally fairly common. ⚫ ♨ ⋙ ⋙ ®

Masked Finch *Poephila personata* 13cm Small, brownish grass-finch, yellow-beaked and with a pointed tail. Upperparts cinnamon, with black mask and bib contrasting with rich yellow conical beak. Rump white, contrasting in flight with black tail with distinctively elongated and pointed central feathers. Underparts buff, with white lower belly and undertail crossed by vertical black flank stripe. Northeastern birds have whitish cheeks and pale buff underparts. Immature duller and greyer, lacking mask and with a blackish beak. Often gregarious, immatures predominating, but flocks rarely large. Usually terrestrial. Rump and tail prominent in flight. *Voice:* brief, low, 'twat' and louder 'teeaah'. *Habitat:* dry grassy areas with scattered trees and scrub, usually near water. Fairly widespread in north; generally quite common. ♨ ⋙ ®

Long-tailed Finch *Poephila acuticauda* 16cm Small, but comparatively large among grass-finches. Elegant and extremely long-tailed. Crown, cheeks and nape dove-grey, with black mask from beak to eye, and black throat. Body pinkish-fawn, darker above than below. Rump and undertail uniquely patterned with wasp-like bands of black, then white, very distinctive in flight. Tail black, central feathers very long and pointed. Beak conical, relatively powerful, yellow with black tip in western birds; reddish-orange in east. Immature duller with shorter tail and blackish beak. Active; often terrestrial or in long grass, moves gracefully. *Voice:* sad but penetrating descending 'peee-ew', alarm call a chattering 'cheek-chee-chee-cheek'. *Habitat:* dryish grass woodlands to open plains with scattered trees, usually close to water. Locally fairly common. ♨ ⋙ ®

Zebra Finch (adult ♂)

Double-barred Finch (adults, eastern race)

Masked Finch (adult, Queensland race)

Long-tailed Finch (adult, Queensland race)

Pictorella Mannikin *Heteromunia pectoralis* 11cm Small, dull, but
distinctive grass-finch. Crown, nape, back and tail brown; wings brown with
faint broken white wingbars. Black face and throat outlined by chestnut bar
over eye and round ear-coverts. Upper breast and sides of neck white with
dense black crescentic barring. Rest of underparts dark pinkish-buff. Beak
comparatively long, strong, and conical; steel-grey. Female has duller face
and throat pattern, lacking in immature which is also paler below. Gregarious
but shy. Terrestrial or in long grass, often with other mannikins. *Voice:* sharp
'chip' or 'pick', sometimes 'teet'. *Habitat:* open grassland, or with scattered
trees and scrub, sometimes spinifex. Favours longer grasses, usually near
water. Discontinuous; generally uncommon but locally quite numerous. ⬛Ⓡ

Chestnut-breasted Mannikin *Lonchura castaneothorax* 10cm
Tiny, robust, and distinctively patterned. Crown and nape grey; back brown
tinged with bronze; rump and tail distinctive golden-brown. Face and throat
black, with characteristic black-edged broad chestnut breast band. Belly
white, barred black on flanks, undertail black. Beak conical and powerful,
steel-blue. Female similar but paler and duller; immature plain brown above,
fawn below. Gregarious outside breeding season. Often terrestrial or in
grasses. Undulating flight, flocks perform mass aerobatic turns. *Voice:* high,
clear bell-like 'teet' amalgamating into a steady tinkling as flock takes off.
Habitat: open grassland, swamps, reeds, weedy areas, farmland,
occasionally mangroves, *Lantana*, rice and other cereals. Relatively
widespread naturally, with some feral pockets founded on aviary escapes.
Patchy and erratic, often common in northern area of range. 🌾⬛ⅠⓇ

Yellow-rumped Mannikin *Lonchura flaviprymna* 10cm Tiny,
distinctively brown-and-yellow mannikin. Pale fawn hood, often appearing
nearly white. Back and wings rich brown; rump and tail golden-brown. Breast
and belly distinctive canary-yellow; undertail coverts black. Powerful blue-
grey conical beak. Immature much paler. Interbreeds occasionally with
Chestnut-breasted producing plumages intermediate between the two. Often
terrestrial or in tall grasses. Gregarious. *Voice:* bell-like penetrating 'teet'.
Habitat: tall grasses along watercourses, open grassland with scattered trees
and shrubs. Relatively restricted and generally uncommon, but local pockets
of abundance occur. 🌾⬛Ⓡ

Black-headed Mannikin *Lonchura malacca* 11cm Small, simply-
patterned, dark introduced mannikin. Hood black; back, rump and relatively
long tail dark chestnut-brown. Breast and belly chestnut; undertail black.
Beak conical, silver-grey. Immature appreciably paler, brown and fawn. Nods
head while singing. *Voice:* shrill 'peep-peep'. *Habitat:* usually reed beds or
other rank waterside tall grasses. Introduced in south-east; now apparently
gone. 🌾Ⓡ

Nutmeg Mannikin *Lonchura punctulata* 11cm Small, brown,
introduced mannikin, more familiar as a cage and aviary bird. Crown, nape,
face, mantle and back brown, darkest on face and forehead; rump and tail
golden-brown. Underparts white, densely covered in distinctive vee-shaped
brown markings. Beak conical, powerful, dark grey. Often with Chestnut-
breasted. *Voice:* penetrating 'kit-tee' or 'ki-ki-tee-tee'; croaking sharp 'tret-tret'
of alarm. Jangling tinkling song. *Habitat:* wetter rank grasslands, swamps, tall
weedy areas, crops, occasionally suburban gardens. Introduced, now
flourishing along eastern coastal belt; locally common, even abundant.
🌾⬛Ⓡ

Pictorella Mannikin (adult)

Chestnut-breasted Mannikin (adult)

Yellow-rumped Mannikin (adult)

Black-headed Mannikin (adult, breeding)

Nutmeg Mannikin (adult, breeding)

Metallic Starling *Aplonis metallica* 21cm Medium-sized. Entire plumage glossy black with purplish and greenish sheens. Eye strikingly red. Slim-bodied outline emphasized by long pointed tail. Immature dull brown above; paler below with brown streaks, grey mottling on flanks. *Voice:* wheezy chatterings, song brief fluting warble. *Habitat:* rainforest, coastal woodland and scrub, mangroves, sometimes gardens, where tame. Fairly restricted in northeast; locally quite common. ◀ ⬅ 💺 ⣿ ♨ ®

Common Starling *Sturnus vulgaris* 21cm Medium-sized. Distinctive plump appearance with short tail and characteristic triangular wings in flight. In breeding season blackish, with iridescent sheen and bristling throat feathers. Non-breeding adult duller, flecked with white. Immature grey-brown. *Voice:* amazing trilling, cackling and whistling, with much mimicry. Shrill shrieks of alarm. *Habitat:* urban areas, farmland, pastoral lands and other open grassy or scrubland areas. Introduced, now widespread in southeast, often numerous; sometimes a fruit pest. ◀ ⬅ ♨ ⣿ ⌶ ®

Common Mynah *Acridotheres tristis* 24cm Medium-sized. Body rich brown above and below, with darker head and nape. Yellow patch of skin round eye; legs yellow. Tail black with white terminal bar; wings blackish with conspicuous and characteristic white patch at base of primaries. Immature similar but browner. *Voice:* varied creaking and growling notes, occasional fluting passages, shriek of alarm. *Habitat:* urban regions, farmland of many types. Widely but discontinuously distributed down east coast; locally common. Introduced. ◀ ⬅ ®

Yellow Oriole *Oriolus flavocinctus* 26-30cm Medium-large. Upperparts greenish-olive with yellow wash and sparse darker streaks. Darker brownish wing and white-tipped tail feathers show pale green or gold fringes. Underparts greenish yellow. Eye orange. Legs grey. Beak reddish-pink, relatively long, stout and pointed. Immature paler and duller, more streaked. *Voice:* three- or four-note warbling 'yock-yock-yoddle', clear 'peee-kweeek', harsh alarm notes. *Habitat:* rainforest, riverine woodland, swamp woodland, mangroves; also orchards, parks and gardens, all usually near water. Discontinuous but fairly widespread; generally quite common. ⬋ ⣿ ♨ ⌶ ®

Olive-backed Oriole *Oriolus sagittatus* 26-28cm Medium-large. Head and mantle pale olive-green, finely streaked black. Wings and relatively long white-tipped tail darker grey-brown, with greenish feather fringes. Underparts characteristic, with greenish throat, white breast and belly all copiously spotted dark brown. *Voice:* characteristic rolling 'orry-orry-ole' and 'olio'. Scolding alarm call. *Habitat:* wooded areas, orchards, gardens, often associated with water. Widespread; in many areas fairly commmon. ⬅ 💺 ⣿ ♨ ⌶ ®

Figbird *Sphecotheres viridis* 28cm Medium-large. Male has golden-green back and rump, with blackish flight feathers and white-edged, white-tipped black tail. Underparts vary from grey-green in the south to yellow in the north. Head black, with a distinctive reddish face patch. Female and immature mottled brown above; yellowish (in north) or whitish below with brown streaks. *Voice:* yelping 'keeyer' or 'jok-yer', descending 'see-kew'. Song melodious but repetitive 'tu-tu-heer, tu-heer tu-heer'. *Habitat:* rainforest, forest and woodland, riverine woodland, sometimes mangroves, orchards, gardens. Widespread; erratic, generally quite common. ◀ ⬅ ⣿ ♨ ⌶ ⌶ ®

Metallic Starling (adult)

Common Starling (adult)

Common Mynah

Yellow Oriole ♂

Olive-backed Oriole ♂

Figbird (northern race) ♂

Spangled Drongo *Dicrurus bracteatus* 28-30cm Medium-large.

Generally black, with glossy green sheen on wings and iridescent streaks on head and body. Beak strong, broad and black. Eye red. Tail characteristic, black, relatively long, splayed out in fish-tail at tips. Legs short and dark; upright perching posture. Immature dusky black speckled with white. Chooses prominent perches, dashing out in pursuit of prey. *Voice:* noisy harsh metallic chattering and harsh rasping calls. *Habitat:* forest and woodland edges and clearings, riverine woodland, open land with mature trees. Regular and reasonably common in north, scarce at southern end of distribution. 🐦🐦🏵🏵🏵 ⏚ ®

Golden Bowerbird *Prionodura newtoniana* 23cm Medium-small.

Male unmistakable: bright golden-yellow from throat to tip of underside of tail; face olive-brown. Back, wings and upperside of tail brown, washed yellow. Eye strikingly golden. Female and immature dull brown above; paler below with whitish throat. *Voice:* rattling calls, frog-like croaks, plentiful mimicry during display. *Habitat:* rainforest at high altitude, usually in excess of 900m. Confined to small part of northeast Queensland; locally fairly common. 🐦 ®

Satin Bowerbird *Ptilonorhynchus violaceus* 27-33cm Largish; male

spectacularly rich glossy blue-black all over. Tail relatively short and broad. Legs strong and grey. Eye pale grey; beak grey, short, stout and deep, characteristically feathered along ridge of upper mandible and on chin. Female and immature dull olive-green above with browner wings and tail. Faint double white wingbar. Underparts whitish, conspicuously scalloped with brown feather fringes. *Voice:* loud, whistling 'whee-you'; wheezing and whirring at bower. *Habitat:* rainforest and other wet, often eucalypt, woodland, normally at some altitude (over 500m). Discontinuous distribution. Locally common, perhaps diminishing with spread of habitation. 🐦🏵🏵🏵 ®

Regent Bowerbird *Sericulus chrysocephalus* 24-28cm Medium-

sized. Breeding male unmistakable, with black face and underparts, golden tinge on forehead, yellow beak and bright golden eye. Crown, nape and mantle bright yellow; back, rump and tail black. Wings have black shoulders and primaries, contrasting strikingly with golden secondaries and tertials. Black 'T' of tail, back and wing shoulders against primarily yellow wings gives very characteristic flight pattern. Female brown, darker above with pale markings on mantle and back; paler below with dark scaly markings. *Voice:* rarely heard chattering, rattles, and soft warbles. *Habitat:* rainforest and coastal scrub, occasionally thickets or scrubby clearings. Restricted but locally fairly common. 🏵🐦🏵🏵🏵 ®

Spotted Bowerbird *Chlamydera maculata* 25-30cm Medium-sized,

like an oversize thrush. Upperparts brown with bold rufous-buff spots. Characteristic iridescent pink erectile bristly crest and greyish patch on nape. Underparts buff, speckled on chin and throat. Female has smaller crest; immature darker, lacks crest. *Voice:* very varied, with much mimicry in display, grating and churring notes. *Habitat:* inland scrubs and dry open woodlands. Widespread; only locally common. 🏵🏵 ®

Spangled Drongo

Golden Bowerbird ♂

Satin Bowerbird ♂

Satin Bowerbird ♀

Regent Bowerbird ♂

Spotted Bowerbird

Western Bowerbird *Chlamydera guttata* 24-28cm Medium-sized.
Upperparts and throat black, spotted creamy-buff. Underparts buff, mottled paler on blackish throat. Characteristic erectile iridescent pink nape crest. Female smaller, with less marked pink crest. Immature lacks crest. *Voice:* as Spotted. *Habitat:* inland arid scrub and dry open woodland, often in rocky hill areas with wild fig. Discontinuous distribution across west central and western areas. Widespread but only locally fairly common. ♨ ⬜ ®

Great Bowerbird *Chlamydera nuchalis* 32-38cm Large. Upperparts
grey-brown, mottled darker on back, with pale scalloped markings on dark-brown wing shoulders. Underparts pale grey-fawn. Lilac patch on nape inconspicuous except when raised during display. Peculiar gait and behaviour, like an inquisitive but cautious chicken. *Voice:* wide range of high-pitched whistling and cackling calls, liquid churring and mimicry of other birds. *Habitat:* dry eucalypt woodland and scrub, often near watercourses. Relatively widespread; locally common. ⬜ ♨ ⬜ ®

Fawn-breasted Bowerbird *Chlamydera cerviniventris* 25-30cm
Medium-large. Upperparts pale grey-brown, scaly on mantle. Cheeks flecked brown and white. Tail brown, relatively short, square and wide. Throat pale buff; rest of underparts rich yellow-buff, lightly spotted brown on sides of neck. *Voice:* hoarse grating calls, a little mimicry. *Habitat:* mangroves, tea-tree and other scrub, usually with tall grasses. Confined to eastern Cape York Peninsula; locally fairly common. ♨ ⬜ ⬜ ♨ ⬜ ®

Tooth-billed Bowerbird *Scenopoeetes dentirostris* 24-27cm
Medium-sized, stocky. Upperparts plain olive-brown, with pale brown eye-ring. Beak blackish, deep and distinctively stout, with serrations near tip. Underparts whitish to pale fawn, densely streaked with brown. Male sings with mouth wide open, showing yellow gape; throat feathers bristling showing yellow bases. *Voice:* loud varied medley of sound, starting with chuckles and melodious whistles, moving into rich mimicry of birds and other animals. *Habitat:* tropical rainforest, usually from 500-1500m. Restricted, but locally common. ⬜ ®

Spotted Catbird *Ailuroedus melanotis* 26-30cm Medium-large. Beak
whitish, distinctively stout. Upperparts brilliant green, with slim double white wingbar and white-tipped green tail. Underparts paler green, streaked with white. Immature duller and darker. Distinctive calls aid location. *Voice:* loud, characteristically like a howling cat; nasal 'here-I-arr', sharp clicks followed by three loud cries. *Habitat:* tropical rainforest, often montane, on eastern Cape York Peninsula. Locally common. ⬜ ®

Green Catbird *Ailuroedus crassirostris* 26-30cm Medium-large.
Upperparts bright green, flecked with white on nape, with double white wingbar. Tail green above, grey below, with white tips. Underparts pale green, streaked with white. Calls a good indication of presence. *Voice:* loud and distinctively cat-like; high-pitched double or triple wailing and whistling calls; various clicks; raucous 'here-I-arr' like Spotted. *Habitat:* rainforest, forested gullies, often montane. Restricted distribution in eastern Queensland to southern NSW; locally common. ⬜ ⬜ ®

340

Western Bowerbird

Great Bowerbird

Fawn-breasted Bowerbird

Tooth-billed Bowerbird

Spotted Catbird

Green Catbird

Paradise Riflebird *Ptiloris paradiseus* 25-30cm Medium-large bird. Male dark, iridescent and spectacular; largely velvet-black, with iridescent purple-green throat, breast and belly spots, and emerald crown visible in good light. Beak distinctive: black, long, slim, pointed and downcurved. Female dark olive-brown above, with characteristic dull chestnut wings and tail, and clear white stripe over eye. Throat white, with dark moustachial streaks, breast and belly pale buff scalloped brown. Unobtrusive, behaves like a giant treecreeper, acrobatic on fruit. *Voice:* characteristic rasping, almost explosive 'ya-aa-aa-ss' like rustling fabric or paper, also shorter double 'yaas-yaas' and mellow whistles. *Habitat:* rainforest, often montane to 1200m. Restricted; locally fairly common in north of range. 🐾 🎵 ®

Victoria's Riflebird *Ptiloris victoriae* 23-25cm Medium-sized, similar to Paradise but slightly smaller and appreciably shorter-beaked. Male largely velvet-black, with green iridescent crown, purple-green throat and broad purplish breast band. Stands upright, fanning wings like a parabolic reflector during display. Female olive-brown above, greyer on head, with a white stripe over eye. Chin white, with blackish moustachial streaks. Breast pale cinnamon-buff, sparsely marked with brown scalloping. Wings and tail dull chestnut. *Voice:* characteristic explosive 'yaas', single or double; rustling like fabric. *Habitat:* rainforest, often montane. Note restricted range; locally fairly common. 🐾 ®

Magnificent Riflebird *Ptiloris magnificus* 28-33cm Medium-large. Male spectacular, with filamentous plumes; velvety black, with a long black beak, slim and downcurved. Crown iridescent green; breast an expansive erectile bib of very iridescent glistening greenish-purple feathers ending in a green and reddish-black band across breast above a sooty black belly. Filamentous plumes on flanks. Displays on high branches, spreading wings and shuffling feathers. Female olive above with dull chestnut wings, with pale stripe over eye and bold dark moustachial streaks, but distinctively and copiously finely barred brown. *Voice:* double whistling 'weeoo-wit', display song of three clear 'wee-oo' notes followed by an abrupt 'who'! *Habitat:* tropical rainforest, monsoon forest and dense scrub. Note range: confined to tip of Cape York Peninsula, but locally fairly common. 🐾 ®

Trumpet Manucode *Manucodia keraudrenii* 27-32cm Medium-large bird of paradise, rather like a giant starling. Entire plumage black with purplish, violet or greenish sheens, with a loose fine crest on nape. Eye red. Beak short and thrush-like, blackish. Tail relatively long, slightly expanded and fan-like at tip. Often single or in pairs. Shy and inconspicuous in canopy, calls being best indication of presence. Noisy display, similar to Riflebird, upright and facing female with spread and fanned wings. *Voice:* resounding long, loud, trumpet-like blast, sometimes more of a squawk or croak. *Habitat:* rainforest, eucalypt woodland and dense scrub. Note restricted range on Cape York Peninsula. Locally fairly common. 🐾 ®

Paradise Riflebird ♀

Victoria's Riflebird ♂

Magnificent Riflebird ♂

Trumpet Manucode

White-breasted Woodswallow *Artamus leucorhynchus* 17cm

Small. Upperparts dark grey-blue, contrasting strikingly with white rump and belly. Immature browner with scaly markings above, buff below. Flight swooping and graceful, on distinctively triangular wings showing white undersides. *Voice:* sharp metallic 'pirt pirt', chattering song with mimicry. *Habitat:* usually over or close to water; rivers, lakes swamps and floods, occasionally mangroves. Widespread but erratic and patchy; localy fairly common. ◢ ◣ ⚏ ⚞ ⚟ ▮ ®

Masked Woodswallow *Artamus personatus* 17-19cm

Medium-small. Male grey above with darker wings and a white-tipped tail. Distinctive black face contrasting with pale-grey underparts. Female duller, with an obscure mask. Immature grey above, spotted white; buff below with grey face and throat patch. *Voice:* fluting 'chap chap', sweetly melodious but simple song. *Habitat:* open forests, woodlands, pastures and orchards, golf courses and parks. On migration over almost any habitat. Widespread, but erratic. Locally common. ◢ ⚏ ⚟ ⫿⫿ ⚞ ⚟ ▮ ®

White-browed Woodswallow *Artamus superciliosus* 20cm

Medium-small, colourful. Male blue above with white stripe over eye and white tail tip. Underparts rich chestnut except for blue throat. Female less richly coloured above; pale cinnamon on breast and belly. Immature similar but more mottled. *Voice:* in flight, tuneful 'chap chap'; song quiet, melodious, with mimicry. Call harsh and scolding. *Habitat:* widespread, but sporadic outside southeastern Australia. ◢ ⚏ ⚟ ⫿⫿ ⚞ ⚟ ▮ ®

Black-faced Woodswallow *Artamus cinereus* 18-20cm

Medium-small, variable woodswallow. Upperparts grey-brown (some appreciably paler), with darker wings and tail with characteristic double white mark on tip. Underparts slightly paler, and underwing paler grey still, sometimes white. Small black face-patch. Undertail coverts variable, white in east, black in central regions. Black-and-white banded forms also occur. *Voice:* harsh 'chip' or 'chaff' notes, usually double. Agitated chattering song with mimicry. *Habitat:* open landscapes of most types including arid areas, with or without trees or scrub. Widespread; often common. ⚟ ⫿⫿ ⚞ ⚟ △ ®

Dusky Woodswallow *Artamus cyanopterus* 18cm

Small. Adult brown, with indistinct blackish patch round eye. Wings blackish, with distinctive but difficult to see white webs to outer primaries. Tail relatively long; dark brown with white-blocked tips to outer feathers. In flight, shows contrastingly pale whitish underwings. Immature brown, with bold whitish streaks. *Voice:* soft 'vut vut', sharp 'peet' and various chirruping calls. *Habitat:* open forests and woodlands, paddocks, scrub, orchards, golf-courses, suburbs. Discontinuous distribution; erratic, locally common. ⚟ ⫿⫿ ®

Little Woodswallow *Artamus minor* 12cm

Small. Plumage largely dark chocolate-brown, with small darker smudge round eye and with slightly iridescent dark-grey wings, similar to Dusky but lacking white margins to primaries. Tail brown with distinctive double white patches on tip. Immature paler and streaked whitish. *Voice:* brisk 'peet' in flight, sometimes double, sometimes repetitive. Twittering musical song. *Habitat:* scrub and grassland, usually with rocky areas or gorges, often near water. Widespread but patchy and erratic; generally uncommon. ⚟ ⫿⫿ ⚞ △ ®

White-breasted Woodswallow (adult)

Masked Woodswallow (adult ♂)

White-browed Woodswallow (adult ♂)

Black-faced Woodswallow (adult)

Dusky Woodswallow (adult)

Little Woodswallow (adult)

White-winged Chough *Corcorax melanorhamphos* 42-47cm

Large, relatively slim, distinctively long-tailed black bird with white patches visible in wings in flight. Uniformly sooty black, with bright red eye and characteristic moderately long, slender, pointed and slightly downcurved black beak. In flight, shows distinctive white webs to primaries. Immature similar but duller black with a brown eye. Largely terrestrial when feeding, taking bold strides with head jerking back and forth. Usually flies low to cover, raising tail on landing. *Voice:* fluting descending whistle, grating 'hass' of alarm. *Habitat:* widespread but patchy across southeast; locally common. 🐜 ⁂ ⛩ ®

Apostlebird *Struthidea cinerea* 29-32cm

Medium-large, dull but even so distinctive. Body dull, lead-grey, with darker eye-patch and dark-brown wings. Tail long and black, wedge-shaped. Beak dark grey, robust, almost triangular. Legs short, giving awkward horizontal posture, with tip of long tail on ground. Flies low, with frequent glides. Often gregarious. Terrestrial when feeding; walks, hops or runs actively; often aggressive. *Voice:* harsh tearing and chattering 'ch-kew'; nasal call transcribed as 'git-out'. *Habitat:* open forest, woodland, scrub, usually fairly dry. Occasionally orchards, around habitation, and along roads. Discontinuous and patchy distribution; only locally common. ⁂ ⁂ ⛩ ®

Australian Magpie-lark *Grallina cyanoleuca* 26-30cm

Medium-large, neither magpie nor lark, but one of two members of a family of uncertain affinities. Conspicuous and familiar, resembling small-beaked lightweight crows. Male has black back, head and breast, relieved by white supercilia and white cheek and nape patches. Rest of underparts and rump white. Wings and tail black and white. White patches at sides of base of black tail are distinctive in flight. Female generally similar, but supercilium and cheek patch merge, and throat is white. Beak whitish, eye bright yellow; legs black. Immature greyer with dark eye. Often in noisy pairs or family parties, associating with other flocking birds. *Voice:* varied, but commonly duetting 'tee-hee' with response 'pee-oo-wee' accompanied by wing-raising. Alarm call a piercing repeated 'pee'. *Habitat:* catholic, but avoids dense forest and desert. Widespread; often common. 🐦 🐦 ≋ ⁂ ⛩ ≋ ⚯ ®

Black Butcherbird *Cracticus quoyi* 32-45cm

Large, heavy-beaked and rather crow-like; with two colour forms. Dark form adult entirely dark blue-black, with a dark eye and a long, powerful, straight, black-tipped grey beak, slightly hooked. Immature dull black. Northeast Queensland race *rufescens* is deep chestnut-brown, mottled darker above, barred blackish on underparts as immature, but black as adult. Normally shy, but will come to food in gardens. *Voice:* fluting 'caw-caw-cooka-cook', simple soft song. *Habitat:* rainforest, monsoon forest, riverine woodland, coastal scrub and mangroves, sometimes farmland. Discontinuous distribution; generally fairly common. 🐦 ≋ ⁂ ⁂ ⛩ ®

White-winged Chough

Apostlebird

Australian Magpie-lark ♂

Black Butcherbird

Grey Butcherbird *Cracticus torquatus* 24-30cm Medium-sized, black, white and grey bird with characteristic butcherbird beak. Black crown and cheeks, and grey mantle, contrast with white rump and white-tipped black tail. Conspicuous white crescentic patch behind ear. Underparts greyish-white. Race *argentatus* (called Silver-backed) from the extreme north is paler silver-grey on back, white below. Flight fast and darting on shallow wingbeats, showing white rump. Beak long, straight and strong, grey with black tip, slightly hooked. *Voice:* musical mellow piping song, deep in tone, sometimes with mimicry. Harsh rattling alarm call. *Habitat:* rainforest, other forest and woodland margins, open woodland, coastal and inland scrub, riverine woodland, farmland and suburban areas with trees. Widespread but patchy; nowhere really common. 🐾 🦡 ⛟ ♨ ▦ ®

Black-backed Butcherbird *Cracticus mentalis* 25-28cm Medium-sized and familiar, boldly pied with a grey rump and typical butcherbird beak. Upperparts largely black, with white collar mark, grey rump and white-tipped black tail. Wings black with bold white bars. Underparts white apart from small black chin patch. Immature paler on upperparts, with buffer wingbars. Beak long, straight and strong, grey with black tip, slightly hooked. *Voice:* soft mellow yodelling calls, frequently mimics other birds. *Habitat:* open forest and woodland, riverine woodland, farmland and suburban areas with trees. Restricted, but common. 🐾 🦡 ⛟ ♨ ▦ ®

Pied Butcherbird *Cracticus nigrogularis* 32cm Large, black-hooded, pied butcherbird. Crown, nape, throat and breast black, separated from black back by white collar. Wings black with bold white bars; rump white contrasting with black tail with white tips to outer feathers. Belly and undertail white. Beak long, straight and powerful, grey with black tip, slightly hooked. Immature browner above, duller white elsewhere. *Voice:* superb melodious song of unusual range, fluting from high-pitched to low mellow notes. Expert mimic. *Habitat:* open woodland, scrub, riverine woodland, pastoral land with trees, fields and suburban areas. Widespread; patchy in places but generally common. ▪ 🐾 🦡 ⛟ ♨ ▦ ®

Australian Magpie *Gymnorhina tibicen* 37-44cm Large and familiar, with variable pied plumage. All races have black throat and breast, with white undertail coverts and white underside to black-outlined, black-tipped tail, conspicuous in flight, as are distinctive black underwings with prominent white leading edge to forewings. Wings black with bold white bar. Crown black, nape white in all races, but amount of white on back and rump varies from all-white (race *hypoleuca*, coastal southeast) to black with white only on upperside of tail (the widespread race *tibicen*), with various intermediates. Eye red. Beak long, dagger-shaped and pointed (compare with butcherbirds), grey with black tip. *Voice:* familiar and renowned rich fluting yodel, subsong with mimicry. Harsh shriek of alarm, descending 'peeew' call. *Habitat:* catholic in the extreme, any open grassy area with trees. Widespread; scarce in arid regions but often common elsewhere. ▪ 🐾 🦡 ⛟ ♨ ▦ ®

Black-backed Butcherbird (adult)

Grey Butcherbird (adult)

Pied Butcherbird (adult)

Australian Magpie (race *tibicen*)

Australian Magpie (race *hypoleuca*)

Pied Currawong *Strepera graculina* 42-49cm Large, crow-like, bell-magpie. Generally black, with heavy black beak. Distinguished by contrasting white base and tip to tail, white undertail coverts, and striking white patch in wing particularly conspicuous in flight. Eye strikingly yellow. Immature duller grey-brown, with dark eye. More southerly birds have less white in tail, much less in extreme southeast. Congregates in small flocks outside breeding season. *Voice:* varied tunefully mellow whistles, plus harsh shrieks and variants of 'currawock' and 'currawong'. *Habitat:* essentially a forest bird which has adapted to well-treed farmland, scrub and city parks and gardens. Widespread in the east; often common. ▲ ⋏ ⚑ ♒ ⁑ ⌗ ®

Black Currawong *Strepera fuliginosa* 47cm Large, robust, heavy-beaked, largely black bell-magpie. Plumage largely black, with small white tips to flight feathers and white terminal band to relatively long tail, more visible in flight. Eye boldly yellow. Beak black, long and strong, slightly hooked, ridge of upper mandible convex. In flight, looks long-tailed, with broad fingered wings. In pairs or small flocks, usually in foliage. Easy, flopping, but deceptively skilful flight. *Voice:* noisy, nasal but musical calls, 'kar-week, week-kar' and other short metallic notes. *Habitat:* forests, including montane forest, woodland heath and grazing farmland with trees, parkland and suburbs. Confined to Tasmania and Bass Strait islands; generally common. ⋏ ⚑ ♒ ⁑ ⌗ ≈ ®

Grey Currawong *Strepera versicolor* 45-50cm Large, variably grey bell-magpie with variable amounts of white in wing. Body grey, rather darker on head, with white undertail coverts. Tail long, dark-grey to blackish, with white terminal band. Wings may show white tips to tertials, white bases to primaries (conspicuous as 'flash' in wing in flight) or no white at all. Body colour almost black in inland birds. Eye golden yellow. Beak blackish, long and strong, slightly hooked at tip. *Voice:* distinctive and useful in identification, a ringing 'chling chling' or 'chding, chding' and strident 'creee'. *Habitat:* open forests and woodlands, coastal scrub, mallee inland, farmland with trees, occasionally suburban areas. Fairly widespread but patchy; only locally fairly common. ⋏ ⚑ ♒ ⁑ ⌗ ≈ ®

Australian Raven *Corvus coronoides* 47-56cm Large, familiar, and the largest Australian crow. Entirely glossy black, with an oily sheen in sunlight. Throat feathers of adult bushy and bristly, especially during calling, when body is characteristically held horizontal. Eye white in adult. Beak long, strong and black, with slightly convex ridge to upper mandible. Immature duller with brown eye. Mated pairs characteristically sedentary, roaming flocks of non-breeders small, not cohesive as in very similar Little Raven. *Voice:* loud and strong drawn-out 'aah-aah-aah-aaaaah' in slow tempo, ending in gurgle; also unexpectedly high-pitched descending wail. *Habitat:* catholic, but avoiding dense closed-canopy forests. Widespread; often common. ⋏ ⁑ ⌗ ≈ ▾▾ ®

Pied Currawong

Black Currawong

Grey Currawong (eastern form)

Australian Raven (adult)

Forest Raven *Corvus tasmanicus* 52cm Large, with the largest beak among the Australian corvids. All-black, with an oily sheen. Eye white. Throat feathers not distinctively bushy. Beak black, long, strong and powerful, with convex ridge to upper mandible. Immature duller. Generally appears heavy and short-tailed in flight although isolated New England race *boreus* relatively longer-tailed than southern birds. Note habitat choice and voice, otherwise similar in behaviour to Little, flocks of several hundred birds occurring. *Voice:* deepest of the corvids, a distinctive repeated 'korr' sometimes with the last call of a series drawn-out. *Habitat:* catholic in Tasmania (Australian and Little Ravens absent); on mainland generally in damp eucalypt forests. Discontinuous distribution; locally fairly common on mainland, common in Tasmania. 🐎🚂🏂🏔🚠☂🅡

Little Raven *Corvus mellori* 50cm Large, comparatively lightly-built raven with characteristic call. All-black, with an oily sheen. Eye white. Lacks distinctive bushy throat of Australian Raven when calling, each call being accompanied by a characteristic rapid flick of the wings. Gregarious at all times, often breeding in loose colonies, and forming nomadic flocks outside breeding season. Flies high, fast and straight. Often seen feeding in trees, unlike other ravens. *Voice:* distinctive quick-fire, harsh 'car, car, car, car, car' of even tone and tempo, each note clear-cut. *Habitat:* catholic, but avoiding closed-canopy forests. Widespread but erratic; patchy but often common across southeast. 🐎🏂🏔🚠☂🅡

Little Crow *Corvus bennetti* 41-48cm Large, but smallest of the Australian corvids. About the size of an Australian Magpie. All-black with an oily sheen (immature duller). Characteristic comparatively slim and neat build. Lacks shaggy throat. Eye white in adult. Tail comparatively long and slim in flight. Often tame, usually gregarious, breeding colonially and forming non-breeding flocks over 100 strong. *Voice:* usefully distinctive, nasal and monotonous 'nark-nark-nark-nark', of even tone, with each call extended but produced in a rapid series. *Habitat:* fairly catholic - most landscapes with at least a few trees, scavenging in urban areas. Widespread, patchy and erratic in the interior, locally common. 🏔🐎🏂🏔🚠☂☂🅡

Torresian Crow *Corvus orru* 50-55cm Large, similar to Australian Raven but lacking shaggy throat. All-black, with an oily sheen (immature duller). Eye white in adult. In hand, shows distinctively white down, sometimes visible in field beneath wind-ruffled feathers. Difficult to separate with ease from the two ravens except by call and behaviour. Frequently 'shuffles' wings, especially after landing, but does not flick wings when calling (Little). Occasionally gregarious (adult pairs probably sedentary), sometimes with Little Crow. *Voice:* distinctively high-pitched, nasal and abrupt series of 'uk-uk-uk-uk-uk' or 'ok-ok-ok-ok-ok', lacking the broad 'aar' and 'oarr' sounds of Australian Raven. *Habitat:* fairly catholic, including coastal beaches and mudflats; scavenges round habitation. Widespread northerly distribution; patchy and erratic in places, locally fairly common. 🐎🏂🏔🚠☂☂🅡

House Crow *Corvus splendens* 43cm Large, but on the small side for a corvid. Combination of greyish neck and lower breast, dark eyes and strange head shape created by short, steep forecrown and large, long bill renders this crow unmistakable. Avid scavenger. *Voice:* repeated short 'caw' notes. *Habitat:* catholic, usually in association with human habitation. Introduced (occasionally self-introduced on visiting ships); apparently not successfully established; rare. 🏔

Forest Raven (adult, southern race)

Little Raven (adult)

Little Crow (adult)

Torresian Crow (adult)

House Crow

FIELD EQUIPMENT

Fundamental to the enjoyment of birdwatching in any habitat is to be properly dressed for the conditions – both those prevailing at the outset and those that may develop in the course of the day. Good, comfortable walking boots or shoes are a basic requirement, along with thornproof or waterproof clothing, sun protection cream and/or insect repellent, according to the area being visited. A small first-aid pack and emergency rations may also be appropriate.

Field-guides and notebooks are part of every birder's 'kit', and many will also take along a camera, but one item of specialized equipment that is truly invaluable is a good pair of binoculars. It is quite possible to see and enjoy birds without them, but with them whole new worlds are opened up. Distant birds cease to be mere dots against an expanse of water or sky, and develop distinct colours and shapes, while close-up views show that feathers have an intrinsic beauty of their own. The use of binoculars also dramatically increases the observer's ability to identify birds correctly, with the added bonus of offering fascinating opportunities to spy on birds going about their daily lives undisturbed.

Because binoculars are so important as a piece of birdwatching equipment, it is worth taking great care in their choice. The first rule is to test them, personally and outdoors. Implicit in this is an avoidance of mail-order offers unless they allow a similar testing opportunity, with easy return and guaranteed cash refund if the test is unsatisfactory. Check for balance, that they sit easily and comfortably in the hands, with the controls within easy fingertip reach. Do the eyecups keep out stray light? Is the image of good, natural colour, free from 'rainbow' colour fringes or haloes (a common fault with cheap lenses). Find and look at a vertical line – a telephone pole will do: it should not seem bent and should be in sharp focus right across the field of view (although a little less detail at the extreme margins may not matter too much).

Choice of magnification depends very much on the sort of birdwatching likely to be undertaken. Good 'all-purpose' magnifications are x7, x8, x9 and x10. Watching to a considerable extent in open habitats, such as coasts, estuaries or grasslands, demands rather higher power, at least x9 and preferably x10 or x12, but such binoculars are normally comparatively large and carry a weight penalty. In contrast, woodland birdwatching benefits from a lower magnification, say x7 or x8, coupled with lenses designed to give a wide field of view, very useful when locating birds up in the tree canopy. Wide-field binoculars may also be comparatively bulky. High-magnification binoculars normally have smaller fields of view and may let in less light and so be less suitable for evening work.

Binoculars are normally marked with two figures (e.g. 8 x 30). The first figure is the magnification, the second the diameter (in mm) of the larger lenses. Divide the second figure by the first (30 ÷ 8 = 3.75, or for 10 x 50, 50 ÷ 10 = 5.0) to obtain a rough guide to their poor-light suitability. A factor of 5 means better light transmission (and thus better evening viewing) than 3.75. Expensive binoculars may not necessarily be the best birdwatching value – there are many excellent, reasonably-priced binoculars available. Beware also of gimmicks: very high magnifications and low-cost zoom lenses for example – neither is likely to give a good optical performance.

For long-distance work – on the shore, over large lakes or for detailed observation of groups offering considerable identification challenges, like the waders – a telescope (and a rigid tripod to support it) is a thoroughly worthwhile investment. Most modern telescopes are compact, with much better light transmission than their forebears. Most have variable magnification, which allows the target bird to be located (not always easy) on low magnification/wide field, and, once centred in the field of view, be then studied in detail on high magnification, with its inevitably smaller field of view. Once again, personal testing in the field is a 'must' before a final choice is made. Other birdwatchers will happily let you try their favourites, and this is by far the best way of gaining experience.

CONSERVATION

In recent years, environmental issues have gained ever-widening public support, and there is no doubt that our wildlife is endangered by a number of factors. Destruction of habitats is one major threat, and the widespread use of fertilizers and pesticides is another practice with far-reaching and sometimes unpredictable long-term effects. The introduction of the fox and the incidence of feral cats have threatened many species and indeed extinguished some. The dumping of industrial waste and sewage sludge around our coasts, and chemical seepage into inland waters, are further causes for anxiety.

However, before condemning out of hand the activities of farmers and developers, it is as well to admit to our own vested interests. Farmers do use fertilizers and pesticides, but we expect to buy produce that is uniform in quality, size and colour, and blemish-free. With every kilometre of new road, habitats are destroyed: but motorists like to reach their destinations quickly, and industrialists and householders alike expect swift delivery of goods and services. We expect our businesses to be efficient to ensure that the national economy is in the best possible shape. Heavy industry, and perhaps particularly mineral extraction, has a vital part to play in this – but is appallingly destructive of both habitat and landscape in the process. We demand more and more land for new homes and new industries, and make little protest when derelict or city-centre land is not re-used in the same way that domestic materials can be recycled. We are the ones who demand that new land is opened up, particularly along the coasts and on offshore islands, to allow recreational development, appropriate (we think) for the oncoming twenty-first century. The answer is for conservationists and developers to work ever more closely together and to pool their resources of expert knowledge so that serious mistakes – like the clearing of native grasslands for agriculture in semi-arid Australia – are avoided in the future. Increased political pressure by concerned people, as well as the knowledge of birdwatchers, is needed to ensure proper management of these grassland habitats and their wildlife. We can also participate in bird projects run by the RAOU or local ornithological societies. All of such measures, combined with firm governmental support, are essential if our immense national heritage of wildlife and habitat is to be protected from accelerating erosion.

Organizations and Addresses

Below are the names and addresses of various organizations which promote an interest in birds.

Australian Bird Study Association
P.O. Box, A313, Sydney South, NSW 2000

Bird Observers Club of Tasmania
G.P.O. Box 68A, Hobart, Tasmania 7001

Bird Observers Club of Australia
Head Office 183 Springvale Road, Nunawading, Victoria 3131
(Postal: P.O. Box 185, Nunawading, Victoria 3131) Phone: (03) 877 5342

Canberra Ornithologists Group
P.O. Box 301, Civic Square, A.C.T. 2608

Cumberland Bird Observers Club
P.O. Box 550, Baulkham Hills, NSW 2153

Illawarra Bird Observers Club
P.O. Box 56, Fairy Meadow, NSW 2519

Hunter Bird Observers Club
P.O. Box 24, New Lambton, NSW 2305

NSW Field Ornithologists Club
P.O. Box C436, Clarence Street, Sydney NSW 2000

Queensland Ornithological Society
P.O. Box 97, St Lucia, Queensland 4067

Royal Australasian Ornithologists Union (RAOU)
Head Office: 407–415 Riversdale Road, Hawthorn East, Victoria 3123
Sydney Office: Level 10, 8-12 Bridge Street, Sydney, NSW 2000
(Postal: Locked Bag 600, St James Post Office, Sydney, NSW 2000
Phone: (02) 252 1403 Fax: (02) 252 1460
Perth Office: Perry House, 71 Oceanic Drive, Floreat, W.A. 6014
(Postal: P.O.Box 199 Jolimont, W.A. 6014)
Phone: (09) 383 7749
Northern NSW
Group: c/o The Chairman, 173 Allingham Street, Armidale, NSW 2350

South Australian Ornithologists Association
c/o South Australian Museum, North Terrace, Adelaide, South Australia 5000

Bibliography

There are many books and publications dealing with the various aspects of Australian Birds. Those listed below will lead you further into this extensive literature.

Higgins, P.J., & Marchant, S., *RAOU Handbook of Australian, New Zealand and Antarctic Birds* . OUP, Vol. 1 *Ratites to Ducks*, 1991; Vol. 2 *Raptors to Lapwings, 1993*, with further volumes in preparation

Pizzey, G., *A Field Guide to the Birds of Australia*. Collins Australia, 1980 (revised 1991)

Reader's Digest Complete Book of Australian Birds. Reader's Digest (Sydney), 1976 (revised 1986)

Simpson, K. & Day, N. *Field Guide to the Birds of Australia: A Book of Identification*, Lifetime Distributors 1989 (revised 1993)

Slater, P., Slater P. & Slater, R. *The Slater Field Guide to Australian Birds*. Lansdowne Press, 1986 (revised 1989).

Trounson, A.D. & M., *Australian Birds*. P. R. Bowles, Sydney, 1989

Acknowledgements

Photograph sources are as listed below:

National Photographic Index of Australian Wildlife, The Australian Museum: G. Anderson 211br, 219bl; K. Atkinson 67tl, 163m; Australian Museum 195tl; V. Bail 293bl; G.B. Baker 203tl; H. & J. Beste 79mr, 99tr, 105br, 115bl, 125tr, 181bl, 291tl, 321tr, 337mr, 339tr; D. & V. Blagden 45br, 73mr, 73bl, 105tl, 105m, 123tr, 173br, 177m, 181m, 207br, 215bl, 229bl, 303mr, 319tr, 329tl, 339br, 345br; E. Beaton 107tr; W.J. Belson 153mr, 351bl; R. Borland 347tr; N. Brothers 71m; R. Brown 101br, 103bl, 105bl, 113tr, 121m, 173mr, 217tl, 223tl, 233tr, 345ml, 347tl; M. Carter 51tr, 53tl, 55mr, 59tl, 61tr, 61br, 63tr, 67m, 69bl, 95bl, 139tl, 151mr, 213br, 227m, 335tl; N. Chaffer 199bl, 277tl, 283m, 329br, 341mr; G. Chapman 73tl, 99mr, 105tr, 107mr, 117bl, 123bl, 125tl, 127tl, 131mr, 131br, 133tl, 157tl, 157br, 161m, 165tl, 169tr, 169bl, 173tl, 173ml, 181tr, 191tl, 199br, 223tr, 235bl, 239bl, 241bl, 245tr, 247tl, 247bl, 247br, 249m, 253br, 255tr, 255ml, 257bl, 263mr, 271bl, 273mr, 275bl, 277tr, 283br, 293mr, 295tl, 297bl, 301tr, 303bl, 307tl, 307ml, 311mr, 313ml, 313bl, 315bl, 315br, 317tr, 317bl, 323bl, 325tr, 325br, 353bl; B. Chudleigh 61ml, 75ml, 75br, 79ml, 89br, 93br, 103tr, 109bl, 125m, 125bl, 127ml, 127br, 129tl, 129ml, 129br, 131tl, 133br, 135tr, 135mr, 137bl, 137br, 139mr, 139bl, 139br, 141tl, 141tr, 141m, 141br, 145tr, 145ml, 145mr, 145bl, 147tr, 147mr, 159mr, 169tl, 179tr, 217bl, 223br, 227tr, 233bl, 233br, 237tl, 327ml, 337tr; B. Coates 57br, 103m, 107tl, 127mr, 153tr, 157bl, 165br, 211bl, 213bl, 219ml, 221tr, 225mr; M. Cohen 333br, 347bl; David Cottridge 125br, 135ml, 137tl, 137ml, 143m, 143bl, 145tl; G. Cumming 121bl, 159bl, 247tr, 267tl; J. Dart 287br; A. Dominelli 243m, 249br; F. Dowling 305tr; V.A. Drake 325tl; R. Drummond 65tr, 85br, 93tr, 119bl, 129mr, 151br, 181br, 183tl, 189bl, 193tl, 201bl, 203tr, 221mr, 231tr, 241tl, 253tl, 255br, 281bl, 319br; A. Eames 49m; J. Estbergs 101tl, 111br, 193br, 207mr, 283bl, 313mr; A. Evans 299bl; J. Fennell 91mr, 91bl, 239m; Geoff du Feu 155mr; J. Fields 45tr, 51tl, 51bl, 75mr, 79br, 85ml, 93m, 119mr, 225tl, 225ml, 297ml, 337ml; K. Fisher 149bl, 155ml, 341bl; A.T. Foster 111m, 205mr; P. Fullagar 59mr, 69tr, 143br; T. & P. Gardner 43bl, 45tl, 75tl, 79tl, 79bl, 81tl, 85mr, 89tl, 89bl, 91tr, 91br, 95tr, 95br, 97ml, 101bl, 115tl, 119tr, 119br, 129tr, 131bl, 133m, 133bl, 135bl, 141bl, 149br, 153tl, 153mr, 161tl, 167bl, 189tr, 189br, 197tl, 201mr, 205tl, 205tr, 205bl, 209br, 229br, 241br, 251br, 255mr, 255bl, 259tl, 267br, 275br, 279tl, 287bl, 293tl, 297tr, 303tl, 309tr, 309ml, 309br, 313tr, 319mr, 321tl, 329bl, 333tl, 333tr, 339tl, 339bl, 341tr, 343tl, 353tr; R. Garstone 99bl, 191tr, 191ml, 191br, 273ml, 305br; C.L. Gill 97tl; Michael Gore 147bl, 155br; J. Gray 187tl, 255tl, 257tl, 281tl, 291bl, 311bl; R.H. Green 43tl, 45m, 201br, 235br, 307br, 309mr, 323tl, 351tr; D. Hadden 55tl, 55bl, 57tl, 63mr, 63bl, 65mr, 83m, 83br, 89mr, 117br, 153br, 161tr, 177bl, 349bl, 349br, 351br; James Hancock 109tr; J. Handel 177tl, 199tr, 199m, 245tl, 275tr, 297br; P. Harper 59br, 61bl; G. Harrington 113br; J.L. Hayward 149m; C. Andrew Henley 67br, 77br, 87tr, 87ml, 87mr, 109m, 121br, 167br, 191bl, 237ml, 295bl, 295br, 299tr, 305tl, 307mr, 309tl; A. Hertog 301mr; J. Hicks 77tl; D. Horning 49bl, 53blr; M. Howard 163tr, 269tl; Tony Howard 47tl, 47mr, 47br, 55tr, 55br, 63br, 87br, 91ml, 109tl, 111tl, 111tr, 151tl, 159tr, 171br, 177tr, 185br, 187m, 213tr, 341tl, 353tl; I. Hutton 57ml, 59bl, 67bl, 69br, 73bl, 77bl, 123m, 163br; K. Ireland 85tl, 121tr, 133tr, 159br, 161br, 203mr, 211t, 231bl, 303br, 349tl; James Karmali 85tr; R. & D. Keller 173bl; R. King 73tr, 77m; P. Klapste 49br, 81mr, 149tl, 155bl, 157m, 161bl, 171m, 221br; F. Kristo 101tr, 113bl, 205br; W. Labbett 81bl, 211ml, 217tr, 249bl, 259bl, 261tl, 261br, 263b, 281tr, 283tl, 289tr, 293ml, 297mr, 303tr, 307bl, 311br, 337bl, 345mr; W. Lawler 221bl; F. Lewitzka 97br, 107br; T. Lindsey 301bl; G. Little 43tr, 93bl, 285br, 319tl; J. Lochman 121tl, 131tr, 173tr, 175bl, 331tl; W. Longmore 135tl; R.H. Lovell 167m; T.G. Lowe 143tr; A. McBride 61tl, 65ml, 65bl, 65br, 151bl, 155tr; J. McCann 103tl, 175tl, 209tl, 311tl, 349mr; E. MacKrill 147br, 149tr; P. Mannell 65tl, 201ml; P. Menkhorst 159tl; D. Merton 57mr; Bob Miller 237br; C. Minton 145br; M. & I. Morcombe 97tr, 99tl, 273tl; I. Morgan 279bl; I. Morris 115ml, 285m; P. Munchenberg 179tl, 185mr, 323br; J. Napier 245br; Philip Newman 147tl; A. Olney 345bl; U. Olsson 139tr; Tony Palliser 53tr, 57tr, 59tr, 143bl, 151ml; R. Palmer 171tr, 239tr, 273tr, 283tr, 315tl, 319ml, 323tr; F. Park 237tl, 257br; W. Peckover 139ml, 169mr, 179bl, 179br, 185tl, 209tr, 215tr, 215br, 265tl, 265tr, 301ml, 341ml; W. Peckover & R. Schodde 343br; L. Pedler 113m, 193bl, 197br, 223bl, 273bl, 275tl, 277ml, 281m, 281br, 289ml, 291tr, 319bl; A.Y. Pepper 111bl; T. Pescott 43br; J. Purnell 83bl, 115tr, 217br, 219tr, 231tl, 249tr, 253bl, 265m, 285tl, 287ml, 291br, 293tr, 293br, 297tl, 317tl, 337tl; H. Rechler 125bl; P. Roberts 81tr, 277bl; R. Roberts 47bl; G. Robertson 47tr, 47ml, 49tl, 69m, 77tr; L. Robinson 81ml, 119tl, 165tr, 165m, 171tl, 185bl, 189ml, 189mr, 193ml, 195tr, 197mr, 197bl, 207bl, 235ml, 235mr, 237bl, 259tr, 261m, 271tl, 275m; A. Rogers 51br; G. Rogerson 107bl, 123br, 237mr, 239br, 315ml; I. Rowles 185tr, 265bl, 305ml; P. Sagar 151tr; A. Salter 289br, 295m, 299mr; A. Schick 87tl; D. Schick 163tl; G. Schick 201tr; L.F. Schick 49tr, 87bl, 107ml, 181tl, 269br, 287tr, 351tl; A. Selby 233tl, 345tr; C. Seller 81br, 343bl; V. Serventy 83tl; M. Seyfort 177br, 225bl, 225br, 239tl, 267bl, 269tr, 345tl; R. Shepherd 123tl, 243br, 307tr; J.C. Sinclair 53bl; E. Slater 221tl; E. Smith 97mr, 203br; M.F. Soper 63tl, 63ml, 67tr, 155tl; G. Spanner 253tr; K. Stepnell 179ml, 179mr; Paul Sterry 115br; E. & N. Taylor 289bl; G. Taylor 193tr; G. Threlfo 165bl, 183bl; Roger Tidman 69tl, 71tr; D. & M. Trounson 45bl, 83tr, 85bl, 95tl, 127bl, 167tl, 175tr, 183tr, 201tl, 207tr, 229m, 231m, 235tl, 241m, 243tr, 247mr, 269mr, 299br, 303ml, 309bl, 327mr, 327br, 331tr, 331ml, 331mr, 331br, 335m, 335bl, 349tr; B. Turner 109br; M. Unkovich 143tl, 265br, 333bl; D. Val 317br; C. Veitch 163bl; R. Viljoen 73ml, 169br, 187br, 203ml; T. Waite 279br, 287mr, 295tr, 311ml; J. Warham 57bl, 59ml, 251tl; J. Waterhouse 169ml, 231br, 237tr, 277mr, 289mr, 299tl, 315tr, 321bl, 335tr; D. Watts 53m, 55ml, 75tr, 75bl, 97bl, 99br, 101m, 103br, 127tr, 187bl, 189tl, 197tr, 207bl, 269ml, 323m, 329tr; G. Weber 79tr, 215bl, 245bl, 247mr, 251tr, 279ml, 301br, 311tr, 313tl, 325bl; C. Webster 91tl, 183br, 203bl, 227tl, 229tl, 249tl, 259ml, 267tr, 271br; B. & B. Wells 117tl, 119ml, 135br, 159ml, 171bl, 175br, 195tr, 195ml, 235tr, 241tr, 245m, 257tr, 259mr, 259br, 261b, 263tr, 269mr, 269bl, 271tr, 271ml, 289tl, 305bl, 313br, 315mr, 329m, 331bl, 353m; Dick Whitford 89tr, 95m, 211mr, 243tl, 243bl, 277br, 279tr, 287tl, 301tl, 337br, 343tr, 347br; M. Willis 175m, 183ml, 219br, 221ml, 339ml, 339mr, 341br; W. Worrad 131ml, 285tr, 321br; M. Wright 99ml, 273br; J. Yates 117tr; S. Young 157tr; E. Zillmann 199tl, 209bl, 219tl, 229tr

Ardea 147ml (J.B. & F. Bottomley); Janet Baker 71tl, 113tl, 251bl, 167tr, 187tr, 213tl, 327bl; Eric and David Hosking 225tr, 227bl; K. Scriven 115mr; I. Sinclair 61mr, 71b; Ray Tipper: 93tl, 129bl, 137tr, 137mr, 227br, 267m, 335br, 353br

357

INDEX
Common Names

INDEX
Scientific Names